HUMANITARIAN INTERVENTION AND THE RESPONSIBILITY TO PROTECT

Humanitarian Intervention and the Responsibility to Protect

Who Should Intervene?

JAMES PATTISON

OXFORD
UNIVERSITY PRESS

Great Clarendon Street, Oxford OX2 6DP

Oxford University Press is a department of the University of Oxford.
It furthers the University's objective of excellence in research, scholarship,
and education by publishing worldwide in

Oxford New York

Auckland Cape Town Dar es Salaam Hong Kong Karachi
Kuala Lumpur Madrid Melbourne Mexico City Nairobi
New Delhi Shanghai Taipei Toronto

With offices in

Argentina Austria Brazil Chile Czech Republic France Greece
Guatemala Hungary Italy Japan Poland Portugal Singapore
South Korea Switzerland Thailand Turkey Ukraine Vietnam

Oxford is a registered trade mark of Oxford University Press
in the UK and in certain other countries

Published in the United States
by Oxford University Press Inc., New York

British Library Cataloguing in Publication Data

Data available

Library of Congress Cataloging in Publication Data
Library of Congress Control Number: 2009939963

Typeset by SPI Publisher Services, Pondicherry, India
Printed in Great Britain
on acid-free paper by the
MPG Books Group, Bodmin and King's Lynn

ISBN 978–0–19–956104–9

Contents

Acknowledgements

Several people have helped this book take shape. First, I would like to thank my ex-supervisors, Simon Caney and Peter Jones. This book draws on parts of my doctoral research on who should undertake humanitarian intervention and their comments on this research were extremely insightful and constructive. I am also very appreciative of their support, assistance, and guidance since this time. I would also like to thank the members of the Newcastle Political Philosophy Group, including Derek Bell, Thom Brooks, Graham Long, and Ian O'Flynn, who provided extensive comments on my work during my time in the north-east. Thanks are also due to the Economic and Social Research Council, who funded my doctoral research.

From 2007 to 2009, I was based in the Department of Politics, Philosophy, and International Relations at the University of the West of England, Bristol. I am grateful to my colleagues from that time, including Christien van den Anker, Ed Lock, and Simon Thompson, for useful discussions and suggestions. I am particularly indebted to Nick Buttle. Our frequent conversations on ethics and political philosophy helped me to clarify and to develop the arguments of the book, and his careful comments on the final manuscript were invaluable.

I have presented material from the book at over fifteen conferences and workshops, including at Birmingham, Cambridge, Cork, Edinburgh, Exeter, Manchester, Newcastle, Newport, Oxford, Pavia, Reading, Southampton, St. Andrews, and Warwick. I would like to thank the participants for their comments, criticisms, and suggestions. I also benefited greatly from discussions on humanitarian intervention and who should intervene with Simon Chesterman, Sue Mendes, Joel Rosenthal, and Tom Weiss. Several people provided comments on draft material from the book. I am grateful in this respect to Chris Armstrong, Eric Heinze, Darryl Howlett, Seth Lazar, Andy Mason, Enzo Rossi, Steve Smith, and Jennifer Welsh. I am especially indebted to Suzanne Keene, John Lango, Ulrich Petersohn, Ibrahim Seaga Shaw, and Richard Vernon, all of whom read through a draft of the full manuscript. The suggestions and comments that they made were vital for improving the clarity, precision, and quality of the argument. In addition, I would like to thank Dominic Byatt at Oxford University Press for his help and enthusiasm, and the Pattisons for numerous stylistic suggestions.

Some material from this book has been published in an earlier form elsewhere, although I have modified and revised many of my arguments. An earlier version of Chapter 2 was published as 'Humanitarian Intervention and International Law: The Moral Significance of an Intervener's Legal Status', *Critical Review of International Social and Political Philosophy* (2007), 10/3: 301–19 and a version of Chapter 5 appeared as 'Representativeness and Humanitarian Intervention', *Journal of Social Philosophy* (2007), 38/4: 569–87. Parts of Chapters 1, 3, and 7 draw on material from 'Whose Responsibility to Protect: The Duties of Humanitarian Intervention', *Journal of Military Ethics* (2008), 7/4: 262–83. Chapter 4 draws on material from 'Humanitarian Intervention, the Responsibility to Protect, and *jus in bello*', *Global Responsibility to Protect* (2009), 1/3: 364–91. An extended version of the discussion of the proposals for a UN force can be found in 'Humanitarian Intervention and a Cosmopolitan UN Force', *Journal of International Political Theory* (2008), 4/1: 126–45. I am grateful to the publishers for permission to use this material.

Last, I would like to thank my wife, Claire, whose help, love, and support have made this book possible.

List of Abbreviations

AMIS	African Union Mission in Sudan
AMISOM	African Union Mission in Somalia
ASEAN	Association of Southeast Asian Nations
AU	African Union
DPKO	United Nations Department of Peacekeeping Operations
DR Congo	Democratic Republic of Congo
DUPI	Danish Institute of International Affairs
ECOMOG	ECOWAS Monitoring Group
ECOWAS	Economic Community of West African States
EU	European Union
EUFOR Tchad/RCA	European Union Force Chad/Central African Republic
ICISS	International Commission on Intervention and State Sovereignty
ICRC	International Committee of the Red Cross
INTERFET	International Force for East Timor
MONUC	United Nations Mission in the Democratic Republic of Congo
NGO	Non-governmental organization
Operation Artemis	European Union Mission in the Democratic Republic of Congo
Operation Licorne	French Mission in Côte d'Ivoire
Operation Turquoise	French Mission in Rwanda
PMC	Private military company
R2P	The responsibility to protect
RUF	Revolutionary United Front
SHIRBRIG	Standby High Readiness Brigade for United Nations Operations
UNAMID	United Nations Mission in Darfur
UNAMIR	United Nations Assistance Mission for Rwanda
UNAMSIL	United Nations Mission in Sierra Leone
UNEPS	United Nations Emergency Peace Service
UNMIL	United Nations Mission in Liberia
UNPROFOR	United Nations Protection Force
UNSAS	United Nations Standby Arrangements System

1

The Problem of Who Should Intervene

This book is concerned with a seemingly straightforward question: when the world is faced with a serious humanitarian crisis, such as in Rwanda in 1994, Kosovo in 1999, and Darfur since 2003, which international actor, if any, should undertake military intervention to help those suffering? That the question arises is largely due to a shift in the legal, political, and moral norms of the international system since the end of the bipolar, divisive international system of the Cold War. Although there are still many that object to humanitarian intervention, there has been a growing sense in the international community that humanitarian intervention can be morally (and perhaps legally and politically) permissible on occasion. This has been reflected in the number of humanitarian interventions since 1989. These include:

- The Economic Community of West African States (ECOWAS) intervention in Liberia in 1990 to restore law and order.
- The French, British, and American intervention in northern Iraq in 1991 to create safe havens and to implement no-fly zones to protect thousands of endangered Kurds.
- The US-led intervention in Somalia in 1992 to open up humanitarian corridors.
- The US-led intervention in Haiti in 1994 to restore the democratically elected Jean-Bertrand Aristide.
- NATO's bombing of Bosnian-Serb positions in 1995 to end the civil war in the former Yugoslavia.
- ECOWAS intervention in Sierra Leone in 1997 to restore peace and stability after heavy fighting.
- NATO intervention in Kosovo in 1999 to protect the Kosovan Albanians from ethnic cleansing.
- The Australian-led intervention in East Timor in 1999 after Indonesian brutality.
- The UN action (including a European Union (EU) force) in eastern parts of the Democratic Republic of Congo (DR Congo) since 1999.
- The UK intervention in Sierra Leone in 2000 to strengthen the faltering United Nations Mission (UNAMSIL).

- The ECOWAS, the UN, and the US intervention in Liberia in 2003 after the renewal of fighting.
- The French and UN intervention in Côte d'Ivoire in 2003.

Indeed, it is much harder to find someone who completely supports non-intervention nowadays. The lack of action in Rwanda (or, more accurately, lack of effective action) and the subsequent genocide has had a massive impact on the theory and practice of intervention. Even those who are deeply suspicious of armed humanitarian intervention and deeply sceptical about its prospects of success may still admit that it might, in theory, be justified when a humanitarian crisis is sufficiently serious.[1] As a result, the questions of *if* and *why* humanitarian intervention is justifiable, which previously received sustained attention in the literature, are now less pertinent.[2] There is wide-spread support for the view, if not complete agreement, that humanitarian intervention can be justifiable in exceptional cases to tackle large-scale human suffering. More of a concern is *who* should undertake humanitarian intervention and *when* it is justifiable for them to do so. For instance, is a humanitarian intervention justifiable only when undertaken by a multinational force with the authorization of the UN Security Council and in response to genocide or mass killing? Or, can humanitarian intervention be justified when undertaken by a single state without Security Council support and in response to severe oppression?

At the same time, there has been a shift towards an alternative conception of sovereignty. As traditionally conceived, the principle of sovereignty emphasizes a state's freedom from external interference, so that it can pursue whatever policies it likes within its own boundaries. Although this notion of sovereignty as *authority* seemed to provide a legal and normative barrier that weaker states could use to fend off the interference of larger states, it presented the leaders of certain states with what was essentially a free hand to violate their citizens' human rights with impunity. Humanitarian intervention, from this perspective, is largely unjustifiable. Indeed, a key aspect of the traditional notion of sovereignty is the non-intervention principle. This principle is encapsulated by Article 2 (4) of the UN Charter, which states:

> All Members shall refrain in their international relations from the threat or use of force against the territorial integrity or political independence of any state, or in any other manner inconsistent with the Purposes of the United Nations.

This notion of sovereignty as authority, however, is no longer sacrosanct.[3] As the notion of universal human rights has grown in standing in the international community, there has been an increasing shift to an alternative conception that views sovereignty as *responsibility*, the responsibility to uphold citizens' human rights. A key development in this context has been the report by the International Commission on Intervention and State Sovereignty (ICISS) 2001, *The Responsibility to Protect.* Commissioned by the Canadian government in response to a request from the then UN Secretary General, Kofi Annan, and led by former Australian foreign affairs minister, Gareth Evans, this report argues that a state has the responsibility to uphold its citizens' human rights. If it is unable or unwilling to fulfil this responsibility, such as in cases of mass killing, its sovereignty is temporarily suspended. In such cases, the responsibility to protect these citizens transfers to the international community. The international community's responsibility to protect involves the 'responsibility to prevent' the crisis, the 'responsibility to react' robustly to it, and the 'responsibility to rebuild' after. The 'responsibility to react' may, on occasion, require humanitarian intervention, providing that certain 'precautionary principles' have first been met (just cause, legitimate authority, right intention, last resort, proportional means, and reasonable prospects).

Although far from being fully implemented, the notion of a 'responsibility to protect'—'R2P' for short—has had some success in getting onto the international agenda. UN, state officials, and non-governmental organizations (NGOs) regularly use the language of the responsibility to protect in relation to serious humanitarian crises and military intervention. For instance, the Report of the UN High-Level Panel on Threats, Challenges and Change in 2004, *A More Secure World*, argues that '[t]here is a growing recognition that the issue is not the "right to intervene" of any State, but the "responsibility to protect" of *every* State' (UN 2004: 56). Similarly, in the report, *In Larger Freedom*, Kofi Annan argues that we must 'move towards embracing and acting on the "responsibility to protect"' (2005: 35). Most notably, at the 2005 UN World Summit (the High-Level Plenary meeting of the 60th session of the General Assembly, with over 160 heads of state and government in attendance), states agreed that there exists a universal responsibility to protect populations. In doing so, they indicated their preparedness to undertake action 'should peaceful means be inadequate' and when 'national authorities are manifestly failing to protect their populations from genocide, war crimes, ethnic cleansing and crimes against humanity' (UN 2005: 30).[4]

On the face of it, this agreement was something of a watershed moment for humanitarian intervention. It seemed to mark the worldwide acceptance of the responsibility to intervene in response to the mass violation of basic human rights. As Andrew Cottey notes, it 'indicated a significant shift in the balance of international opinion, with a widening group of states accepting the argument that state sovereignty cannot be viewed in absolutist terms and the principle that military intervention within states may be justified in some circumstances' (2008: 437). More generally, the development of the doctrine of the responsibility to protect has been hailed by Ramesh Thakur and Thomas Weiss as the 'most dramatic development of our time—comparable to the Nuremberg trials and the 1948 Convention on Genocide' (2009: 23) and by historian Martin Gilbert as the 'most significant adjustment to national sovereignty in 360 years' (in Axworthy and Rock 2009: 69).

There remain, however, significant ambiguities with the responsibility to protect doctrine. One major issue is that, when intervention is required, it is unclear *who*, in particular, in the international community should discharge the responsibility to protect. To be sure, the primary responsibility to protect lies with the state suffering the humanitarian crisis. The difficulty arises when this responsibility transfers to the international community because this state is failing to protect its citizens' human rights and other measures short of force fail, or are likely to fail. The problem, as Thomas Weiss, notes, is that the term 'international community' is vague and 'without a policy edge. Using it allows analysts to avoid pointing the finger at which specific entities are responsible when the so-called international community fails to respond or makes a mess of things' (2001: 424).[5] As such, referring to the international community does not help us to identify who should actually intervene when humanitarian intervention is called for under the responsibility to protect doctrine. The ICISS (2001*a*: XII) report does make it clear that, whoever intervenes, the UN Security Council should authorize the action. States at the 2005 World Summit adopted a similar (and arguably stronger) view. Yet the requirement for Security Council authorization identifies only a *procedure* that agents should follow when discharging the responsibility to protect. It does not identify which particular *agent* has this responsibility.

More generally, it is unclear who should undertake humanitarian intervention because, as things stand, there is not an *obviously* legitimate institution—or, as Bernard Williams (1995: 67) puts it, a *salient* institution—to undertake humanitarian intervention. In (most) domestic societies, the question of who should stop violations of basic human rights (such as murder and rape) tends not to arise because an effective and credible police service exists to tackle these crimes. However, there is no direct analogy to the domestic police in the international system. To see this, consider the following leading candidates for humanitarian intervention, none of which stand out as an obvious choice to intervene given their track records. I will offer only a brief sketch of the current problematic situation here. The problems highlighted will be considered more extensively later.

The UN might appear, at first glance, to be the most appropriate agent. Its jurisdiction, as outlined in the UN Charter, is universal and includes matters of peace and security. It is also widely accepted as being able to undertake or to authorize humanitarian intervention legally. Yet, two events have cast significant doubts on its ability and credibility as a humanitarian intervener. The first was its failure to act effectively in response to the Rwandan genocide. There was a 2,500-strong UN peacekeeping force—the United Nations Assistance Mission for Rwanda (UNAMIR)—in Rwanda at the time of the outbreak of the genocide. In February 1994, UNAMIR's force commander, Major General Roméo Dallaire, obtained death lists of the names of Tutsi and moderate Hutu targets. It was clear that genocide was on the cards, but Dallaire was denied his request for permission to capture and destroy arms caches. Instead, in the middle of the crisis, the size of UNAMIR was decreased, leaving only a token force. The second infamous crisis on the UN watch was only one year later. This was in Srebrenica in July 1995, which at the time was a UN 'safe haven'. As such, it was supposed to enjoy the protection of the United Nations Protection Force (UNPROFOR), the UN force in Bosnia. UN member states were, however, unwilling to provide the ground troops necessary for effective protection. As a result, Bosnian Serbs overran Srebrenica and massacred several thousand Bosnian Muslims. The Supplementary Volume to the Responsibility to Protect (ICISS 2001*b*: 93) argues that Srebrenica has since become synonymous with the gap between Security Council rhetoric and effective action.[6] There are, then, serious questions about the UN's capability as an intervener.

In light of these difficulties when the UN acts itself, one alternative is an international mandate by the Security Council, given to a state, a coalition of the willing, or regional organization, to undertake humanitarian intervention. *Prima facie*, this appears to be the ideal solution to the problem of who should intervene. It seems to avoid the excesses of unilateralism, overcomes the problems with the UN's lack of capability to intervene, and still maintains a sense of internationalism. Indeed, the 1999 Security Council-authorized, Australian-led intervention in East Timor appeared to bear out the optimism about this mandate option. Australia provided the necessary troops for successful intervention, suffered little by way of military casualties, received a stamp of international authorization, and largely halted the immediate crisis.

Yet the UN-authorization option is perhaps not as good a solution as it first appears. The Security Council's representativeness and functioning (especially the veto powers of the permanent members) are morally problematic, and this means that it is far from obvious that interveners authorized by the Security Council are legitimate. Furthermore, the Security Council often fails to authorize humanitarian intervention when it is desperately needed. The most infamous case was its decision not to authorize NATO's 1999 intervention in Kosovo. Both the history of the Milosevic regime during the Bosnian War and its behaviour in Kosovo in late 1998 and early 1999 indicated that another state-sponsored ethnic cleansing was imminent. NATO member states sought Security Council authorization to undertake what was essentially pre-emptive action, but the mandate was not forthcoming, largely because of Russia's ties to the Milosevic regime.

Despite the lack of Security Council authorization, NATO intervention in Kosovo was largely successful in preventing a humanitarian crisis on the scale of Bosnia. There was, however, significant controversy surrounding this unauthorized action. NATO action was criticized for undermining international law and order and, in particular, the general prohibition on the use of force. Moreover, the means used by NATO, which included cluster bombs and excluded ground troops, seemed to be highly objectionable. Therefore, humanitarian intervention by collective security organizations such as NATO and, more generally, unauthorized intervention (action without the authorization of the Security Council), is also not an obvious solution to the problem of who should intervene.

Intervention by regional organizations has its difficulties as well. Take, for instance, ECOWAS intervention in Liberia in 1990. Although this Nigerian-led operation—the ECOWAS Monitoring Group (ECOMOG)—had some success in achieving peace around the capital city and protecting civilians within its control, it was not able to establish security elsewhere. The Nigerian troops committed abuses against civilians and supplied arms to some of the factions, thereby contributing to the proliferation of the conflict (Nowrojee 2004).[7]

It is a similar story for humanitarian intervention by a state or coalition of states. The French-led intervention in Côte d'Ivoire (Operation Licorne), for instance, struggled to sustain neutrality. The force first incurred the wrath of the rebels for blocking their advances on Abidjan, but then pro-government militias attacked French interests and expatriates, and President Laurent Gbagbo's supporters claimed that the operation had been siding with the rebels. The French were left with essentially no option but to muddle through. They could not pull out, since exiting would mean that Côte d'Ivoire would be plunged even further into civil war, and they could not overthrow Gbagbo, for fear of an international outcry.

Therefore, there are several potential agents of humanitarian intervention, but there is no standout candidate. Which of these agents should intervene is far from being a foregone conclusion. The issue is instead surrounded in controversy, complexity, and ambiguity. Furthermore, despite the agreement at the 2005 World Summit, many egregious humanitarian crises go largely unchecked. For instance, according to the United Nations Department of Peacekeeping Operations (DPKO), an estimated 300,000 have died and 2.5 million people have been displaced in Darfur since 2003 (UN 2008*a*). In Somalia, the conflict and lack of authority have led to 1.1 million people being displaced since January 2006 (International Crisis Group 2008*b*). In addition, the conflict in the DR Congo has led to an estimated 5.4 million deaths since 1998 (International Rescue Committee 2008). To help tackle such crises, and to avoid future crises, we need to have a stronger sense of which agent should be responsible for undertaking humanitarian intervention when the situation demands.

Who then should intervene? I will provide a detailed analysis of this question. I will consider which agent of intervention should intervene if, and when, there is a humanitarian crisis in the future that requires humanitarian intervention. Should we prefer intervention by the UN, NATO, a regional or subregional organization (such as the African Union AU), a state, a group of states, or someone else?

To make this choice, we need to know which qualities of interveners are morally important. I will therefore determine who should intervene by, first, evaluating which qualities of interveners are morally significant. I do this by assessing the relevant factors when deciding who should intervene. This normative analysis forms much of the ensuing discussion. Chapters 2–6 examine and evaluate the importance of various potential factors. Some of the issues that I consider are as follows. How much moral weight should be assigned to an intervener's legal status according to the international law on humanitarian intervention? How important is it that an intervener will be effective and what does this mean in practice? Can an intervener be legitimate if its intervention is costly in terms of lives and resources for those within its own borders? How important are the effects of an intervener's actions on international peace and security? Should an intervener follow closely principles of *jus in bello* (principles of just conduct in war) even if this undermines its effectiveness at tackling the crisis and, if so, which particular principles should it follow? Must an intervener be welcomed by those it is trying to save? Should an intervener have the support of its home population before undertaking humanitarian intervention? Is it important that an intervener has a humanitarian motive and intention, and achieve a humanitarian outcome?

Having determined which qualities are morally relevant, I will, secondly, consider the more empirical question of whether (and to what extent) the current agents of humanitarian intervention actually possess these qualities, and therefore should intervene. How effective can we expect UN action to be in the future? Is NATO likely to use humanitarian means? Are Western states likely to have the support of those suffering the humanitarian crisis?

Overall, I will develop a particular normative conception of legitimacy for humanitarian intervention that answers the question of 'who should intervene?' or 'who should discharge the responsibility to protect?', based on what I call the 'Moderate Instrumentalist Approach'. Using this conception of legitimacy, we will be able to assess whether a particular intervener, such as NATO, is legitimate. In addition, this conception of legitimacy will help to evaluate potential reforms to the mechanisms and agents of humanitarian intervention. Accordingly, I will consider not simply who, out of the current agents of intervention, should undertake humanitarian intervention. I also will go on to delineate what sort of changes should be made to improve the willingness and legitimacy of humanitarian interveners.

The rest of this chapter will set the scope for this analysis. In Section 1.1, I say more about the problems caused by the lack of clarity surrounding who should intervene and, in doing so, identify two specific questions that I am concerned with ('who has the *right* to intervene?' and 'who has the *duty* to intervene?'). Section 1.2 discusses in more detail the issue of who should intervene in relation to the responsibility to protect and, in particular, considers how this question varies according to how the responsibility to protect is interpreted. I then turn to consider two central questions in the ethics of humanitarian intervention: whether humanitarian intervention is a duty or only a right (Section 1.3), and when can there be a just cause for humanitarian intervention (Section 1.4). Section 1.5 considers two conceptual issues: what I mean by, first, 'humanitarian intervention' and, second, 'legitimacy'. The aim, then, is to provide a normative and conceptual framework within which we can begin to consider who should undertake humanitarian intervention.

1.1 THE IMPORTANCE OF THE TOPIC

There are several reasons, both political and moral, why the issue of who should undertake matters. Perhaps most significantly, which particular agent undertakes humanitarian intervention has substantial implications for (*a*) those suffering the humanitarian crisis. Thousands of peoples' lives, security, and future depend on which particular agent intervenes. Yet it is not just those subject to the intervention who are affected by which particular agent intervenes. This may seem an obvious point, but who intervenes also has significant implications for (*b*) those individuals who collectively form the intervener. These individuals may face increased taxation, decreased spending on public services, military casualties, but, at the same time, may enjoy an improved international standing. Moreover, there are (c) significant implications for the international system as a whole. On the one hand, a legitimate intervener might improve the standing of the UN and promote the rule of international law. Conversely, an illegitimate intervener might undermine the credibility of the UN, including its status as the locus of decision-making on the use of force, weaken international law and order, and the general prohibition on the use of force. It may also destabilize certain regions and areas (for instance, by creating refugee flows) and perhaps damage the standing and credibility of the doctrine of humanitarian intervention so that there will be fewer humanitarian interventions in the future.

Yet, there is a general reluctance of potential interveners to step forward and, as a result, several humanitarian crises currently go unabated. Why then should we be concerned with the issue of who should intervene? In this context, David Miller argues that we 'should not try to lay down in advance conditions for who may intervene, but rather be guided by the simple maxim "who can, should"' (2007: 10).[8] So, rather than being concerned with which particular agent has the right to intervene, we should be more concerned with delineating threshold conditions for humanitarian intervention. Above the threshold conditions, any agent can exercise their right to act. Providing extra restrictions on who may act will mean that there will be fewer interveners to choose from when we need them most.

There are several points to note about this objection. First, it is precisely the lack of willing and committed interveners ready to step forward that necessitates a more detailed analysis of the issue of agency and humanitarian intervention. We first need to know who are the most suitable agents to undertake intervention before we can identify how to increase their willingness to act. Once we know who should act, we can design a strategy to ensure that they do so. Having a stronger sense of the agency issues for humanitarian intervention will also help in identifying what is needed to *improve* the abilities of potential interveners, so that in the future we will have more—and better—interveners from which to choose. Indeed, towards the end of the book, I will consider ways of achieving these goals, drawing on the conception of legitimacy defended throughout the book.

Second, as Miller (2007: 4) recognizes, the lack of willingness to intervene is, in part, related to the ambiguity surrounding these issues. He outlines the collective action problem of 'diffused responsibility'. That is, the more potential rescuers there are, the less the likelihood of the chances of rescue. But when there is only one potential intervener or a clearly identified agent, the likelihood of rescue increases. Similarly, without having a stronger sense of who should act, states and other agents can use the ambiguity surrounding who should intervene and the responsibility to protect to circumvent their duty to tackle egregious humanitarian crises. Thus, Alex Bellamy asserts, 'there is a real danger that appeals to a responsibility to protect will evaporate amid disputes about where that responsibility lies' (2005: 33).

To put this another way, the responsibility to protect (according to the ICISS version) implies that there currently exists an *unassigned* responsibility to intervene (in certain cases) which falls on the international community in general but on no one in particular. For this responsibility to protect to be realizable, it needs to be assigned to a specific agent. Thus, the Supplementary Volume to the ICISS report argues that if citizens' human rights are to be protected, 'it is necessary to identify not only counterpart obligations but also specific obligation-bearers' (ICISS 2001*b*: 147).

Kok-Chor Tan (2006*a*) frames the issue in the language of perfect and imperfect duties. Unless an agent is identified as the primary agent of protection, he argues, the duty to protect will remain an imperfect one—it is a duty that cannot be morally demanded of any particular state. To generate a perfect duty to protect—that is, a duty that *can* be demanded of a specific agent and therefore is effectively claimable—a condition is needed to identify a particular agent (what Tan 2006*a*: 96 calls an 'agency condition'). The language of perfect and imperfect duties can be misleading (which Tan 2006*a*: 95–6 admits) because it differs from the normal use of these terms in political philosophy to denote the lack of specificity of claimants (rather than of agents).[9] Nevertheless, the central problem is clear: '[i]f agency is not specified, one can easily see why potential agents can have the discretion of not acting in *all* cases of humanitarian crisis if for each case there are alternative agents who can as well perform the action required by duty' (Tan 2006*a*: 95–6). We therefore need to assign the duty to protect for it to be effectively claimable. As Miller and Tan recognize, this does not necessarily involve the *formal* assignment of who should intervene in the form, for instance, of new legal criteria for intervention, which may limit the opportunities for future potential interveners. It may instead be more informal, such as a widely accepted norm that the most legitimate intervener should act, with room for other actors still to act if necessary.

The third point to note is that since we cannot assume that our preferred choice(s) of intervener will always act, it is important to consider who would be the next best choice(s). Accordingly, we need a nuanced account of who should intervene in order to provide some normative guidance when political realities strike hard and the most legitimate agent fails to act. The account of legitimacy that I present will do this.

Fourth, having a stronger sense of who should intervene may have a deterrent effect. The need for humanitarian intervention may generally decrease as potential abusers of human rights know that, if they violate human rights, they will face intervention by a particular agent.

Fifth, although the bigger problem might be a general lack of willing interveners, illegitimate intervention is a major concern. It is vital that when intervention *does* occur it is morally permissible—that the interveners are morally justified in their action. Although it sounds plausible to suggest that we should follow the maxim, 'who can, should', after the threshold conditions for humanitarian intervention have been met, this potentially risks ignoring specific issues that are raised when choosing amongst potential interveners. Most accounts of the threshold conditions do not consider questions of internal legitimacy, such as whether the intervention will be excessively costly to the intervener and whether it will have support from its domestic population. The ICISS's 'precautionary principles' (2001*a*: 31–7), for instance, make no reference to these concerns, which I will argue should affect our views on the suitability of potential interveners. We may think, for example, that our choice on who should intervene ought to be affected by the fact that intervention is likely to be excessively costly for State A but not for State B.

That said, it is possible to construct a threshold level for when intervention may be permissible that does consider questions of internal legitimacy. We might hold that, in addition to meeting the more standard requirements, such as having a reasonable expectation of success, intervention must not be excessively costly for the intervener and must have the support of its population. Any agent that meets this amended threshold can justifiably intervene and therefore has the right to act. In fact, one of the main roles of the normative account of legitimacy that I will develop (the Moderate Instrumentalist Approach) is to set out a threshold level for the justifiability of humanitarian intervention that takes into account such agency-related issues. This account of legitimacy will identify a level above which it is permissible for interveners to act—when their intervention will be sufficiently legitimate. Put simply, it will prescribe *when* interveners have the *right* to act. I will also go on to consider which current agents are likely to pass this threshold level and therefore may permissibly intervene. Thus, I consider the question: 'who has the right to act?'

There is, however, more to the issue of choosing amongst interveners than simply setting a threshold level for sufficiently legitimate humanitarian intervention. Suppose that a number of potential interveners are likely to pass the threshold level. States A, B, and C are likely to possess a sufficient degree of legitimacy, which means that they have the right to act. How are we to choose amongst interveners? The maxim, 'who can, should', does not help us to make this choice. By contrast, according to the account of legitimacy that I will provide, we can look to the intervener that, amongst those that meet the threshold level of sufficient legitimacy, will be the *most* legitimate.

In addition, if we take humanitarian intervention to be a *duty* (as I suggest in Section 1.3), and if a number of potential agents are likely to have the *right* to act because they meet the threshold level, then this raises questions of *how* the duty to intervene should be assigned. Assigning this duty raises issues of what Miller (2001) calls 'distributing responsibilities'.[10] These issues cannot be captured by simply setting a threshold level for when an agent's intervention is morally permissible. They concern *how* the duty to intervene should be distributed amongst potential agents. For example, amongst those that meet the threshold conditions, should it be the most *capable* intervener that acts? Should it be the intervener that has *historical ties* with those suffering the crisis? Is it important that the duty to intervene should be distributed *fairly* amongst interveners? Thus, I also consider the question: 'who has the duty to act?'

To recap, I am concerned with two central questions:

1. 'Who has the right to intervene?' or 'who *may* intervene?' and
2. 'Who has the duty to intervene?' or 'who *should* intervene?'.

I answer both questions with the conception of legitimacy defended through-out the book (the Moderate Instrumentalist Approach). In the answer to the first question ('who has the *right* to intervene?'), any intervener that possesses *an adequate degree of* legitimacy according to this account will have the *right* to intervene (providing that there is also just cause and they are engaged in 'humanitarian intervention'). This sets a threshold level for *when* humanitar-ian intervention will be permissible. In answer to the second question ('who has the *duty* to intervene?'), I will argue that it is the *most* legitimate agent that has the duty to intervene. If this agent fails to intervene, the duty falls on the next most legitimate intervener, and so on. For stylistic reasons, from now on I will use the phrase 'who should intervene' to denote who may intervene as well. Nothing substantive will turn on this.

1.2 HUMANITARIAN INTERVENTION AND THE RESPONSIBILITY TO PROTECT

On the face of it, the question, 'who should intervene?', seems very similar to the question, 'who has the responsibility to protect?' Both questions ask us to consider which international actor should be tasked with tackling a serious humanitarian crisis. It is important to note, however, that the responsibility to protect is both *broader* and *narrower* than humanitarian intervention, and, more generally, the status of the responsibility to protect is still subject to much dispute.

On the one hand, the responsibility to protect is much *broader* than humanitarian intervention. It comprises three central responsibilities—the responsibility to prevent, the responsibility to react, and the responsibility to rebuild. Military intervention falls only under the responsibility to *react*. First and foremost, the international community has a responsibility to *prevent* the crisis to avert the need for robust action. Measures here include development assistance, mediation (such as by Kofi Annan in Kenya in 2008 after the post-election violence), and the preventative deployment of a peacekeeping force.[11] When such efforts flounder, and a serious humanitarian crisis arises, the international community has the responsibility to react. Even then, humanitarian intervention is only one part of the toolbox of the responsibility to react. The international community should also pursue other measures, short of military intervention, such as military, diplomatic, and economic incentives and sanctions, and the use of international criminal prosecutions (e.g. referral to the International Criminal Court). Moreover, in the post-conflict phase, there is the responsibility to rebuild to ensure that the conditions that prompted the military intervention do not repeat themselves.[12]

More broadly, the responsibility to protect is concerned with encouraging states to live up to their responsibilities to protect their citizens' human rights—to realize that sovereignty entails responsibility. Humanitarian intervention is only one part of this much larger effort. Indeed, defenders of the responsibility to protect are often at pains to highlight that one of the major implications of the doctrine is to move away from the narrow choice of military intervention or no action, to a broad array of non-military measures before, during, and after the crisis.[13] For reasons of space, I will have little to say on these other measures. Nevertheless, it is important to reiterate that humanitarian intervention will sometimes still be necessary. And, when it is, we need to know who should actually intervene.

On the other hand, the responsibility to protect doctrine is *narrower* than humanitarian intervention. As I will define it (in Section 1.5), 'humanitarian intervention' can be undertaken in response to a variety of humanitarian crises and does not require Security Council authorization. Humanitarian intervention under the responsibility to protect umbrella is much more circumscribed. The degree to which this is the case depends on the particular account of the responsibility to protect adopted. Let me explain.

The responsibility to protect doctrine is still in its infancy and is not yet fixed (see Wheeler and Egerton 2009: 124–5). As it has been extended to the international arena, the responsibility to protect doctrine has evolved away from that envisaged in the original ICISS report. For instance, the UN High-level Panel Report on Threats, Challenges and Change in 2004, *A More Secure World*, published in the build-up to the 2005 World Summit, makes no mention of action outside the auspices of the Security Council (unlike the ICISS report). Most notably, the agreement reached at the World Summit waters down the ICISS account of the responsibility to protect in a number of ways (although many of the central aspects of the responsibility to protect, such as sovereignty as responsibility, remain). As a result, Weiss (2007: 117) labels it 'R2P Lite'.[14] Which version of the responsibility to protect we prefer affects how we view the issue of who should intervene and which forms of humanitarian intervention can be included under the responsibility to protect.

To see this, consider some of the key differences between the ICISS doctrine and the agreement at the World Summit.[15] On the ICISS version of the responsibility to protect, (*a*) the responsibility to protect transfers to the international community when the state involved is unable or unwilling to look after its citizens' human rights. (*b*) Military intervention will meet the just cause threshold in circumstances of 'serious and irreparable harm occurring to human beings, or imminently likely to occur' and, in particular, actual or apprehended ' "large-scale loss of life" or "large-scale ethnic cleansing" ' (ICISS 2001*a*: XII). (*c*) When the state primarily responsible for its people fails to act, reacting robustly to the crisis is a fall-back responsibility of the international community in general (ICISS 2001*a*: 17). (*d*) The Security Council should be the first port of call for humanitarian intervention, but alternative sources of authority (such as the Uniting for Peace procedure) are not to be completely discounted (ICISS 2001*a*: 53). (*e*) Intervention must meet four additional precautionary principles (right intention, last resort, proportional means, and reasonable prospects) (ICISS 2001*a*: XII).

By contrast, according to the agreement reached at the World Summit, (*a*) the responsibility to protect transfers to the international community only when 'national authorities are *manifestly failing* to protect their populations' (UN 2005: 30; emphasis added). (*b*) Military intervention will meet the just cause threshold only in the more limited circumstances of 'genocide, war crimes, ethnic cleansing and crimes against humanity' (UN 2005: 30). (*c*) Reacting to a crisis is not a fall-back responsibility of the international community. Instead, states are only 'prepared' to take collective action 'on a *case-by-case* basis' (UN 2005: 30; emphasis added). (*d*) Any action is to be collective and to be taken through the Security Council.[16] (*e*) No reference is made to criteria for intervention.

These five central differences affect what it means to ask 'who should intervene?' in the context of the responsibility to protect. If we endorse the ICISS version of the doctrine, the question is:

> Amongst the interveners that meet the precautionary principles, who has the duty to intervene when a state is unable or unwilling to halt actual or apprehended large-scale loss of life or ethnic cleansing within its borders?

By contrast, if we defend the version of the doctrine agreed at the Summit, the question is:

> Who has the right to intervene when a state is manifestly failing to prevent genocide, war crimes, ethnic cleansing, and crimes against humanity within its borders and when the Security Council authorizes intervention?

In what follows, I will answer both questions. The normative account of legitimacy that I will present—the Moderate Instrumentalist Approach—can be applied to both the broader and narrower conceptions of the responsibility to protect.

1.3 A DUTY OR ONLY A RIGHT?

Having delineated the central questions that I am concerned with, it will help now if I outline my position on two key issues in the ethics of humanitarian intervention. In this section, I consider whether humanitarian intervention is a duty or only a right. In Section 1.4, I will assess when there can be just cause for humanitarian intervention. In outlining my position on these issues, it is important to note that there is reasonable disagreement on both questions. The account of legitimacy that I will present—the Moderate Instrumentalist Approach—will also be relevant for those who hold different positions (i.e. for those who believe that humanitarian intervention is only a right and for those who assert that intervention should be limited to exceptional circumstances).

I will start, then, by considering whether humanitarian intervention is a duty or only a right. It helps to distinguish between two positions. According to what I will call the 'General Duty Approach' (in essence, the approach adopted by the ICISS), there is a general, unassigned duty to undertake humanitarian intervention. To assign this duty to intervene, we need to look to the qualities of potential interveners, such as their capability. By contrast, according to what I will call the 'General Right Approach', there is a general right to intervene, but not a general, unassigned duty to do so.

On this approach, there exist *negative* duties to non-compatriots, for instance, not to cause them harm. Yet there exist few, if any, *positive* duties to non-compatriots, particularly one as demanding as humanitarian intervention. For most agents, humanitarian intervention is only supererogatory: it is morally permissible, but not morally obligatory. That said, according to this General Right Approach, a certain agent might still have the duty to intervene. For it to do so, however, there needs to be a strong reason why it should act, such as it being responsible for the humanitarian crisis or having close ties with those suffering.[17] It is not simply a case of *assigning* the duty to intervene. Rather, the duty to intervene needs to be *generated*.

The General Right Approach is problematic. To start with, the notion that we have a general duty to intervene (as suggested by the General Duty Approach and the ICISS doctrine) is intuitively compelling. Consider the alternative in which there is no such duty and inaction in the face of extreme human suffering is acceptable. If this were the case, states did nothing wrong, for example, by failing to tackle the genocide in Rwanda.

More substantively, the General Right Approach's claim that we possess only *negative* duties to those beyond our borders can, in fact, still generate a general, unassigned duty to undertake humanitarian intervention (as endorsed by the General Duty Approach). Thomas Pogge's institutional cosmopolitan defence (1992*a*) of humanitarian intervention is relevant here.[18] It is not only tyrants and interfering states that are responsible for humanitarian crises. The lines of causality are far more complex, and we are all, to a certain extent, implicated in the imposition of a global institutional scheme that leads to severe humanitarian crises. This is by, for instance, upholding the system of resource privileges that can lead to significant, bloody conflicts over the right to sell natural resources. In doing so, we violate our negative duty not to harm others. It follows that we possess a duty to tackle the human rights violations produced by the existing international institutional scheme. The duties here include to redistribute wealth to those who do badly out of the current arrangements, as well as a duty to undertake humanitarian intervention in certain circumstances.

Even if one finds these causal claims unpersuasive, the duty to intervene, as Tan (2006*a*) asserts, seems to be a logical corollary of the right to intervene. Given the stringency of the conditions that are necessary for humanitarian intervention to be permissible, it follows that humanitarian intervention must be a duty (Tan 2006*a*: 94). In his words, '[i]f rights violations are severe enough to override the sovereignty of the offending state, which is a cornerstone *ideal* in international affairs, the severity of the situation should also impose an obligation on other states to end the violation' (Tan 2006*a*: 90). In this context, John Lango (2001: 183) argues that if we have established that there is a right to intervene, and therefore override a *prima facie* obligation not to intervene, there is a burden of proof required to show that humanitarian intervention is not a duty. Yet, satisfying this burden of proof is difficult.[19]

One reason why the symmetry between a right and a duty to intervene is sometimes denied is the excessive costs of humanitarian intervention, both in terms of soldiers' lives and resources (see Lango 2001). These costs mean that a state does not have an obligation to intervene—it is instead supererogatory. What this overlooks, however, is that, if intervention is excessively costly to its people, an intervener would not have a *right* to intervene. To see this, suppose that the Mozambican government decides to intervene in Zimbabwe with the purpose of resolving the humanitarian crisis. Mozambique's minimal financial resources are all tied up in the intervention and, as a result, it is unable to provide vital services, such as clean water provision, for its home population. In this scenario, the Mozambican government would violate its fiduciary obligation to look after the welfare of its citizens and would therefore have neither a *duty* nor a *right* to intervene. This leads us to an important point. To have the *right* to intervene, an intervener needs to possess the qualities necessary for its intervention to be justifiable. It needs, for instance, to follow international humanitarian law, to be welcomed by the victims of intervention, and to have a reasonable expectation of success. It follows that, to have a *duty* to intervene, an intervener would first need to meet these permissibility criteria so that it has a *right* to intervene. Otherwise, it could not act on this duty; it would not have the right to do so.

Here we face a serious objection to the notion that humanitarian intervention is a general duty, however. This concerns what Allen Buchanan (1999), in his discussion of the internal legitimacy of humanitarian intervention, terms the 'discretionary association view of the state' (Buchanan goes on to reject this view). This view understands the state as:

> the creation of a hypothetical contract among those who are to be its citizens, and the terms of the contract they agree on are justified by showing how observance of these terms serves *their* interests. No one else's interests are represented, so legitimate political authority is naturally defined as authority exercised for the good of the parties to the contract, the citizens of this state (Buchanan 1999: 74–5).

Accordingly, government is taken to be solely the agent of the associated individuals and its role as the furthering of these individuals' interests. As such, it 'acts legitimately only when it occupies itself *exclusively* with the interests of the citizens of the state of which it is the government' (Buchanan 1999: 75; emphasis added). On this view, humanitarian intervention could not be a duty. Intervention cannot be demanded of a state because it would require the state to pursue the interests of non-citizens over citizens and would therefore break the fiduciary obligation implicit in the social contract.[20]

There is, I think, something to this view. Indeed, in Chapter 5, I argue that the potential contravention of this fiduciary obligation is one of the 'special characteristics' of humanitarian intervention, which means that it requires internal support. Yet we can admit this point and still assert that humanitarian intervention is a duty.

First, and most straightforward, humanitarian intervention that *is* in the interests of the citizens of the intervening state does not contravene the terms of the contract. In such cases, the duty to intervene cannot be rejected on the basis of breaking the fiduciary obligation. It is only purely altruistic humanitarian interventions that are subject to this objection. Moreover, in Chapter 6 I draw on constructivist international relations literature to defend a broad interpretation of a state's self-interest (against narrow materialist accounts of self-interest). On this wider, ideational definition, many humanitarian interventions will be in the interests of the state and therefore not subject to this criticism.

Second, when humanitarian intervention is what in Chapter 5 I call 'internally representative' (i.e. when it has internal support), it may be a duty. When citizens *do* support humanitarian intervention, it can still be demanded that the state acts according to the terms of the social contract. It may be responded that support for the intervention has to be unanimous, which is highly unlikely. Otherwise, humanitarian intervention would violate the terms of the contract for those who oppose intervention. Even if there were majority support for the intervention, it would use at least one citizen's resources in a manner that they do not agree to and therefore not be justified in its rule over them (see Buchanan 1999: 76). However, on this view, humanitarian intervention could almost never be a right either. Thus, the discretionary association view is too strong. This takes us to the next problem.

Third, as Buchanan (1999: 78) points out, the discretionary association view denies that government possesses any obligations to those beyond the borders of the state. It follows that, on the one hand, almost any action (e.g. imperialism, colonization, and exploitation) could be justified on this view if it would advance the interests of those within the state, regardless of the harm caused to those beyond its borders. On the other hand, it also follows that any governmental action that is *not* in its citizens' interests, such as the removal of unfair trade barriers, is unjustifiable. Instead of a strict discretionary association view, we can admit that governments possess special obligations to promote their citizens' interests, but deny that these obligations should always outweigh those to non-citizens. In other words, a government does not have to occupy itself *exclusively* with the interests of its citizens. Rather, the point is that the *primary* role of government is to promote its citizens' interests. By viewing this fiduciary obligation as primary, this more moderate approach allows room for a government to possess certain obligations to those beyond its borders, including the duty to intervene when a humanitarian crisis is serious. (In less serious cases, humanitarian intervention may go beyond the scope of a government's obligations to those beyond its borders.) Hence, it is only (*a*) when states have no interest, (*b*) there is little internal support for the intervention, and (*c*) in less serious humanitarian crises that the general duty to intervene may be denied.[21]

There are further reasons for adopting the General Duty Approach. Henry Shue (2004) argues that basic rights imply correlative duties to enforce these rights, including to undertake humanitarian intervention (I discuss basic rights further in Chapter 3). Likewise, the ICISS (2001*a*: XI) claim that the foundations of the responsibility to protect (and, as a corollary, the duty to intervene) lie in: the concept of sovereignty; the responsibilities of the Security Council; the developing practice of states, regional organizations, and the Security Council; and legal obligations under human rights and human protection declarations and other legal instruments.

From an interactional cosmopolitan approach, Carla Bagnoli (2006) argues that the duty to intervene stems from the moral obligation to respect humanity, independent of any consideration of special relationships. To flesh this out further, we can say that there is a duty to prevent, to halt, and to decrease substantial human suffering, such as that found in large-scale violations of basic human rights. This duty to prevent human suffering is not dependent on high levels of interdependence. Instead, it is universal, generated from the fundamental moral premise that human suffering ought to be tackled.[22] This duty to prevent human suffering translates, firstly, into an *unassigned, general* duty to intervene for sufficiently legitimate interveners (i.e. for those that meet the threshold level). Second, it translates into an *assigned* duty for those whose intervention would possess the greatest legitimacy according to the Moderate Instrumentalist Approach.

For those agents that cannot intervene justifiably (perhaps because they would not be effective or would not be able to intervene without excessive cost to themselves), there is no duty to undertake humanitarian intervention. Instead, the more general duty to prevent human suffering translates into other, more specific duties, which also ensue from the duty to prevent human suffering. These might include duties to do the following: to work towards becoming more effective interveners (perhaps by improving capability); to prevent human suffering in other ways (such as by using diplomatic pressure and giving aid); to assist (and not to resist) those that are attempting to tackle human suffering; and to press for reforms to the current mechanisms and agents of humanitarian intervention so that human suffering is tackled (including the development of a new institutional arrangement for humanitarian intervention).

1.4 JUST CAUSE

Let me now turn to consider the 'just cause' question: how serious does a humanitarian crisis have to be in order for military intervention to be justified? Is humanitarian intervention justifiable, as Michael Walzer suggests, in response to acts that 'shock the moral conscience of mankind' (2006: 107)? Or, can it be justifiable to intervene in many more cases, such as in response to arbitrary detention or, as Fernando Tesón (2005c: 157–60) argues, severe tyranny and anarchy?

I cannot explore all the complexities of this issue here.[23] I will instead consider briefly the reasons for setting the bar for humanitarian intervention high and offer an account of just cause that can be used to frame the assessment of who should intervene. Also note that the question of just cause is only one part of when humanitarian intervention can be justifiable. Just cause concerns the circumstances in the target state that *potentially* render humanitarian intervention permissible. For an intervener to act permissibly, it would *also* need to possess the other qualities identified by the Moderate Instrumentalist Approach, such as having a reasonable prospect of success and being welcomed by those subject to the crisis.

There are a number of possible reasons to maintain a proscribed view of just cause. The first is communal integrity. As Walzer (1980) argues, the circumstances in the target state that potentially justify intervention should be limited because of a community's right of self-determination. A community should generally be free to form its own government. As such, there is just cause for humanitarian intervention only in cases where it is 'radically apparent' that there is no 'fit' between a government and its people (Walzer 1980: 214, 217). However, a community's right of self-determination is not a persuasive reason to limit just cause for humanitarian intervention. A community's right to self-determination seems less valuable when there is a major humanitarian crisis within its borders, regardless of whether there is a fit between the majority of the population and the government (a minority may be suffering the crisis).[24]

Walzer (1980: 212) also points to epistemic reasons—foreigners are not well placed to evaluate whether there is a 'fit' between a government and its people. Although the existence of a fit may be morally irrelevant, epistemic difficulties of judging the existence of a humanitarian crisis do provide reason to be cautious when engaging in humanitarian intervention. Yet, this is a practical issue. Simon Caney (2005: 237) argues that, although it may sometimes be difficult to assess the existence or seriousness of the crisis, in other cases an external party may have substantial evidence of human suffering. As the ICISS (2001*a*: 35) note, reports by UN organs and agencies, international organizations, and NGOs can be helpful in this regard, and the Secretary General or the Security Council can send special independent fact-finding missions. Moreover, if an intervener is responsive to the opinions of the victims of the humanitarian crisis and the burdened bystanders (as I argue in Chapter 5 it should), there would potentially be a more reliable internal assessment of the crisis. In addition, it would be less clear that humanitarian intervention would violate a community's right of self-determination because it would have notable support from within the community.

A related defence is the assertion that there can be only very limited occasion for intervention to be permissible because a state's sovereignty should be respected. More specifically, it is only when the state can no longer be said to exist as a sovereign entity (e.g. in cases of failed states and civil war) that intervention can be permissible. This is an unpersuasive view of sovereignty. It treats the state essentially as a black box: what goes on within its borders is solely the responsibility of the state, not outsiders. This is problematic because it gives leaders impunity to violate their citizens' human rights without fear of reprimand. By contrast, according to the view of sovereignty as responsibility, such as defended by the ICISS (2001*a*), a state's right to be sovereign and free from external interference depends on the treatment of its population. On this view, a state's sovereignty is conditional on its internal legitimacy, and its internal legitimacy is conditional on the treatment of its population (e.g. the general protection of citizens' human rights). It follows that sovereignty does not provide justification to oppose humanitarian intervention when a state is unable or unwilling to uphold its citizens' rights. In such cases, its sovereignty is temporarily suspended.

There are, however, a number of other potential reasons to set the bar for humanitarian intervention high. To start with, it may be that states have the right to use their citizen's resources to undertake humanitarian intervention only when a humanitarian crisis is severe. This argument builds on the discussion of a state's fiduciary obligations in Section 1.3. The suggestion is that there is a moral requirement to use your country's military and financial resources to help those beyond your borders only when these individuals face extreme degrees of human suffering. As I suggested earlier, although there is something to this view, humanitarian intervention in less serious cases may be in the interests of the intervener's population and therefore will not always contravene a state's fiduciary obligations to its citizens.

More pragmatically, we may think that we should restrict humanitarian intervention to exceptional cases because of the importance of international order. That is, humanitarian intervention should be only a rare occurrence because this will best protect the stability of the international system. If humanitarian intervention can be undertaken in response to less serious cases, there are likely to be many cases of intervention and this will create instability in the international system. Accordingly, humanitarian intervention should be limited to only the most serious cases. It is unclear, however, that intervention in less serious cases will necessarily undermine international order. Even less serious humanitarian crises may have destabilizing effects for surrounding regions and therefore intervening in response to them may, in fact, be beneficial to international order. Moreover, even if it were true that humanitarian intervention in less serious cases undermines international order, it is unclear what the value of international order is if it protects the status quo in which many humanitarian crises—and high levels of human suffering—go unchecked (Caney 2005: 240).

Perhaps the most plausible reason to maintain the bar for humanitarian intervention links just cause to the importance of the likelihood of success (which I defend strongly in Chapter 3). If intervention is to increase the enjoyment of human rights, that is, if it can be reasonably expected to be successful, the intervener needs to be responding to a situation in which it has the opportunity to do enough good to outweigh the harm that its intervention will cause. As Eric Heinze asserts, '[w]hether or not the use of military force can be expected to avert more harm than it brings about thus depends crucially on how large-scale or severe the situation to be corrected is' (2005: 173). This is because humanitarian intervention involves military action and so is likely to harm the human rights of some of those in the political community that is subject to the intervention. It is also likely to harm the human rights of those undertaking intervention. For instance, the intervener may suffer casualties and intervention may be a heavy drain on its resources. Furthermore, intervention may destabilize international order to a certain degree. If the infliction of these three sorts of harms is to be legitimate, the humanitarian crisis must be of such a magnitude that the good that might be secured by intervention is sufficiently large to outweigh the badness of those harms. In particular, the crisis will have to be such that intervention will improve the human rights situation sufficiently to offset the harms that it will cause. As Heinze argues unless a

> government is engaging in large-scale, systematic and gross physical abuse
> of its people, then the costs of deposing such a regime via military invasion is

likely to only bring about severe harm that would have otherwise not occurred. Since interveners risk killing people, maiming them, and otherwise physically harming them in the conduct of intervention, then intervention must only take place to avert this same type and severity of harm (2005: 172).

Therefore, there is reason to have two sorts of limits on when humanitarian intervention can be justifiable. The first is *qualitative*: the rights being violated must be what Shue (1996) calls '*basic* rights', such as the right to physical security (including the right not to be subject to murder, rape, and assault) and the right to subsistence (Abiew 1999: 31; Holzgrefe 2003: 18). The violation of other, *non-basic* rights, such as the right to a fair trial, equal pay for equal work, and the right to political representation is not sufficient justification for humanitarian intervention. The second limit is *quantitative*: there must be a substantial number of individuals whose basic rights are being violated. Humanitarian intervention should not be used, R.J. Vincent (1986: 127) argues, for the 'everyday' violation of basic rights; rather, it is reserved for gross or massive violations. Together, these two limits assert that humanitarian intervention can be justifiable only in cases where a *large number* of violations of *basic* rights are being frustrated. Any good achieved by responding to, first, a large number of violations of *other human rights* (which are not basic) or, second, a *small* number of violations of *basic* rights, are unlikely to outweigh the harms caused by intervention. An intervener can be expected to be effective overall only in cases where a *large number* of violations of *basic human rights* are being frustrated. For instance, suppose that the Mauritanian government detains opposition politicians without trial, denies the freedom of the press, and does not follow proper judicial processes. Military intervention in Mauritania, however, would cause much more hardship for the Mauritanians than their current situation. Intervention in this case is therefore unlikely to be effective overall because the situation, although bad, is not bad enough. Suppose further that genocide is currently ongoing in Guinea-Bissau. Although intervention in Guinea-Bissau may cause harm to some of its citizens, for instance, by damaging vital infrastructure with stray bombs, the situation is bad enough for the intervener to be effective overall. By tackling the genocide, the intervener will make a large enough increase in the enjoyment of basic human rights to outweigh these harms.

These qualitative and quantitative limits mean that, ultimately, we should generally endorse a just cause criterion similar to that outlined by the ICISS (2001*a*: XII). This asserts that, for humanitarian intervention to be warranted, there must be serious and irreparable harm occurring to human beings or imminently likely to occur. In particular, there must be circumstances of actual or apprehended (*a*) 'large-scale loss of life', with or without genocidal intent or not, which is the product of deliberate action or neglect or (*b*) 'large-scale ethnic cleansing', whether carried out by killing, forced expulsion, or acts of terror or rape.

Such practical concerns provide the strongest case for generally maintaining that the bar for humanitarian intervention should be set high. There may, however, be particular instances when intervention in response to a less serious crisis is likely to cause little harm. There would be little reason to reject such a case as morally problematic, providing that the intervener undertaking the intervention was legitimate. Suppose, for instance, that an intervener can successfully prevent the assassination of a large number of political prisoners *without* putting at risk many of its own soldiers and civilians in the target state. Suppose further that it has internal support from its population, will be welcomed by those subject to the intervention, has the authorization of the Security Council, and will follow closely strict principles of *jus in bello* (listed in Chapter 4). We should not necessarily oppose such a case, even though there is reason to hold that in general the circumstances for justifiable humanitarian intervention must be very serious. Thus, for pragmatic reasons the bar for humanitarian intervention should be high, but in principle the target state's internal legitimacy is the determinant of whether there is just cause for humanitarian intervention.

1.5 DEFINITIONS

Having outlined my view on two central issues in the ethics of intervention, this section will clarify what I mean by two key terms: 'humanitarian intervention' and 'legitimacy'.

1.5.1 Defining 'humanitarian intervention'

The term 'humanitarian intervention' is frequently employed to denote a wide array of international actions, from the distribution of humanitarian aid to virtually any form of military intervention, regardless of whether it is in response to a serious humanitarian crisis. The recent wars in Iraq and Afghanistan have further muddied the waters, as there has been a tendency for these wars to be viewed (wrongly) as 'humanitarian interventions', even by those who believe that they lacked any humanitarian rationale. It is therefore necessary to define what I mean by 'humanitarian intervention' to help set the scope of what follows.

Before beginning, it is important to distinguish the definitional issue of the qualities that an agent needs to be *engaged* in humanitarian intervention from the normative issue concerning the qualities it needs to be engaged *legitimately* in humanitarian intervention. By defining humanitarian intervention, the ensuing discussion will provide an account of certain qualities that an intervener must have if it is to be engaged in 'humanitarian intervention'. These qualities help to define a humanitarian intervener, rather than what counts as a *legitimate* humanitarian intervener. This is not to prejudge the *legitimacy* of an intervener: an intervener that is engaged in 'humanitarian intervention' according to the definition that I outline might still be illegitimate. This contrasts with a definition of *justifiable* humanitarian intervention, which, by including a number of normative criteria, builds the rectitude of humanitarian intervention into its definition. The difficulty with this sort of definition is that it risks twisting the definition of humanitarian intervention to exclude morally problematic cases of humanitarian intervention, which, despite their difficulties, are still generally regarded as instances of 'humanitarian intervention'.

It should also be noted that the ICISS (2001*a*) argue for the abandonment of the term 'humanitarian intervention' in favour of the language of the 'responsibility to protect'. The reasons they give include the international opposition to the notion of 'humanitarian intervention' (ICISS 2001*a*: 9) and that the language of the humanitarian intervention focuses attention on the claims, rights, and prerogatives of interveners rather than potential beneficiaries (2001*a*: 16–18).

The rejection of the notion 'humanitarian intervention' is unhelpful, however. As noted earlier, the responsibility to protect doctrine is both broader and narrower than humanitarian intervention. The risk is that general opposition to humanitarian intervention will transfer to the notion of the responsibility to protect, and therefore risk jeopardizing the potential contributions of the latter beyond humanitarian intervention (e.g. the acceptance of sovereignty as responsibility (see Bellamy 2009*a*: 112). It is better then, as Bellamy (2009*b*: 198) argues, to distinguish sharply between the responsibility to protect and humanitarian intervention to avoid the responsibility to protect being seen solely as humanitarian intervention in disguise. To do this, we need separate terms. Indeed, the ICISS (implicitly) seem to recognize the need still for the notion of humanitarian intervention, since they repeatedly use the cumbersome phrase 'intervention for human protection purposes' throughout their report as a synonym for humanitarian intervention.[25]

There are four defining conditions of humanitarian intervention. The first concerns the activity of intervention. To start with, humanitarian intervention is *military* (e.g. Roberts 1993: 445). This distinguishes it from a number of actions that we do not commonly regard as humanitarian intervention, including economic interventions (such as sanctions, trade embargoes, and boycotts) and diplomatic interventions (such as denunciation, the restricting of certain individuals' ability to travel, and the cutting of diplomatic ties).

In addition, intervention must be *forcible* (Holzgrefe 2003: 18; Windsor 1984: 50). According to Simon Chesterman (2001: 3), non-forcible means are not part of the notion of humanitarian intervention but should be included instead in the concept of 'humanitarian assistance'. Thus, humanitarian intervention differs from humanitarian assistance (such as that delivered by humanitarian organizations like Oxfam, World Vision, and ActionAid).

This position seems commonsensical, but the question arises: against whom must humanitarian intervention be forcible? Many of the more statist definitions of humanitarian intervention argue that it must be contrary to the wishes of the government of the political community that is subject to the intervention. In other words, humanitarian intervention must lack the consent of the government of the target state. Jeff McMahan (2010), for instance, argues that it is a conceptual condition of humanitarian intervention that it does not occur at the request or with the consent of the government. The point is that action that has been consented to is not intervention because it does not violate state sovereignty (Chesterman 2001: 3; Coady 2002: 10; Holzgrefe 2003: 18; Roberts 1993: 429).

The requirement for contravention of state consent should not be viewed too strictly, however. What is important is that the action is against *someone's* wishes, such as those of militias, warlords, or criminal gangs, and in particular those who are responsible for the humanitarian crisis. This is the case even if it is not necessarily contrary to the wishes of the government of the target state. In fact, insisting on a strict view of state consent risks excluding five possible situations where humanitarian intervention does not contravene governmental consent. First, there may be no effective government to consent to the action, as in the US-led intervention in Somalia in 1992. Second, the consent may be obtained by duress. For instance, the Australian-led 1999 intervention in East Timor received consent from the Indonesian government after significant international pressure. Third, the recognized government may agree to intervention because a significant part of its territory is under rebel control. For example, the government of Sierra Leone hired the private military company (PMC), Executive Outcomes, to combat the rebel faction, the Revolutionary United Front (RUF), which was in control of large parts of the country. Fourth, the recognized government may have been forcibly removed in a coup or rebel movement and consent to outside help to restore its power, such as after the overthrow of the democratically elected General

Aristide in Haiti in 1994. Fifth, the intervention may provide military muscle in support of a UN or regional organization peacekeeping mission that originally received state consent. For example, in 2000, the UK deployed 1,000 paratroopers and five warships to strengthen the UN's faltering mission in Sierra Leone.[26] These five possibilities have led to cases that are widely cited as instances of humanitarian intervention, but would be excluded if the requirement for the contravention of state consent were asserted too strongly.[27]

 ✗ The second defining condition concerns the circumstances of intervention: humanitarian intervention takes place where there is actual or impending grievous suffering or loss of life. This condition concerns only the circumstances in the target state that enable us to say that an intervener is *engaged in* 'humanitarian intervention' rather than those that relate to its being *justifiably* engaged in humanitarian intervention. Of course, as argued earlier, for humanitarian intervention to be *justifiable*, this humanitarian crisis may have to be serious.

 ✗ The third defining condition concerns who can undertake humanitarian intervention. In short, humanitarian intervention is conducted by an external agent. This means that a state resolving its own humanitarian crisis or an insurrection by a group within the state to end a crisis are not examples of a 'humanitarian intervention', whereas a state intervening to resolve another state's humanitarian crisis is. Thus, humanitarian intervention must be transboundary. Such 'outside parties' can range from the UN to other states to PMCs.

 ✗ Fourth, it is widely held that humanitarian intervention must have a humanitarian intention (e.g. Seybolt 2007: 7; Tesón 2005c). That is to say, to be 'humanitarian', an intervention must have the predominant *purpose* of preventing, reducing, or halting actual or impending loss of life and human suffering, whatever the *underlying reasons*—its 'motives'—for wishing to do so. Chapter 6 defends this claim, and the difference between an intervener's motives and its intentions, in more detail (I also reject the definitional significance of humanitarian motives and outcomes). For now, it will suffice to note that an agent's intentions are key to classifying its actions and, as such, to be engaged in the action of 'humanitarian intervention', it is necessary that an intervener has a humanitarian intention. It follows that humanitarian intervention is not the same as intervention *for other purposes*, such as intervention for self-defence and collective security (unless these interventions contain a significant humanitarian purpose). The main objective of an intervener must be to tackle an ongoing humanitarian crisis in the target state, such as ethnic cleansing, genocide, and the mass violation of basic human rights. Of course, this need not be the only objective—a state may have a number of reasons for intervening. But the humanitarian impulse must be predominant.

Thus, to be engaged in 'humanitarian intervention', an intervener needs to meet four defining conditions: it needs (*a*) to be engaged in military and forcible action; (*b*) to be responding to a situation where there is impending or ongoing grievous suffering or loss of life; (*c*) to be an external agent; and (*d*) to have a humanitarian intention, that is, the predominant purpose of preventing, reducing, or halting the ongoing or impending grievous suffering or loss of life. Accordingly, I define humanitarian intervention as:

> forcible military action by an external agent in the relevant political community with the predominant purpose of preventing, reducing, or halting an ongoing or impending grievous suffering or loss of life.

Interventions that fall under this definition will be the focus of this book. It is important to reiterate, however, that these four defining conditions do not prejudge the legitimacy of an intervener. An intervener could possess these qualities, and therefore be engaged in 'humanitarian intervention', yet still be illegitimate.

This view of humanitarian intervention has similarities with what Cottey (2008: 440) calls 'classical humanitarian intervention'. Classical humanitarian intervention lacks the consent of the government of the target state, has a significant military and forcible element, is in response to high levels of ongoing violence, and is typically undertaken by states or coalitions of the willing. Examples include Tanzania's intervention in Uganda in 1979, the US, the UK, and France's imposition of no-fly zones in Iraq in 1991, and NATO's intervention in Kosovo in 1999. Although the UN Security Council may authorize such intervention under Chapter VII to use all necessary means to restore international peace and security (if it does, the operation is in effect a peace enforcement mission), the UN would not be likely to undertake this sort of intervention itself. Recently, however, there have been fewer classical humanitarian interventions than in the heydays of the 1990s. This is partly because the major interveners were the Western powers and their military forces have been tied up in Iraq and the War on Terror.

Classical humanitarian intervention clearly differs from 'traditional' or 'first generation' peacekeeping. Traditional peacekeeping concerns Chapter VI of the UN Charter, has the agreement of all parties to the conflict, and is based on principles of consent, neutrality, and the non-use of force (Evans 2008*b*: 120). It involves 'the stationing of neutral, lightly armed troops with the permission of the host state(s) as an interposition force following a cease-fire to separate combatants and promote an environment suitable for conflict resolution' (Diehl 2008: 15). Examples include UN missions in

Cyprus, Western Sahara, and Lebanon. The mandate and rules of engagement of these types of peacekeeping missions are not, on most accounts, strong enough for them to be deemed 'humanitarian intervention'.

The distinction between classical humanitarian intervention and traditional peacekeeping has begun to blur, however. As Cottey (2008) asserts, a 'grey area' of peace operations between these two types of operation has been growing (also see Breau 2006: 445–53). Operations in the grey area are typically deployed after a peace agreement has been signed, but this agreement is frequently fragile and there is often low-level violence with significant spoilers (Cottey 2008: 433). Although the government of the target state may consent to the operation, this consent may be coerced or the deployment may contravene the wishes of some of the parties (Cottey 2008: 433–4). Such operations are also increasingly 'hybridized', undertaken by a combination of agents performing different roles (see Chapter 7). Significantly, these operations have also increasingly been more robust in their use of force and often involve aspects of peace enforcement.[28] There has been growing pressure to protect civilians and to respond to spoilers, and this has challenged the traditional obligation on peacekeepers to remain impartial (Evans 2008*b*: 121). Consequently, most new UN missions have a civilian protection role and a Chapter VII mandate (Evans 2008*b*: 123). In this context, Weiss (2007: 9) identifies two types of military objectives, both of which have similarities to the objectives of classical humanitarian intervention. The first, 'compelling compliance', includes methods that require deadly force, such as the forcible demobilization of soldiers, the destruction of weapons, and the forcing of parties to the negotiating table (Weiss 2007: 9). The second, 'coercive protection', involves the robust protection of civilians, such as maintaining humanitarian corridors in the face of attack and the creation and protection of safe havens (Weiss 2007: 9–10). The clearest example of peace operation that has employed such measures is the UN Mission in the DR Congo (MONUC). This has used significant force proactively against rebel factions, including helicopter gunships, and is authorized to use all necessary means to protect civilians under imminent threat of physical violence. In April 2005, for instance, it attacked two rebel camps in Bunia after they failed to surrender their weapons (BBC 2005*b*).[29]

Certain operations in this grey area between classical humanitarian intervention and traditional peacekeeping can also be regarded as cases of humanitarian intervention, providing that they meet the four defining conditions (i.e. if they will be military and forcible, be responding to a major crisis, be an external agent (or agents), and possess a humanitarian intention). The inclusion of these operations reflects the shift in peace operations and humanitarian intervention, and will make the ensuing analysis of who should intervene and discharge the responsibility to protect more relevant to contemporary practice. It is also worth noting that there is much less international opposition to these new forms of humanitarian intervention than to classical humanitarian intervention. This is largely because of their multilateralism: they are typically led by the UN or a regional organization, and authorized by the Security Council, and this reduces the fear of abuse. Thus, in what follows, I am concerned with both the classical type of humanitarian intervention and the grey area of robust peacekeeping. Although the doctrine of the responsibility to protect encompasses other measures, such as traditional forms of peacekeeping, diplomatic mediation, and economic sanctions, my focus is limited to the coercive, military operations that meet the four defining conditions.

1.5.2 Defining 'legitimacy'

The concept, 'legitimacy', is also employed in a number of different ways. Those concerned with political science tend to treat legitimacy as depending on the beliefs of the individuals subject to authority. This approach is often called 'sociological' (or 'attitudinal') legitimacy. It holds that an agent is legitimate if its subjects *perceive* that it possesses the right to rule. By contrast, normative legitimacy is largely prescriptive. On this view, legitimacy is determined by moral considerations, such as whether an institution is democratic, has received its citizens' consent, and protects their human rights. Thus, an institution is legitimate if it has the right to rule and, on some accounts, if its subjects have a duty to obey its commands. As Daniel Bodansky notes, there is 'a conceptual difference between saying, "the Security Council *is* legitimate", and "the Security Council is *accepted as* (or *perceived as*) legitimate"' (1999: 602).

When used in conjunction with humanitarian intervention, legitimacy is used to mean that humanitarian intervention is legal, accepted by the international community, procedurally justified, authorized by the Security Council, and/or morally justifiable. These uses confuse a number of the central issues when deciding who should intervene. It is therefore necessary to demarcate what I mean by this term. Clarifying how I will use 'legitimacy' is also essential for the understanding of the normative arguments that are made in the later chapters. In particular, the analysis of the concept of legitimacy will (*a*) make clear what exactly it is that we are concerned with when we consider who should intervene, (*b*) clarify how the various factors in the legitimacy of an intervener hang together, (*c*) make explicit the relevance of *ex ante* and *ex post* questions of legitimacy in this context, and (*d*) identify the various types of legitimacy that will be encountered in this book.

To start with, since the question of who should intervene is, first and foremost, a moral one, I use this term in the normative sense, that is, to imply moral justifiability. In particular, my use of the concept of legitimacy draws to a certain extent on Buchanan's account of political legitimacy. For Buchanan, legitimacy is 'about the conditions that must be satisfied if it is to be morally justifiable to use force to secure compliance with principles of justice' (2000: 73). It follows that '[w]hether an entity is politically legitimate depends only upon whether the agents attempting to wield political power in it are morally justified' (Buchanan 2004: 239).[30] So, legitimacy pertains to agents—it is an 'agent-justifiability question'. To answer this question, we need to know the qualities of an agent that would mean that it could justifiably wield political power. When we apply this understanding of legitimacy to humanitarian intervention, the focus is on the agent undertaking the humanitarian intervention—the intervener. The intervener requires certain qualities to be legitimate. These features make it an appropriate agent to wield political power (i.e. to undertake humanitarian intervention). A central aim of this book is to determine what these features are. That is, I will answer the question of who should intervene by assessing the qualities needed for an intervener to be legitimate and then examining which interveners, if any, have these qualities.

It is worth noting here that this account of legitimacy does not insist on a necessary connection to political obligation or authority. It simply holds that an intervener whose action is morally justifiable is legitimate. Those subject to its intervention do not necessarily possess a content-independent reason to obey its commands.[31] Although this is a narrow meaning of legitimacy, it is widespread (e.g. Farer 2005*a*; Tesón 2003). It also avoids three confusions, all of which are common in the literature on humanitarian intervention, and which obfuscate a number of issues.

First, it avoids confusing normative and sociological accounts of legitimate humanitarian intervention. Legitimacy is often used in the sociological sense of denoting conformity with widespread beliefs and common understandings about the established laws, norms, and mores of international society. The legitimacy of an act, on this view, 'depends on the extent to which the act is undertaken in accordance with widely shared norms and understandings about what is right, which are manifested in international law and morality' (Heinze 2009: 115). Legitimate humanitarian intervention, in this sense, is intervention that is perceived to be legitimate with the norms, laws, and mores governing the use of force for humanitarian purposes. Yet, this can lead, on the one hand, to the interpretation of widely held beliefs and common understandings about the established laws, norms, and mores of international society as being morally justifiable. On the other, it can lead to viewing that which is morally justifiable as being perceived to be legitimate. This conflates a number of central issues when deciding who should intervene, such as the moral importance of international approval for humanitarian intervention. For conceptual clarity, I shall refer to such sociological accounts of the legitimacy as 'perceived legitimacy'. This is not to deny the importance of perceived legitimacy. On the contrary, it can be paramount to the importance of the effectiveness of an intervention that it is perceived to be legitimate (see Chapter 3).

Second, it avoids confusing legitimacy and legality. Sometimes 'legitimate humanitarian intervention' is used as a synonym for legal humanitarian intervention. This is especially prevalent amongst international lawyers. Those who use legitimacy in this legal sense on occasion drift between using it to imply legality and using it to imply morally justified power. The implicit assumption made then is that which is legal is morally justifiable and that which is illegal is not. By contrast, my use of the term legitimacy does not imply legality. Whether the law is in fact legitimate—meaning morally justifiable—needs to be subject to argument (see Chapter 2).

Third, this use avoids confusing legitimacy with procedural justice. That is, sometimes legitimacy is thought to depend, for example, on whether an institution follows procedures that are democratic, have been consented to, and are legal. Legitimacy is then contrasted with substantive justice, which depends, for example, on whether an institution has good laws and is effective (e.g. Kurth 2006; McDougall 2004; Stanley Foundation 2004). This purely procedural account of legitimacy rules out a consequentialist understanding of legitimacy, such as that presented by Joseph Raz (1986). It is better, then, to treat legitimacy as involving issues to do with both procedural and substantive justice. The consequentialist conception of legitimacy can then be incorporated into our general understanding of legitimacy.

Thus, I will use 'legitimacy' in the narrow sense of meaning morally justifiable power. Although using the term in this sense removes much of the content from the term, it keeps separate key normative, political, and legal issues.

Scalar and forward-looking

I need to make two additional clarifications about my use of legitimacy. First, I take legitimacy to be scalar, that is, a matter of degree. We can distinguish between an intervener possessing *full* legitimacy and an intervener possessing an *adequate degree of* legitimacy. An intervener possessing an adequate degree of legitimacy is morally acceptable. It is desirable, however, to have an intervener with a *more than adequate degree of* legitimacy and, in particular, an intervener that is *fully* legitimate, for the simple reason that such an intervener's use of power would be more morally justified.

A number of different qualities contribute to the legitimacy of an intervener. To be *fully* legitimate, an intervener needs to have all the relevant legitimating qualities. But an intervener does not have to possess all of these qualities in order to have *an adequate degree of* legitimacy. It may, for instance, be effective, representative, and legal, but not use humanitarian means, and yet still be legitimate overall. An intervener can also have varying degrees of the qualities, possessing high levels of one quality but less of another. Any combination of qualities is acceptable, as long as they each contribute enough legitimacy so that, *when added together*, the intervener possesses an adequate degree of legitimacy.

Some characteristics will make a large contribution to an intervener's legitimacy, others will be less significant. But each of the qualities is limited in how much it can contribute and therefore an intervener needs to possess a number of the qualities in order to reach an adequate degree of legitimacy. In other words, most of these legitimating qualities, taken singularly, are not necessary or sufficient conditions for an *adequate degree of* legitimacy. (That said, I argue in Chapters 3 and 4 that effectiveness, given its importance, is a *necessary* condition for an intervener to be legitimate—and can be a *sufficient* condition in certain circumstances.) Hence, this approach is cumulative: the legitimacy of an intervener depends on the combined contribution of the various qualities it possesses.

Therefore, I shall use the term 'legitimate' to encompass all of the qualities that are morally relevant for identifying an actor as the appropriate intervener. A 'fully legitimate' actor would possess all of these qualities and the 'most legitimate' actor would possess them in greater measure than any other. With the conception of legitimacy detailed, we will be able to assess whether a particular intervener, such as NATO, is legitimate.

This approach differs from a categorical approach, such as that sometimes found in Just War Theory. According to some accounts of Just War (e.g. US Catholic Bishops 1992), war can be justly waged only when the criteria of *jus ad bellum* are met (typically, these are just cause, reasonable prospect of success, legitimate authority, right intention, formal declaration of war, last resort, and proportionate response). Many theorists have used the same categorical approach for humanitarian intervention. The most significant example is the ICISS (2001*a*) report, which requires an intervener to meet six criteria (just cause, proportionate means, last resort, reasonable prospects, right intention, and legitimate authority).[32] So, on a categorical approach, an intervener would need to possess all of the relevant qualities in order to be legitimate. If it were to lack even one quality, it could not be legitimate. For example, if intervention is not the last resort, then it should not occur, even though it may be a proportionate response to a just cause undertaken for the right reasons and with a good chance of success. The main difference between the scalar approach I use in this book and the categorical approach favoured by some accounts of Just War is that, on my position, fulfilment of *all* the criteria is not always necessary. On occasion, an intervener that lacks one quality could still possess an adequate degree of legitimacy (depending on the other qualities it possesses). Notwithstanding, to be fully legitimate, an intervener will need to possess all of the relevant qualities.[33]

The second clarification is temporal. Two types of question might be raised when considering the legitimacy of humanitarian intervention. One is backward-looking (*ex post*) and is concerned with whether an intervener *was* legitimate in a particular case. The other is forward-looking (*ex ante*) and is concerned with whether an intervener *will be* legitimate. My concern is largely with the forward-looking (*ex ante*) question. The concern of this book is who should intervene if there is a humanitarian crisis that requires intervention in the future. *Ex post* questions of legitimacy—questions of whether an intervener was legitimate—are not directly relevant, although they can help to provide historical evidence on which to base future decisions, such as an agent's track record of undertaking successful humanitarian intervention.

Internal and external legitimacy

For a fuller understanding of legitimacy for humanitarian intervention, we need to note the two types of legitimacy that an intervener can have. This distinction will recur in various forms throughout this book. The first concerns the intervener's use of political power over those who make up its citizens. This is what Buchanan (1999) calls an intervener's 'internal legitimacy'. It depends on whether an intervener is morally justified with respect to the population under its normal jurisdiction, such as a state's citizens. This does not (necessarily) mean that these individuals need to believe that the intervener is legitimate. Instead, an intervener needs to act in a certain way or to have a particular structure that means it is legitimate for these individuals. Note here that my focus is on an agent's internal legitimacy for a *particular intervention* rather than its internal legitimacy *more generally as an institution*. It is possible that an intervener that is generally internally illegitimate as an institution (e.g. it is a state with an authoritarian government) might still be able to undertake internally legitimate intervention (e.g. in this instance its intervention is internally effective and reflects its citizens' opinions on the intervention).[34]

The second type of legitimacy is what Buchanan calls 'external legitimacy'. External legitimacy depends on 'whether intervention by one state or by a collection of states can be justified to the state that is the object of intervention, or to the community of states as a whole' (Buchanan 1999: 72). Again, this does not mean that these individuals must *believe* the intervener to be legitimate. Rather, it means that the intervener is structured or acts such that its power over them (its intervention) is morally justified. It helps to distinguish between two sorts of external legitimacy. The first sort of external legitimacy—what I shall call 'local external legitimacy'—depends on whether an intervener is morally justifiable for those in *the political community that is subject to its intervention*. The second sort of external legitimacy—what I shall call 'global external legitimacy'—depends on whether it is morally justifiable for those in *the wider international community* (apart from those who have been taken into account under the other two notions of legitimacy). On the one hand, an intervener may successfully halt a mass violation of human rights in a particular community—and therefore possess local external legitimacy—whilst, on the other hand, its intervention may destabilize the surrounding region, cause widespread loss of life elsewhere, and set a precedent which undermines international law—and therefore lack global external legitimacy.

To illustrate fully the different types of legitimacy an intervener can possess, consider Operation Turquoise, the French intervention in Rwanda in 1994. The internal legitimacy of France in this case depended on whether it was morally justifiable in domestic terms, that is, with regard to French citizens. For instance, two factors that might have influenced the internal legitimacy of Operation Turquoise was whether it took into account the opinions of French citizens on whether they wanted to intervene in Rwanda and the level of casualties amongst French soldiers. France's local external legitimacy depended on whether it was morally justifiable for Rwandan citizens. This could be influenced, for instance, by whether Operation Turquoise helped to end the genocide and whether the Rwandans wanted intervention. Lastly, the global external legitimacy of France's intervention depended on whether it was morally justifiable for the wider international community. Factors that might influence this include its effects on international law and whether the exodus of the *interahamwe* (the Hutu militia largely responsible for the Rwandan genocide) into eastern DR Congo, and that region's subsequent destabilization, was caused by Operation Turquoise.

1.6 THE ROAD AHEAD

This chapter has outlined the analytical framework for the rest of the book. We have seen the importance of the topic and the two central questions that I will be concerned with: 'who has the right to intervene?' and 'who has the duty to intervene?' We have also seen how the different versions of the responsibility to protect (the ICISS report and the World Summit agreement) affect these questions. In addition, I set out my position on two central issues in the ethics of humanitarian intervention: I argued that humanitarian intervention is a duty and, in general, is justifiable only in response to the mass violation of basic human rights, although there may be particular exceptions. In Section 1.5, I considered two conceptual issues. First, there are four defining qualities that an agent must possess in order to be engaged in 'humanitarian intervention'. Second, I defined what I mean by 'legitimacy'—the morally justifiable use of political power.

Over the next five chapters, I will consider the normative qualities that are required for an intervener to be legitimate. The next chapter, Chapter 2, begins this analysis by evaluating the moral relevance of an intervener's legal status. Here I consider—and largely reject—a number of possible arguments for the importance of an intervener's legal status, including the claim that illegal humanitarian intervention is abusive and undermines international order. I will also consider what the international law on humanitarian intervention is, which is vital to understanding the international picture in which the normative debates about humanitarian intervention take place.

Chapter 3 considers the importance of what I argue is a much more significant factor—an intervener's effectiveness. I outline and defend the 'Moderate Instrumentalist Approach'. This holds that an intervener's effectiveness is the primary determinant of its legitimacy. More specifically, I distinguish between three types of effectiveness—internal effectiveness, global external effectiveness, and local external effectiveness—and go on to argue that effectiveness is a necessary condition of an intervener's legitimacy. The second part of this chapter fleshes out the Moderate Instrumentalist Approach in more detail. It considers what sort of timescale and comparison should be used to measure an agent's effectiveness (and, consequently, considers the importance of intervention being the last resort), and delineates the qualities that an intervener needs to possess in order to be effective. I also consider two possible alternatives to this approach. The first, the 'Non-instrumentalist Approach', holds that an intervener's effectiveness is of little moral concern. The second, the 'Extreme Instrumentalist Approach', gives exclusive weight to an intervener's effectiveness.

To show that this second approach is unpersuasive, in Chapter 4 I outline the importance of an intervener's following principles of *jus in bello*. I defend a stricter account of the principles of discrimination and proportionality than found in traditional Just War Theory, before going on to assert two principles of 'internal *jus in bello*'. The importance of fidelity to these sets of principles, I claim, needs to be taken into account in a complete conception of legitimacy for humanitarian intervention. This, I argue, is one of the key attractions of the Moderate Instrumentalist Approach.

Chapter 5 argues that, in addition to fidelity to the principles of *jus in bello*, there are two further non-consequentialist factors that should affect who intervenes—what I call an intervener's 'internal representativeness' and its 'local external representativeness'. The importance of these two factors, I claim, further demonstrates the inadequacy of the Extreme Instrumentalist Approach and, as a corollary, further establishes the persuasiveness of the Moderate Instrumentalist Approach.

Chapter 6 considers the claim that an intervener's humanitarian credentials—its reason for intervening—are an important determinant of its legitimacy. After distinguishing between an intervener's intentions and its motives, I largely reject the non-instrumental importance of both qualities (although I assert that an intervener's intentions have definitional and instrumental importance). I use this analysis, first, to argue that an intervener can be selective in its intervention and still be legitimate and, second, to reject the humanitarian credentials of the 2003 war in Iraq.

Chapter 7 begins by bringing together the findings of the previous six chapters to provide a complete conception of legitimacy for humanitarian intervention legitimacy—the Moderate Instrumentalist Approach. It goes on to use this approach to consider to answer the two central questions: (*a*) 'who has the right to intervene?' and (*b*) 'who has the duty to intervene?' It first suggests that any agent that has an *adequate degree of* legitimacy has the right to intervene. Second, it argues that the duty to intervene should fall on the *most legitimate* intervener. Assigning the duty to intervene raises additional issues, such as that of fairness. The chapter therefore defends the view that the most legitimate agent has the duty to intervene against three leading alternatives and the claims that this is unfair. The third section considers who, out of current agents (NATO, states, the UN, regional organizations, and private military companies), (*a*) has an adequate degree of legitimacy, and therefore the *right* to intervene, and (*b*) is the most legitimate agent, and therefore has the *duty* to intervene. It concludes that, although some agents of intervention possess an *adequate degree of* legitimacy, no current agent is *fully* legitimate.

For this reason, Chapter 8 considers some proposals for improving the agents and mechanisms of humanitarian intervention so that we can legitimately tackle egregious violations of human rights on a much more frequent basis. More specifically, I evaluate five sets of proposals and defend two in particular, one long-term, one short-term. I conclude in Chapter 9 by considering how we can realize these reforms by re-emphasizing our duties, offering some proposals for amending states' perceptions of their national interest, and emphasizing that humanitarian intervention is an important, but limited, part of the responsibility to protect.

NOTES

1. For instance, in the extensive consultations across Africa, Asia, and Latin America in the build-up to the International Commission on Intervention and State Sovereignty's report, Ramesh Thakur and Thomas Weiss note that '*nowhere* did *anyone* argue that intervention to sustain humanitarian objectives is *never* justifiable' (2009: 36).
2. For discussions of these issues, see Caney (2005: 226–62), Heinze (2009), Smith (1998), and Tesón (2005c). Some still do reject the general justifiability of humanitarian intervention, such as Atack (2002), Ayoob (2002), Chandler (2002), and Mehta (2006).
3. Chopra and Weiss (1992) were amongst the first to make this claim.
4. The Security Council has also endorsed the responsibility to protect in Resolution 1674 and mentioned it in relation to Darfur in Resolution 1706. As I discuss in Section 1.2, however, the notion of the responsibility to protect agreed to at the World Summit, and endorsed by the Security Council, differs somewhat from the notion outlined by the ICISS.
5. For a discussion of the problems with defining 'international community', see Hodge (2003), Kovach (2003), and Lucas (2003b).
6. Overall, as many as 230,000 people died in Bosnia during UNPROFOR's watch (ICISS 2001b: 93).
7. In addition, the legal basis of this intervention was dubious: there was no Security Council authorization (although it did receive retrospective authorization) and the ECOWAS treaty did not permit it to deal with internal conflicts (ICISS 2001b: 81).
8. Miller draws on Michael Walzer's (2002: 23–7) defence of the same maxim, 'who can, should'. Walzer uses the maxim to imply that the agent that has the greatest capability to act—'the most capable state, the nearest or the strongest' (2002: 25)—

should intervene. This gives the maxim more normative content: in essence, 'who will be the most capable, should'. I defend a similar position in later chapters.

9. See, further, Terry Nardin (2006: 14–18) on perfect and imperfect duties in relation to who should intervene. As Nardin notes, this distinction is also sometimes used in the more Kantian sense to distinguish between duties of justice and duties of ethics.

10. Miller (2007), Pattison (2008c), and Tan (2006a; 2006b) consider issues concerning distributing responsibilities in relation to humanitarian intervention. Also see Miller (2001) and Thom Brooks (2002) on distributing duties more generally.

11. That said, humanitarian intervention could also be included under the responsibility to prevent if the contravention of the target state's government's express consent is *not* a requirement for a military action to be deemed 'humanitarian intervention' (as I argue in Section 1.5.2). In his report on the responsibility to protect, *Implementing the Responsibility to Protect*, Ban Ki-Moon (2009: 19) cites UK intervention in Sierra Leone in 2000 and the EU-led Operation Artemis in DR Congo in 2003 as examples of preventative action. These are widely regarded as instances of humanitarian intervention, even though they had the consent of the target state. Also see Wheeler (2008: 27), who argues that more consideration needs to be given to how far prevention requires a coercive military element.

12. For analysis of the normative issues raised by the responsibility to rebuild, see Gheciu and Welsh (2009).

13. See, for instance, Axworthy and Rock (2009: 59), Ban Ki-Moon (2009: 6), Bellamy (2009b: 3–4), and Evans (2008b: 56–9). In addition to the non-military measures that receive more attention, there are also a broad array of military measures that might be used, from traditional forms of peacekeeping to robust armed interventions (including different forms of humanitarian intervention). In this context, Lango (2009b: 119–20) argues that it should be recognized that there is a gamut of options for UN peace operations, including naval blockades, air power to impose no-fly zones, and a small-scale reaction mission.

14. It should be noted that Weiss (2010) has since stepped back from the caricature of the World Summit agreement as 'R2P Lite'. Also see Bellamy's (2009b: 196–7) rejection of this label.

15. For a more detailed analysis of these changes, see Bellamy (2008: 623) and A. Brown (2008). Bellamy (2009b: 66–97) also has a detailed discussion of how this agreement was reached and the politics behind it.

16. Bellamy (2006b: 168) argues that the Outcome Document does not explicitly exclude the possibility of unauthorized intervention and so leaves the door open for defences of unauthorized intervention said to be in conformity with the UN Charter. Also see Focarelli (2008: 200) and Stahn (2007).

17. In Chapter 7, I consider being responsible for the humanitarian crisis and having close ties with those suffering as alternative ways of assigning the duty to intervene.

18. Institutional cosmopolitanism 'maintains that principles of justice apply to "institutions"' whereas an interactional approach 'maintains that principles of justice apply even in the absence of a common institutional background'

(Caney 2005: 105–6). For a defence of institutional cosmopolitanism see, more generally, Pogge (2008).

19. There is sometimes a distinction made between obligation and duty (an obligation is voluntarily agreed and a duty is non-voluntary). My concern is with the non-voluntary moral requirements to prevent human suffering and to undertake humanitarian intervention. However, like Tan (2006a: 112 n.1), for stylistic reasons I will use obligation and duty interchangeably.

20. This is not to deny that *individuals* within the state possess extensive obligations to those beyond their borders. Indeed, these obligations could plausibly include a duty to encourage and support humanitarian intervention. This is consistent with the notion that the primary role of *government* is to promote its citizens' interests.

21. A further response is made by Richard Vernon (2008). He argues that humanitarian intervention *is* justified on the Lockean version of the social contract. This is because the benefits enjoyed in successful civil societies can be justified only when those who benefit are willing to aid the victims of failed or abusive states. Also see Tesón (2005c: 132–5).

22. To be sure, however, this duty to tackle human suffering is not always an overriding duty. Sometimes there are countervailing moral reasons against fulfilling it (e.g. that its fulfilment would cause more suffering and would undermine valuable personal relationships, such as family relationships). In addition, Chapter 7 suggests a subtle amendment to the duty to prevent human suffering to make it less demanding for those agents that have already done their fair share.

23. For a much more detailed discussion of this issue, see Heinze (2009). This issue may be complicated further if, as McMahan (2005) notes, humanitarian intervention can act as a contributing just cause. This means that it does not singularly provide just cause for war, but can do so in combination with other reasons for military action (such as self-defence). When humanitarian intervention is a contributing just cause, the bar for humanitarian intervention may not need to be so high since the other reasons for the military action will also do justificatory work.

24. For rejections of Walzer's restrictive account of humanitarian intervention, see Beitz (1980), Caney (2005: 236–7, 247), Doppelt (1980), Luban (1980a; 1980b), and McMahan (1996).

25. The ICISS also want to move away from the notion of the 'right to intervene'. This can be seen as an attempt to persuade international actors to view the tackling of serious humanitarian crises as morally and politically obligatory. In other words, the ICISS (2001a: 17) want to move towards the view that there is a 'duty to protect'. This does not require, however, an abandonment of the term 'humanitarian intervention'. In addition, the ICISS (2001a: 16) argue that the language of humanitarian intervention loads the dice in favour of intervention before the argument has begun. In Chapter 6, I argue that humanitarian intervention is neither *prima facie* right nor *prima facie* wrong. As such, the apparent 'humanitarianism' of the action should not prejudge the ethical issues.

26. Although one of the aims of this intervention was the protection of British citizens, this was not the only objective of the action. Paul Williams (2002) notes that other

objectives included wanting to 'do something' in the face of the impeding humanitarian crisis, the defence of democracy, the commitment to an ethical foreign policy, and defending the credibility of the UN.

27. For further discussion of consent-based humanitarian intervention, see Wheeler (2008: 10–12).

28. Susan Breau (2006: 446) argues that the recent UN peacekeeping operations in Burundi, Côte d'Ivoire, and the DR Congo are, in reality, peace enforcement.

29. For an application of Just War Theory to these sorts of robust peacekeeping missions, see Lango (2009*b*).

30. My use of legitimacy does differ, however, in some measure from Buchanan's account. This is because Buchanan (2004: 235) is concerned with the justifiability of political power, where to wield the political power is to attempt to exercise supremacy within a jurisdiction. By contrast, an intervener may not attempt to achieve supremacy.

31. Some, such as Simmons (1999), take legitimacy to be much stronger than this, by for instance implying political obligation owed to the institution. Buchanan's (and my) use of the term 'legitimacy' is much closer to Simmons' account of 'justification'.

32. Other notable examples include Farer (2005*a*), the report of the UN Secretary General's High-level Panel on Threats, Challenges and Change (UN 2004: 57–8), *A More Secure World: Our Shared Responsibility*, and Kofi Annan (2005: 33), who, in the report, *In Larger Freedom*, calls for the use of force to meet certain criteria.

33. The scalar approach is not new. Another endorsement of this sort of approach in the context of humanitarian intervention can be found in Tesón (2005*c*: 143–4).

34. For an alternative view, see Tesón (1998: 59).

2

Humanitarian Intervention and International Law

Building on the Just War principle of 'right authority', it is often claimed that humanitarian intervention must be authorized by the appropriate body, by which most mean the UN Security Council. As discussed in Chapter 1, in their endorsement of the responsibility to protect, states at the 2005 World Summit asserted that any robust action should be undertaken through the Security Council (UN 2005: 30). This reflects a common view amongst many states: an intervener's having proper legal authorization is a *necessary* condition of its moral justifiability. Their fear—especially those in the Global South—is that illegal humanitarian intervention will be abusive, destabilize their region, or be conducted against them. These concerns have been exacerbated by the US- and UK-led war in Iraq (Badescu 2007), which at times was claimed to be a case of humanitarian intervention but lacked Security Council authorization. On this view, then, we should look to an intervener's legal status when considering who should intervene: illegal intervention is unjustifiable.[1]

The agreement reached at the World Summit shifted away from the original ICISS doctrine, which admits the possibility of justifiable action outside the Security Council as a last resort. Nevertheless, the ICISS asserts that '[t]here is no better or more appropriate body than the United Nations Security Council to authorize military intervention for human protection purposes' (ICISS 2001*a*: XII). On this second view, proper legal authorization is a *highly significant factor* in an intervener's legitimacy. Although this leaves open the possibility that illegal humanitarian intervention could be justified in exceptional cases, it is generally regarded as morally unacceptable. More specifically, the ICISS (2001*a*: 48, 55) argue that humanitarian intervention approved by the UN is regarded as legitimate because it is authorized by a representative international body. By contrast, unauthorized intervention is seen as illegitimate because it is self-interested. Without the discipline and constraints of UN authorization, they claim, unauthorized intervention will not be conducted for the right reasons or with the right commitment to the necessary precautionary principles.

Only two years prior to the publication of the ICISS report, however, NATO undertook action in Kosovo that was, according to most international lawyers and commentators, illegal because it lacked the requisite Security Council authorization.[2] Nevertheless, NATO's action was, to a certain extent, successful at preventing rights violations on the scale of the Bosnian war and did receive notable support in the international community. Indeed, the Independent International Commission on Kosovo concluded that NATO's action was 'legitimate, but not legal, given existing international law' (2000: 289).[3] NATO's intervention in Kosovo raises doubts, then, over the significance that many give to an intervener's legal status: if humanitarian action can be successful at halting egregious violations of human rights without having the proper legal basis, why should we care whether an intervener has the legal right to intervene? In addition, there has been a lack of effective action in response to the human rights violations in Darfur, DR Congo, northern Uganda, and elsewhere.[4] If an illegal but effective intervener were to intervene in one of these states, should we support it? Or should we maintain that only those interveners whose intervention would be legal can justifiably undertake humanitarian intervention?

The primary aim of this chapter is to assess the commonly held position that those undertaking humanitarian intervention must have legal authority from international law to do so. I argue that an intervener's legal status according to current international law plays *little or no role* in its legitimacy. It follows that an intervener's legal status is a poor basis on which to assess who should intervene; we need to look instead to other factors to make this decision.

Note that throughout the chapter my concern is with the significance that we should give to *current international law* in determining where we should place the responsibility to intervene, not international law *per se*. Thus, I do not conduct a broad inquiry into the relationship between law and morality in international affairs. Although some of the issues that I raise can be applied to international law more generally, I focus on the specific moral and political issue of the moral significance of the current international law on humanitarian intervention when deciding who should intervene.

The chapter proceeds as follows. I start by briefly exploring the current status of the international law on humanitarian intervention. This analysis is necessary because we need to know what the law on humanitarian intervention is before we can assess its worth. Then, in the main part of the chapter, I critically examine four prevailing reasons for treating an intervener's legal status according to current international law as morally significant (and therefore an appropriate basis on which to decide who should intervene). In particular, I consider the arguments that an intervener's legal status is morally significant because: (*a*) legal interveners derive their authority from morally valuable procedures; (*b*) illegal humanitarian intervention is itself abusive; (*c*) illegal humanitarian intervention leads to abusive intervention; and (*d*) illegal humanitarian intervention undermines international order.

2.1 THE LEGAL PICTURE: INTERNATIONAL LAW ON HUMANITARIAN INTERVENTION

Let us start by looking at the current status of the international law on humanitarian intervention. There are a number of different readings of the current law, but I shall focus on two of the most informative: international legal positivism and Fernando Tesón's natural law theory. The debate between these two approaches should be helpful for our purpose of determining what the law on humanitarian intervention is.[5] Why is this relevant? First, and most obviously, if we are to assess the moral importance of an intervener's legal status according to current international law, we need to know what this law is. Second, understanding the international law on humanitarian intervention is central to grasping the international framework in which the normative debates about humanitarian intervention must work. It is important then to grasp the international legal picture before deciding who should intervene.

2.1.1 An international legal positivist reading of international law

International legal positivism is a subspecies of legal positivism. It holds the 'separability thesis', asserting that there is a conceptual distinction between what international law is and what morality demands. As such, *lex lata*—the law as it is—is not the same as *lex ferenda*—the law as it ought to be. Its account of legal validity, and therefore of what international law is, is highly voluntaristic. International law is said to emanate exclusively 'from the free will of sovereign independent states. There is no law except what is "posited" by sovereign powers' (Wight 1991: 36). There are two ways in which sovereign states 'posit their will', that is, consent to international law. The first is by agreeing to a treaty; the second is by engaging in a practice which becomes a customary rule of international law over time as it is repeated (and which meets the requirements of *opinio juris*).[6] In other words, for international legal positivism the two sources of international law are treaty and custom and, as such, moral considerations are not necessary for legal validity.

International legal positivists generally take the following position on the legality of humanitarian intervention. Article 2(4) of the UN Charter provides a general prohibition on the use of force. This states that:

> [a]ll Members shall refrain in their international relations from the threat or use of force against the territorial integrity or political independence of any state, or in any other manner inconsistent with the Purposes of the United Nations.

There are only two significant legal exceptions: unilateral or collective self-defence and Security Council enforcement action under Chapter VII of the UN Charter.[7] Most international legal positivists reject the existence of a third possible exception to Article 2(4), which would hold that *unauthorized* humanitarian intervention is legal because there is a customary international law for this practice. Their argument, in brief, is that there is insufficient state practice to establish such a customary international law (e.g. DUPI 1999; Byers and Chesterman 2003). It follows that humanitarian intervention— which violates Article 2(4)—can be legal only when undertaken for self-defence or when the Security Council authorizes it. We can dismiss the former because humanitarian intervention will be very rarely, if ever, legal on the basis of self-defence, so defined in international law.[8] Interveners therefore need to have Security Council authorization in order to be legal.

This reading of the law on humanitarian intervention is disputed by some legal positivists who regard it as too broad (e.g. Joffe 1994; Hehir 2008: 13–32). Their argument is that the Security Council is restricted by the UN Charter, which, in Article 2(7) claims that the UN cannot intervene 'in matters which are essentially within the domestic jurisdiction of the state'. And, although Chapter VII measures concerning 'international threats to peace and security' are excluded from this article, the argument runs, humanitarian intervention rarely constitutes an international threat to peace and security. As such, the Security Council has no legal basis to authorize humanitarian intervention. What this overlooks, however, is that according to Article 39 of the Charter, it is the Security Council that determines what constitutes an 'international threat to peace and security'. Since the early 1990s, the Council on occasion has broadened its interpretation of a threat to international peace and security to include intra-state war and internal oppression, and has been willing to authorize humanitarian intervention in such cases. Moreover, the recent discussions of the responsibility to protect and, in particular, the agreement reached at the World Summit, seem to indicate that states view the Security Council as empowered to authorize humanitarian intervention (Focarelli 2008: 212), even in the absence of a clear threat to international peace and security.[9]

In addition, there are three other (but perhaps less significant) exceptions to the requirement for Security Council authorization. The first is when the target state expressly agrees to the intervention. As such, humanitarian intervention that has been consented to by the government of the target state is legal, since it does not violate its sovereignty.[10] The second is intervention undertaken by certain regional organizations, most notably the African Union (AU). Article 4 (h) of the Charter of the AU permits it to intervene in grave circumstances (war crimes, genocide, and crimes against humanity) in countries who have signed up to the treaty. That said, it is questionable whether humanitarian intervention authorized by regional organizations can be legal without accompanying (perhaps *ex post*) authorization by the Security Council (Badescu 2007: 59–60). A third option, cited by the ICISS (2001*a*: VIII), is the Uniting for Peace procedure of the General Assembly. This allows the General Assembly to make recommendations on enforcement action when the Security Council is unable to decide, providing that the action wins two-thirds majority backing (ICISS 2001*b*: 159). The problem with this procedure, however, is that humanitarian intervention which does not receive Security Council authorization is highly unlikely to win two-thirds majority approval in the General Assembly, given notable opposition amongst states to intervention outside the auspices of the Security Council.[11]

Before moving on to assess the naturalist view of the law on intervention, it is worth mentioning the legal status of responsibility to protect on a positivist understanding. The responsibility to protect doctrine is often described as an 'emerging norm', on its way to becoming binding law (e.g. Matthews 2008: 147). The Outcome Document of the 2005 World Summit and Resolution 1674 of the Security Council (which affirms the Council's commitment to the notion of a responsibility to protect) lends credence to this view, as does Resolution 1706 of the Security Council, which affirms the responsibility to protect in the context of Darfur. As the responsibility to protect continues to be invoked, the argument runs, it will become part of customary international law.

This line of reasoning, however, to a certain extent confuses matters, since the particular requirements of responsibility to protect are still subject to much debate and most of the main statements of the responsibility to protect (such as the Outcome Document, *A More Secure World*, and the ICISS report) differ in emphasis, such as on how serious a humanitarian crisis has to be before the responsibility transfers to the international community. As such, the responsibility to protect is far from being a clear norm in international law. Instead, it is more fruitful to look at some of the specific elements that comprise the responsibility to protect. And, when we do, we find that much of the doctrine, in terms of its legal requirements, is old wine in new bottles.

Take the doctrine's assertion that states have an obligation to look after their citizens' interests. As Carsten Stahn (2007: 118) argues, this legal obligation is well established in universal and regional human rights conventions. The same is also true of the central claim of the responsibility to protect that states cannot cite sovereignty as a legal barrier against external interference. As detailed earlier, current international law sometimes permits humanitarian intervention. The central proviso is that the intervention receives Security Council authorization. This is akin to the Outcome Document's requirement that intervention be authorized by the Council.

In fact, different interpretations of the responsibility to protect have a greater claim to legal validity than others. It is doubtful whether the wider conceptions of the responsibility to protect, such as that endorsed by the ICISS, are legally binding. This is because of their stronger view on the obligations of the international community to intervene. Although states are legally obliged to act in cases of genocide under the Genocide Convention, the issue is whether, as the ICISS argues, they are required to act in other cases of the mass violation of human rights. Stahn (2007: 119) thinks that this is doubtful and this puts in question the legal validity of the ICISS account of the responsibility to protect.[12] By contrast, the agreement reached at the 2005 World Summit is, in part, legally binding on a legal positivist reading. This is because, as Stahn (2007: 109) also notes, the agreement at the 2005 World Summit largely rejects the view that the international community has a legal obligation in such cases. The legal validity of this agreement is not because of a dramatic legal shift since the development of the responsibility to protect concept. On the contrary, it is because this particular limited version of the responsibility to protect largely mirrors existing international law (on a positivist reading).

2.1.2 A naturalist reading of international law

Some view this positivist understanding of the law on humanitarian intervention and the responsibility to protect to be too restrictive. A prominent example is Tesón (2005c), who, from the perspective of natural law, argues that those undertaking humanitarian intervention do not need to have express Security Council authorization to be legal.

Like all naturalist accounts, Tesón rejects the separation of legal validity and morality. His account, which is based on Ronald Dworkin's interpretive natural law theory, asserts that what the current status of the law is on a certain issue, such as humanitarian intervention, also depends in part on what the law ought to be. In other words, *lex ferenda* affects *lex lata*. Tesón's naturalism includes a large role for positive law but, in contrast to legal positivists, he argues that neutral analysis of the two traditional positive sources of international law—custom and treaty—is impossible, and we should therefore interpret these sources according to the best moral theory of the purposes of international law. This theory, according to Tesón (2005c), is a human rights-based approach that sees individuals as the subjects of international law and the role of international law as the protection of human rights.

On the basis of this human rights-based approach, Tesón argues that those undertaking humanitarian intervention act legally, even if they lack express Security Council authorization. He reaches this conclusion principally by claiming that the selection and reading of possible precedents, which could establish or deny the existence of a customary law permitting humanitarian intervention, is inevitably affected by the interpreter's views on the role of international law. Given that international practice tends to be chaotic and contradictory, and that any attempt to find normative patterns of behaviour is result-orientated (Tesón et al. 2003: 941), he claims that we need to appeal to moral–political values to interpret potential precedents (Tesón 2005c).

Using a human rights-based interpretation of state practice, Tesón (2005c: 219–329, 343–414) argues that there are a number of precedents for humanitarian intervention: India's 1971 intervention in East Pakistan; Tanzania's 1979 intervention in Uganda; France's 1979 intervention in the Central African Republic; US interventions in Grenada in 1983 and Panama in 1989; ECOWAS action in Liberia in 1991 and Sierra Leone in 1997; the US, the UK, and France's 1991 intervention in northern Iraq to protect the Kurds; the US-led 1992 UN intervention in Somalia; the US-led 1994 action in Haiti; the French-led 1994 intervention in Rwanda; NATO's 1994 intervention in Bosnia, NATO's 1999 intervention in Kosovo, and the US-led interventions in Afghanistan in 2001 and Iraq in 2003. On the basis of these precedents, Tesón asserts that there is a legal right to intervene in customary international law for *both* authorized and unauthorized interveners.

It is hard to see how this conclusion can be sustained, however. The central problem is this: although intervention authorized by the Security Council is legal, too few *unauthorized* humanitarian interventions have met the requirements of *opinio juris* for it to be plausibly claimed that unauthorized humanitarian intervention is legal according to customary international law.

According to the International Court of Justice, the *opinio juris* condition of customary international law requires:

> [e]ither the States taking such action or other States in a position to react to it, must have behaved so that their conduct is 'evidence of a belief that this practice is rendered obligatory by the existence of a rule of law requiring it' (in Chesterman 2003: 58 n.26).

Most of the unauthorized interveners that Tesón cites did not behave in a way that evidences a belief that humanitarian intervention is legally obligatory. In particular, they did not claim that their action was legal according to the international law on humanitarian intervention (they instead cited other legal justifications, such as self-defence), nor was world opinion inclined to regard these interveners' actions as legal (Chesterman 2003: 49–50). For instance, neither Tanzania in Uganda, India in East Pakistan (at least primarily), nor France in Central African Republic invoked a humanitarian justification for their action, nor was there widespread support for the legality of humanitarian intervention at the time (see Byers and Chesterman 2003; DUPI 1999; Wheeler 2000).

That said, it could be reasonably claimed that *some* unauthorized humanitarian interventions have met the requirements of *opinio juris*. For example: the 1992 intervention in northern Iraq by the UK, the US, and France was justified in conformity with Security Council resolution 688, but also asserted a right of humanitarian intervention (albeit a limited one which required a supporting Security Council resolution) (Wheeler 2000: 169); ECOWAS declared a right of humanitarian intervention in its interventions in Liberia (1990) and Sierra Leone (1997) (ICISS 2001*b*: 166); and NATO's legal justification for intervening in Kosovo rested on some assertion of a right of humanitarian intervention or humanitarian 'necessity' (Stromseth 2003: 251).[13]

It is doubtful, however, whether any customary right of unauthorized humanitarian intervention can be reasonably interpreted to exist solely on the basis of these few interventions. Customary international law is formed by states engaging in a repetitive and ongoing practice. As the practice is repeated over time, it becomes law. The problem is that there have been too few instances of unauthorized humanitarian intervention that meet the requirements of *opinio juris* for unauthorized humanitarian intervention to be said to be a 'repetitive and ongoing practice'. Thus, at best such a law is in the process of emerging; it is not yet established.

Hence, it seems clear then that legal positivists are right on this point: according to current international law, legal interveners are those with express Security Council authorization and illegal interveners are those without it.

This is not to reject *in general* the natural law position defended by Tesón. It is simply to assert that, on this particular issue, the law seems to cohere with how most legal positivists view it. In fact, a natural law theorist may disagree with Tesón's particular reading of the law on humanitarian intervention and instead believe that, although possible precedents should be interpreted using a human rights-based approach, there is insufficient customary international law to establish a legal right of humanitarian intervention for unauthorized interveners.

2.2 THE MORAL SIGNIFICANCE OF AN INTERVENER'S LEGAL STATUS

Having seen what the current international law on humanitarian intervention is, how important is it that those undertaking humanitarian intervention do so legally? Or, to put it another way, is it morally significant that interveners have received Security Council authorization?

2.2.1 Legal proceduralism

It should be noted here that although I have endorsed the legal positivist understanding, this is not to presume the moral justifiability of the current international law on humanitarian intervention. To that extent, it is important to distinguish between international legal positivism and what I shall call 'legal proceduralism'. International legal positivism makes no direct normative claims *itself*. It is simply a theory of what constitutes international law, that is, of legal validity. It holds that the two sources of law are treaty and custom (rather than moral considerations), but does not make any *normative* claim about the moral significance of these procedures. Legal proceduralism, by contrast, is normative. It asserts that the procedures by which international law is formed are *morally* valuable and, consequently, international law has moral significance (because it is formed by these procedures).

Many legal positivists also happen to assert legal proceduralism, but the two need not go hand in hand. On the contrary, a legal positivist can coherently assert that an intervener needs to have Security Council authorization in order to possess the legal authority to undertake humanitarian intervention, but, at the same time, hold that whether an intervener has Security Council authorization—and therefore has the legal authority to undertake humanitarian intervention—is of little moral significance. Indeed, in this chapter, I accept the international legal positivist reading of the current international law on humanitarian intervention, but reject the claim that this law is morally significant.

There are, in fact, significant problems with legal proceduralism in the context of humanitarian intervention. This approach asserts that an intervener's legal status is morally important because of the moral value of the processes by which this law is formed, that is, by, firstly, state consent to international law and, secondly, Security Council authorization.

State consent

As already discussed, state consent is the process by which international law is created (by treaty and custom) and therefore the way in which interveners authorized by the Security Council ultimately gain their *legal* authority. State consent may also be claimed to be *morally* valuable, and consequently that international law has moral significance because it is formed by state consent. On this line of reasoning, then, the legality of interveners is important because legal interveners ultimately derive their authority from state consent.

There is no clear analogy, however, between individual consent and state consent, so it does not follow that because individual consent matters state consent matters as well.[14] Nor can it be plausibly claimed that state consent is somehow representative of individual consent, for many states are undemocratic and even some apparently democratic states are often unrepresentative of their citizens on specific issues, including foreign policy issues. In these cases, Buchanan argues, 'leaders cannot reasonably be regarded as agents of their people' and 'it cannot be said that state consent is binding because it expresses the people's will' (2003: 152). One might reply that states represent their citizens even though their citizens have not expressly consented. Yet this claim has limited credibility. It is plausible only when there is some formal system of representation in place (this does not necessarily have to be liberal democracy) and when states do not seriously violate their citizens' human rights.[15] So, although this argument is not fully convincing, neither is it wholly unsuccessful: state consent can be said to have some, albeit minor, moral value because, in some states, it expresses the wishes of that state's citizens.

A seemingly more promising defence of the moral worth of state consent, and therefore of an intervener's legality, is presented by David Chandler (2002). He argues that state consent is necessary for the formal equality of states, which he assumes is morally valuable. More specifically, he argues that state consent is a crucial part of the 'equality of derivation', which along with the 'equality of application', is required for international law to be based on the formal equality of states. In his words: 'international law derives its legitimacy from the voluntary assent of nation-states.... Without a notion of consent, the distinction between law...and repression...disappears' (Chandler 2002: 137; also see Hehir 2008: 27–32).

The trouble with this argument is that it shifts the problem from justifying state consent to justifying the formal equality of states, and it is unclear why the formal equality of states has moral value. The formal equality of states cannot be plausibly defended on democratic or egalitarian grounds. It does not reflect an equal consideration for individuals (which is perhaps one of the most convincing arguments for the democratic ideal) since, firstly, many states are unrepresentative of their citizens on a number of issues and, secondly, states of massively varying population size (e.g. Luxembourg and India) would be treated equally if we were to follow this principle (Buchanan 2004: 318). And even if we overlook these difficulties and assume that the equality of states is valuable, there is not a strong link between the *formal* equality of states and the *actual* equality of states. Powerful states have a much greater ability to consent to international law (they are more likely to be the authors of customary international law and have greater bargaining power in treaty negotiations) and are less likely to have international law applied against them.

This leads us to a larger problem with arguments that use state consent to make the case for the moral value of an intervener's legal status: in practice, international law is not founded on the free consent of sovereign states. The first element of this problem is that, when states consent to international law, their consent is often not freely given. It is widely held that consent needs to be free from duress and that there need to be reasonable options available if it is to be morally valid, but such requirements are frequently not met in the process of international law. Hence, Buchanan argues 'what counts as consent in the system is not qualified by any requirement of voluntariness that would give what is called consent normative punch' (2004: 303). The second element of this problem is that states have not consented to many aspects of international law. Although treaty-based law may appear less susceptible in this regard, it still suffers from a lack of free consent. Perhaps the best example of this, as H.L.A. Hart (1994: 226) notes, is the automatic assumption that newly formed states are bound by international treaties, even though they have not consented to them. Given the number of states achieving independence in the past 100 years, this is a serious consideration. What is more, even if states subsequently withdraw their consent to a particular aspect of (some realm of) international law, they are still held to be bound by it (Hall 2001: 3). Hence, the traditional view of international law, in which sovereign states are free to posit their will as they like and are bound by the law only when they choose, is in conflict with the experience and complexity of international law. In short, international law is not, in large part, based on the free consent of states.

Thus, these defences of the moral value of state consent are largely unpersuasive and, even if they were persuasive, the extent to which states have freely consented to international law is questionable. It follows that state consent to international law provides little reason for holding that the legality of an intervener matters. Let us now consider a second possible procedural reason for the moral significance of an intervener's legal status.

The functioning of the Security Council

Security Council authorization is for a large part the process by which the international law in a particular case of humanitarian intervention is determined and is therefore, like state consent, a central way in which interveners gain their legal authority. And again, as with state consent, some argue that the functioning of the Security Council is morally valuable and, as a corollary, that legal interveners gain in legitimacy because their authority derives from this process.

To be sure, most of those who make this argument admit that the Security Council is far from meeting the requirements of an ideally functioning institution (e.g. Caron 1993: 566; Krisch 2002: 333). But, like E.H. Carr in *The Twenty Years' Crisis* (2001 [1939]), they claim that the current international system is conflictual and dominated by powerful states and, because of this, it is highly unlikely that we would be able to develop an international system that completely matches the ideal in the foreseeable future. If we overlook these realities of the international system, we would be guilty of a form of naive idealism, which is morally problematic for two reasons. First, if we construct an international system based on an ideally functioning international institution, powerful states would not agree to join it or to be constrained by it. This would reduce the capability of the institution to govern. More seriously, it would have terrible consequences for the international system: powerful states would not be constrained by the law, and so would be free to dominate, to violate others' sovereignty, and to do generally what they want, or even worse, to engage in wars with each other. This danger, Carr (2001[1939]: 29–31) argues, can be observed in the failure of the League of Nations, largely because it was too idealistic and therefore failed to constrain powerful states, and was therefore unable to prevent the Second World War. Hence, there is (what I shall call) a 'moral–political' demand to include powerful states within our international institutions, even if this means sacrificing some of (what I shall call) the ideal–moral demands for the functioning of the institution.

Second, constructing an international system based on an ideally functioning international institution would be counter-productive with respect to the ideal–moral demands. Since powerful states would refuse to be constrained by such an institution, any institutional arrangements based on ideal functioning would not locate these ideal principles where they are needed most—to constrain the decision-making of the powerful. If we wish to realize the 'ideal–moral' demands, it would be more productive to reduce these demands so that powerful states are included in the institution and therefore the ideal principles, although weakened, govern the decision-making of the powerful. The best solution is therefore an international institution that recognizes the realities of the international system and which balances the ideal–moral demands for an institution that has a representative make-up and a fair and democratic decision-making procedure with the moral–political demands for including powerful states.

The Security Council is claimed to strike such a balance (e.g. DUPI 1999: 123). By giving China, France, Russia, the UK, and the US permanent membership and veto power, it provides some of the most powerful states in the international system with a reason to engage with the UN. In addition, the functioning of the Council attempts to respond to ideal–moral demands by including ten non-permanent members which provide it with a sense of universal representation (Doyle 2001: 223) and also by giving each of these members a vote. In short, the Council's functioning includes powerful states in the international legal system and subjects them to a formalized decision-making procedure, whilst still being based on a sense of universal representation and the rule of law. Interveners that are authorized by the Security Council are desirable because they gain their authority to intervene from this carefully balanced and morally valuable process.

The theoretical premises of this argument have some force, but its empirical claims do not. That is to say, although it is true that we need to balance ideal–moral demands carefully with moral–political ones for including powerful states, the functioning of the Security Council does not reflect such a balance. It is *too* much of a compromise with power and has *too* little concern for ideal–moral demands for its functioning to legitimize the interveners that it authorizes. To start with, the representativeness of the Security Council is unduly limited. There are only ten non-permanent members and these states have limited power within the Council. More representative bodies, such as certain NGOs and the UN General Assembly, have little input into the procedures of the Council. Moreover, the Security Council is highly unrepresentative, not only of *states*, but also, much more significantly, of *individuals*.

Furthermore, the Council's decision-making lacks almost any consideration for ideal–moral demands. As Allen Buchanan and Robert Keohane (2004: 9) assert, there is no justification for the veto given that it creates a radically unequal distribution of decision-making authority; it seriously impugns the legitimacy of the legal status quo. Moreover, Brian Lepard (2002: 313) argues the veto is contrary to a system based on fair and democratic decision-making and the Council operates a 'closed-door' approach, which means that non-permanent members are often not consulted. It also has an uneasy relationship with other UN organs and lacks both coherence and consistency in its decisions, which often reflect the particular self-interests of the permanent five (Lepard 2002: 324–5).

This leads us to the second point, which is that the current balance of the Security Council is morally problematic because not only does it disfavour ideal–moral considerations, it also jeopardizes the moral–political considerations. This is because it is doubtful whether the Security Council does, in fact, constrain powerful states. The permanent members mostly act as they please, whether it be engaging in unauthorized and unjust wars, violating their citizens and non-citizens' rights, refusing to sign up to climate change protocols, or conducting nuclear tests. Moreover, it could be claimed that giving these five states permanent status reinforces their power. By being permanent members, they are always involved in UN decisions on the use of force, and by having the veto, they are essentially free from the governance of the Council (see Lepard 2002: 310–30). Similarly, it is doubtful whether the Council is effective in its governance. For years it was stymied by the Cold War. Yet even in the less divisive international system of the past two decades, the Council has failed in a number of areas. Most notably, it did not adequately respond within any acceptable time frame to a number of humanitarian crises, such as those in Rwanda, Chechnya, Bosnia, Sudan, and Indonesia. It has also failed to enforce its resolutions or to fulfil its supposed purpose of achieving international peace and security. What is more, part of the ineffectiveness of the Council may be due to the demands to include powerful states. The requirement for consensus amongst powerful states within the Council has led to either a lack of a decision or a watered-down resolution that represents the lowest common denominator of agreement between member states (Lepard 2002: 314). Hence, the Security Council compromises the ideal–moral requirements for a democratic, fair, and representative system without sufficiently securing the compensating moral–political benefits of constraining the great powers and promoting effective governance.

It is important not to overstate the arguments against the Council, however. It *sometimes*, if perhaps infrequently, restrains powerful states and at times it *does* act robustly and effectively. Likewise, it is not wholly unrepresentative and its decision-making is not completely morally redundant (compare a system where only one state or one individual makes all the decisions). In other words, the Council is not wholly illegitimate. It is easy to conceive of a worse institution to be in charge of international peace and security. My point, instead, is that the Security Council lacks the requisite efficacy and procedures for its authorization to be a necessary, or even significant, factor for the legitimacy of an intervener.

So, we have seen that the importance of an intervener's legality cannot be persuasively established by the two main arguments for the moral value of the procedures by which interveners achieve their legal authority. I will turn next to consider whether the moral importance of an intervener's legality can be successfully demonstrated by arguments that claim that there are links between abusiveness and illegal humanitarian intervention. Unlike the procedural arguments, which are concerned with whether the intervener's legality derives from a morally valuable international legal process, these arguments are concerned with the moral value of the content of international law and, in particular, with its effects when obeyed and disobeyed, that is, with the consequences of interveners being legal or illegal. The first of these, the Trojan Horse Objection, is concerned with the effects of an intervener's legal status on its local external legitimacy. The second objection, the Bad Precedent Objection, is concerned with effects of an intervener's legal status on its global external legitimacy.

2.2.2 Abusive humanitarian intervention—the Trojan Horse Objection

One of the most common arguments given in favour of the importance of an intervener's legal status amongst scholars, practitioners, and many states is that illegal humanitarian intervention involves abuse. This argument is best seen as involving two quite distinct objections to illegal humanitarian intervention. The first objection is that illegal humanitarian intervention is *itself* abusive. This is what I shall call the 'Trojan Horse Objection': states use humanitarian intervention as a cover to engage in abusive humanitarian intervention. Consequently, we should use an intervener's legal status to decide who should intervene because this avoids abusive humanitarian intervention.

The Trojan Horse Objection's accusation of 'abusive humanitarian intervention' is ambiguous. It is sometimes meant to imply imperialistic or neo-colonial intervention, where the intervener's primary intention is to gain territorial, economic, or strategic advantage (e.g. Chandler 2002; Krisch 2002). But, as suggested in Chapter 1 (and defended in detail in Chapter 6), those undertaking 'humanitarian intervention' must possess a primarily humanitarian intention. It follows that this first version of the Trojan Horse Objection misses its target: imperialistic or neocolonial action is clearly not *humanitarian*—its intention is not to halt violations of human rights—and, as such, should not be regarded as an instance of 'humanitarian intervention' (also see Tesón 2005c: 112). Accordingly, it is incoherent to claim that illegal humanitarian intervention is 'abusive' in the sense of being imperialistic. Although illegal *non*-humanitarian intervention can be abusive in this sense, illegal *humanitarian* intervention cannot. That said, it may still be claimed that illegal humanitarian intervention *leads* to abusive, non-humanitarian intervention by making humanitarian justifications more acceptable reasons for breaking the prohibition on the use of force. This is what I will call the 'Bad Precedent Objection', which I consider in Section 2.2.3.

It may also be responded that having the Security Council authorize humanitarian intervention avoids the potential problem of *accidental* abuse, that is, where an intervener conducts what it believes to be humanitarian intervention, but it is mistaken in its judgement. It may, for instance, overestimate the seriousness of the humanitarian crisis. The procedures and mechanisms of the Security Council and the greater number of actors involved, the argument runs, will improve judgement on such issues. The problem with this argument, however, is that, first, there do not seem to be many cases where the intervening force has got it wrong (i.e. mistakenly judged the seriousness of a humanitarian crisis). Second, the Security Council might be politically influenced in its assessment of the crisis. For instance, Russia and China may downplay the seriousness of a crisis given their general opposition to humanitarian intervention or because they have links with the government of the target state. Or, the other permanent members (i.e. France, the UK, and the US) may underestimate the gravity of a crisis for fear that they will be called on to fund or undertake humanitarian intervention themselves.[16]

Another version of the Trojan Horse Objection uses 'abusive' to mean motivated by self-interest: illegal humanitarian intervention is abusive because those undertaking such interventions do so with self-interested motivations. Ian Brownlie, for instance, asserts that when humanitarian justifications have been made by interveners, 'circumstances frequently indicated the presence of selfish motives' (1963: 339). This contrasts with legal humanitarian intervention, which, it may seem, is much less likely to be self-interested given the processes of the Security Council. So, this second version of the Trojan Horse Objection claims that an illegal intervener's *motives* undermine its legitimacy: self-interested reasons are inappropriate motives to conduct war in defence of human rights.

As I will argue in Chapter 6, however, there are significant problems with the reliance on the concept of an intervener's motivation. For instance, there are the difficulties of identifying whose motives matter and of determining particular individuals' motives. It is not clear that the mindset of those intervening is a morally significant factor, especially compared to the other factors that are relevant to an intervener's legitimacy (such as its effectiveness). That aside, it may be morally desirable that an intervener *is* motivated by a degree of self-interest. A strong element of self-interest, for instance, could make it more likely that the intervener will secure the necessary commitment for effective humanitarian intervention.

So, if 'abusive humanitarian intervention' is meant to denote humanitarian intervention with a self-interested motivation, that sort of intervention is not necessarily objectionable. There is little stock, then, in the argument that an intervener's legal status is morally significant because illegal interveners are motivated by self-interest. Thus, the Trojan Horse Objection, which claims that illegal humanitarian intervention is abusive itself, is unconvincing because if (*a*) it takes 'abusive' intervention to be imperialistic intervention, this is not *humanitarian* intervention, and if (*b*) it takes 'abusive' intervention to be self-interested, being abusive is not that morally problematic.[17]

2.2.3 Future abusive intervention—the Bad Precedent Objection

Let us now consider the second claim often made about illegal humanitarian intervention and abuse, which, like the next reason I consider, is instrumentalist. I will call it the 'Bad Precedent Objection'. The allegation is that illegal humanitarian intervention *leads* to abusive intervention. 'Abusive' intervention here is meant to imply imperialistic or neocolonial intervention, where the purpose of the intervention is to gain territorial, economic, or strategic advantage, as discussed earlier in the first version of the Trojan Horse Objection. This objection has become more popular since 2003 with some theorists (e.g. Wheeler 2005*b*: 240) suggesting that the illegal intervention in Kosovo set a precedent for the war in Iraq.

The Bad Precedent Objection has two parts: (*a*) illegal humanitarian intervention leads to humanitarian reasons being regarded as more acceptable reasons for breaking the prohibition on the use of force (perhaps, but not necessarily, in the form of a legal right to undertake humanitarian intervention in international law); (*b*) if humanitarian reasons are regarded as more acceptable reasons for breaking the prohibition on the use of force, states will be more inclined to engage in abusive (non-humanitarian) interventions.

Therefore, we should prefer legal to illegal interveners because they do not have the negative effect of creating additional abusive interventions. It should be noted that the argument is not that it is impossible to distinguish between, on the one hand, genuine humanitarian intervention and, on the other, abusive intervention that is falsely claimed to be humanitarian. We can distinguish between the two by looking at the intervener's rhetoric, conduct during the intervention, and track record of waging war for humanitarian reasons. Rather, it is that by establishing humanitarian reasons as permissible reasons to breach Article 2(4) of the UN Charter, unauthorized humanitarian intervention increases the opportunities for abusive intervention because, in the future, other states will be able to cite humanitarian reasons to justify their abusive actions.

The two parts of the causal relationship between illegal humanitarian interveners and abusive intervention that underlie this argument are not strong. To start with, although it is probably true that (*a*) illegal humanitarian intervention leads to humanitarian reasons becoming more acceptable reasons to breach the prohibition on the use of force, this is also true of legal humanitarian intervention. Indeed, the Security Council-authorized interventions of the 1990s have already gone a long way towards establishing the acceptability of humanitarian reasons for the use of force in the international community.

The second part of the causal link (*b*) is also questionable. This objection to illegal humanitarian intervention is similar to the argument given by some of those who reject a new, broader legal right to intervene: formally establishing humanitarian justifications as permissible justifications for using force (in the form of a legal right) will lead to abusive (non-humanitarian) interventions (Brownlie 1973: 147–8; Chesterman 2001: 6).[18]

The difficulty with this argument is that establishing humanitarian reasons as acceptable reasons for using force is unlikely to provide many *additional* occasions for states to engage in abusive interventions with the purpose of gaining territorial, material, or strategic advantage. This is not to deny that states have used humanitarian justifications mendaciously in the past. Nor is it to deny that if humanitarian reasons became more acceptable reasons for breaking the prohibition on the use of force, sometimes states would maliciously and mendaciously invoke a humanitarian justification for their actions. Rather, my point is that, since states *already* invoke self-defence as the justification for so many actions, increasing the acceptability of humanitarian reasons for using force is unlikely to provide many new opportunities for abuse. And although it might seem that there would be at least a few more cases of abusive (non-humanitarian) intervention as a consequence of further establishing the permissibility of humanitarian reasons for using force, this has not been borne out by recent state practice. Humanitarian reasons have become increasingly acceptable (at least politically and perhaps legally too) reasons to violate the prohibition on the use of force, but there has not been a corresponding increase in the number of abusive interventions that mendaciously allege a humanitarian justification. Wars and interventions in recent decades have instead relied on self-defence as the justification for their action.[19] As Mark Stein rightly asserts, the 'idea that humanitarian interventions will lead to nonhumanitarian wars has been somewhat overtaken by events' (2004: 37).[20] Furthermore, and again as Stein asserts, in the future, the US' recent assertion of the right to 'anticipatory self-defence' is far more likely to undermine the prohibition on the use of force and lead to abusive intervention than 'the possibility, feared by opponents of unauthorized humanitarian intervention, that like cases will lead to unlike cases' (2004: 37).[21]

In addition, if humanitarian justifications were to become acceptable reasons to use military force without Security Council authorization, the norm or law that would develop would be unlikely to be a carte blanche to any intervener. On the contrary, it would be likely to include important restrictions on humanitarian intervention. These restrictions might, for instance, assert that action outside the Security Council is permissible only when authorized by regional organizations, the Security Council must approve the intervention *ex post*, and the humanitarian crisis must be of exceptional gravity. Such restrictions would limit the possibility for abuse of the norm or law by non-humanitarian interveners.

What is more, even if the two claims (*a*) and (*b*) were true, the good achieved by the original illegal humanitarian intervener could outweigh the harm done by subsequent abusive intervention. Although abusive intervention may lead to oppression, domination, and the violation of human rights, these negative, long-term effects could be balanced by illegal humanitarian intervention's positive, immediate effects of ending serious violations of human rights. Furthermore, if it is true that (*a*) illegal interveners establish the acceptability of humanitarian reasons as reasons for breaching Article 2 (4), then in addition to abusive interventions where humanitarian justifications are claimed mendaciously, there may also be additional *genuine* humanitarian interventions. These genuine humanitarian interventions could further offset any harm done by abusive interventions. In fact, the greater danger with maintaining a strict prohibition on unauthorized interventions may be abusive *non*-intervention or what Chesterman (2003: 54) labels as 'inhumanitarian nonintervention'. These are cases, such as Rwanda, where potential interveners fail to act for self-interested reasons. Insisting on Security Council authorization may make it easier for states to hide behind the lack of authority for their refusal to fulfil their responsibility to act in such cases. Thus, the worry that illegal humanitarian intervention will lead to abusive non-humanitarian intervention is largely misplaced.

2.2.4 International order

Some question, however, the ability of humanitarian intervention to do more good than harm (e.g. Brownlie 1973: 146). Their argument is that illegal humanitarian intervention undermines international order. Kofi Annan, for instance, argues that 'actions without Security Council authorization threaten the very core of the international security system founded on the Charter of the United Nations' (in Wheeler 2000: 294). Similarly, the ICISS asserts that

> [t]hose who challenge or evade the authority of the UN as the sole legiti-
> mate guardian of international peace and security in specific instances run
> the risk of eroding its authority in general and also undermining
> the principle of a world order based on international law and universal
> norms (2001*a*: 48).

We have just encountered and rejected one version of this argument: that illegal humanitarian intervention leads to additional abusive interventions, and therefore undermines international order. Chandler (2002: 157–91) offers a more general argument. He argues that by circumventing the international legal system, an illegal humanitarian intervener reintroduces chaos into international affairs and fundamentally challenges the pre-existing structures of international order, thereby pushing us towards a Hobbesian international system. This is because it leaves the judgement to the individual state, rather than deferring to the UN, and therefore removes consensus and certainty from international law.

This overexaggerates the potential destabilizing effects of illegal humanitarian intervention on international order. As Buchanan (2003: 147–8) argues, international law is not a seamless web: cutting one thread—violating one norm such as the law on humanitarian intervention—would not destroy the whole fabric and send us towards chaos. Indeed, the experience of illegal humanitarian intervention does not suggest that it destabilizes the international legal system. On the contrary, illegal humanitarian intervention is often condoned by the international community, as in the cases of Tanzania's intervention in Uganda and (to a certain extent) NATO's intervention in Kosovo (see Wheeler 2000).

Moreover, Ryan Goodman (2006) argues that increasing the acceptability of humanitarian reasons for going to war, contrary to expectations, can be *beneficial* for international order. This is because, even if a norm permitting unauthorized intervention is cited mendaciously by states, states ultimately become tied to the humanitarian justifications that they present (through 'blowback'), and this can have a pacifying effect. That is, a humanitarian framework may make an interstate dispute less escalatory and provide greater opportunities for resolution and settlement to the conflict (Goodman 2006: 116).

Notwithstanding, there might be a better argument relating to international order for the importance of an intervener's legal status. This argument appeals to the *positive* effects of *legal* interveners (instead of the *negative* effects of *illegal* interveners) for international order, and runs as follows. Since legal interveners require Security Council authorization in order to be legal according to current international law, when legal interveners act, it means that the Security Council is behaving as an effective system of international governance—it is fulfilling its purposes of governing and authorizing the use of force. And although the functioning of the Security Council is *procedurally* problematic (for the reasons outlined earlier), in terms of the *substantive* question of international order, an effectively functioning Security Council is likely to be beneficial because it will strengthen the rule of law and the stability of the international system by centralizing decision-making on the use of force. As such, legal interveners are preferable to illegal ones, not because illegal interveners have disastrous effects on international order, but because legal interveners have a greater positive effect on international order.

This provides reason, at the very least, for interveners to bring their case to the Security Council and attempt to receive the Council's authorization. It is important, however, not to overstate the force of this argument. It does not provide a strong reason for disfavouring illegal humanitarian intervention, but only a reason for favouring legal humanitarian intervention. Furthermore, the positive effects of a Security Council-authorized intervention on the international system and on international order may be insignificant, at least on the grand scale of things. That the Security Council authorizes a particular humanitarian intervention is unlikely to have a significant, positive effect on overall international law and order.

Moreover, this argument is instrumentalist. It highlights the importance of an intervener's having the legal authority to intervene because of the consequences that this will have for the international system. In Chapter 3, I suggest that such concerns can be included under a broader notion of effectiveness—what I call an intervener's 'global external effectiveness'. As such, international order does not provide an *independent* reason for favouring Security Council authorization. If the importance of an intervener's legality can be subsumed to effectiveness, it follows that we should not necessarily oppose illegal humanitarian intervention that will be effective.

Having Security Council authorization may also improve the likelihood of the success of an intervener in tackling the humanitarian crisis (what in Chapter 3 I call its 'local external effectiveness'). This is because a legal intervener may be more likely to be perceived to be legitimate, first, by those in the political community subject to its intervention (who may be less likely to resist the intervention). Second, it may be more likely to be perceived to be legitimate by other international actors. As discussed earlier, many states in the Global South reject intervention without Security Council authorization and they may oppose an illegal intervener, making a successful resolution to the crisis more difficult. But, again, these provide only instrumental, rather than independent, reasons for favouring those authorized by the Security Council.

Moreover, the potential positive effects of an intervener's legality on its success might be quite small. Indeed, it is far from certain that previous humanitarian interventions that have received Security Council authorization have been more effective than those that have not. Compare, for example, the lack of success of the US-led intervention in Somalia, UNPROFOR in Bosnia, and French intervention in Rwanda, all of which had the requisite legal authority, with the UK, the US, and France's implementation of no-fly zones in Iraq and NATO's action in Kosovo, which lacked clear legal authority but were arguably effective.

2.3 CONCLUSION

My suggestion, then, is that a humanitarian intervener's legal status according to current international law is of little moral importance, significantly less than commonly assumed. It is neither a necessary condition of, nor a morally significant factor in, an intervener's legitimacy. So, when deciding who should intervene, an intervener's legal status according to the current international law on humanitarian intervention should play only a small role in our thinking. This position therefore differs from the views defended by the ICISS and states at the World Summit. We will need instead to look to other factors, such as those considered over the course of the next four chapters. All we can say is that an intervener with Security Council authorization is mildly preferable to an intervener without such authorization. But this does no more than establish the minor, instrumental contribution of an intervener's legality to its legitimacy.

This is not to say that the Security Council, *in general*, has no moral value. On the contrary, for uses of force *apart from* humanitarian intervention, such as the 2003 war in Iraq (which lacked Council approval), the 2001 action in Afghanistan, and other security-related uses of force, it is probably morally desirable, for instrumental reasons at least, that the Council authorizes the action. In cases of humanitarian intervention, however, if an intervener responds to a grave humanitarian crisis but is unable to achieve Security Council approval, perhaps due to the self-interested actions of the permanent five, it would be wrong to reject its action merely because it is illegal. Hence, Security Council authorization should not be considered a critical warrant for action. Similarly, if we face a choice between an ineffective but legal UN action, and a justifiable yet illegal humanitarian intervention by another agent, we should prefer the latter, other things being equal.

It follows then that there is too great a gap between the current international law on humanitarian intervention and the demands of morality: *lex lata* bears little relation to *lex ferenda*. If we want an intervener's legal status to matter more, we need to reform international law. But, given my arguments earlier, why should we want an intervener's legal status to matter more? The very limited significance that I give to law relates primarily to international law and arrangements *in their current form*, not to international law *as such* (although there is, of course, some overlap). Therefore, international law and international legal institutions could be reformed such that we should give them greater moral significance. Indeed, a strong case can be made for the necessity of such reform. States and other international institutions have been reluctant to intervene and the current international law exacerbates this situation. Interveners without express Security Council authorization are widely regarded as illegal and this discourages agents that are unlikely to win Security Council approval from undertaking what could otherwise be justifiable humanitarian intervention.

This reform is perhaps not best achieved by changes in customary international law. The problem with this approach is that it leaves too much to fortune.[22] Nor should reform simply be a matter of legalizing all unauthorized humanitarian interveners or legalizing all unauthorized humanitarian interveners that meet certain criteria. A more desirable solution, which I expand upon in Chapter 8, is an approach that would develop additional formal bases for authorizing humanitarian intervention in certain regional organizations, which would supplement the powers of the Security Council. Additional treaty-based law would be created to give these organizations the legal authority to authorize and to undertake humanitarian intervention within their regions, and perhaps the responsibility to do so. This more integrated response would start to tackle the problems of the lack of states' willingness to intervene, as well as some of the legal issues raised in this chapter. And although this solution would not be ideal, it would be a lot better than the morally deficient international law on humanitarian intervention we have at the moment.

NOTES

1. For a more detailed analysis of the reasons why states regard Security Council authorization as important, see Welsh (2004).
2. The list of scholars who regarded the Kosovo intervention as illegal is too long to document here, but a sample of them are Buchanan (2003), Byers and Chesterman (2003), Chandler (2002), Chesterman (2001), Franck (2003), the Independent International Commission on Kosovo (2000), Krisch (2002), Lepard (2002), Mayall (2000), and Nardin (2003).
3. Although some lawyers automatically equate legality and legitimacy, as discussed in Chapter 1, I do not adopt this position.
4. Although there have been interventions in Darfur and the DR Congo by the AU and the UN, both missions, despite some success, have been unable to halt the egregious violations of human rights.
5. Other ways of framing the debate about the legality of humanitarian intervention include 'restrictionists' against 'counter-restrictionists' and 'legal realism' against 'classicism' (see Farer 1991; 2003). These alternative ways of framing the legality of intervention cut across the positivism/naturalism divide on some issues.
6. See Section 2.1.2 for a statement of the requirements of *opinio juris*.
7. 'Unilateral' is sometimes used by international lawyers to refer to action by any number of states that lack UN Security Council authorization. This usage is confusing. I will use 'unilateral' to refer to an intervention carried out by one state on its own and 'unauthorized' to refer to an intervention that lacks Security Council authorization.
8. The International Court of Justice has ruled that claims of self-defence can be made only in response to 'an armed attack' (in ICISS 2001*b*: 160).
9. A further argument in this context has been recently advanced by Patrick Macklem (2008). He argues that international law requires UN Security Council members to provide reasons in support of their decisions about the legality of humanitarian intervention. Their failure to do so might undermine the legal validity of their decision. For instance, if one of the permanent five members vetoes humanitarian intervention without supplying valid supporting reasons, their veto may be illegal.
10. It is worth noting here that in practice the Council tends not to authorize military intervention against a functioning state without its consent (Welsh 2004: 181). That said, the consent may be achieved by duress and many of the states suffering

serious humanitarian crises, and therefore relevant to humanitarian intervention, are not functioning states.

11. It is also not clear whether the Uniting for Peace procedure does provide an alternative legal basis. See Chesterman (2001: 118, 2002), Welsh (2004: 182), and Wheeler (2008: 20–1).

12. For an alternative view, see Arbour (2008). For further analysis of the legal status of the responsibility to protect doctrine and the impact of international human rights law, see McClean (2008).

13. In Chapter 6, I argue that the war in Iraq, another unauthorized intervention cited by Tesón, was not a case of humanitarian intervention.

14. See Beitz (1979) and Caney (2005: 236) on the problems of the domestic analogy, on which such claims rest.

15. An example of such a society might be Rawls' account (1999*b*: 63–7) of a 'decent hierarchical society'.

16. I consider further whether the Security Council should be charged with deciding whether the factors for legitimate humanitarian intervention have been met in Chapter 7.

17. Tesón (2005*c*: 126–7) presents a similar response to the claim that humanitarian intervention *in general* is abusive (i.e. his focus is broader than illegal humanitarian intervention).

18. For a detailed discussion of whether we should establish such a new, broader legal right to intervene, see Chapter 8.

19. See Gray (2000). For instance, self-defence was the main reason given by the US and the UK for the 2003 war on Iraq (their attempts to justify the war for humanitarian reasons were always secondary to the main argument of self-defence).

20. Similarly, Farer (2005*b*: 246) argues that the Kosovo intervention did not set a precedent for Iraq.

21. See, further, Tesón (2003: 113), who argues that the prohibitive costs of humanitarian interventions mean that the chaos feared by opponents of allowing humanitarian intervention is unlikely.

22. See Buchanan (2003) for a detailed discussion of this sort of reform.

3

Effectiveness and the Moderate Instrumentalist Approach

In the previous chapter, I argued that the importance of an intervener's legal status is significantly less than is commonly assumed. So, when deciding who should intervene, whether an intervener has UN Security Council authorization should not be the primary concern. I focus now on what is a much more important factor for an intervener's legitimacy—its effectiveness. Indeed, I argue that an intervener's effectiveness is the most important factor for the legitimacy of an intervener. It follows that, when considering who should intervene, we should primarily look to the intervener that would be the most effective. To help make this case, I develop what I call the 'Moderate Instrumentalist Approach'. I argue that the Moderate Instrumentalist Approach, which asserts that an intervener's effectiveness is the primary determinant of its legitimacy, provides a compelling answer to how much weight we should give to an intervener's effectiveness.

This chapter proceeds as follows. I begin (Section 3.1) by giving a brief introduction to consequentialism and outline the basics of the Moderate Instrumentalist Approach. I then make the case for the persuasiveness of this approach. I first highlight the intuitive appeal of consequentialist thinking on humanitarian intervention. I then distinguish between three types of effectiveness and suggest that an intervener's effectiveness is a necessary condition of its legitimacy. Having defended the basic premise of the Moderate Instrumentalist Approach—that an intervener's legitimacy is primarily dependent on its effectiveness—the second part of this chapter (Section 3.2) fleshes out this approach in more detail. In particular, I consider what timescale we should use to measure an agent's effectiveness, outline what sort of comparison we should make to judge effectiveness (and, consequently, consider the importance of intervention being the last resort), and delineate the qualities that an intervener needs to possess in order to be effective. I go on to argue that the Moderate Instrumentalist Approach provides a compelling answer to how much weight we should give to an intervener's effectiveness and, in doing so, claim that effectiveness is a necessary condition of an intervener's legitimacy. Having defended the Moderate Instrumentalist Approach, I then consider (in Section 3.3) two alternative approaches to the importance of an intervener's effectiveness. I first consider the 'Non-instrumentalist Approach', which holds that an intervener's effectiveness is of little moral concern. I then consider another alternative—the 'Extreme Instrumentalist Approach'.

3.1 THE MODERATE INSTRUMENTALIST APPROACH INTRODUCED

Let me start then by outlining the Moderate Instrumentalist Approach. The key assertion of this approach is that an intervener's effectiveness is the *primary* determinant of its legitimacy. When deciding who should intervene, the Moderate Instrumentalist Approach focuses on the intervener that will be the *most effective*. Unlike the Non-instrumentalist Approach (considered in Section 3.3.1), it gives significant weight to the importance of an intervener's effectiveness. And unlike the Extreme Instrumentalist Approach (considered in Section 3.3.2), it does not hold that this is the *only* determinant of an intervener's legitimacy. Other, non-consequentialist factors, such as an intervener's representativeness and fidelity to the principles of *jus in bello*, matter to a certain degree, although they are less important than effectiveness. Their value can be included under the Moderate Instrumentalist Approach. Therefore, the Moderate Instrumentalist Approach is, *in large part*, although not *completely*, consequentialist. In fact, as we will see later, it holds that achieving good consequences is *necessary*—and sometimes *sufficient*—for an intervener's legitimacy.

So, the Moderate Instrumentalist Approach asserts that there are a number of different sorts of moral value at stake which cannot be captured by a purely deontological, procedural, or consequentialist framework. Although value pluralism makes the moral picture messier, and means that careful assessments of the relative weight of particular values will be required, this approach is in keeping with most thinking on the ethics of humanitarian intervention. Tesón (2003: 114), for instance, asserts that defences of humanitarian intervention will combine deontological and consequentialist concerns. More generally, a value pluralist approach is common when thinking about the ethics of warfare. Most accounts of Just War Theory combine deontological, procedural, and consequentialist concerns. For instance, the standard principles of *jus ad bellum* include a reasonable prospect of success and proportionality (more consequentialist concerns), just cause and right intention (arguably more deontological), and legitimate authority and formal declaration (more procedural).

Note here that I do not use legitimacy and effectiveness to denote separate qualities. Instead, like Raz's influential consequentialist account (1986) of legitimacy, I will assert that an agent is primarily legitimized by its effectiveness. For Raz, as for the Moderate Instrumentalist Approach, achieving good consequences is not the sole way to determine an agent's legitimacy, but the *normal* and *primary* way to do so.[1] On this view, then, effectiveness is not distinct from legitimacy, but a central part of it.

3.1.1 Consequentialism and the good

Since the Moderate Instrumentalist Approach is, in large part, a consequentialist approach, it is worthwhile considering what consequentialism is in general and then relating this to the effectiveness of an intervener. Putting it in its most simple form, consequentialism judges things by their consequences. If something—such as an action, rule, institution, or practice—promotes (or is expected to promote) a good outcome, then that makes it morally right. What consequentialism is concerned with therefore is the intrinsic value of certain 'states of affairs'. Actions, rules, and institutions are instrumentally valuable to the extent that they have (or are expected to have) the consequence of achieving the intrinsically valuable state of affairs. As Philippa Foot puts it: '[a] consequentialist theory of ethics is one which identifies certain states of affairs as *good* states of affairs and says that the rightness or goodness of actions (or of other subjects of moral judgement) consists in their positive productive relationship to these states of affairs' (1988: 224–5). Utilitarianism, which for a long time has been the most prominent form of consequentialism, identifies the 'good' as utility (roughly meaning welfare) and claims that the rightness of something depends on whether it promotes utility. The structure of consequentialism, however, does not require that the good is always utility, since other values, such as human rights, can be specified as the intrinsically good state of affairs.

There are several possible accounts of the good that is to be increased by an intervener.[2] There are two potential difficulties that any account of the good for humanitarian intervention must overcome, however. On the one hand, the account of the good may be too *narrow* and exclude from an intervener's effectiveness important concerns that should be included. Indeed, this is a serious concern for four typical measurements of an intervener's success: whether it (*a*) secures the peace, (*b*) fulfils its mandate, (*c*) protects civilians, or (*d*) ends the killing. Such measures of the good exclude other important concerns. For example, if we take an intervener's effectiveness to be judged by whether it secures the peace and fulfils its mandate, it may be regarded as effective even though it fails to protect civilians. Or, if we treat the good to be maximized as the lack of killing, we will exclude whether the intervener improves the security of those suffering the crisis in other ways, such as by the tackling of systematic rape, torture, and physical assault. On the other hand, the account of the good may be too *broad* and include in an intervener's effectiveness measures that we think should not be included. For example, if we take utility to be the good, then an intervener may be deemed effective because it promotes overall utility (say by improving many individuals' wealth), but does little to tackle the crisis.[3]

For this reason, the Moderate Instrumentalist Approach, as I formulate it, takes the good that is to be increased as the enjoyment of human rights (specifically the rights listed in the Universal Declaration of Human Rights).[4] As such, an intervener that increases the enjoyment of human rights is effective.[5] Note here that some human rights may be themselves justified consequentially, but many may not be, and instead justified non-consequentially. Indeed, it is in the nature of consequentialism that it must make its case by reference to a goal which is morally ultimate—the good state of affairs— and which cannot therefore be justified consequentially. These features of consequentialism in general, and of human rights in particular, are consistent with the claim of the Moderate Instrumentalist Approach that the primary determinant of an intervener's legitimacy is consequentialist.

This account of the good avoids the two pitfalls above. On the one hand, it is not too narrow since an agent's intervention that (*a*) secures the peace, (*b*) fulfils its mandate, (*c*) protects civilians, or (*d*) ends the killing can be deemed effective, providing that this intervention improves the enjoyment of human rights. Indeed, this account captures what is morally important about these measurements of the good—they typically improve the human rights situation of those currently suffering. Also note here that an intervener's effectiveness on this account is not solely a function of tackling the *immediate* rights violations. Its effectiveness can also include addressing the root causes of the conflict and putting in place stable institutions in order to prevent future rights violations, thereby ensuring the *future* enjoyment of human rights. This inclusion of addressing the root causes fits in with the emphasis of the responsibility to protect on avoiding a reoccurrence of the crisis (rather than a quick 'in and out' intervention). On the other hand, this account of the good is not too broad since actions that have little impact on human rights are excluded. The effects of the intervention, for instance, on individuals' wealth (above the threshold level needed for subsistence) would be largely excluded.

To make this account of the good more focused still, we can distinguish between types of human right and, in particular, between what Shue (1996) calls 'basic' rights and 'non-basic' rights. An intervener's effect on basic rights should be the primary determinant of its effectiveness.[6] Basic rights include the right to physical security (including the right not to subject to murder, rape, and assault) and the right to subsistence (including the right to adequate food, clothing, and shelter).[7] What makes such rights basic is that their enjoyment is necessary for the enjoyment of all other human rights (Shue 1996: 18–20). The justification for this privileging of basic rights is that these rights need to be established before other human rights can be secured (Shue 1996: 20). Physical security and subsistence are necessary, for instance, for the right to democratic participation to be enjoyed. As Heinze puts it, '[n]o individual can fully enjoy any right that is guaranteed by society if someone can credibly threaten him or her with bodily harm of any kind (rape, beating, torture, starvation, etc.)' (2009: 43). In addition to this *conceptual* prioritization of basic rights, the content of basic rights means that they should be *normatively* privileged. That is, the right to physical security and the right to subsistence are, I suggest, the most morally urgent rights. This is not only because they are necessary for the enjoyment of other rights, but also because they concern the protection of individuals' fundamental interests and welfare. Again as Heinze puts it, the good protected by these rights represents 'the absolute minimum required for one to lead a recognizably human existence' (2009: 44). Protecting basic rights, more than any other human rights, will have the largest impact on individuals' welfare and quality of life.

This is not to deny that other human rights are important. On the contrary, an intervener's effectiveness should also be measured by its effect on the enjoyment of non-basic human rights. These should play a secondary role in assessing its effectiveness. My suggestion, then, is that the degree to which an intervener has an effect on individuals' enjoyment of basic rights is the *most important* determinant of its overall effectiveness. In addition, its effect on other human rights still *plays some* role in determining overall effectiveness.

3.1.2 The intuitive appeal of effectiveness

Why should we take the consequences of an intervener's action seriously? The notion that an intervener should be effective is intuitively appealing. Indeed, the effectiveness of an intervener is central to many of the normative issues in the ethics of humanitarian intervention. It is important for whether humanitarian intervention can be justified in general—that is, *if* humanitarian intervention is justified. Those who are sceptical of intervention can cite the failure of the 1991 UN and US interventions in Somalia and UN action in Bosnia as examples of the ineffectiveness of intervening to save lives. Those more favourable to intervention, on the other hand, can highlight the successes of US, British, and French action in northern Iraq and UN-authorized, Australian-led action in East Timor.[8] Despite their differing empirical judgements, what both sides agree on is the importance of intervention being successful and a certain consequentialist logic: if intervention in another political community is to be undertaken in order to achieve a humanitarian outcome, it matters that it should achieve that humanitarian outcome.

The likely effectiveness of humanitarian intervention is also central to whether it should occur in *a particular case*—that is, *when* humanitarian intervention is justified. If humanitarian intervention is not successful, then it should not occur; but if it is, perhaps it should. In other words, to have the right to intervene—for its intervention to be permissible—an intervener needs to be likely to be effective. If the UN, for instance, is to intervene in Guinea-Bissau, it should do so effectively. This is a frequent requirement made of interveners both in the academic literature and by those involved with the practice of humanitarian intervention.[9] Furthermore, the *jus ad bellum* criteria of Just War Theory typically require war to have a reasonable prospect of success and to be proportionate. These two criteria, when applied to humanitarian intervention, require interveners to be effective and to have a good prospect of success (see Fixdal and Smith 1998: 304–6).

At the very least, then, a degree of consequentialist thought on humanitarian intervention is appealing and the debate surrounding humanitarian intervention is often couched in terms of its likely success. This helps to provide some initial backing for the Moderate Instrumentalist Approach, which claims that an intervener's effectiveness is a *primary*, *necessary*, and sometimes *sufficient* determinant of its legitimacy.

3.1.3 Three types of effectiveness

To see more clearly why an intervener's effectiveness is such an important consideration, it helps to distinguish between three types of effectiveness. First, '*local external effectiveness*' depends on whether an intervener promotes or harms the enjoyment of human rights of those in the political community that is subject to its intervention. Second, '*global external effectiveness*' depends on whether an intervener promotes or harms the enjoyment of human rights in the world as a whole. Third, '*internal effectiveness*' depends on whether an intervener promotes or harms its own citizens' enjoyment of human rights.

To illustrate these categories by way of example, the local external effectiveness of Tanzania's 1979 intervention in Uganda depended on whether Tanzania promoted the enjoyment of the human rights of Ugandans. Its global external effectiveness depended on whether it promoted the enjoyment of the human rights in the world at large. Third, its internal effectiveness depended on whether it protected the human rights of Tanzanians. According to the Moderate Instrumentalist Approach, all three types of effectiveness are important for an intervener's legitimacy. Together, they explain why an intervener's effectiveness is the primary determinant of its legitimacy. I will make the case for each in turn.

The first type of effectiveness most clearly demonstrates the significance of an intervener's effectiveness and why it is the primary determinant of an intervener's legitimacy. This is an intervener's local external effectiveness, which depends on whether an intervener is likely to promote or harm the enjoyment of human rights of those in the political community that is subject to its intervention. In other words, to be locally externally effective, an intervener needs to be successful at tackling the humanitarian crisis. For instance, if the UN were to intervene in Malawi (suppose there were a major humanitarian crisis) with the purpose of helping the Malawians, it would be vital that its intervention would benefit the Malawians. If it were likely to make the situation even *worse*, then it would be locally externally ineffective and (in all probability) would not be legitimate.

Why is local external effectiveness a highly significant factor for an intervener's legitimacy? If an agent is to go to the extreme of undertaking *military* action in another state, with the risk of great harm to the citizens of this state, in order to end, decrease, or prevent a serious humanitarian crisis and assist (some of) these individuals, it seems paramount that it will actually assist these individuals. More specifically, my reasoning is as follows. *Qualitatively*, the sort of suffering typically involved in a serious humanitarian crisis— torture, killing, rape, physical injury, death, starvation, and so on—is perhaps the greatest moral wrong that can happen to an individual. We tend to think that rape, torture, death from disease, and murder are more morally problematic than a restriction of freedom of speech, inequality, and so on. *Quantitatively*, a humanitarian crisis usually involves this suffering on a *massive* scale. As such, it involves the worst moral wrong on a massive scale: *mass* killing, *mass* rape, *mass* torture, and so on. Accordingly, it is of the utmost moral importance that the humanitarian crisis is effectively tackled, given that it involves such a high degree of severe human suffering. It follows that an intervener's local external effectiveness is vital. This is because a local externally effective intervener will tackle the humanitarian crisis and therefore prevent, reduce, or halt the worst moral wrong on a massive scale.

Moreover, humanitarian intervention involves military force and there is a risk that the use of force will *increase* the amount of human suffering in the target state. For this reason, Farer argues that '*there must be a high probability that the use of force will achieve a positive humanitarian outcome*' because the 'one sure thing about force is that it destroys things . . . to propose to invade a society, to thrash around breaking things, and then to leave without significantly ameliorating and possibly even aggravating the situation is unacceptable' (2005*a*: 219).

The second type of effectiveness is 'global external effectiveness'. This depends on whether an intervener is likely to promote or harm the enjoyment of human rights in the world at large. But in order to avoid double-counting an individual's enjoyment of human rights, global external effectiveness excludes those already included under internal effectiveness and local external effectiveness. Thus, global external effectiveness depends on whether an intervener promotes or harms the enjoyment of human rights in the world at large, apart from the intervener's citizens and those subject to its intervention.

It is perhaps a little more difficult to see the significance of global external effectiveness for an intervener's legitimacy. In the vast majority of cases, the most important thing seems to be whether the intervener promotes the enjoyment of human rights of those suffering the humanitarian crisis, not whether the intervener promotes the overall enjoyment of human rights worldwide. Yet global external effectiveness is a key consideration. Perhaps the best way of seeing this is to consider not the importance of an intervener's *promoting* the worldwide enjoyment of human rights, but the importance of its *not significantly harming* the worldwide enjoyment of human rights. In other words, the significance of an intervener's global external effectiveness is best seen in its negative aspect: an intervener that undertakes humanitarian intervention that severely harms the enjoyment of human rights in the world at large (minus those included under local external effectiveness and internal effectiveness) loses legitimacy.[10] The following are some examples where global external effectiveness is important. An intervener could destabilize the neighbouring states of the target political community (perhaps by creating a large refugee flow) and therefore severely harm the enjoyment of human rights of those in neighbouring states. Alternatively, an intervener's action may undermine international order by setting a dangerous legal precedent that weakens the prohibition on the use of force. The international instability that results may undermine the enjoyment of human rights of a large number of individuals in the international community. Or, an intervener's action may cause great power antagonism and, ultimately, nuclear war.

The third type of effectiveness is an intervener's internal effectiveness, which depends on the consequences for the intervener's own citizens. This requirement tends to receive less attention than global and local external effectiveness, yet it is still significant. My claim is this: an intervener's legitimacy depends, at least in part, on its looking after its citizens' enjoyment of basic human rights.[11]

Like global external effectiveness, internal effectiveness is less obviously important for an intervener's legitimacy than local external effectiveness. It is also typically best seen in its negative aspect. In most cases, we would not expect an intervener to make an *improvement* in its own citizens' enjoyment of human rights, given the costs of humanitarian intervention in terms of lives and resources. Instead, humanitarian intervention is likely perhaps to *decrease* some of its citizens' enjoyment of human rights, for example, those of its soldiers who are wounded and killed in action. But this decrease must not be excessive: an intervener that undertakes reckless humanitarian intervention, which will *severely* decrease its own citizens' enjoyment of human rights (perhaps by incurring heavy casualties amongst its own forces or by bankrupting the state), loses legitimacy. Thus, according to the Moderate Instrumentalist Approach, an intervener's legitimacy depends also on its internal effectiveness and typically how internally *in*effective it is. Although an intervener could be legitimate even though it does not promote its own citizens' enjoyment of human rights, its legitimacy will be reduced if its intervention causes excessive harm to its home population (so that it is ineffective overall).

In fact, there is a case for giving internal effectiveness greater weight in the overall assessment of the legitimacy of an intervener than the other two types of effectiveness. This is because of the fiduciary obligations that an intervener owes to its citizens (see Chapters 1 and 5). To that extent, I agree with Walzer's claim (although not necessarily his broader communitarian philosophy) that '[t]he leaders of states have a right, indeed, they have an obligation, to consider the interests of their own people, even when they are acting to help other people' (2002: 26).[12] To be legitimate, an intervener needs to ensure that it does not cause significant harm to its home population, even if it benefits a *greater* number of non-citizens. So, an intervener that saves the lives of 100,000 foreigners, but costs the lives of 90,000 of its citizens, may be illegitimate.

There are two limitations to the case for giving greater weight to an intervener's internal effectiveness. First, giving internal effectiveness greater weight is not plausible when humanitarian intervention will prevent the rights violations of a *significantly greater* number of non-citizens than the number of interveners' citizens it will harm. This is because, as asserted in Chapter 1, an intervener's fiduciary obligations are not absolute. It can subject its home population to some harm when helping a *much greater* number of individuals beyond its borders. In such cases, the duty to intervene to help foreigners outweighs the duty to its citizens. Second, giving greater weight to internal effectiveness seems plausible only when we are considering potential *harms*, rather than *benefits*, to the intervener's citizens. It is unconvincing to assert that an intervener can engage in humanitarian intervention that *benefits* the enjoyment of human rights for some of its citizens, but harms a greater number of non-citizens. So, an intervener that costs the lives of 100,000 non-citizens, but saves the lives of 90,000 citizens, would be illegitimate. To put this another way, despite fiduciary obligations, humanitarian intervention still needs to prevent more suffering than it causes *overall*. *Excessive* internal costs provide reason to reject the potential legitimacy of an intervener. But internal costs do not justify the intervener causing more human suffering than it prevents, even if it benefits its citizens.

Given the importance of an intervener's being effective in these three senses, it follows that an intervener's *overall effectiveness* is a *necessary* condition of its legitimacy. If, when combining its local external effectiveness, global external effectiveness, and internal effectiveness, an intervener is ineffective overall, it cannot be legitimate. If an intervener's effectiveness were not a necessary condition of its legitimacy, an intervener could be legitimate even though it (*a*) failed to make an improvement in the humanitarian crisis (and so lacked local external effectiveness), (*b*) undertook intervention that was excessively costly to the enjoyment of human rights worldwide (and so was globally externally ineffective), and/or (*c*) undertook intervention that was excessively costly to its citizens (and so was extremely internally ineffective). Accordingly, an intervener must be likely to make an overall improvement in the enjoyment of human rights to be legitimate. A similar point is made by Jane Stromseth:

> [l]egitimate humanitarian intervention should have a reasonable prospect of success in stopping the atrocities that triggered intervention in the first place. Otherwise, the intervenors will simply be exposing their soldiers and the target population to life-endangering situations without the hope of success that justifies the risks to be borne (Stromseth 2003: 268).

The standard way that the intervener will be effective overall is by being locally externally effective, that is, by successfully tackling the humanitarian crisis. It follows that, in most cases, an intervener's local external effectiveness is a necessary condition of its legitimacy. An intervener (usually) cannot be legitimate if its intervention is likely to worsen the situation of those suffering the humanitarian crisis.

There are, however, two potential exceptions. These are when the intervener could be locally externally *in*effective, yet effective overall, and so still be legitimate. The first sort of case is when an intervener would be effective overall because of the contribution made by its global external effectiveness. For instance, State A may intervene with the purpose of tackling the humanitarian crisis in State B, but will make the situation worse for those in State B. It would prevent, however, an even worse humanitarian crisis arising in a neighbouring state, State C. Overall, State A's intervention would be effective and therefore legitimate according to the logic of the Moderate Instrumentalist Approach, even though it would lack local external effectiveness. The second sort of case is when an intervener would be effective overall because of the contribution made by its internal effectiveness. For instance, State X may intervene in State Y to tackle the humanitarian crisis in State Y, but its intervention would worsen the situation for those in State Y. State X would avert, however, an even worse impending humanitarian crisis within its own borders. Overall, State X's intervention would be effective—it would increase the overall enjoyment of human rights—and it would therefore be legitimate according to the logic of the Moderate Instrumentalist Approach, even though it lacks local external effectiveness.[13] Although it is important to acknowledge the existence of these two potential exceptions, they are hypothetical. In nearly all real-world cases, an intervener's local external effectiveness is a necessary condition of its legitimacy.

To summarize: an intervener's effectiveness is the primary, and a necessary, determinant of its legitimacy. This is because an intervener's internal effectiveness, global external effectiveness, and local external effectiveness are important considerations when deciding who should intervene. The importance of global external effectiveness and internal effectiveness are perhaps best seen in a negative sense. Local external effectiveness, by contrast, is obviously crucial. Indeed, in most cases, this is a necessary condition of an intervener's legitimacy. Although there are two potential exceptions to this, these two exceptions still support the central point: an intervener's effectiveness, generally speaking, is a necessary condition (and the primary determinant) of its legitimacy.

3.2 DETAILS OF THE MODERATE INSTRUMENTALIST APPROACH

The previous two sections have outlined and defended the basics of the Moderate Instrumentalist Approach. I first argued that the notion that consequences have a large role in the legitimacy of an intervener is intuitively compelling and that this helps to explain some of the initial attractiveness of the Moderate Instrumentalist Approach. Next, I distinguished between three types of effectiveness: internal effectiveness, global external effectiveness, and local external effectiveness. Together these help to explain why an intervener's effectiveness is the primary, and a necessary, condition of its legitimacy. This section will now consider some details of the Moderate Instrumentalist Approach.

1. Timescale and the Moderate Instrumentalist Approach

Let us start with whether the Moderate Instrumentalist Approach should measure an agent's intervention—and therefore its effectiveness—by its short- or long-term expected success. Measuring an intervention in terms of the likely short-term success means that effectiveness is to do with how well the intervener can be expected to tackle the impending or ongoing humanitarian crisis. The long-term view, on the other hand, requires the intervener not only to resolve the humanitarian crisis, but also to prevent it flaring up again, thereby securing individuals' enjoyment of human rights. This longer-term view is favoured by advocates of the responsibility to protect: an intervener's effectiveness is not simply about the responsibility to react to the immediate crisis, but also about the responsibility to prevent a reoccurrence of it and the responsibility to rebuild afterwards (e.g. by putting in place functioning political institutions). Nicholas Wheeler suggests that we should regard the short- and long-term humanitarian outcomes as issues of rescue and protection: 'the former [rescue] referring to the success of intervention in ending the supreme humanitarian emergency, and the latter [protection] being defined in terms of how far intervention addresses the underlying political causes that produced the human rights abuses' (2000: 37).

Overall, the long-term perspective is preferable because it includes expected short-term gains in its calculation of expected long-term enjoyment of human rights—it includes rescue as well as protection. The short-term perspective, conversely, excludes expected long-term gains—it includes only rescue. As Walzer (2002: 30) argues, the short-term view, in the form of an 'in and quickly out' rule, can lead to a recurrence of the humanitarian crisis after the intervener has left. So, assuming that both short- and long-term gains in the enjoyment of human rights are morally significant, we should favour the long-term perspective because it takes into account *both* types of increase in the enjoyment of human rights. Long-term humanitarian intervention does not mean that short-term expected results are of lesser importance. Where possible, the intervention 'must be tailored to suit these long-term objectives, though . . . securing an immediate cessation of hostilities will, in some cases, trump other objectives' (Clarke 2001: 3). For example, if a state's intervention is expected to save 50,000 lives in the short term but cost 40,000 lives in the long term, this is still a positive outcome in the long term (10,000 lives have been saved).

2. Comparison, last resort, and the Moderate Instrumentalist Approach

A related issue here is the standard of comparison by which we should judge an intervener's effectiveness. The absolute option treats an effective intervener as one that increases enjoyment of human rights in the long term, compared to *the situation at the time its decision to intervene was made.* By contrast, the relative option treats an effective intervener as one that increases enjoyment of human rights in the long term, compared to *other potential courses of action*—the counterfactual—such as the use of diplomatic pressure, economic sanctions, and non-intervention. To illustrate the distinction, suppose that Tanzania were to intervene in Mozambique (where suppose there is a serious humanitarian crisis). On the first position, Tanzania would be expected to be effective if it were likely to improve the enjoyment of human rights in the long run, compared to the situation at the time that President Jakaya Kikwete agrees with his ministers to intervene in Mozambique. On the second position, Tanzania would be expected to be effective if it were likely to improve the enjoyment of human rights in the long run, compared to other courses of action, such as economic sanctions and non-intervention. Which position should we prefer? Note that both options are forward-looking in that they are concerned with *ex ante* judgement of the *likely* effectiveness of an intervener, rather than the *ex post* assessment of the effectiveness of the outcomes it *has* achieved (I reject the case for including humanitarian outcomes in the legitimacy of an intervener in Chapter 6).

I will use the second position for the Moderate Instrumentalist Approach. The justification for using counterfactual calculations in determining effectiveness is that this properly accounts for the role of humanitarian intervention in *preventing* atrocities. The problem with the first approach is humanitarian interventions that prevents or stops a crisis from worsening would often be deemed ineffective. For example, although NATO's intervention in Kosovo originally exacerbated the situation and, overall, the post-intervention situation was probably worse than the pre-intervention situation in Kosovo, had NATO instead stood by and not intervened, the situation in Kosovo would have become far worse (Franck 2003: 226). It is right to call this intervention 'effective', even though it did not improve the pre-intervention situation. As Caney notes, 'it is implausible to criticize humanitarian intervention as "unsuccessful" when it is more "successful" in meeting the humanitarian objectives than any of the other courses of action' (2005: 244). Thus, the second approach is preferable and we should measure all three types of effectiveness (global external effectiveness, local external effectiveness, and internal effectiveness) by comparison with the counterfactual of non-intervention and other courses of action.[14]

This account of the effectiveness of intervention can incorporate some of the importance of the Just War principle of last resort. Let me explain. The principle of last resort is often interpreted literally so that every option short of the use of force must be attempted first (see Orend 2006: 57–8). In the context of humanitarian intervention, this may be morally problematic because the time taken to pursue these other options could result in a significant worsening of the humanitarian crisis and, furthermore, the other options, such as economic sanctions, might cause more harm than military intervention. Instead, Lango (2007) argues that we should see last resort as requiring that *every reasonable alternative measure be attempted first*.[15] Unreasonable options—those that are likely to be worse than military intervention—need not be attempted. It follows that, on this view of last resort, the intervener has to have good reason to believe that humanitarian intervention is more likely to be successful than *any other course of action*. It has to be more likely to be effective than, for instance, economic sanctions, non-intervention, or diplomatic pressure. Any other courses of action that it is reasonable to believe would be more likely to be effective should be pursued first. In this sense, then, some of the significance of the principle of last resort can be included under the importance of effective humanitarian intervention.[16]

The consequences of military action can be extremely harmful (e.g. causing high numbers of civilian casualties). For this reason, it is often held that there is a 'burden of proof' for military intervention (e.g. Lango 2007). This is because the harm that humanitarian intervention is likely to cause may be greater than the other options. To outweigh this harm, there needs to be an expectation of a higher degree of effectiveness than for other options. For instance, humanitarian intervention may be expected to lead directly to the deaths of 1,000 civilians, whereas diplomatic pressure will not directly cause any casualties. For intervention to be effective, it will need to save at least 1,000 more lives than diplomatic pressure to make up for this harm. Thus, for military intervention to be reasonably expected to be the most effective option, it must be likely to produce a significant amount of good (in terms of the enjoyment of human rights) to outweigh the harm that it is likely to cause and, furthermore, to be likely to be more effective than any other option.

That said, any counterfactual improvement need not necessarily be that large. Hypothetically, an intervener could be deemed effective overall, even if it prevented the violation of only a small number of individuals' human rights, if the other courses of action are likely to be less effective still. More generally, an intervener does not need to tackle completely the humanitarian crisis, resolve all its underlying causes, and put in place fully working institutions to prevent a reoccurrence of the crisis for its intervention to be effective. As long as its intervention makes an improvement in the crisis, its underlying causes, and its likely reoccurrence, compared to the other potential courses of action, this is sufficient for it to be deemed effective. Of course, the greater the intervener's effectiveness, the better. The more it increases the overall enjoyment of human rights (particularly basic rights), the greater its legitimacy.

This relates to an important point about what we can expect of interveners. Too often there are unrealistically high expectations of what interveners can achieve. This has three effects. First, it can lead to the problem of 'moral hazard', where those suffering a humanitarian crisis exacerbate the crisis or reject political solutions out of expectation that an intervention would considerably improve their humanitarian political situation (see Kuperman 2001; T. Crawford and Kuperman 2006). In Darfur, for instance, the promise of a UN force raised expectations amongst armed rebel movements and their supporters and led to them viewing any political compromises or offer of peacekeepers from the African Union Mission in Sudan (AMIS) as 'an unacceptable second-best' (de Waal 2007: 1046). Second, unrealistic expectations can lead to dissatisfaction with, and ultimately disdain for, the interveners amongst the local population, which can further hamper its effectiveness. In Rutshuru, in the DR Congo, for instance, the local population targeted the UN force, MONUC, in September 2008 (IRIN 2008). Third, inflated expectations may mean that an intervention is wrongly seen as unsuccessful because it has not tackled all the problems that a society faces, even though it has made a notable improvement in the enjoyment of human rights—the situation is much better than it would have been without intervention (or any other course of action). Indeed, inflated expectations of what a humanitarian intervention can achieve are part of the reason for the perception that humanitarian intervention is never effective (I consider and reject this claim in Section 3.4). We should expect instead that a humanitarian intervener will be limited in what it can do.[17]

So, the legitimacy of an agent depends on whether, at the time the decision to intervene is made, it can be reasonably expected to be effective at increasing enjoyment of human rights (primarily basic rights) in the long term compared to the counterfactual of alternative courses of action, including non-intervention. To have a reasonable expectation of success, an agent should follow a course of action that it judges is likely to be successful and, crucially, base that judgement on information that it has good reason to believe is accurate. An agent of intervention cannot have a reasonable expectation of success if it acts on the basis of what it regards as a suitable course of action, yet this judgement is not supported by information that it has a good reason to believe is accurate. Hence, Farer asserts that

> [t]he question for those assessing an intervention after the fact would be whether, at the time the decision was taken, the decision makers could reasonably have believed that their planned tactics, strategies and material investment were likely to achieve the required outcome. In law this is what we call the 'reasonable person' standard (2005b: 245).

The use of 'reasonable' may be claimed to be vague and open to abuse. Yet, as Gordon Graham (1987: 142) asserts, although there is flexibility in the term— so that well-informed and well-intentioned parties may disagree—it does not follow that there are no clear cases of reasonable (or unreasonable) expectation, nor does it follow that the majority of cases are disputable.[18]

3. Qualities of effectiveness

Given that I hold that an intervener's effectiveness has much moral significance, it is important to see what exactly is required for an intervener to be effective. In addition, this analysis will be vital when it comes to Chapter 7's assessment of who exactly should intervene. It is also needed to respond to the claim (considered in Section 3.3.1) that an intervener's effectiveness is solely dependent on circumstances.

Direct qualities of effectiveness

The most obvious quality an intervener needs is the *capability* to intervene successfully. It has to possess the resources necessary for it to be expected to carry out intervention effectively. Military resources are central. They are necessary for not only the initial coercive action, but also for post-war reconstruction and the opening up of a 'humanitarian space' in which NGOs can deliver aid. To have sufficient military resources, an agent requires the following: (*a*) a high number of armed, motivated, and trained—and, ideally, experienced—military personnel; (*b*) military equipment such as helicopters and armoured-personnel carriers; (*c*) strategic lift capacity (in both air and sea forms) to be able to move personnel and equipment to wherever the humanitarian crisis is in the world; and (*d*) logistical support to sustain this force abroad (without it resorting to looting, etc.) (see O'Hanlon 2003). Although some of these are not always required—Tanzania obviously did not need sea and airlift capacity for its 1979 action in Uganda—many humanitarian interventions require all four capacities.

Military capability alone is far from sufficient to achieve success, however. If a successful and enduring solution is to be achieved, non-military resources are required to accompany the military ones. To put it crudely, military resources are important for winning the war and non-military resources are important for winning the peace. More specifically, political and economic resources are required for tackling the causes of the conflict, running any transitional authority, and reconstructing the political community. For instance, in addition to the military resources required to secure a stable environment, a successful intervener will need personnel to run the vital infrastructure (such as electricity, fresh water, and sewerage) in the affected political community, facilities for training the affected political community's civil service, and election monitors. Hence, Michael Bhatia notes that it 'is the nonmilitary and political dimension that determines overall success or failure' (2003: 124).

To use military and non-military resources successfully, an agent of intervention needs to have a suitable strategy for both aspects. Agents of intervention often have a clear military strategy for halting the humanitarian crisis— for winning the war—but fail to develop a proper post-war strategy—for establishing and maintaining the peace and preventing a reoccurrence of the crisis (a central part of the responsibility to protect). As a result, the success of their intervention has often been harmed as post-war policy is formed on the hoof. Perhaps the best example of this is the 2003 war on Iraq (although not a case of humanitarian intervention—see Chapter 6), which suffered from an apparent lack of such planning and was followed by severe instability. Furthermore, the strategy must be realistic. For decisions about whether and how to intervene to have a good chance of success, Alan Kuperman argues that 'they must be informed by realistic appraisals of the prospects of humanitarian intervention rather than wishful thinking about the ease of saving lives with force' (2001: 119). An intervener needs to make an accurate assessment of the situation on the ground and how it can tackle it with its resources, noting its own limitations.[19]

Now, all the men, machines, and materials in the world, backed up by a suitable strategy, do not mean much unless the agent is prepared to use them. To be an intervener, an agent needs, at the very least, to have the *willingness* to use its resources to intervene. And, to be an effective intervener, it also needs to be *committed* to using all the resources required for achieving a long-term successful outcome. Thus, Stromseth argues that success for intervention depends profoundly on the international commitment to providing adequate resources:

> [o]ften the impulse to assist suffering civilians is a mile wide and an inch deep—it is not accompanied by a corresponding willingness to commit forces or provide resources needed to respond effectively to the atrocities

and their underlying causes. Yet if insufficiently equipped and trained forces are deployed to carry out over-ambitious or ill-defined missions, the likelihood of failure is considerable (2003: 270).

Hence, the Stanley Foundation report asserts that '[c]ommitment . . . is also very much a part of effectiveness. . . . Commitment means more than just mustering the political will to get involved; it also means providing adequate resources, both material and political' (2000: 28). An agent of intervention lacking commitment may be willing to use only airpower or it may be unwilling to take casualties, which will mean that it is more likely to put civilian lives at risk, which is also likely to harm the prospects of success. Alternatively, the agent may be willing to commit military resources necessary to achieve a short-term successful outcome, but not be willing to commit non-military resources necessary for long-term success.

Kuperman argues that 'experiences in the 1990s demonstrated that although the international community has sufficient will to intervene in many conflicts, it rarely has sufficient will to devote the resources necessary to intervene effectively' (2001: 116). This apparent lack of commitment leads some to claim that effective interveners require 'mixed motives'. Indeed, in Chapter 6, I will argue that an intervener that possesses mixed motives is more likely to provide the commitment necessary for effective humanitarian intervention, such as sustained military resources.

This point about mixed motives links to an argument for an intervener's being local or regional. A regional intervener is more likely to be effective because its geographical proximity to the humanitarian crisis means that it will typically have a vested interest in resolving the crisis (ICISS 2001b: 210). A nearby humanitarian crisis may cause border incursions, an influx of refugees, financial hardship, and political instability for the whole region. For instance,

> African countries pay a high price for mass human-rights abuses and killing on their continent—a price that European and North American countries do not pay, at least not directly. Flows of hundreds of thousands of refugees, cross-border incursions of militia groups, social and political upheaval, and damage to already struggling economies can hurt entire regions, as happened in West Africa, Central Africa and the Horn of Africa in the end of the Cold War (Gompert 2006: 15–16).

Indeed, it would be odd if regional interveners did *not* benefit from humanitarian intervention in their region. This element of self-interest makes commitment to the intervention much more likely, which, as discussed above, is crucial for effective intervention.[20] In addition, fewer financial and military resources are required for regional intervention. Air and sealift capabilities are rarely needed, and the costs involved in sustaining troops abroad are lower. Regional interveners may also have greater understanding of the crisis, its causes, and the main actors involved. It is important not to overstate the case, however. The link between successful intervention and regional interveners is not always certain since regional interveners are often ill-equipped and lack the financial resources to undertake humanitarian intervention (see Chapter 7).

The final direct quality an agent needs in order to be expected to be effective is the ability to respond in a timely manner. This has two aspects. First, an intervener needs to be able to intervene when the situation is *ready* for intervention. In many cases, this means an early intervention since early tackling of the humanitarian crisis can often be the most effective type of humanitarian intervention. Intervening early may be better than economic sanctions, leaving the crisis to worsen whilst diplomatic efforts are exhausted, and so on. Yet, the ability to undertake only early humanitarian intervention is insufficient because early humanitarian intervention might not be preferable. It can make a humanitarian situation worse; other methods of diplomatic action might need to be tried first to avoid domestic and international resistance to the intervention, and waiting may secure Security Council approval. More important, as Gerardo Munck and Chetan Kumar (1995: 180) argue, is that the intervener is able to wait until the situation is *ripe* for intervention. The second aspect of timeliness is that an intervener needs to be able to use its resources *quickly*. Kuperman rightly claims that, 'once humanitarian military intervention is deemed necessary, time becomes of the essence because most violence can be perpetrated in a matter of weeks, as also demonstrated by the cases of Rwanda, Kosovo, and East Timor' (2001: 111). To a certain extent, this is again a question of the agent's capabilities and commitment, since it needs the necessary military and non-military resources for quick intervention.

Indirect qualities of effectiveness
The discussion so far has been concerned with direct qualities of effectiveness; an improvement in an intervener's capability, commitment, strategy, and timeliness can be expected to increase directly its effectiveness. There are other qualities, however, that improve expected effectiveness, albeit indirectly. They can be indirect in three related senses: (*a*) they improve effectiveness *overall* despite sometimes detracting from it; (*b*) they improve effectiveness in the *long term*, rather than in the short term; and (*c*) they increase the amount of *perceived legitimacy*, which in turn increases effectiveness.

This last point merits explanation. For an intervener to be expected to be effective, those in the political community that is subject to its intervention need to *believe* that it is legitimate.[21] This makes the running of any occupation much smoother, since those subject to the intervention are more willing to yield to its demands and rules, and therefore the chances of achieving long-term peace and stability are greatly increased. Constant opposition amongst most of the population will make the achieving of a successful long-term humanitarian solution almost impossible (as can be seen in Iraq and Afghanistan). Yet an intervener does not need to have the support of everyone within the political community in which it intervenes. Political elites and certain factions within the population might have vested interests in continuing the crisis, perhaps because their power is dependent on it, or perhaps because they do well materially out of the current structures. Instead, it is important that there is strong grass-roots support for the intervener amongst the affected political community.

In addition to the importance of perceived legitimacy in the political community subject to intervention, it is also important, as certain international relations constructivists and English School theorists claim, that an intervener is perceived *globally* to be legitimate. Without global perceived legitimacy, an intervener may face global pressures that can make success harder to achieve.[22] It may, for instance, lack military and financial support for the intervention from other agents and any interim government that the intervener puts in place may not be formally recognized internationally. Moreover, global perceived legitimacy can also affect whether a particular agent can undertake humanitarian intervention in the first place. Actors are bound by the 'logic of appropriateness'. States and other actors are socialized into behaviour that is seen as appropriate internationally. As Wheeler argues, 'state actions *will be constrained if they cannot be justified in terms of a plausible legitimating reason*' (2000: 4). Thus, agents that are widely perceived to be illegitimate may not be able to engage in humanitarian intervention as they cannot offer a plausible case for their intervention.[23]

There are a number of indirect qualities that affect an intervener's effectiveness in these three ways. Indeed, in later chapters, I argue that certain qualities have an instrumental value, thereby contributing to an intervener's effectiveness. In Chapter 5, for instance, I argue that an intervener that is internally, locally externally, and globally externally representative is more likely to be effective. The next chapter suggests the same for an intervener that follows the principles of *jus in bello*. And, in Chapter 2, I suggested that an intervener whose intervention is legal—that has Security Council authorization—is perhaps more likely to be globally externally effective (partly because of increased local and global perceived legitimacy). I shall not repeat the argument for the instrumental value of these qualities here. My point is that the qualities of an intervener can affect its effectiveness both directly and indirectly.

To summarize, an effective intervener will have, and will be committed to using, sufficient military and non-military resources, based on a sound and suitable strategy, and in a timely manner. It may also have Security Council support, follow principles of *jus in bello*, and be internally and locally externally representative, which can affect an intervener's effectiveness indirectly.

3.3 ALTERNATIVE APPROACHES

We have seen that the Moderate Instrumentalist Approach asserts that an intervener's effectiveness should be the primary determinant of legitimacy. We have also seen that there are three types of effectiveness, that effectiveness should be measured in terms of the effect on the enjoyment of human rights (with basic rights prioritized) over the long term and compared with the counterfactual, and that there are several direct and indirect qualities an intervener needs to possess in order to be effective. But is the Moderate Instrumentalist Approach the most persuasive approach to the importance of an intervener's effectiveness? Would an approach that (*a*) gives less weight or (*b*) gives greater weight to an intervener's effectiveness be preferable to this Moderate Instrumentalist Approach?

My aim now is to show that the Moderate Instrumentalist Approach is preferable to two alternative approaches to the significance of consequences for humanitarian intervention. The first I call the 'Non-instrumentalist Approach' and this gives little weight to an intervener's effectiveness. The second I call the 'Extreme Instrumentalist Approach'. This gives exclusive weight to an intervener's effectiveness and no weight to other factors. By showing that these two other approaches to the significance of consequences are mistaken, I hope to strengthen the case for the Moderate Instrumentalist Approach.

3.3.1 The Non-instrumentalist Approach

The most palatable version of the Non-instrumentalist Approach claims that an intervener's effectiveness is of little moral concern. A stronger version of the Non-instrumentalist Approach, which holds that an intervener's effectiveness is of absolutely *no* moral concern, is highly counterintuitive. That an intervener could have no expectation of success, and still be a legitimate intervener, seems nonsensical. As John Rawls argues: '[a]ll ethical doctrines worth our attention take consequences into account in judging rightness. One which did not would simply be irrational, crazy' (1999a: 26).[24]

There are a number of arguments that might be deployed in support of the more palatable version of the Non-instrumentalist Approach. The first is that an intervener's effectiveness is of minor significance for its legitimacy since humanitarian intervention is unlikely to be successful. For instance, Graham argues that intervention relies

> upon the actions now and in the future of the third parties through which the intervening states must work—foreign diplomats, rebel forces, and governments installed by the power of the intervener. As the governments of the South Vietnam, Kampuchea, Afghanistan, Uganda, and Lebanon illustrate, such third parties are rarely satisfactory instruments of the po-licies of their backers. Intervention, consequently ... may not have a very much higher chance than not intervening at all (1987: 143).

Similarly, Charles Beitz (1980: 391) concludes, 'the prospects of reform inter-vention in unjust states are normally uncertain whereas the costs in blood and treasure are certainly extreme'. These arguments, however, do not provide persuasive reasons for rejecting the importance of an intervener's effectiveness. It is simply not true that humanitarian intervention is never likely to be successful. There have been a number of cases of effective humanitarian inter-vention (as defined above as the improvement in the enjoyment of human rights), such as those of India in Bangladesh in 1971, Tanzania in Uganda in 1979, the US, the UK, and France in northern Iraq in 1991, Australia in East Timor in 1999, and NATO in Kosovo in 1999.[25] Furthermore, even if it were true that humanitarian intervention is never likely to be successful, the proper conclusion would not be to reject the importance of an intervener's effectiveness, but to maintain that intervention should not occur.

A second pragmatic argument for holding the Non-instrumentalist Approach also maintains that an intervener will always lack a reasonable expectation of success. But, unlike the first argument, it relies not upon the claim that humanitarian intervention *cannot* be successful, but on the claim that we can never *know*, at the time the decision is made to intervene, whether it will be successful. Graham argues that this is because of the complexity of humanitarian crises, which 'makes the outcome of political actions to a large degree uncertain' (1987: 143). Hence, this epistemological objection claims that an intervener's effectiveness is useless as a moral guide to its legitimacy. We cannot *predict* whether an intervener will be successful and, for that reason, (expected) effectiveness cannot determine legitimacy.

This line of reasoning is also unsustainable. It is possible to make fairly accurate predictions of the likely success of humanitarian intervention, especially if an effort has been made to obtain accurate information and intelligence. We can judge, for instance, that a multilateral, large-scale, force to help the government of State A to fend off an attack from a poorly equipped rebel group is likely to be successful, but would face difficulties intervening in State B where there is much opposition to intervention and the humanitarian crisis is spread over a large geographical area. As Andrew Mason and Nicholas Wheeler argue, '[t]here are many dangers attached to humanitarian intervention... But surely in practice there can be cases in which we know that humanitarian intervention has a reasonable chance of success, and the potential gains are such that the risk is worth taking' (1996: 105).[26]

A third potential reason to endorse this Non-instrumentalist Approach is that an intervener's effectiveness is of little significance for its legitimacy because the effectiveness of humanitarian intervention is completely contingent upon circumstances. It is not the characteristics of the agent that determine the success of humanitarian intervention; it is the cause that it is tackling. In this regard, Munck and Kumar (1995) argue that it is the specific circumstances within the political community that is subject to intervention which have the greatest effect. So, when deciding who should intervene, the effectiveness of an intervener should be of no moral concern because it is entirely circumstantial. The particular qualities of the intervener do not determine its effectiveness and, for that reason, do not determine its legitimacy. It will be harder to achieve a successful outcome in China or Russia than in a war-torn collapsed state with deeply ingrained ethnic conflict and influential systems of patronage, and this, in turn, will be more difficult than to assist in the supplying of aid to a poverty-stricken region with the support of most of those involved. On the Moderate Instrumentalist Approach, an intervener is likely to be effective and therefore legitimate in the last case, but ineffective and therefore illegitimate in the first. This highlights the hollowness of this approach, so the objection continues, since an agent's legitimacy will depend on the circumstances of intervention rather than on its structural qualities. We should therefore look to other values in assessing an intervener's legitimacy, such as its motives and representativeness.

This third reason for the Non-instrumentalist Approach therefore provides a strong challenge to the Moderate Instrumentalist Approach. If it were true that an intervener's effectiveness is wholly determined by circumstances, then the Non-instrumentalist Approach would be preferable to the Moderate Instrumentalist Approach. As argued above, however, we can predict, to a certain extent, that an intervener that has certain qualities will be more likely to be effective than an intervener that lacks these qualities. All these qualities depend on the structure of the intervener, so that institutional form does play a significant role in the agent's expected effectiveness. Indeed, even in the same, or very similar, circumstances, two different interveners may achieve very different results.[27]

All that said, circumstances do, to some extent, determine an intervener's effectiveness. In fact, circumstances can determine whether an intervener's effectiveness is sufficient for its legitimacy according to the Moderate Instrumentalist Approach. Let me explain. The overall effectiveness of an intervener depends, firstly, on the degree to which it has requisite characteristics and, secondly, on the circumstances in which it is acting. Just as different interveners will achieve different results in the same circumstances, the same intervener will achieve different results in different circumstances.

Circumstances affect an intervener's effectiveness in two ways. First, an intervener will have a different expectation of success in different circumstances. For instance, there may be more local resistance to the intervention by State A in State B than in State C. Hence, the *probability* of success varies according to the situation. Second, an intervener will have greater opportunity to achieve a large-scale success in some situations than in others. Where there is a terrible humanitarian crisis and the potential for great harm to a large number of individuals, such as genocide, there is more scope for an intervener to achieve extremely beneficial consequences by tackling the crisis and preventing the harm. Other less (although still) serious situations, such as the oppression of political opposition, present less scope for an intervener to achieve extremely beneficial consequences. Hence, the *magnitude* of the potential success varies according to the circumstances. Thus, an intervener's effectiveness varies in both probability and magnitude according to the circumstances. It is important not to overemphasize this point, however. An intervener's effectiveness is not completely dependent on circumstances. An intervener with the characteristics outlined above is much more likely to be effective than one that is not. My point is rather that, in addition to whether it has these characteristics, circumstances also determine an intervener's effectiveness.

Now to the crux of the matter: on the Moderate Instrumentalist Approach, when an intervener has a *high probability* of achieving a success with a *large magnitude*, effectiveness can be *sufficient* for it to have an adequate degree of legitimacy. An intervener can be legitimate, for instance, simply because it is highly likely to prevent genocide. This is the case even if it lacks other qualities. Recall here that, in Chapter 1, I proposed a scalar approach to legitimacy. On this scalar approach, a legitimate intervener does not need to possess all of the morally relevant qualities; it needs to have only enough of these factors in order to possess an adequate degree of legitimacy. An intervener can have an adequate degree of legitimacy by being expected to achieve hugely beneficial consequences. The likely achievement of these extremely beneficial consequences means that extreme levels of human suffering can be expected to be prevented. The likely good achieved by this intervention would outweigh any other moral problems which come from the intervener's not having other qualities. Suppose, for example, if in the beginnings of the genocide in Rwanda, Uganda had been willing to intervene and was highly likely to do so effectively. Given that this could have saved hundreds of thousands of lives, the fact that Uganda lacked other qualities (e.g. it may not have been internally representative since it was undemocratic at the time and might not have consulted with the Rwandans) would not have undermined Uganda's general legitimacy as an intervener.

So, in unusual circumstances when hugely beneficial consequences are more than likely, effectiveness can be sufficient for an adequate degree of legitimacy according to the Moderate Instrumentalist Approach. In most cases, however, effectiveness will not be sufficient because an intervener will not have a very high probability of achieving a very sizeable success. Normally, then, an intervener's legitimacy will also depend on the degree to which it possesses other, non-consequentialist qualities, such as fidelity to the principles of internal and external *jus in bello* and internal and local external representativeness (I establish the importance of these qualities in the next two chapters).

Moreover, even when hugely beneficial consequences are more than likely, and effectiveness is sufficient for an intervener to have an *adequate degree of* legitimacy, the intervener will not be *fully* legitimate unless it has all the relevant qualities. Hence, effectiveness can, at most, be a *sufficient* condition for an *adequate* degree of legitimacy. In the majority of circumstances, it is not even sufficient for this.

3.3.2 The Extreme Instrumentalist Approach

This chapter has attempted to establish that the Moderate Instrumentalist Approach provides a persuasive account of the weight that we should give to an intervener's expected effectiveness. In short, effectiveness is a substantial consideration when deciding who should intervene. It is a necessary condition of legitimacy and even occasionally sufficient for an adequate degree of legitimacy.

But why is effectiveness only sufficient for an *adequate* degree of legitimacy in *exceptional* cases? Why is it not sufficient for *full* legitimacy *in all cases*? On what I call the 'Extreme Instrumentalist Approach', effectiveness is not a *primary* determinant of legitimacy. It is the *only* determinant. This approach therefore presents a different sort of challenge to the Moderate Instrumentalist Approach. It claims that the Moderate Instrumentalist Approach, which holds that effectiveness is the primary determinant of an intervener's legitimacy, does not go far enough.

One of the attractions of the Extreme Instrumentalist Approach is its simplicity. It holds that an intervener's legitimacy is entirely dependent on its consequences. If an agent of intervention is effective at bringing about good consequences, that is, the enjoyment of human rights, it is legitimate, but if it is ineffective, it is illegitimate. For instance, on this approach the International Force for East Timor (INTERFET)—the Australian-led, Security Council-sanctioned force—was a legitimate intervener in East Timor solely because it was effective. Other putative criteria for this force's legitimacy, such as whether it was representative or used humanitarian means, are not intrinsically important, but only instrumentally valuable to the extent that they improved its effectiveness. Thus, on the Extreme Instrumentalist Approach, an intervener's effectiveness is the sole determinant of its legitimacy, or, to put it another way, effectiveness is always both necessary *and* sufficient for legitimacy.

In placing all moral weight on consequences, however, the Extreme Instrumentalist Approach disregards other moral qualities, which are also significant for an intervener's legitimacy. The legitimacy of an intervener also depends on three other qualities that have non-consequentialist value: the intervener's fidelity to principles of *jus in bello*, its internal representativeness, and its local external representativeness. The task of Chapters 4 and 5 is to establish the importance of these other, non-consequentialist factors and, in doing so, to repudiate the Extreme Instrumentalist Approach.

In the next chapter, I will concentrate on the non-consequentialist value of an intervener's fidelity to principles of *jus in bello*. Of the three non-consequentialist values, the importance of fidelity to the principles of *jus in bello* provides the clearest demonstration of the inadequacy of the Extreme Instrumentalist Approach to the legitimacy of an intervener. In fact, the inability of the Extreme Instrumentalist Approach to take into account properly the importance of this value reflects a commonly cited difficulty with a purely instrumentalist approach: it is insensitive to the means by which consequences are achieved. By contrast, the Moderate Instrumentalist Approach leaves room for such non-consequentialist values in its account of legitimacy and so is not subject to this problem.

NOTES

1. In addition to an institution's effectiveness, Raz (1986) includes secondary reasons which help to establish legitimacy. These include two types of 'identification': (*a*) consent to the authority and (*b*) respect for its laws (Raz 1986). Raz waters down the role of consequences further with his belief that authorities must satisfy what he calls the 'Condition of Autonomy'. These are matters 'on which it is more important that people should decide for themselves than that they should decide correctly' (Raz 1989: 1180). This condition takes into account the intrinsic desirability of people conducting their own life by their own lights (Raz 1989: 1180) and has some affinity with my argument in Chapter 5 for local external representativeness.
2. For instance, Heinze (2009: 33–56) employs human security as the 'good' to be promoted by humanitarian intervention, Victoria Holt and Tobias Berkman (2006) use civilian protection, and Taylor Seybolt (2007: 30) measures an intervener's success by its effectiveness at saving lives.
3. Thomas Hurka (2005) identifies similar problems with accounts of the 'good' when considering proportionality in the morality of war generally.
4. For a defence of the list of rights in the Universal Declaration, see Nickel (2007: 92–105, 186–7).
5. This position is therefore similar to what Robert Nozick (1974: 28) calls the 'utilitarianism of rights'.
6. The inclusion of the right to subsistence may mean that an intervener can be effective because, for instance, it feeds a starving population, despite doing little to tackle physical abuse.
7. Unlike Shue (1996: 65–87), I do not include the right to liberty (including political participation) as a basic right since it is not a right that is necessary for the enjoyment of other rights. See Heinze (2009: 154–5 n. 43). Shue (1996: 82–7) also raises some doubts over the inclusion of the right to liberty as a basic right.
8. See, for instance, Seybolt's table on the success (and failures) of interventions in the 1990s, from which he concludes that intervention 'succeeded more often than it failed' (2007: 272).
9. Those who argue for the importance of an intervener being effective include deLisle (2001), Heinze (2009), ICISS (2001*a*; 2001*b*), Lucas (2003*a*), Seybolt (2007), Peter Singer (2002), Stromseth (2003), Walzer (2002; 2004), and Wheeler (2000).
10. This is not to endorse what J.J.C. Smart (1973) calls 'negative utilitarianism', which attempts to minimize the bad rather than maximize the good. Although I argue that the importance of global external effectiveness is best seen in its negative aspect, it is also possible for global external effectiveness to be important because an intervener has a positive impact on the enjoyment of human rights in the world. For further discussion of relevant goods and evils in the context of warfare, see Hurka (2005: 39–50).

11. Note here that I focus on the intervener's citizen's enjoyment of *human rights* (and especially their basic rights) rather than their *interests*. This is first for reasons of consistency—so the same measure of good is used for the different types of effectiveness. Second, it is to avoid the counterintuitive view that an intervener could be judged as internally effective because it promotes the interests of its citizens, say, by promoting their access to oil. Third, suppose that an intervener's internal effectiveness is measured by its success at promoting its citizens' interests and that internal effectiveness is given equal or greater weight than the two other types of effectiveness. It would follow that an intervention could be judged effective overall because of a significant effect on its citizens' interests (e.g. by increasing their wealth), despite doing little to tackle the humanitarian crisis. (See, further, the two potential exceptions to local external effectiveness being a necessary condition discussed later.)

12. See, further, Andrew Mason (2000: 199–200), who argues that a state can legitimately engage in humanitarian intervention, but when doing so it should give proper weight to the special obligations it owes to its citizens.

13. To be sure, such an intervener must still have a humanitarian intention. Its main objective must be to tackle the humanitarian crisis. Furthermore, as noted above, if the intervener were to advance only its citizens' interests in ways not involving the enjoyment of their human rights (such as by increasing their access to oil), it would not be legitimate. It can be legitimate on this line of reasoning only if it improves their enjoyment of human rights by, for instance, preventing a terrible humanitarian crisis.

14. Although counterfactual judgements are often tricky, this does not mean that they are impossible. For a defence of counterfactual reasoning in the context of humanitarian intervention, see Seybolt (2007: 30–8).

15. Likewise, Caney interprets last resort as 'the least awful option', according to which 'intervention . . . may be resorted to only having considered less awful options (such as, say, diplomacy)' (2005: 249). The ICISS assert that '[e]very diplomatic and non-military avenue for the prevention or peaceful resolution of the humanitarian crisis must have been explored' (2001*a*: 36). Yet, they argue, 'this does not mean that every such option must literally have been tried and failed . . . But it does mean that there must be reasonable grounds for believing that, in all the circumstances, if the measure had been attempted it would not have succeeded' (ICISS 2001*a*: 36).

16. Last resort may not be able to be completely subsumed to effectiveness, however. First, there may also be epistemic reasons for favouring other options. We may have greater certainty that military intervention will cause harm than other options and the expected gains (although potentially larger) may be more uncertain. Second, the principle of last resort traditionally concerns only effectiveness (i.e. consider whether another course of action will be more likely to be effective). There may be a case for extending the principle of last resort to reflect other normative concerns, such as being responsive to the wishes of those suffering the crisis (i.e. to consider whether another course of action be more likely to be

responsive to these individuals' concerns). See, further, Lango (2007: 13). If there is some non-instrumental value to last resort, this would have to be included under the threshold conditions for when intervention can be justifiable (i.e. for when interveners have the right to act).

17. As one of the participants at the Stanley Foundation's Thirty-Fifth United Nations of the Next Decade Conference observed, the intervener could not and 'should not fix "everything" in these countries. "You don't need to turn Rwanda into Pennsylvania"' (2000: 39).

18. See Chapter 7 for a more detailed discussion of the issue of vagueness and how we should decide when the relevant factors of legitimacy have been met.

19. For more on this issue, see Seybolt (2007), who claims that the appropriate strategy is a central factor in an intervener's success. Similarly, Alex de Waal (2007) argues that one of the main problems with the UN action in Darfur was that it was not located within the broader political strategy.

20. Conversely, for non-regional intervention, such as Western and UN engagements in Africa, there has been a notable lack of commitment necessary for effective intervention (de Waal 2000: 93; Gueli 2004: 133).

21. Analogously, Les Green argues that 'a belief in legitimacy tends to increase its [the state's] stability and effectiveness' (1988: 1).

22. Heinze (2009: 117–25) asserts that global perceived legitimacy can come from acting multilaterally, a state's internal legitimacy (i.e. its democratic credentials and the protection of its own citizens' human rights), and the agent's position in the prevailing international political context.

23. For an example of the effects of global perceived legitimacy and how it can make possible intervention, see Wheeler and Dunne's analysis (2001) of Australian-led intervention in East Timor.

24. Scheffler (1988: 1) makes a similar point.

25. Also see Seybolt (2007), who uses quantitative data to show that a number of humanitarian interventions have been successful.

26. Similarly, J.L. Holzgrefe argues that it is true that 'the task of testing a claim that this or that humanitarian intervention will (or would) affect human well-being in this or that way is fraught with methodological and practical difficulties' but although 'these problems are formidable, they are not insurmountable. One can crudely measure how a humanitarian intervention will affect human well-being by comparing the number of people who actually died in a similar intervention in the past with the number of people who would have died had that intervention not occurred' (2003: 50; emphasis removed).

27. More broadly, a potential intervener has some control over its effectiveness in future situations. It can decide, for instance, to develop its rapid-reaction capability and the training of its troops in non-combat roles, so that it is ready to respond effectively to a humanitarian crisis in the future.

4

An Intervener's Conduct: Humanitarian Intervention and *Jus in Bello*

The problematic conduct of those undertaking humanitarian intervention has often been documented. In Somalia in 1992, for example, the Canadian airborne division was subject to allegations of torture, murder, and racist behaviour. Similarly, NATO's use of cluster bombs and its targeting of Serbian infrastructure during its intervention in Kosovo were heavily criticized. UN personnel on operations in Burundi, Côte d'Ivoire, DR Congo, Haiti, and Liberia have been subject to allegations of serious sexual abuse. Accordingly, an intervener's conduct is often mentioned as an important consideration in its legitimacy (e.g. Ramsbotham and Woodhouse 1996: 226). For example, the UN's 'Capstone Doctrine' (2008d), which outlines principles and guidelines for UN peace operations, asserts that participating troops should observe the principles and rules of international humanitarian law.[1] Others frame this requirement in terms of Just War Theory and, in particular, with reference to the principles of *jus in bello*, principles of just conduct in war (e.g. Caney 2005: 254–5).

Yet interveners' conduct—the '*in bello*' issue—rarely receives detailed and systematic attention in the literature on the ethics of humanitarian intervention.[2] Instead, the focus has largely been on '*ad bellum*' issues, that is, the conditions that must be met before an intervener can justifiably engage in humanitarian intervention (e.g. just cause, reasonable prospect of success, right intention, and legitimate authority). The recent shift in the debate away from the notion of humanitarian intervention towards a responsibility to protect has, if anything, exacerbated the focus on *ad bellum* issues. Contemporary legal and political discussions have concentrated on legitimate authority (e.g. whether Security Council authorization is necessary for intervention) and just cause (e.g. how serious the humanitarian crisis has to be in order for military intervention to be appropriate).[3] By contrast, Just War Theory does consider in detail *jus in bello*, but this is seldom, if ever, specifically in relation to humanitarian intervention.

In this chapter, I consider the moral importance of an intervener's conduct when deciding who should intervene. I argue that an intervener's fidelity to principles of *jus in bello* is non-instrumentally important and cannot be captured by a purely consequentialist account of legitimacy. In doing so, I not only establish the importance of a central factor in an intervener's legitimacy, I also repudiate the Extreme Instrumentalist Approach considered in the previous chapter. This approach, recall, claims that achieving consequences is all that matters for an intervener's legitimacy. By showing that there is non-consequentialist importance to an intervener's fidelity to the principles of *jus in bello*, this claim will be shown to be mistaken. Indeed, of the three non-consequentialist values I consider, the importance of fidelity to the principles of *jus in bello* provides the clearest demonstration of the inadequacy of the Extreme Instrumentalist Approach. It also shows that the Moderate Instrumentalist Approach, which leaves room for such values in its largely consequentialist account of legitimacy, is more persuasive.

I start by outlining which particular principles of *jus in bello* an intervener should follow. I distinguish between 'external' and 'internal' principles of *jus in bello* and claim that, since an intervener is using force for humanitarian purposes, these principles should be more restrictive than those found in both traditional and recent Just War Theory. An intervener's likely fidelity to the list of principles that I identify should be a central concern when deciding who should intervene. In Section 4.2, I consider some potential consequentialist arguments that could be made for the importance of an intervener following these principles. I argue that these attempts fail, partly because they do not distinguish between 'doing' and 'allowing'. Section 4.3 examines what I call the 'Absolutist Challenge'—that the principles of *jus in bello* that I have defended are *too* important and consequently render humanitarian intervention impermissible. After rejecting the doctrine of double effect as a solution to this challenge, I instead use the scalar account of legitimacy outlined in Chapter 1 to show that this objection can be circumvented.

4.1 THE PRINCIPLES

Which principles should guide an intervener's conduct? There are several principles of *jus in bello* that can be applied to humanitarian intervention. Before examining these, two points of clarification are necessary. First, the principles of *jus in bello* provide restrictions on just conduct *during* war. These criteria are also analytically distinct from questions of who should intervene. This is because the question of who should intervene, as outlined in Chapter 1, implies a forward-looking account of legitimacy. By contrast, the principles of *jus in bello* can affect an intervener's legitimacy only *during* intervention—the legitimacy of the intervener would increase or decrease according to whether it follows these rules—and this would not be helpful when deciding who should intervene *before intervention occurs.*[4] But this does not mean that we should overlook the importance of an intervener's following these principles. I suggest that we consider whether, at the time that the decision to intervene is being made, we can *reasonably expect* an intervener to follow these principles. We can make this judgement by considering, firstly, the intervener's track record of fidelity to the principles of *jus in bello* in previous interventions and, secondly, its institutional characteristics (such as whether it is constituted of low-paid, ill-disciplined troops or highly trained, specialized forces with much experience in dealing with civilians). I make such judgements about the current interveners in Chapter 7.

Second, following Brian Orend (2006: 127–37), we can distinguish between two sorts of principles of *jus in bello*: principles of (*a*) 'external *jus in bello*' and (*b*) 'internal *jus in bello*'. Principles of external *jus in bello*, which I consider first, concern the rules that an agent should follow in connection with the opposition's soldiers and civilians. This is what we normally think about when discussing *jus in bello* (i.e. principles of discrimination, proportionality, and so on). Principles of 'internal *jus in bello*', by contrast, concern the rules that an agent should follow in connection with its own soldiers and citizens.

4.1.1 Principles of external *Jus in Bello*

Let us start by considering the principles of external *jus in bello* that an intervener should follow. There are four central principles of external *jus in bello* according to traditional Just War Theory:

1. A two-part principle of 'discrimination'. Those using force must not do so indiscriminately. Instead, they should distinguish between (*a*) permissible targets (i.e. military objects) and (*b*) impermissible targets (i.e. civilian objects).

   (i) The 'moral equality of soldiers'. Combatants are permissible targets, regardless of the justice of the war that they are prosecuting.
   (ii) 'Non-combatant immunity'. Intentionally targeting civilians or civilian objects is prohibited.

2. A principle of 'proportionality'. The use of force must be proportionate to the military advantage gained. The excessive use of force against combatants is prohibited.

3. A prohibition on the use of certain weapons and methods, such as biological warfare and antipersonnel mines.
4. The humane treatment of civilians, persons *hors de combat*, and prisoners of war.

The ensuing discussion focuses on the first two of these principles, that is, discrimination and proportionality. The other two principles are relatively uncontroversial and I shall assume that all parties, including interveners, should follow them. Let us consider, then, the applicability of the principles of discrimination and proportionality to humanitarian intervention. As will become apparent, these two principles need revising in the context of using military force for humanitarian purposes and the responsibility to protect. There are, in fact, two sorts of revision. The first rejects traditional Just War Theory's separation of *jus in bello* from *jus ad bellum* and exclusion of moral responsibility. The second asserts that there are stricter rules that interveners should follow when engaged in humanitarian intervention.

The first set of revisions: revising traditional Just War Theory

Traditional Just War Theory treats the principles of discrimination and proportionality as distinct from *jus ad bellum*. That is to say, the principles apply both to those fighting a just war—a war that meets the requirements of *jus ad bellum*—and to those fighting an unjust war—a war that does not meet these requirements. In the context of the responsibility to protect, they apply to both those undertaking legitimate humanitarian intervention and those who unjustly oppose the intervener, such as local militia. In addition, for the most part, these principles do not take into account combatants' moral responsibility for their part in the war. For instance, conscripts who are forced to fight an unjust war are as liable to attack as volunteer soldiers who consent to do so. These principles are part of what can be called the 'conventional rules of war'. They are drawn from existing legal rules and norms governing the use of force and designed to reflect a number of pragmatic considerations. Walzer's *Just and Unjust Wars* (2006), for instance, can be viewed largely as a defence and interpretation of the conventional rules of war.

Recent work in Just War Theory, however, has raised doubts about the adequacy of the moral underpinnings of the traditional, convention-based Just War Theory. Most notably, McMahan (2004*a*; 2008) offers what he calls an account of the 'deep morality' of the rules of war. This is less concerned with existing conventions and pragmatic considerations. The focus instead is on offering an account of the principles of *jus in bello* which better reflect underlying moral principles and, in particular, individual rights. And, on this 'deep' view, both the separation of *jus in bello* from *jus ad bellum* and the exclusion of individual moral responsibility are mistaken.

This can be most clearly seen for the moral equality of soldiers. Traditional Just War Theory asserts that, regardless of the justice of the war that they are prosecuting, soldiers are permissible targets because, in Walzer's terminology (2006: 145), they are dangerous men. The problem with this view, McMahan (2004*a*) asserts, is that it is not clear why soldiers prosecuting *just* wars—wars that meet the requirements of *jus ad bellum*—should be acceptable targets. He suggests that individual liability to attack in war is 'by virtue of being morally responsible for a wrong that is sufficiently serious to constitute a just cause for war, or by being morally responsible for an unjust threat in the context of war' (McMahan 2008: 22). So, in prosecuting a just war, just combatants do nothing wrong. They do nothing to forgo their right not to be killed.

It also follows that it is not clear why those who are *not* morally responsible for prosecuting an unjust war (e.g. conscripts and child soldiers) should be liable to attack. Since they are not morally responsible, they also do not seem to do anything wrong and, likewise, are not acceptable targets. Of course, there may be certain cases when it is difficult to determine an opposing soldier's moral responsibility. However, in other cases it may be more clear-cut. McMahan (2004*a*: 724–5) cites the example of the first Gulf War, where it was reasonable to assume that the Iraqi Republican Guard (a highly paid, elite volunteer force) were more responsible for their action than the poorly armed Iraqi conscripts who were forced to fight by threats to themselves and their families.

The requirements of *jus in bello* seem to depend, then, both on *jus ad bellum* and individual moral responsibility. Thus, although they may be 'engaged in harm', both those prosecuting a just war and those with little choice but to fight can be said to be 'morally innocent' combatants: they are not responsible for unjust aggression and should therefore not be liable to attack.[5]

This rejection of the separation of *jus in bello* and *jus ad bellum* and the inclusion of individual moral responsibility has potentially important implications for humanitarian interveners. If an intervener is legitimate, it is not permissible to target its soldiers. Those subject to humanitarian intervention cannot justly use force against the intervener. For instance, it seems right that a murderous rebel faction cannot justly target those working for a UN multinational force attempting to secure a peaceful resolution to the humanitarian crisis.[6]

How do these revisions affect the means that an intervener can use to tackle the humanitarian crisis? If the intervener is illegitimate (if, for instance, it lacks a reasonable prospect of success, local external and internal representativeness, and so on) and if opposing the intervention is just, then the intervener cannot justifiably target enemy combatants fighting against it. Even if the intervener is legitimate, there are still limits on which enemy combatants it can target. More specifically, it may be prohibited from targeting enemy combatants who are not morally responsible for their unjust resistance. For instance, it may be unjust to target conscripts who have little choice but to defend their tyrannical ruler against the intervener, since such soldiers are not culpable for the threat that they pose.[7] Similarly, child soldiers do not have sufficient moral capacity to be morally responsible for their actions, and therefore should not be liable to attack.[8]

Here we face a potential problem, however. Since it would not be permitted to target morally innocent soldiers (such as certain conscripts and child soldiers), an intervener could be severely limited in any operation that involves fighting against these soldiers. This could make prosecuting the intervention difficult, and perhaps practically impossible, and, as a result, the victims of the humanitarian crisis would be left to suffer. One response is to argue that such soldiers can be targeted because they are *causally*, if not *morally*, responsible for the humanitarian crisis that prompts intervention, such as ethnic cleansing or genocide. Perhaps this answer is the only plausible justification for the targeting of morally innocent soldiers. McMahan (2008: 23) calls this the 'lesser evil justification': targeting those who are morally innocent is necessary to tackle a much greater evil (e.g. ethnic cleansing or genocide).

But even granting that such an instrumentalist logic may sometimes take over, the requirement to avoid harming morally innocent agents still seems to impose a number of restraints on interveners, including a stricter principle of proportionality.[9] First, the targeting of morally innocent combatants should be avoided where possible. Second, other means apart from lethal force should be pursued first. Third, morally responsible combatants, such as volunteer, genocidal forces, should be the primary targets of any military action by an intervener. The targeting of morally innocent combatants should be the last resort. Fourth, interveners are required to accept greater risk to themselves (and their soldiers) to minimize harm to morally innocent combatants. Suppose, for instance, that an intervener is to conduct an aerial-bombing campaign against an enemy commander, with child soldiers nearby. If it would increase accuracy, the intervener would be required to conduct this campaign at low altitude, at greater risk to its pilots, in order to decrease the likelihood of injuring the child soldiers.

It is important to note here that these revisions do not mean that interveners can justly target *civilians* who are morally responsible for the unjust aggression, such as politicians and media figures who whip up genocidal hatred. In other words, the principle of non-combatant immunity should *not* be amended to take into account individual moral responsibility or *jus ad bellum*. As McMahan (2004*a*; 2008) notes, there are epistemic and conse-quentialist reasons for maintaining the general prohibition on targeting civilians. For instance, given the difficulties of determining moral responsi-bility, a rule that would allow an intervener to target morally responsible civilians would be dangerous since it could lead to the mistaken targeting of morally innocent civilians. On the contrary, I argue below that it is even more important that an intervener follow the principle of non-combatant immu-nity when engaged in humanitarian intervention. In fact, rather than remov-ing a restriction on warfare by weakening non-combatant immunity, the revisions I propose to, first, the moral equality of soldiers and, second, proportionality provide *additional* restrictions on the use of force. As such, if one side mistakenly perceives that it is fighting a just war or targets morally innocent combatants, the result would be regrettable. But such soldiers could have been permissibly targeted anyway under the conventional account of these principles.

The second set of revisions: using military force for humanitarian purposes

I have suggested that by drawing on recent accounts of Just War Theory it becomes clear that both the principles of discrimination and proportionality should be revised to reflect *jus ad bellum* considerations (or, more specifically, an intervener's legitimacy) and individual moral responsibility. These first set of revised principles are more restrictive than traditional accounts of Just War Theory. The rejection of the separation of *jus ad bellum* and *jus in bello* and the inclusion of moral responsibility of opposing combatants can take us only so far, however. The problem is that these principles are still too permissive because they focus on war in general. Most notably, proportionality is com-patible with the use of substantial force against morally responsible comba-tants who are prosecuting an unjust war. If this were applied to humanitarian intervention, it could be acceptable for a legitimate intervener to kill a large number of opposing volunteer soldiers (assuming that they are morally responsible) if militarily necessary. This seems mistaken. When undertaking humanitarian intervention, the principles of external *jus in bello* should be more stringent and more important still.[10] Let us consider, then, the second set of revisions to the principles of *jus in bello* that an intervener should follow.[11]

Few humanitarian interventions, if any, involve outright war. Instead, many missions (especially those in the 'grey area' between peacekeeping and classical humanitarian intervention) take place in response to low-intensity conflicts and are tasked with a mix of monitoring, keeping, building, and enforcing the peace (e.g. MONUC in the DR Congo).[12] In fact, humanitarian intervention can sometimes be conceived of as closer to domestic law enforcement than outright war (see Kaldor 1999: 113–33; 2008: 196). That is to say, an intervener's task is not to defeat an opposing army but to establish and maintain the rule of law against potential spoilers. The analogy with domestic law enforcement gains plausibility if we conceive humanitarian intervention not as a permissible act of war to halt an exceptional mass violation of basic human rights in an otherwise Hobbesian international system, but as an obligatory discharging of the responsibility to protect in order to uphold the international rule of law. Of course, the analogy is not perfect. Interveners often have to deal with situations where there is little or no law to enforce, and so have to rely on significant, destructive force in order to achieve their humanitarian aim.

This difference in type of operation necessitates more restrictive principles of external *jus in bello*.[13] In particular, it requires less aggressive conduct by intervening forces than permitted under the Just War notion of proportionality. Unlike in regular warfare, attempting to destroy enemy forces using significant force is not appropriate.[14] The intervener's conduct should instead be driven, like the domestic police, by the objectives of the protection of civilians and the maintenance of the peace. Thus, George Lucas Jr. (2003*a*: 77) argues that, if ground troops had have been deployed in Kosovo, the mission would not have been to make war upon the Serbian military in a conventional manner. Rather, it would have been to prevent those forces from firing on Kosovar civilians and to prevent exchanges of fire between the Serbs and Kosovar militia. Of course, on occasion the deliberate targeting of enemy combatants and infrastructure and a clear show of force is necessary to tackle the humanitarian crisis. However, notions of military necessity and the minimum use of force under traditional Just War Theory and the laws of armed conflict lead soldiers to consider only the most force *permissible*. As Tony Pfaff, a Lieutenant Colonel in the US Army, argues,

> [g]iven the logic of warfare, it is always in the commander's interest to place as much force as is morally and legally permissible on any particular objective in order to preserve soldiers' lives. This means when commanders and their soldiers determine what is necessary, they are always asking themselves how much force is allowable, not how little is possible. What is necessary when resolving the tension between due care and due risk is minimizing risk, not force. The most force allowable then becomes the necessary force since it is what is necessary to preserve soldiers' lives without violating the law or morality of war (2000: 2).

By contrast, those engaged in peace operations should consider what is the least force *possible*, and avoid using force as a first resort (Pfaff 2000: 5).[15]

The aims of the operation also mean that more stringent principles of external *jus in bello* are necessary. In short, the intervener is conducting intervention for *humanitarian* purposes. This is particularly relevant for the principle of non-combatant immunity. Let me explain. As suggested in Chapter 1 (and as will be argued in more detail in Chapter 6), to be engaged in 'humanitarian intervention', an intervener needs to possess a humanitarian intention. Without a humanitarian intention, its action could not be classified as 'humanitarian'. One of the main ways to determine an agent's intention is to look to its conduct. It is unlikely that an intervener that kills civilians indiscriminately could be said to possess a 'humanitarian' intention. Its apparent indifference to civilian casualties counts against its other humanitarian credentials. For instance, NATO's use of cluster bombs and reliance on aerial bombing in Serbia certainly weakened (if not fatally) the humanitarian credentials of its intervention. What is called for, then, is consistency of means and ends: an intervener should use humanitarian means when attempting to achieve humanitarian ends (see Bellamy 2004: 229; Heinze 2004; Lucas 2003*a*).

This is not simply a definitional question. Interveners should follow these principles because part of what makes it permissible to undertake military intervention, in contravention of state sovereignty, is being humanitarian. As Lucas argues,

> the justification for such acts to begin with, and subsequent prospects for their enduring legitimacy, rest upon understanding the purpose of the intervening forces as primarily the enforcement of justice, the protection of rights and liberties currently in jeopardy, and the restoration of law and order, rather than straightforwardly defeating (let alone destroying) an opposing military force (2003*a*: 77).

The importance of possessing a humanitarian intention lies then as a *permissible* reason to use military force (see, further, Chapter 6). There is a strong case to maintain a general prohibition on the use of force (e.g. for reasons of global stability), with only a few exceptions. The use of force in order to tackle a serious humanitarian crisis—humanitarian intervention—is generally regarded as one of these exceptions (as defended by the responsibility to protect doctrine). And to be such an exception, humanitarian intervention requires a humanitarian intention. Otherwise, it would be a different sort of intervention (e.g. intervention for economic gain) that is *prima facie* morally impermissible because it violates the general prohibition on the use of force (unless it falls under another exception to prohibition on the use of force, such as self-defence in response to aggression). But the humanitarian purposes that (sometimes) permit overriding state sovereignty are compromised if the intervening forces deliberately or inadvertently behave unjustly (Lucas 2003*a*: 77).

By analogy, suppose that a concerned neighbour breaks into a house in order to stop an abusive mother hurting her children. Since the neighbour knows that he may be attacked by the abusive mother too, he uses nerve gas to weaken her strength and to minimize the risk to himself. In doing so, he knowingly harms some of the children. Although his actions ultimately result in more good than harm (e.g. he harms one child but protects five others), there seems to be something deeply problematic about his use of nerve gas. What makes his action permissible—just as what makes it permissible for interveners to violate state sovereignty when attempting to tackle a humanitarian crisis—is having a humanitarian purpose. But the humanitarian permission for him entering the house is significantly weakened by his use of non-humanitarian means.

This example also indicates that those saving lives should be willing to incur risks to themselves when necessary. This may, for instance, require an intervener to risk casualties amongst its soldiers in order to avoid harming civilians and to use minimum force against other combatants. In response, it might be argued that requiring interveners to incur risks is problematic because it could reduce potential interveners' willingness to intervene, given the fear of casualties. Although this is a reasonable expectation, it does not mean that the requirements on interveners should be watered down to overcome such fears. If interveners are willing to act only with very high levels of force protection and, as a result, insist on deflecting risk onto the civilian population and enemy combatants, the conclusion should be that the intervention would be morally problematic, rather than that we should weaken the requirements of *jus in bello*.

Another potential objection runs as follows. According to my account of external *jus in bello*, (*a*) civilians, (*b*) certain enemy combatants, and (*c*) intervening soldiers are (typically) all morally innocent and therefore not liable to attack. In this sense, they are all morally equal. Yet the stricter principle of proportionality that I have defended may require intervening soldiers to accept a greater degree of risk to themselves when dealing with other morally innocent individuals. Such a requirement seems to give greater weight to the lives of civilians and (innocent) enemy combatants, and therefore seem to deny the equal moral worth of intervening soldiers. There are two potential lines of response here. First, in their role as agents of humanitarian intervention, intervening soldiers may be required to accept a greater degree of risk to themselves in order to protect civilians, just as we may think that the police have to accept greater risk to themselves in their role of protectors of society. Second, any additional risk required of intervening soldiers would, in practice, be limited by instrumental considerations. Given that most interveners face shortages in military personnel, more lives would be saved by protecting, as far as possible, the welfare of intervening soldiers and using them in the most optimal way of protecting civilians, rather than sacrificing a large number of intervening soldiers to protect only a few civilians.[16]

Therefore, interveners should adopt the following principles of external *jus in bello*, which should be incorporated not only in the deep morality of warfare but also form part of the conventions of Just War Theory and international humanitarian law.

1. A two-part principle of 'discrimination'. Those using force must not do so indiscriminately. Instead, they should distinguish between (*a*) permissible targets (i.e. military objects) and (*b*) impermissible targets (i.e. civilian objects).
   (i) Permissible targets. Combatants prosecuting a *justified* intervention cannot be permissibly targeted. For its part, an intervener can justifiably use limited force against *morally responsible* combatants who are fighting an unjust war. They can also use limited force against *morally innocent* combatants who are fighting an unjust war, as long as this is unavoidable, is a last resort, and providing that they attempt to minimize the harm to these combatants by accepting risk themselves.
   (ii) Non-combatant immunity. Intentionally targeting civilians or civilian infrastructure is prohibited. Foreseeable civilian casualties are also impermissible, even if unintended. Interveners should accept risks themselves in order to minimize harm to civilians.
2. A principle of 'proportionality'. The use of force against morally responsible combatants must be limited to the least force possible. The use of force must always be driven by the objectives of the protection of civilians and the maintenance of the peace, rather than defeating the enemy.[17]

4.1.2 Principles of internal *jus in bello*

I have argued that an intervener should follow stricter principles of discrimination and proportionality. The traditional version of these principles should be revised (*a*) to reflect *jus ad bellum* and individual moral responsibility and (*b*) the context of using force for humanitarian purposes. An intervener's likely fidelity to these stricter principles of external *jus in bello* is an important consideration for its legitimacy and therefore when determining who should intervene.

Let us now consider the principles of 'internal *jus in bello*'. These have received much less attention in both Just War Theory and discussions of humanitarian intervention. These principles concern how an intervener should behave towards its own citizens and soldiers. For our purposes, there are two central principles of internal *jus in bello*.

The first restricts the sort of soldiers that an intervener can use to undertake humanitarian intervention. It seems clear that an intervener cannot justifiably employ child soldiers. Likewise, it can be argued that the use of conscripts should be avoided. This is not because of anything objectionable about the use of conscripts for humanitarian intervention in particular. It can be argued that, if conscription were justifiable, it would be as justifiable for humanitarian intervention as for any other purpose (such as self-defence), given that the conscripts would be used to tackle mass suffering.[18] Rather, the problem with the use of conscripts is more general: conscription undermines individual autonomy and freedom of conscience in that it sometimes forces individuals to fight against their will. In addition, the use of private military companies in roles that involve combat should generally be avoided, given the problems caused by the lack of effective national and international regulation of their services, such as the undermining of democratic accountability (see Chapter 7). Accordingly, it is only regular, volunteer soldiers that can be justifiably used for humanitarian intervention.

It may be argued, however, that the use of regular, volunteer soldiers is objectionable as well, since humanitarian intervention contravenes the terms of the implicit soldier-state contract that soldiers agree to when joining. Martin Cook (2003: 150–3) most clearly expresses this concern. He argues that this contract obliges military personnel to accept great risks and engage in morally and personally difficult actions on the understanding that the circumstances under which they will act will be when the nation's defence or vital interests require action. But when using force altruistically for humanitarian purposes, 'the military person may say with moral seriousness, "This isn't what I signed up for"' (Cook 2003: 151). To be sure, Cook asserts that soldiers and citizens may be willing to accept a certain 'threshold of pain' when fighting humanitarian wars, but claims that this will be rather low.

It is important to acknowledge the strength of Cook's objection. If force protection needs to be high in order to minimize casualties amongst the intervener's soldiers, the result in all but the least risky of missions would be either non-intervention, as potential interveners choose not to act, or the deflection of military risk onto those subject to humanitarian intervention (for instance, as interveners conduct only aerial-bombing campaigns from a high altitude). In the latter case, high levels of civilian casualties are likely and humanitarian intervention may therefore be unjustifiable. Accordingly, if the soldier-state contract implies that force protection standards must be high for humanitarian intervention, and if the use of other military personnel apart from volunteer regular soldiers, such as conscripts and PMCs, is objectionable (as I have suggested), there is reason to prohibit humanitarian intervention in all but the least risky of cases.

We need not reach this conclusion, however. This is because the soldier-state contract is not limited to defence of a state's vital interests. A soldier can expect when signing up that they will take part in humanitarian and peace operations, given the frequency of such operations. Indeed, some armed forces (such as the British Navy) have expressly used the possibility of conducting humanitarian intervention in their recruitment campaigns. Moreover, as Cook (2003: 146) also argues, the US has tended to employ humanitarian and universalizing rhetoric to justify their wars, such as advancing human rights, freedom, and democracy and opposing tyranny and despotism, rather than simply national defence (and the point can be extended to a number of other states). Such rhetoric is likely to have an impact on individuals signing up: they can expect that their state will engage in a variety of military operations, including sometimes humanitarian intervention, for the benefit of those beyond the borders of their state. Moreover, on the broader notion of national interests defended in Chapter 6, humanitarian intervention, even when apparently altruistic, may be in the intervener's self-interest and therefore within the remit of the narrow view of the soldier-state contract.

Let me now turn to a second principle of internal *jus in bello*. Although interveners are required to accept risks themselves, and therefore should avoid maintaining high standards of force protection at the expense of civilians and enemy combatants, they should still attempt to minimize casualties amongst their own soldiers. Thus, the second principle of internal *jus in bello* asserts that an intervener possesses a responsibility of care for those fighting on its behalf. Those in the military profession put their lives on the line and, in doing so, sacrifice many political and civil rights and other liberties. In return, an intervener owes its soldiers special treatment, for instance, looking after their families if they are injured in action and providing its soldiers with the equipment (such as flak jackets, radio systems, and working rifles) necessary to be able to undertake humanitarian intervention without putting their lives in needless danger.[19]

This is not to claim that an intervener should never put its soldiers' lives at risk. On the contrary, the intervener may be required to put at risk its soldiers' lives in order to avoid harming civilians and sometimes enemy combatants.

In other words, interveners have a responsibility of care for their soldiers, although this does not mean that they should maximize force protection at the expense of violating the principles of external *jus in bello*. Rather, the point is to insist that the intervener has a duty to ensure that those fighting for it are not subject to *reasonably avoidable* harm by, for instance, providing them with the right equipment and sufficient back-up. Although soldiers may willingly agree to be placed in combat situations that are dangerous, such individuals do not forgo their human rights. Their lives should still be cherished.

4.2 CONSEQUENTIALISM AND DOING AND ALLOWING

We have seen, then, that those undertaking humanitarian intervention should follow a number of principles of external and internal *jus in bello*. An intervener's likely fidelity to these principles is, I claim, a key factor in its legitimacy and should guide the decision on who should intervene. The Extreme Instrumentalist Approach outlined at the end of the last chapter cannot fully account for these principles of just conduct in war in its conception of legitimacy. By placing all moral weight on an intervener's effectiveness, it marginalizes the importance of an intervener's expected fidelity to these principles of *jus in bello*. In this context, Heinze claims that a purely consequentialist account 'has serious problems when employed as part of a theory of the morality of war based on human rights, because it suggests that aggregate human suffering is the *only* moral concern that need be addressed' (2004: 549; emphasis added). He claims that if, for instance, a purely consequentialist principle alone were used to determine proportionality in NATO's intervention in Kosovo, NATO would have been permitted to pursue its primary end of the capitulation of the Milosevic regime unconditionally, regardless of civilian casualties (Heinze 2004: 550).

One potential consequentialist argument against requiring an intervener to follow these principles is that they could reduce the effectiveness of its attempt to halt the humanitarian crisis. Insisting on a strict principle of proportionality, for instance, may make it more difficult for an intervener to use robust military force against those perpetrating the crisis. More strongly, the Extreme Instrumentalist Approach would seem to hold that *all that is important* is the successful tackling of the humanitarian crisis and an intervener should not be restricted in its use of means to achieve this goal.

That said, there are three potential consequentialist arguments that could be made for the importance of an intervener being expected to follow these principles. The first is act consequentialist (particularly, direct act consequentialist): fidelity to the principles of *jus in bello* will directly increase an intervener's effectiveness.[20]

This act consequentialist argument clearly fails. For it to work, an intervener's strict fidelity to the rules of *jus in bello* would need to maximize the good *in each and every situation* during intervention. But, on many occasions, an intervener will be more effective if it abandons these principles. These rules may prohibit the use of methods that can be highly effective in achieving strategic aims and that might be expected to decrease civilian casualties overall. For instance, an intervener may be more effective if it tortures captured soldiers in order to obtain information that will help it to achieve a swift resolution to the humanitarian crisis.

The second argument is rule consequentialist.[21] The argument is this: interveners should follow rules of *jus in bello* because these rules, when sufficiently complied with, maximize the good—the enjoyment of human rights. Although an intervener may be more effective in the short-term by disregarding these rules, the rules of *jus in bello* will generally increase its effectiveness. In this context, R.B. Brandt argues that 'the moral justification of these rules lies in the fact that their acceptance and enforcement will make an important contribution to long-range utility' (1972: 147).[22] For instance, although torturing captured soldiers may increase the good in a particular instance, a rule against torture will generally maximize the good because such methods will reduce the perceived legitimacy of the humanitarian intervener and mean that it will face greater resistance.

Although this rule consequentialist argument seems promising, there is an inherent problem with rule consequentialism: it collapses into act consequentialism. This objection to rule consequentialism is made by J.J.C. Smart:

> [s]uppose that an exception to a rule *R* produces the best possible consequences. Then this is evidence that the rule *R* should be modified so as to allow this exception. Thus we get a new form of the rule 'do *R* except in circumstances of the sort *C*'. That is, whatever would lead the act-utilitarian to break a rule would lead the Kantian rule-utilitarian to modify the rule. Thus an adequate rule-utilitarian would be extensionally equivalent to act-utilitarianism (1973: 10–11).[23]

This difficulty also arises with the rule consequentialist defence of the importance of an intervener's expected fidelity to these principles when deciding who should intervene. Suppose that a rule—call it R1—requires interveners to follow principles of *jus in bello*. If complied with, this rule is generally expected to increase the enjoyment of human rights. Suppose, further, that in a particular case, an intervener can be more effective by abandoning one of the details of the rule R1. When intervening in a militarily strong state, for instance, an intervener may be more effective if it abandons the provision of external *jus in bello* against using conscripts (which would allow for a larger force). According to the logic of consequentialism, the appropriate response would be to modify the rule R1 so as to take into account this exception. We then have rule R2, which says that interveners should follow principles of *jus in bello*, except when intervening in a militarily strong state, where they can be more effective by using conscripts. R2 is better at maximizing overall enjoyment of human rights than R1 because it takes into account this exception. Suppose, further, that in another case, one particular type of intervener (such as a PMC) would be more effective if it abandoned one of the details of R2—such as the strict prohibition on targeting non-combatants. Again, according to the logic of consequentialism, the most appropriate response would be to modify the rule R2 to take into account this second exception. We then have rule R3, which is better at maximizing overall enjoyment of human rights than both R2 and R1 because it takes into account this new exception. Such modifications will continue *ad infinitum* so that the rule of fidelity to principles of *jus in bello* maximizes enjoyment of human rights.

The problem then for rule consequentialism is that, by making continuous modifications to these rules, there will be a rule for each intervener and for each situation. It therefore becomes equivalent to act consequentialism. The rule consequentialist may reply by arguing that we need not make these continuous amendments. If we were not to make these continuous amendments, however, then the rule of fidelity to principles of *jus in bello* would not be *optimal*—it could not be justified on the consequentialist grounds of maximizing enjoyment of human rights. In short, it would be 'rule worship' (Smart 1973: 10).[24]

The third consequentialist defence is an indirect consequentialist argument and runs as follows.[25] An intervener should follow these principles because this is likely to maximize its effectiveness at tackling the humanitarian crisis overall, even if on particular occasions it will not. As suggested in the previous chapter, perceived legitimacy is an important factor in an intervener's effectiveness. An intervener that is willing to kill civilians (even unintentionally), it might be claimed, will quickly stop being legitimate in the eyes of those in the political community that is subject to its intervention. This will increase resistance and hostility to the intervener, and severely hamper its effectiveness. Likewise, the argument runs, an intervener that is more careful and limited in its use of force against enemy combatants (for instance, by attempting to secure their surrender before using lethal force) is more likely to be able to disarm, co-opt, and rehabilitate these soldiers in the long-run (rather than entrenching their position). Moreover, when using a more restrictive principle of proportionality—although still using force robustly when required—it sends a message that the rule of law is being re-established (or established for the first time), rather than allowing the continuation of the conflict. This can help to improve the intervener's chances of long-term success as the intervener is not seen as an enemy occupier prolonging the conflict, but as a facilitator of the peace.

A similar defence can be made of the principles of internal *jus in bello*. It might be argued that an intervener that uses child soldiers, PMCs, or conscripts is less likely to be effective because using these sorts of soldiers will erode the confidence of those in the political community in which it intervenes (and therefore undermine its perceived legitimacy). Likewise, an intervener that fails to fulfil the duty of care to its soldiers will find that its force quickly becomes demotivated and less effective. Hence, an intervener that follows principles of *jus in bello* is more likely to be effective overall and, for this reason, fidelity to the principles of *jus in bello* can perhaps be incorporated into the Extreme Instrumentalist Approach to legitimacy.

This indirect consequentialist argument provides a plausible instrumental justification of the principles of *jus in bello* and therefore helps to respond to the objection that fidelity to these principles undermines an intervener's likely success. Yet it leaves untouched the stronger, extreme consequentialist objection that the successful tackling of the humanitarian crisis is all that matters. That is to say, it leaves the justification of these principles contingent solely on their expected effectiveness, which is a risky strategy. Despite the indirect consequentialist response, the link between an intervener's effectiveness and its fidelity to these principles may not be strong enough to guarantee that following these principles will *always* increase effectiveness overall. There may be occasions when an intervener will be likely to be more effective by abandoning these principles by, for example, using significant force against enemy combatants.

Of course, we might bite the bullet and assert that, if consequentialism cannot guarantee these principles of *jus in bello*, so much the worse for these principles: what matters is solely achieving good consequences. But this seems to be deeply inadequate. By limiting the importance of an intervener's following these principles to their significance for its effectiveness, it misses something morally important. That is to say, there is something more to the importance of an intervener's expected fidelity to the principles of *jus in bello* than simply whether this improves its effectiveness. To see this, consider the following scenario by Philippa Foot, which has been adapted by Warren Quinn:

[i]n Rescue I, we can save either five people in danger of drowning in one place or a single person in danger of drowning somewhere else. We cannot save all six. In Rescue II, we can save the five only by driving over and thereby killing someone who (for an unspecified reason) is trapped on the road. If we do not undertake the rescue, the trapped person can later be freed (1989: 290).

For the consequentialist, we should act in both cases. Yet this seems troublesome. Although in Rescue I it is justifiable to save the lives of five even though one will drown, it is not clear that we should act in Rescue II. What this example relies on is a distinction between *doing* and *allowing*. That is, there is a morally relevant distinction between what one does oneself and what one allows.[26] Thus, there is a significant difference between the killing of the trapped person in Rescue II and the letting of a single person elsewhere die in Rescue I. Rescue I seems permissible because we are not doing harm ourselves. But in Rescue II, it seems that we should not run over the trapped person because we should not *do* harm ourselves. It seems morally better if we *allowed* the other five to die.

The same reasoning can be applied to an intervener's fidelity to the principles of *jus in bello*. In addition to any instrumental justification, a reason why an intervener's likelihood of following the principles of *jus in bello* is important is that an intervener should not itself do harm (specifically, harm that is impermissible according to these principles).[27] It would be better, to a certain degree, if an intervener were to *allow* harm, perhaps thereby being less effective, than for it to target civilians, use indiscriminate weapons, and so on.

One reason why the doing and allowing distinction matters is because when one does the action, it is *oneself* that is violating the right, whereas when one allows the action, it is *someone else* that is violating the right. There is a difference between the government of State A violating State B's citizens' rights and the government of State A not intervening to stop the government of State B violating its own citizens' rights.

But for the extreme consequentialist, there is no moral importance (beyond any instrumental importance) to the distinction between an intervener that does harm (e.g. by killing civilians) and an intervener that fails to prevent harm (e.g. by failing to prevent another agent killing civilians). An agent can justifiably cause harm if this improves its effectiveness. Suppose that, if an intervener were to torture the young children of the members of the oppressive regime of the target state, it would be effective overall at getting this regime to stop human rights abuses. It is morally irrelevant that the intervener would be *doing* harm itself. On the contrary, if the intervener were to refrain from torturing innocent family members, it would be illegitimate because it would be *allowing* harm (it would be failing to stop the regime's human rights abuses). So, on this approach, whether an intervener follows the principles of *jus in bello* is of no independent value. What an intervener *does itself* is essentially morally equivalent to what it *allows others to do*. But, as the discussion above demonstrates, this is highly counterintuitive. An intervener's legitimacy does seem to depend on what it does itself and, in particular, its fidelity to principles of *jus in bello*. For this reason, the Extreme Instrumentalist Approach's reliance solely on instrumental justifications of these principles is unacceptable.

At this point, however, the argument I have presented faces a serious objection, which I shall call the Absolutist Challenge: although the difference between doing and allowing shows that a purely consequentialist account of legitimacy for humanitarian intervention is inadequate, it proves too much—it leads to the conclusion that humanitarian intervention is generally impermissible.

4.3 THE ABSOLUTIST CHALLENGE

The Absolutist Challenge runs as follows. On an absolutist, deontological position according to which the difference between doing and allowing is of absolute moral significance, an intervener could never be legitimate because intervention almost always involves *doing* some harm that is impermissible (see Tesón 2005c: 137–40). That is, since it involves the use of military force, it frequently results in civilian casualties which, according to the strict principle of non-combatant immunity outlined above, are impermissible. It follows that humanitarian intervention can never be justified.[28] This challenge therefore poses a significant problem to my defence of the non-consequentialist importance of an intervener's fidelity to the principles of *jus in bello* and attempt to repudiate the Extreme Instrumentalist Approach. It seems to show that my defence of these principles is *too* strong.

4.3.1 The doctrine of double effect

One potential response to the Absolutist Challenge that is common in the literature on humanitarian intervention is to adopt the doctrine of double effect.[29] In short, this doctrine permits collateral damage, such as civilian casualties, providing that such damage is not *intended*. More specifically, it asserts that a humanitarian intervention that has both a good effect (such as tackling genocide) and a bad effect (such as civilian casualties) can be morally permissible if the following conditions are met:

1. *The good effect is intended.*
2. *The bad effect is unintended.* Although the intervener may *foresee* that the bad effect (e.g. civilian casualties) is likely with its action, it does not *intend* this bad effect. It is a foreseen, but unintentional, side-effect of its action.
3. *The bad effect is not instrumental.* The bad effect (e.g. civilian casualties) must not be a means to achieving the good effect (e.g. the removal of a tyrannical leader). So, for instance, civilian casualties are not used as a means to weaken the morale of enemy soldiers.
4. *The bad effect is proportionate.* The good effect is sufficiently beneficial that it outweighs the bad effect. For example, although the intervention results in 1,000 unintended civilian casualties, by removing a tyrannical leader it ultimately saves 2,000 lives.

So, an intervener that intentionally targets civilian objects in order to force a tyrannical leader into submission acts *impermissibly.* This is because the civilian deaths are intended. But an intervener that targets military objects in order to force the tyrannical leader into submission, in full *knowledge* that civilian objects will also be damaged collaterally, acts *permissibly.* This is because the civilian casualties are an unintended side-effect of pursuing the good end (assuming that the action is proportionate).

This doctrine can provide justification, firstly, for humanitarian intervention *in general,* despite potential harm to civilians in the political community subject to intervention. It can also provide justification, secondly, for a *particular operation* during the intervention, such as the bombing of military infrastructure that will also cause civilian casualties. The intervener's actions may be permissible providing that it does not *intend* to cause civilian casualties, any civilian casualties are not a *means to the end,* and the intervention or action does more good than harm.

The doctrine of double effect allows room, then, for an intervener to cause collateral damage, including civilian casualties, providing that the damage is unintended, not instrumental to the humanitarian end trying to be achieved, and proportionate. As Tesón (2005c: 104) suggests, it can be seen as a midway between deontological and consequentialist approaches. It does not hold the absolutist, deontological position that civilian casualties are *always* impermissible. But it is more restrictive than the Extreme Instrumentalist Approach that potentially justifies civilian casualties (in violation of *jus in bello*) if this is likely to improve the effectiveness of humanitarian intervention. By contrast, the doctrine of double effect asserts that civilian casualties that are intended, disproportionate, or instrumental are impermissible.

The doctrine of double effect is not, however, a persuasive response to the Absolutist Challenge. The general validity of this doctrine is a deep and controversial issue in moral philosophy and I cannot pursue it here.[30] Notwithstanding, there are practical reasons to reject the doctrine as a moral–political principle in the ethics of humanitarian intervention.

The central problem is that it is too permissive since it permits unintended but foreseen civilian casualties. This grants too much in the context of humanitarian intervention. I argued above that those using force for humanitarian purposes must use humanitarian means because what legitimizes their use of military force is being humanitarian. If this is correct, then unintended, but foreseeable civilian casualties should be avoided. As Lucas strongly asserts, military personnel engaged in humanitarian intervention are not entitled 'to inflict unintentional collateral damage on non-military targets or personnel by the principle of double effect', but instead must '*avoid even inadvertent commission of the kinds of acts they are intervening to prevent*' (2003a: 78). Moreover, given that there is a difference between doing and allowing, an intervener should avoid causing foreseeable harm to civilians *itself*, even if unintended.

In his defence of the doctrine, Walzer recognizes that it is too permissive, and so adds a further condition: not only must the intention of the actor be good, 'aware of the evil involved, he seeks to minimize it, accepting costs to himself' (2006: 155). Yet even with this extra restriction, the doctrine still allows too much. Suppose, for instance, that an intervener cannot avoid hitting a school when using long-range missiles against a military barracks of genocidal soldiers. It cannot use ground troops since there is an early-warning system that means that the genocidal soldiers would flee before the intervener's forces could get near (so the intervener cannot minimize the risk any further). Although unintentionally destroying the school would kill hundreds of children, it would help to end the conflict, and potentially save many more lives (so would be proportionate). Such a case would be justified according to the doctrine of double effect, but seems deeply problematic, given the deaths of the school children.

In fact, Shue admits that, since it permits the killing of uninvolved persons and the destruction of ordinary property, granting the permissibility of the doctrine of double effect constitutes a 'giant concession to the fighting of wars' (2003: 107). But in defence of the doctrine, he argues that to reject it would be to adopt a pacifist, unrealistic approach. In a similar vein, Tesón (2005c: 104 n.12) argues that, although the doctrine has problems, rejecting it leads to the result of morally banning all wars. As we will now see, however, these responses are mistaken. One can reject the doctrine of double effect, endorse the difference between doing and allowing, and yet still avoid the non-interventionist position.[31]

4.4 AVOIDING THE ABSOLUTIST CHALLENGE

The Absolutist Challenge can be circumvented without having to invoke the doctrine of double effect. First, we can reject an absolutist, deontological position that rules out humanitarian intervention altogether, yet still endorse the moral importance of the difference between doing and allowing. That is, we do not have to admit that this difference is of *overwhelming* moral significance. Rather, we can say that there is, at least, *some* moral significance to the distinction between doing and allowing. This more moderate position does not necessarily lead to non-interventionism. When deciding who should intervene, it matters, *to a certain degree*, that an intervener will not violate *jus in bello* itself, even though this may ultimately allow more rights to be violated. But *sometimes* it is more important to intervene (and *do* harm) than to refrain from intervention (and *allow* much more harm).[32] Thus, who undertakes humanitarian intervention should be determined *in part* by the non-instrumental importance of an intervener's following the principles of *jus in bello*.

Second, according to the scalar approach to legitimacy I outlined in Chapter 1, an intervener can be sufficiently legitimate, even though it does not have a satisfactory degree of fidelity to the principles of *jus in bello*. As long as the intervener is able to make up the loss of legitimacy that comes from its not following closely the principles of *jus in bello*, its overall level of legitimacy may still be sufficient for it to have an adequate degree of legitimacy. The seriousness of the violation of *jus in bello* will determine how difficult it is for an intervener to make up the loss of legitimacy. For less serious violations, such as the employment of PMCs in combat roles, it may be easier. This also helps to forestall another objection: requiring interveners to follow the stricter principles of *jus in bello* does not impose unrealistic expectations on their behaviour which will, in practice, mean that an intervener will always be illegitimate. A minor violation of *jus in bello* by an intervener generally, or a major violation by only a few soldiers, is unlikely to render an intervention illegitimate. But it may be difficult for an intervener to make up the loss of legitimacy that comes from systematically contravening the principles of *jus in bello*, such as the killing of civilians.

One clear way in which an intervener can make up this loss of legitimacy is if there is a high expectation of achieving extremely beneficial consequences by, for instance, preventing genocide. Suppose that there is mass ethnic cleansing—genocide—in Benin. Tens of thousands of civilians of a certain ethnic group are being slaughtered, maimed, and raped every day by government troops and militias. Nigeria intervenes in Benin to stop this ethnic cleansing, and does so very effectively, but in doing so uses conscripts, a number of whom kill and sexually assault the non-combatants they are supposed to be helping. Although Nigeria's intervention is far from being *fully* legitimate, the fact that it is effective at preventing genocide means that it would have an *adequate degree* of legitimacy overall. Hence, according to the Moderate Instrumentalist Approach, if hugely beneficial consequences are highly likely, then effectiveness may be sufficient for an adequate degree of legitimacy, even if an intervener's fidelity to the principles of *jus in bello* is lacking.

This is not equivalent to endorsing the Extreme Instrumentalist Approach. The Moderate Instrumentalist Approach is much more restrictive. Given the non-consequentialist importance outlined above of an intervener's following the principles of *jus in bello*, an intervener's expected effectiveness is sufficient for an adequate degree of legitimacy only in particular circumstances. As discussed in Chapter 3, these are circumstances in which the intervener has both a *high probability* of achieving a success with a particularly *large magnitude*—in short, when highly beneficial consequences are more than likely. In other cases, effectiveness is not sufficient for an adequate degree of legitimacy because of the non-instrumental significance of an intervener's following these principles. For instance, if the situation in Benin was less serious than ethnic cleansing and genocide—say, for example, that its population suffered political oppression—Nigeria would struggle to possess an adequate degree of legitimacy if it violated principles of *jus in bello*.

Furthermore, even when an intervener has a high probability of achieving a success with a particularly large magnitude by halting an especially egregious violation of basic human rights, it needs to follow principles of *jus in bello* in order to be *fully* legitimate. In the example given above, in which Nigeria intervenes in Benin to halt ethnic cleansing, Nigeria would not be fully legitimate. It would need to use volunteer troops that have a satisfactory degree of fidelity to principles of *jus in bello* (and possess the other qualities of legitimacy). In other words, although the intervention may be justified overall, this does not justify the particular violation of *jus in bello*.

As such, the scalar approach differs from Walzer's account (2006: 251–68) of 'supreme emergency'. When the community is faced with imminent danger of enslavement or extermination, Walzer permits the overriding of principles *jus in bello*.[33] By contrast, the scalar approach does not defend such overriding.

Fidelity to the principles of *jus in bello* is important *at all times*. The point, rather, is that an intervener can be largely legitimized, in exceptional circumstances, by its effectiveness at tackling the mass violation of basic human rights. But even in such circumstances, an intervener should follow the principles of *jus in bello*. If it does not do so, although it might still be legitimate all things considered because of its effectiveness, something will be lacking in its legitimacy because of its failure to follow closely the principles of *jus in bello*. In short, then, there is no exemption to *jus in bello*.

Likewise, the scalar approach does not permit, unlike the doctrine of double effect, unintended but foreseen civilian casualties. An intervener that causes unintended but foreseen civilian casualties may still be legitimate because of its effectiveness in exceptional circumstances. However, unlike for the doctrine of double effect, such an intervener will *lose* legitimacy. Avoiding foreseen civilian casualties is a key factor in its moral justifiability.

Therefore, fidelity to principles of *jus in bello* provides two sorts of constraint on consequentialist thinking on humanitarian intervention. First, in situations where highly beneficial consequences are not expected, an intervener would struggle to have an *adequate degree of* legitimacy if it significantly contravenes the principles of *jus in bello*, even if it is likely to be effective. Second, in situations where highly beneficial consequences are likely, being effective is not enough for *full* legitimacy. A fully legitimate intervener would need to have fidelity to these principles of just conduct.

In contrast to the Extreme Instrumentalist Approach, these two constraints are easily accommodated by the Moderate Instrumentalist Approach. That is because the Moderate Instrumentalist Approach takes effectiveness to be the primary, but not the only, determinant of an intervener's legitimacy. Although effectiveness therefore does much of the normative work, this approach still makes sufficient room for secondary factors, such as fidelity to the principles of *jus in bello*, in its overall conception of legitimacy.

4.5 CONCLUSION

I have argued that an intervener's effectiveness is best seen as the *primary* determinant of its legitimacy, rather than as the sole determinant of its legitimacy (as held by the Extreme Instrumentalist Approach). Although consequentialist thought is dominant in the legitimacy of an intervener, it is not the whole picture: it is important that those intervening follow a number of principles of external and internal *jus in bello*. The principles of external *jus in bello* (e.g. the principles of proportionality and discrimination) are both more stringent and important in the context of the responsibility to protect, given the type of military operation that humanitarian intervention comprises and the humanitarian aims that it has. The importance of an intervener's fidelity to these principles of *jus in bello* cannot be completely captured by consequentialism; it also depends on the difference between doing and allowing. Although the difference between doing and allowing may seem to lead to a problematic absolutist position, we can avoid this position (as well as the problematic doctrine of double effect) by asserting that this difference is not of overwhelming moral significance and by adopting a scalar approach to legitimacy.

Accordingly, it is vital that those undertaking humanitarian intervention abide by these principles of external and internal *jus in bello*. It follows that, firstly, interveners are morally required to ensure that they respect these principles. They should monitor closely the behaviour of their troops, investigate allegations of wrongdoing, and discipline those who violate these principles. To help improve standards of conduct, interveners should increase the training and education of troops in *jus in bello* (R. Murphy 2000). Second, it may be necessary to extend current international mechanisms (such as the International Criminal Court) and develop new mechanisms to ensure the just conduct of interveners (see Archibugi 2005: 224 and the proposals in Chapter 8). The Security Council should also monitor and ensure the just conduct of the interveners that it authorizes (Farer 2005a: 219). Third, as recommended by the Independent International Commission on Kosovo (2000: 184), the International Committee of the Red Cross (ICRC) (or another appropriate body) should prepare a new legal convention for humanitarian intervention and those discharging the responsibility to protect. This convention would impose more constraints on the use of force than currently embodied in conventional Just War Theory, such as the principles of external and internal *jus in bello* that I have outlined.[34] A related, specific improvement would be the establishment of a clear and unified military doctrine for UN forces, particularly for coercive protection which, despite the development of the Capstone Doctrine (UN 2008*d*), is still undeveloped and largely relies on the guidance provided by individual member states (Bellamy 2009a: 121; Cottey 2008: 439).

The inability of the Extreme Instrumentalist Approach to take into account properly the importance of the principles of external and internal *jus in bello* reflects a serious problem with a purely consequentialist approach to humanitarian intervention: it is insensitive to the means by which consequences are achieved and, in particular, it fails to distinguish between doing and allowing. In the next chapter, I make the case for the importance of two further factors for an intervener's legitimacy that cannot be explained solely by instrumentalist concerns: its internal representativeness and its local external representativeness. These two factors are, likewise, neither necessary nor sufficient conditions of an intervener's legitimacy, but are nevertheless important. They will reinforce the objection I have made in this chapter against the Extreme Instrumentalist Approach: that effectiveness is not the only factor determining an intervener's legitimacy. The next chapter will therefore help to establish further the persuasiveness of the Moderate Instrumentalist Approach.

NOTES

1. The Secretary General's *Bulletin on the Observance by United Nations Forces of International Humanitarian Law* (Annan 1999) made it clear that international humanitarian law applies to UN forces. The rules of international humanitarian law also apply to both those involved in international and noninternational armed conflicts (such as rebel groups). See Shraga (2000) and Henckaerts and Doswald-Beck (2005: 3–24).
2. The exceptions include Blocq (2006), the Independent International Commission on Kosovo (2000), Ladley (2005), Lucas (2003*a*), and Pfaff (2000).
3. For useful surveys of these discussions, see Bellamy (2008) and A. Brown (2008).
4. Tesón (2005*b*: 29) makes a similar point regarding the violation of *jus in bello* during the war in Iraq.
5. I cannot explore here all the complexities of McMahan's proposed revisions to Just War Theory (and possible objections). There is a burgeoning debate on the separation of *jus in bello* from *jus ad bellum* and individual moral responsibility in warfare, largely stemming from McMahan's work. See, for instance, Estlund (2007), Hurka (2007), and Steinhoff (2008). Also see McMahan (2006; 2009).
6. I defend this point in more detail in Pattison (2009), where I argue that existing international law should be changed to prohibit attacks on the soldiers of an intervener authorized by the UN Security Council. I also challenge McMahan's claim (2008) that such changes to the moral equality of soldiers should remain part of the deep morality of warfare (largely because of the difficulties in determining *jus ad bellum*).
7. To be sure, a number of conscripts may still be morally responsible for their participation in an unjust war, which may make them morally liable to attack. The conscription may not have been against their will, there may have been reasonable alternatives apart from conscription, the duress may have been only very weak, and there may be reasonable opportunities (which they do not pursue) to desert. In addition, the conscripts may fulfill their role with vigour and to the best of their ability, rather than trying to affect negatively the prosecution of their unjust war by attempting sabotage or being inefficient.
8. It should also be noted here that certain volunteer soldiers may not be morally responsible for their participation in an unjust war. For instance, when joining the

armed force they may have been misled into thinking that their state would be fighting only for just causes, they may have been deceived about the justice of the war, and there may be no reasonable alternative options to participating in an unjust war.

9. A similar list of requirements is presented by McMahan (forthcoming) in his thoughtful discussion of Just War Theory and child soldiers.

10. Some of the reasons that I offer for the increased stringency and importance of *jus in bello* could apply to other uses of force, especially those that occupy enemy territory. In this context, Lango (2009*a*) argues that, for military actions of all sorts, last resort should function also as an *in bello* principle, which means that military commanders must be under the presumption against using military force.

11. Although I focus on the principles of discrimination and proportionality, it may also follow, given the arguments that I present, that it is also more important that those undertaking humanitarian intervention follow the other principles of external *jus in bello* (e.g. the prohibition on certain weapons and the humane treatment of civilians, persons *hors de combat*, and prisoners of war).

12. NATO's campaign in Kosovo is a notable exception. Indeed, the problematic use of means by NATO may, in part, have been due to the fact that it was conceived in some quarters as war rather than humanitarian intervention.

13. Similarly, the ICISS (2001*a*: 37) assert that since military intervention involves a form of military action that is more narrowly focused and targeted than all-out war fighting, an argument can be made that even higher standards should apply.

14. Orend notes that the *in bello* principle of proportionality requires agents to '[u]se force appropriate to the target' (2006: 119; emphasis removed). This is consistent with substantial force against enemy combatants, as long as it is not *excessive*.

15. Pfaff's focus is on traditional peacekeeping, but his arguments can be extended to humanitarian intervention.

16. See, further, McMahan (2010: 63–70) on proportionality and humanitarian intervention.

17. As said above, interveners should also follow other principles of international humanitarian law, such as the prohibition on the use of certain weapons and methods. I have focussed on the principles of discrimination and proportionality as these most obviously require revision.

18. For more on this issue (and on the permissibility of using volunteer soldiers), see Tesón (2005*c*: 132–7). He argues that problems of free riding mean that conscription can be justified for national defence, but not for humanitarian intervention. Also see Vernon's response (2008: 44–5).

19. See, further, Orend (2006: 133–6), who lists a number of soldiers' rights.

20. According to act consequentialism (in its direct form), an agent should try to maximize the good directly with each act it performs.

21. In short, rule consequentialism holds that agents should follow rules that maximize the good.

22. Brandt goes on to offer his own account of the principles of *jus in bello*. R.M. Hare (1972) also presents a rule consequentialist defence of the importance of fidelity to principles of *jus in bello*.

23. In Richard Arneson's words: 'for any construal of rule consequentialism according to which it appears to dictate conduct different from what act consequentialism would dictate, there must be an alternate candidate rule consequentialist code that eliminates the putative conflict with act consequentialism and must be judged superior from the rule consequentialist standpoint' (2005: 236). David Lyons (1965) makes the original statement of this objection.

24. In *Ideal Code, Real World*, Brad Hooker presents a sophisticated version of rule consequentialism that tries to overcome this problem of collapse. His reformulation insists that the rules of rule consequentialism need to be kept simple so that they can be easily internalized (Hooker 2000: 96–7). Iterative amendments to the principles of *jus in bello* would therefore not be endorsed by this sophisticated rule consequentialism—it is more important to keep the rules simple. It is not clear, however, whether his theory is actually rule consequentialist since it ultimately appeals to intuitionism, rather than to a single, underlying consequentialist principle of maximizing the good. Indeed, as Hooker (2000: 188–9) himself admits, his approach does not have an overarching commitment to maximizing the good. It does not appear to conform therefore with the Extreme Instrumentalist Approach. That aside, there are also difficulties with Hooker's account of rule consequentialism in cases of individual acceptance but general noncompliance with the rules, and also with his provision that internalized rules may be broken in cases of disaster. See Arneson (2005), Card (2007), and McIntyre (2005) for discussion of these and other difficulties with Hooker's rule consequentialism. Hooker (2005; 2007) does reply to these concerns, however.

25. As a general theory, indirect consequentialism (specifically indirect act consequentialism) holds that, rather than attempting to maximize the good directly, agents should adopt decision-making procedures, such as dispositions, traditions, and rules of thumb, which maximize the good overall. Note that rule consequentialism and indirect consequentialism are distinct. The central assertion of rule consequentialism is what Hooker (2004) calls the rule consequentialist 'criterion of rightness'. This judges things by whether they comply with rules, the acceptance of which maximizes the good. By contrast, the central assertion of indirect consequentialism is its indirect decision-making procedure, which can be expected to maximize the good indirectly. See, further, Hooker (2004).

26. Samuel Scheffler frames the distinction between doing and allowing in terms of the distinction between primary and secondary manifestations of our agency and claims that 'we operate with an intuitive picture according to which, in general, the norms of individual responsibility attach much greater weight to the primary than to the secondary manifestations' (2004: 216). In his view, '[t]here is little doubt that some idea of this sort has an important role to play in ordinary moral thought' (Scheffler 2004: 215).

27. To be sure, some harm is permissible according to the principles of *jus in bello*. The concern is with *impermissible* harm, such as harm that is suffered by civilians.
28. So, this position is likely to lead to pacifism: since virtually all wars involve civilian casualties, no war can be justified. Atack (2002) gets close to this position.
29. See, for instance, Bellamy (2004: 229–30), Heinze (2004), Shue (2003), and Tesón (2005*c*).
30. One of the most common criticisms of the doctrine is that there is little difference between (*a*) foreseen, unintentional harm and (*b*) intentional harm. See, for instance, May (2008: 283–6) on this point in relation to humanitarian intervention. Recent repudiations of the doctrine in moral philosophy, however, focus on whether the doctrine does any real moral work. See, for instance, McIntyre (2001).
31. It may be responded that those who endorse the doctrine of double effect do not mean it to be an all-embracing moral principle and, as such, other moral principles, such as the difference between doing and allowing, would rule out many problematic cases. This may be true. But the doctrine is often used by its defenders (if mistakenly) in the ethics of war as a catch-all principle that responds to the Absolutist Challenge. My focus is on responding to their account.
32. Indeed, most defenders of the difference between doing and allowing admit that this distinction is not absolute. See, for instance, Quinn (1989).
33. See Caney (2005: 198–9) for criticisms of Walzer's account of supreme emergency.
34. Such a convention would have to be carefully constructed since certain of the revisions proposed may not be best included under international humanitarian law. For instance, international humanitarian law should not be amended to reflect the individual moral responsibility of those who oppose the intervener (e.g. to require interveners to minimize harm to morally innocent combatants, such as certain conscripts). This is because of the difficulties of assessing combatants' moral responsibility, firstly, by the intervener in the midst of an operation and, secondly, more generally in the ethics of warfare. It would be problematic therefore to prosecute intervening soldiers who fail to minimize harm to morally innocent combatants (e.g. by not accepting risk to themselves). Nevertheless, the moral responsibility of opposing combatants can still be included in conventional Just War Theory on a less formal basis under military doctrine. Interveners can issue guidelines for engaging enemy combatants that attempt, where possible, to take into account enemy combatants' culpability (e.g. by suggesting that interveners avoid harming child soldiers). I discuss these potential revisions further in Pattison (2009).

5

Representativeness and Humanitarian Intervention

In Chapter 4, I defended the importance of an intervener's fidelity to the principles of external and internal *jus in bello* when deciding who should intervene. I claimed that the ability of the Moderate Instrumentalist Approach to incorporate these values in its account of legitimacy makes it more persuasive than the Extreme Instrumentalist Approach. In this chapter, I argue for the moral significance of two further factors, both pertaining to an intervener's representativeness. Both factors can be incorporated under the Moderate Instrumentalist Approach. By making the case for these two factors, I will reinforce the objection made against the Extreme Instrumentalist Approach, namely, that effectiveness is not the only morally relevant factor when deciding who should intervene.

The first I shall describe as an intervener's 'internal representativeness'. This requires an intervener's decision-making on the proposed intervention to have internal support. More precisely, internal representativeness depends on whether an intervener's decision-making on the proposed intervention reflects the opinions of *its citizens*. For instance, the internal representativeness of the 1992 American intervention in Somalia turned on whether America represented the opinions of *Americans*. The second is what I shall describe as an intervener's 'local external representativeness'. This depends on whether an intervener's decision-making on the proposed intervention has external support. More precisely, local external representativeness depends on whether an intervener's decision-making on the proposed intervention reflects the opinions of those individuals *in the political community that is subject to the intervention*. To use the same example, the local external representativeness of the 1992 American intervention in Somalia turned on whether America represented the opinions of *Somalis*.

In this chapter, I make the case for the moral importance of these two factors which, like the importance of an intervener's fidelity to the principles of *jus in bello* considered in Chapter 4, have received less attention in the literature on humanitarian intervention and the responsibility to protect.[1]

That is, I argue that an intervener's legitimacy depends on whether it is representative of the opinions on intervention, firstly, of its domestic population and, secondly, of those subject to its intervention. I begin by presenting three (largely complementary) arguments for the importance of an intervener's internal representativeness. The first is consequentialist: an intervener that has public support is more likely to be effective in tackling a humanitarian crisis. The second is the 'Resources Argument'. This asserts that an intervener should be representative of its citizens' opinions because these citizens provide the resources for humanitarian intervention. The third argument emphasizes the value of individual self-government. I then present three arguments for the importance of an intervener's local external representativeness. In some measure, these mirror the arguments for internal representativeness. The first argument is consequentialist: a locally externally representative intervener is more likely to be effective. The second is the 'Burdens Argument', which holds that an intervener should represent the opinions of those subject to its intervention because those individuals are likely to be burdened by its intervention. The third argument again asserts the value of individual self-government. Overall, then, I present six arguments for the significance of internal and local external representativeness for the legitimacy of humanitarian intervention. I conclude by largely rejecting the importance of a third potential factor—'global external representativeness'.

Before we proceed, however, I need to clarify what I mean by 'representativeness'. In her seminal work on the concept, Hanna Pitkin (1967) distinguishes between a number of meanings of representation, all based around the notion of re-presentation, a making present again. For example, formalistic views of representation include the 'authorization view', where a representative is someone who has been authorized to act, and the 'accountability view', where a representative is someone who is to be held to account (Pitkin 1967: 38–55). The problem with these views, Pitkin (1967: 58) notes, is that they cannot tell us anything about what goes on during representation, how a representative ought to act, and whether they have represented well or badly. Alternatively, the descriptive view of representation takes representation to be 'standing for' by virtue of a correspondence or connection between the representative and the represented. The focus is on the representative's characteristics, such as her class, ethnicity, and religion (Pitkin 1967: 61–91).

The most useful meaning of representation for our purposes, however, is 'acting for'. This view is concerned with the activity of representing, what goes on during representing, and the substance or content of acting for others (Pitkin 1967: 113). Accordingly, a representative institution will act for its citizens, by delegation or trusteeship. It is here that we find the 'mandate-independence' controversy. Should a representative represent their citizens' opinions, since they are bound by mandate to do what their citizens want, or should they have the independence to be able to promote their citizens' interests as they see these interests and as best they can? As will become apparent, in relation to humanitarian intervention I take the 'mandate' side of this controversy. That is to say, a representative should represent their citizens' opinions, a representative institution is one that reflects its subjects' opinions in its decision-making, and 'representativeness' is the measure of the extent to which an institution does so.

It is also important to define what I mean by an individual's 'opinions on the intervention'. The most morally relevant opinion is an individual's view on whether humanitarian intervention should be undertaken. Other relevant opinions are an individual's views on the specific form of intervention, on who should intervene, and the structure of the post-war settlement. Those subject to a humanitarian crisis might want intervention, but not want it to be carried out by a particular intervener (such as the US), or they might want regime change, but not long-term occupation. Furthermore, for reasons of practical simplicity (and perhaps of antipaternalism), I am concerned with an individual's *actual* opinions rather than what their opinion would be if they had more information or if their opinions were more freely formed. Although individuals' opinions may be influenced in undesirable ways and contain misperceptions, I argue for their moral significance when they relate to humanitarian intervention.

5.1 INTERNAL REPRESENTATIVENESS

Let us begin with the case for internal representativeness. To be internally representative, an intervener needs to reflect, in its decision-making, its citizens' opinions on the proposed intervention. If the majority of its citizens do not want intervention, an internally representative government would not intervene. If its citizens want intervention to be undertaken in a particular way (such as regime change), then the decision-making of the internally representative government would reflect this.

A would-be intervener can establish the opinions of its citizens—and therefore be internally representative—in a number of ways. For example, it could conduct opinion polls on a sample of the population, hold referenda on humanitarian intervention, and, less scientifically, consider other indicators of the public mood, such as the media, its interactions with the public, and public campaigns. The latter sort of measures are, of course, not completely accurate, given media influence, and, more generally, it can be tricky (but not impossible) to access reliable or genuine assessments of domestic public opinion. But an intervener should nevertheless attempt to garner such information, given the arguments that follow for the importance of internal representativeness. Note here that it is possible for non-democratic states to be internally representative if they accurately reflect their constituents' opinions. That said, democratic states are perhaps most likely—although far from certain—to reflect public opinion on intervention, given the democratic politician's desire to be elected, their sense of duty to reflect their constituents' opinions (and often public opinion more generally), and the likelihood of a concurrence between public opinion and the government's judgement.

An immediate challenge might be this: why does the question of internal representativeness for humanitarian intervention arise? On many issues (such as health, education, and fiscal policy), it seems right that elected politicians should have some independence to use their judgement. They should primarily act in accordance with what they deem to be in the national (or their constituents') interest, without always having to reflect public opinion. In other words, the trusteeship conception of representation according to which a representative can go against constituents' declared opinions and use their own judgement seems appropriate in many contexts. Why should we prefer a delegate conception of representation according to which a representative must reflect the opinions of their constituents in the context of humanitarian intervention? What distinguishes humanitarian intervention from other governmental acts such that it requires politicians to reflect their citizens' opinions?

There are two distinctive features. The first is that humanitarian intervention is a different sort of governmental action because it may not be in the interests of the citizens of the intervening state. The trusteeship model of representation holds that representatives should have the freedom to promote the interests of their citizens (or constituents). Since humanitarian intervention may not be in the interests of the intervener's citizens (or constituents), it transcends the remit of representatives on this model. To put this another way, if we view the primary role of government as the promotion of its citizens' interests, it follows that government contravenes its fiduciary obligation to its citizens by undertaking humanitarian intervention.

We need to tread carefully here, however. In particular, we need to avoid endorsing a similar, but stronger, view—what Buchanan (1999), in his discussion of the internal legitimacy of humanitarian intervention, terms the 'discretionary association view of the state'. This view, discussed in Chapter 1, holds government to be *solely* the agent of the associated individuals and its role as the furthering of these individuals' interests. The problem with this view, recall, is that it is too strong, since it denies that a government possesses *any* duties to those beyond the borders of the state. As such, any governmental action that is *not* in its citizens' interests is unjustifiable.

Nevertheless, the notion that the specialness of humanitarian intervention arises from the breaking of the intervening government's fiduciary obligation to its citizens seems plausible. But we need to be clear about the strength of this obligation. It is not absolute. This is demonstrated by the inadequacies of the discretionary association view. As I suggested in Chapter 1, rather than holding that government acts legitimately only when it occupies itself *exclusively* with the interests of its citizens, we can say that the *primary* role of government is to promote its citizens' interests. By viewing this fiduciary obligation as primary, this more moderate approach allows room for government to possess certain obligations to those beyond its borders, for instance, to avoid causing large-scale environmental pollution in a neighbouring state. Yet, on this approach, these obligations are limited, given the primary role of government. And, as a substantial undertaking, humanitarian intervention— when not in particularly serious cases—seems to go beyond the scope of government's limited obligations to those beyond its borders and is incongruous with government's fiduciary obligation to its citizens.[2] So, unlike the discretionary association view, this more moderate approach can admit that government possesses some limited obligations to those beyond its borders, but, like the discretionary association view, it holds that, by undertaking humanitarian intervention, government sometimes contravenes its fiduciary obligation.

On its own, however, the suggestion that humanitarian intervention is a special case because of its generally altruistic character is incomplete. If we limit the specialness of humanitarian intervention to only its (apparent) altruism, any humanitarian intervention that is in the interests of the citizens of the intervening state can be left to representatives to decide independently.[3] We therefore need to identify a second feature that distinguishes humanitarian intervention from other governmental actions and means that we should reject a trusteeship conception of representation in this context.

My suggestion is that what differentiates humanitarian intervention, in addition to its (apparently) altruistic character, is that it involves the use of military force and, more generally, extremely high moral stakes. Humanitarian intervention (like any use of military force) has significant potential to cause high levels of suffering and devastation to those in the target state, for instance, by killing innocent civilians, destroying vital infrastructure, and creating a power vacuum. Yet a government's decision to undertake humanitarian intervention can also have considerable positive benefits, such as protecting populations from genocide and ethnic cleansing. It follows that the consequences, either good or bad, of an agent's decision if, when, and how to undertake humanitarian intervention will be considerable for those suffering the humanitarian crisis. Furthermore, the effects of an agent's decision to intervene reverberate around the international system, not only by affecting international norms (both legal and normative) by, for instance, the setting of precedents, but also more materially by, for instance, creating refugee flows and destabilizing surrounding regions. The intervener's citizens are also affected by the decision, for (as discussed in Section 5.1.2) they provide the financial and human resources (which can be significant). As such, the consequences, either good or bad, of an agent's decision to intervene will also be highly significant for the international system and the intervener's citizens.

So when making a decision that involves the use of military force and, more generally, has such high moral stakes, it seems right that a government should reflect its citizens' opinions in its decision-making. Unlike for other, less important, decisions, which we can leave politicians to decide for themselves, trusteeship is not appropriate when the moral stakes are so high. Hence, there are two elements to the specialness of humanitarian intervention: first, humanitarian intervention may go against the intervening state's primary (but not absolute) obligation to its citizens; second, it involves the use of military force and, more generally, high moral stakes.

Although we have two reasons why trusteeship is unpersuasive in the context of humanitarian intervention, we do not yet have justification for why the delegate conception of representation should be preferred. In other words, we now need to see why an intervener's decision-making on the proposed intervention should reflect the opinions of its citizens. In what follows, I present three arguments for the importance of internal representativeness for the legitimacy of humanitarian intervention. Note that for the rest of the chapter I will use 'representativeness' in the sense of representation as delegation.[4]

5.1.1 Increased effectiveness

Let us begin the case for the importance of internal representativeness with a consequentialist argument. One of the largest problems faced by humanitarian intervention is insufficient commitment. This has led to critically under-resourced and, ultimately, unsuccessful, interventions. The failure of UN member states to provide UNAMIR, the UN force led by Roméo Dallaire, with the necessary resources to stop the genocide in Rwanda is the most conspicuous example. Many of these problems arise because interveners are unwilling to commit the necessary financial, military, and diplomatic resources to potentially unpopular and controversial interventions. By contrast, an internally representative intervener which knows that it has public support is more likely to be willing to commit the resources required to be successful. It may be more willing, for instance, to risk casualties and so be able to undertake ambitious military manoeuvres, which are necessary for intervention to be successful. Consider, in this context, Australia's 1999 action in East Timor. Since it knew it had the support of the Australian public, the Australian government was prepared to accept some casualties and, as a result, intervened with the level of military force necessary for successful humanitarian intervention (see Wheeler and Dunne 2001).

This consequentialist argument for internal representativeness is, however, contingent on there being a correlation between internal representativeness and effectiveness. On occasion, being internally representative may not ensure that the intervention is successful. The time it takes to establish whether there is public support for intervention may mean that deployment is slowed, which in turn undermines the effectiveness of the operation. Alternatively, public opinion may change during the intervention, but if the intervener were to respond to this change (perhaps by altering its mission objectives), it would be less effective. Likewise, humanitarian intervention can be successful without being internally representative. This raises an important question for both internal and local external representativeness: would an intervener be legitimate if it lacked internal or local external representativeness (or both), yet was likely to be effective at preventing, reducing, or halting the humanitarian crisis?[5]

Both internal and local external representativeness, like the fidelity to principles of *jus in bello*, are neither sufficient nor necessary conditions of legitimate humanitarian intervention. As long as the intervener is able to make up in other ways the loss of legitimacy that comes from not being internally or locally externally representative, its overall level of legitimacy may be sufficient for it to have an adequate degree of legitimacy. One way in which an intervener can make up this loss of legitimacy is if there is a high expectation of its achieving extremely beneficial consequences, such as by preventing genocide. This reflects the dominance of consequentialist thinking on humanitarian intervention, as encapsulated by the Moderate Instrumentalist Approach. What matters most is that the intervener is effective at preventing, reducing, or halting the mass violation of basic human rights.

That is not to deny that internal and local external representativeness are important considerations for the legitimacy of humanitarian intervention. On the contrary, the six arguments set out in this chapter establish that these are significant considerations. The aim here is to make clear the strength of the arguments that follow and, in particular, to avoid overstating the case. Furthermore, in most cases of humanitarian intervention, where extremely beneficial consequences are not on the cards, an intervener would struggle to be legitimate if it were not internally representative and locally externally representative. Moreover, even when extremely beneficial consequences are likely, it remains important that the intervener should be internally and locally externally representative. Indeed, this would be necessary for it to be *fully* legitimate.

5.1.2 The Resources Argument

The second reason why an intervener's internal representativeness matters is what I call the 'Resources Argument'. The central contention is this: since the intervener's citizens provide the resources for humanitarian intervention, their opinions should be reflected in the decision on intervention.

The underlying argument at work here is Lockean: individuals should have some freedom to determine how their own resources (property) are used. Given that humanitarian intervention requires a substantial amount of resources, the intervener should reflect the opinions of those providing the resources for humanitarian intervention—its citizens. Doing so means that these individuals retain some control over their resources. This Lockean argument is not absolute. There are moral constraints on how an individual should use their resources (such as not causing excessive harm to others) and the importance of individual choice here might not be as significant as other moral considerations (such as highly beneficial consequences). Nevertheless, some degree of control over one's own resources is intuitively attractive.

In theory, we could make this argument about any governmental action that uses its citizens' resources. It is more convincing, however, for humanitarian intervention because of the level of resources involved. It is estimated that the ECOWAS interventions in Liberia and Sierra Leone cost $4 billion (de Waal 2000: 81). In their report, the ICISS (2001a: 71) estimates that the cost of the Kosovo intervention (including post-intervention peacekeeping and reconstruction) was $48 billion. The intervener's citizens—in these cases, the citizens of ECOWAS and NATO respectively—ultimately have to foot the bill for humanitarian intervention, perhaps through significantly increased taxation or greatly decreased public spending elsewhere. It is right, therefore, that these individuals should have some input into the decision-making on humanitarian intervention. The Resources Argument gains plausibility if, in addition to financial resources, it includes human resources. The intervener's citizens provide the personnel to undertake humanitarian intervention. Some of these individuals may be injured and killed in combat. There is further reason then for representing the opinions of these individuals.

5.1.3 Individual self-government

The Resources Argument is persuasive as far as it goes, but it may not be relevant for all cases of humanitarian intervention. The resources spent on a small-scale intervention might be insignificant when viewed in relation to overall national spending. In addition, the intervention might not be particularly risky and therefore would not be costly in terms of human resources— it would not put in danger many intervening soldiers' lives. Moreover, the Resources Argument does not go far enough. It does not quite capture the main reason why an intervener's internal representativeness matters: that individuals should have some control over their governing institution because it is *their* governing institution. More specifically, the citizens of the intervener should have their opinions on the intervention represented because it is *their* intervener: it is *their* state or *their* multinational organization that is intervening. This sentiment was discernible in the early stages of the 2003 war in Iraq; many protesters in the UK claimed that the war was conducted 'not in our name'.[6] Their protest was not about the use of resources. It was against the fact that *their* government was undertaking an action which they opposed. Accordingly, I will now outline a third, more Rousseauian defence of the importance of an intervener's internal representativeness.

This third argument relies on the principle of individual self-government, which runs as follows: a governing institution should reflect the wishes of its citizens such that it is as if those individuals were in authority themselves. Individual self-government here possesses significant value. In Robert Dahl's words: '[t]o govern oneself, to obey laws that one has chosen for oneself, to be *self-determining*, is a desirable end' (1989: 89). To be sure, individual self-government is not always an overriding value. Rather, more individual self-government is *by and large* desirable. Other moral factors (such as highly beneficial consequences) can be more important than individual self-government, but this is not to deny its value. Indeed, individual self-government seems to possess non-consequentialist value. The fulfilment of an individual's wishes on how they want to be governed is valuable regardless of whether these wishes, if they were realized, would contribute to their well-being. To see this, consider a (hypothetical) society whose government is hierarchical and unrepresentative. It never consults its citizens on how they wish to be governed—it makes decisions by decree—but is competent at promoting the interests of its citizens. Although such a government would not be *that* morally objectionable because it would be promoting its citizens' interests, something morally important is still missing. That missing element is the value of individuals' having a significant input in how they are governed and how their society is run.

To be fully compatible with the principle of individual self-government, both the structure of government and every law it makes would need to match each individual's opinions on how they wish to be governed. Yet, in all but the smallest of societies, complete self-government is unachievable. This is what Thomas Christiano (1996: 25) calls the 'incompatibility problem'. Given the inevitable conflict of opinions that arises in a society, the ability of a number of individuals to choose how they are governed will be frustrated. But this does not mean that the importance of an institution representing the opinions of its citizens cannot be justified by the principle of individual self-government. The crucial point is that we are not concerned solely with achieving *full* individual self-government within a society (which is a chimera), but with increasing the *amount* of individual self-government. As such, we are concerned with the relative, rather than absolute, level of individual self-government. It follows that an intervener that represents at least the majority of its citizens' opinions on the humanitarian intervention is likely to have *more* individuals who are self-governing on this issue than an intervener that does not. For instance, requiring a supermajority (say of two-thirds of the voting population) for intervention would risk giving those who oppose intervention a greater say than those that support it—and therefore decrease the overall amount of individual self-government on the issue of humanitarian intervention.[7]

The value of individual self-government has a considerable impact on the argument for an intervener's internal representativeness. An intervener's internal representativeness is morally significant because of the importance of individuals' having a voice in the running of their political institutions. As a significant undertaking by the state, it is important that humanitarian intervention be responsive to the concerns of individual self-government by being representative of its citizens' opinions on intervention. An individual's freedom to choose whether there should be intervention, who should do it, how long it should last, and what form it should take, therefore matters. Indeed, given the non-instrumental value of individual self-government, there is reason for an intervener to be internally representative even if its population is mistaken on the issue of intervention. To be sure, this reason may not always be decisive. There may be more morally urgent concerns, such as the likely achievement of extremely beneficial consequences. Nevertheless, individual self-government is a central reason why an intervener's internal representativeness matters. An intervener should be internally representative and respond to its citizens' opinions because they are the opinions of *its* citizens. Suppose, for example, that the Vietnamese government were considering intervening in Laos to tackle a (hypothetical) genocide. The Vietnamese people supported intervention, but only with Security Council authorization. The views of the Vietnamese people matter, on the logic of this self-government argument, not because taking account of those views will best serve international law and order, nor because doing so is the best for the Vietnamese people's enjoyment of human rights, but because it is *their* state, Vietnam, that is considering intervening.

It may help to summarize briefly the argument thus far. The first reason for the significance of an intervener's internal representativeness is consequentialist: an internally representative intervener is more likely to be effective. The second is the Resources Argument, which asserts that the intervener's citizens should have their opinions reflected in its decision-making since they provide the resources for humanitarian intervention. The last reason is the value of individual self-government on humanitarian intervention. Together, these three reasons demonstrate that an intervener's internal representativeness is an important consideration for (and usually a necessary condition of) the legitimacy of humanitarian intervention.

It might be argued at this point that the importance of an intervener's internal representativeness challenges the view (defended in Chapter 1) that humanitarian intervention is a duty. This is because the duty to intervene will be dependent on citizens' support for the intervention, but this may be lacking. There are two points to make in response. First, when humanitarian intervention *is* internally representative (i.e. when it *does* have internal support), it may be a duty. Second, even when humanitarian intervention is *not* internally representative, an intervener may still be morally obliged to intervene. The argument I present for internal representativeness is not absolute. According to the scalar approach to legitimacy, an intervener may lack one quality, such as internal representativeness, but still be the most legitimate intervener if it can make up the loss of legitimacy in other ways (such as by being the most effective at tackling a particularly serious humanitarian crisis). It follows that, if an intervener will be the most legitimate (say, for instance, it is the only agent that could effectively tackle genocide in a neighbouring state), it may still possess the duty to intervene, despite lacking internal representativeness. In other cases (such as less serious crises), its lack of internal representativeness may mean that it would not be legitimate overall. The intervener would not then have the duty to intervene; nor, it should be noted, would it have the right to intervene.

5.2 LOCAL EXTERNAL REPRESENTATIVENESS

Let us now consider the importance of local external representativeness. To be locally externally representative, an intervener needs to represent the opinions of those in the political community that is potentially subject to its humanitarian intervention. For instance, a locally externally representative intervener would not undertake humanitarian intervention if those who would be subject to it do not want intervention. Similarly, if those individuals do not want a particular form of intervention, the decision-making of the locally externally representative intervener would reflect that.[8]

To establish the opinions of those subject to its humanitarian intervention, a would-be intervener should, firstly, attempt to obtain direct access to these individuals. Sometimes there are obstacles to achieving this, but these are not always insurmountable. The ICRC's *The People on War Report* (2000) survey, for instance, comprised a series of comprehensive opinion polls and interviews on humanitarian intervention in a number of war-affected states. Amongst the findings was that 66 per cent of those surveyed wanted more intervention from the international community to deal with humanitarian crises, and only 17 per cent wanted less (ICRC 2000: 54). In addition, they were able to distinguish between combatants and civilians, as well as identifying those who had suffered severe burdens caused by conflict. Of course, such useful information will not always be accessible before the launch of a humanitarian intervention. Access may be denied to researchers and the situation may be too dangerous (the ICRC faced these difficulties with its research as well).[9]

Where direct consultation with those suffering the humanitarian crisis is impossible, a locally externally representative intervener will not simply presume these individuals' opinions on the proposed intervention. Instead, it will use secondary sources or indicators of these citizens' opinions, provided, for instance, by intermediaries. The challenge for the intervener, if it is to be locally externally representative, is to find reliable agents that provide accurate information on the opinions of victims and affected bystanders. One way that the intervener can determine whether an agent provides accurate information is by examining its ethos, track record, and agenda. Another way is to compare the agent's account with that of the few citizens with whom direct access is possible (e.g. refugees). The agents that are perhaps most likely to be reliable are certain NGOs and what Mary Kaldor (1999: 121) calls 'islands of civility' (groups that have political support but are not involved in the violence).

An intervener, therefore, can be locally externally representative in a number of ways. Although these are not always easily achieved, in what follows I argue that an intervener should make a concerted effort to be locally externally representative. A significant part of its legitimacy depends on its doing so. This is the case even if Jacques deLisle is right in asserting that 'most victims will not oppose intervention' (2001: 552). It is important to establish that this is true: that those subject to the humanitarian crisis clearly want intervention. Indeed, much of the opposition to humanitarian intervention revolves around the idea that it is paternalistic, forced upon people who do not want it (e.g. Walzer 1980). One logical corollary of this objection is that, if intervention is to be legitimate, the intervener's local external representativeness is vital. As Tesón notes, 'leaders must make sure before intervening that they have the support of the very persons they want to assist' (2003: 107).

Yet, the question remains: why exactly is it that the intervener should establish and represent the opinions of those in the political community that is subject to its intervention? The three reasons for the importance of an intervener's local external representativeness mirror to a certain degree the three reasons presented for internal representativeness. The first claims that a locally externally representative intervener is more likely to be effective. The second is the 'Burdens Argument', which asserts that those subject to the humanitarian intervention should have their opinions represented because intervention is likely to burden them. The third emphasizes the value of individual self-government.

Together, these three arguments will show that local external representativeness is a significant factor in (and, apart from extreme cases, a necessary condition of) the legitimacy of an intervener. Indeed, local external representativeness perhaps carries greater weight in the overall assessment of an intervener's legitimacy than internal representativeness. This is because we can expect the three arguments presented to be even more significant in this context: (*a*) an intervener's local external representativeness is likely to be of greater consequence for its effectiveness than its internal representativeness; (*b*) the burdens of intervention are likely to have a larger effect on individuals than the contribution of resources to undertake intervention; and (*c*) individual self-government seems to be even more important when you are subject to intervention than when undertaking it.[10]

5.2.1 Increased effectiveness

I begin the defence of the moral importance of local external representativeness with a largely consequentialist argument: an intervener that represents the opinions of those subject to its humanitarian intervention is more likely to be effective at preventing, reducing, or halting the humanitarian crisis. This is because prior consultation with those who would be subject to the intervention can indicate whether there is widespread support for intervention in the target state. This is a key factor in determining whether intervention will succeed (Gizelis and Kosek 2005). Prior consultation can also help to overcome some of the epistemological problems that interveners face when attempting to assess the extent of a humanitarian crisis in another state. It can also help to establish the seriousness of the humanitarian crisis and ensure that the intervener will be responding to a situation of sufficient gravity so that there is room to do more good than harm. Without prior consultation, the intervener might undertake action in response to a less serious (or non-existent) humanitarian crisis that does not meet the requirements of just cause. Or, it might undertake action that is unpopular with the local population and, as a result, face high levels of resistance, making successful intervention difficult.

In addition, a locally externally representative intervener is more likely to know whether a particular course of action or mission during the intervention will be successful. In this context, Jarat Chopra and Tanja Hohe (2004: 291) assert that locals tend to have the best knowledge of the situation, including, we can surmise, the location of conflict hot spots, the terrain and weather conditions, and the underlying political factors. By consulting with locals, therefore, an intervener will have a greater awareness of this situation and, consequently, will be better placed to undertake successful intervention. Moreover, since a locally externally representative intervener reflects, in its decision-making, the opinions of those subject to its intervention, it is more likely to make these individuals feel involved with the intervention. Theodora-Ismene Gizelis and Kristin Kosek (2005) argue that this feeling of involvement is necessary for effective intervention. Conversely, 'a population that is largely uninvolved in a humanitarian intervention is less likely to cooperate with the intervening parties or expend efforts to make the intervention successful' (Gizelis and Kosek 2005: 364).[11] Thus, an intervener that is locally externally representative is likely to be perceived to be legitimate and this will in turn affect its effectiveness.

5.2.2 The Burdens Argument

The second argument for local external representativeness is what I call the 'Burdens Argument'. This asserts that an intervener should represent the opinions of those in the political community that is subject to its intervention because of the potential burdens imposed by humanitarian intervention. Those in this community might have to suffer civilian and military casualties, damage to vital infrastructure, increased levels of insecurity, and other costs associated with being in a war zone. Given that these individuals face these burdens, it is important that the intervener should reflect their opinions on the intervention.

This Burdens Argument is similar to the Resources Argument for internal representativeness in that it relies on the importance of individual choice. Whereas the underlying principle of the Resources Argument is that an individual should have some choice over how their resources are used, the underlying principle of the Burdens Argument is that an individual should have some choice over the burdens that they face. The reason why individual choice regarding burdens matters is that those suffering burdens are negatively affected. More precisely, a burden of humanitarian intervention can be defined as a severe negative impact on an individual's basic human interests caused by that intervention. Examples of burdens therefore include injury, disruption of food supplies, and damage to vital infrastructure (e.g. basic medical services and running water). Hence, the Burdens Argument holds that those subject to the humanitarian intervention should have their opinions represented because intervention may have a negative impact on their basic human interests.[12]

As it stands, this Burdens Argument is both too inclusive and too exclusive. It is too inclusive because it suggests that the intervener should reflect the opinions of *all* those in the political community that is subject to its intervention. This includes the opinions of those carrying out the violations of human rights, which create the need for intervention. For example, on the logic of this argument, NATO should have represented the opinions of the leaders of the Bosnian Serbs before undertaking its air strikes in 1995, since they were essentially the targets and were burdened by this action. We therefore need to amend the Burdens Argument to take into account moral culpability. In this context, Tesón (2005c: 160) asserts that it is the victims of the oppression who must welcome intervention. Elsewhere, he argues

> in a tyrannical regime the population can be divided into the following groups: the victims; the accomplices and collaborators; and the bystanders. . . . Of these groups, only the first, the victims, have (arguably) a right to refuse aid. The accomplices and bystanders who support the regime are excluded for obvious reasons. Their opposition to intervention does not count. And the bystanders who oppose the regime cannot validly refuse foreign aid on behalf of the victims (Tesón 2003: 107).

Although this typology is illuminating, it is too simplistic. I agree that the opinions of accomplices and collaborators should be given no weight. Any burdens of intervention they suffer are a consequence of their own morally reprehensible behaviour.[13] I also agree that we should assign greatest weight to the opinions of the victims. They are not usually morally culpable for the humanitarian crisis, yet often face some of the largest burdens of intervention, such as the bombing campaigns conducted in the regions in which they live. Moreover, if a potential intervener treats each individual's opinions equally, and if the majority of others (such as the bystanders) oppose humanitarian intervention, the victims would be left to suffer the humanitarian crisis.[14] Yet I disagree with Tesón's rejection of the importance of the bystanders' opinions. Although they are less important than the opinions of victims, some bystanders' opinions should be represented as well. In particular, we should include the opinions of those bystanders who are likely to be burdened by the intervention precisely because they are burdened bystanders: they are not (directly) responsible for the humanitarian crisis but might suffer in its resolution. Hence, a locally externally representative intervener will, firstly, give most weight to the opinions of the victims of the humanitarian crisis and, secondly, take into account the opinions of bystanders likely to be burdened by the intervention.[15] Of course, it is not always easy to distinguish between victims, bystanders, collaborators, and accomplices.[16] But, although sometimes the line between the victims and the aggressors is blurred, on other occasions it is all too apparent who are the victims and who are the aggressors.

As it stands, this Burdens Argument is also too exclusive. Some of the burdens of humanitarian intervention may fall on those outside the borders of the target state. An obvious example is the creation of a refugee flow that destabilizes a neighbouring state. Therefore, we need to amend the Burdens Argument so that, when individuals in other political communities will be burdened by the intervention—when they will also be burdened bystanders— the intervener gives some weight to their opinions too. That said, in most cases, the effects on those beyond the borders of the target state might not be significant enough to warrant the consideration of these individuals' opinions.

5.2.3 Individual self-government

Like the Resources Argument in relation to internal representativeness, the Burdens Argument does not provide a complete defence of the importance of an intervener's local external representativeness. That is, it does not encapsulate fully why an intervener should be locally externally representative. For this, we need to turn to the third argument for local external representativeness, which invokes the value of individual self-government.[17]

Let us start with the instrumental argument for individual self-government in this context (and, by implication, for an intervener's local external representativeness). This instrumentalist justification relies on a form of what Albert Weale (1999) terms the 'non-paternalist principle'. To be specific, individuals are the best judge of what enhances their well-being in most cases, although there are obvious exceptions.[18] Individual self-government is valuable, therefore, because self-governing individuals are more likely to realize their well-being. It follows that an institution that is representative, in that it reflects its citizens' opinions in its decision-making, is more likely to promote its citizens' well-being.[19] It also follows that an intervener that represents the opinions of those subject to its intervention—and is therefore locally externally representative—is more likely to promote (or, at least, not harm) these citizens' well-being. This is because the intervener, by reflecting these individuals' wishes, desires, and goals in its decision-making, will help them to attain what they themselves identify as being required for their well-being. For instance, suppose an intervener responds to a humanitarian crisis in a society which has strong religious customs. These customs form part of what constitutes the good life for many individuals. By consultation, a locally externally representative intervener would learn that these religious customs and practices contribute to many individuals' well-being in this society. It would therefore have a better understanding of what is necessary to promote these individuals' well-being. It might follow, for example, that the intervener involves religious leaders in a transitional administration and avoids damaging religious buildings.

I argued earlier that individual self-government matters in itself: it is important that an individual should be self-governing even if their opinions, if realized, would not obviously promote their well-being. This non-consequentialist value of individual self-government adds to the importance of local external representativeness. A state, coalition of states, or multinational organization should not intervene to protect those who do not want their political community to be subject to humanitarian intervention. This is the case even if intervention would promote these individuals' well-being in the short term, for instance, by protecting them from being the victims of oppression and from the violation of their basic human rights.[20] Moreover, it is not only individuals' opinions on whether there should be intervention that matter for the representativeness of an intervener. Although this tends to be the most prominent issue, it also matters that an intervener responds to other opinions of those subject to its intervention, including their opinions on who should intervene, on the form intervention should take, and on how long it should last. The opinions of those subject to the intervention on these issues also have value. For instance, those subject to a humanitarian crisis might desire intervention, but have grievances against the proposed intervener.[21] Responding to such grievances might not directly promote the well-being of those subject to the intervention—an alternative intervener might not be any more effective—but it is still important to be responsive to these opinions as a matter of individual self-government and, ultimately, local external representativeness.

5.3 GLOBAL EXTERNAL REPRESENTATIVENESS

Having seen that an intervener's internal and local external representativeness are important conditions for the legitimacy of an intervener, it might be asked whether it is also important that an intervener represent worldwide public opinion. Should an intervener take into account the opinions of everyone worldwide (minus those who are already considered under internal representativeness and local external representativeness)? In other words, is it important that an intervener is 'globally externally representative'? One indicator of this, especially in democracies, might be the statements of the relevant heads of states and government officials, but a more accurate measure of global external representativeness would be opinion polls carried out in a wide variety of countries, such as those conducted during the Iraq War. Let us now briefly consider this question. I will examine whether the types of arguments made for internal and local external representativeness can also be applied to global external representativeness.

First, is there an argument analogous to the Resources Argument or the Burdens Argument that could be made in favour of global external representativeness? This is doubtful. The Resources Argument and the Burdens Argument rely on the premise that individuals should have some control over the use of their resources and the burdens that they must face (which negatively affect their basic human interests) respectively. But the individuals that are included under global external representativeness (everyone in the world minus those included in the other two sorts of representativeness) are unlikely to provide any significant resources for the intervention or face any burdens that significantly and directly affect their basic human interests. There is no analogous argument, then, because these individuals are essentially international bystanders, generally not directly affected by the intervention. Of course, humanitarian intervention may have global repercussions that affect several thousands. But these effects will have to be sizeable to meet the standard of burdens outlined above ('a severe negative impact on an individual's basic human interests'). And, if they do meet this standard, they can, for conceptual simplicity, be included under local external representativeness. If people of a neighbouring state were burdened by the intervention, for instance, by the creation of a refugee flow, these individuals' opinions would be included under the Burdens Argument. As such, global external representativeness may be important, but the concerns it highlights can be captured by extending local external representativeness.

Second, could an argument for the importance of individual self-government be used to defend the importance of an intervener's global external representativeness? Again, perhaps not, since the individuals in question are not in any way governed or ruled by the intervener. Individual self-*government* cannot be used therefore to justify the importance of an intervener representing these individuals' opinions.

Nevertheless, an intervener's global external representativeness may, third, be instrumentally important. This is because, in practice, it is likely that an intervener that is globally externally representative will go some way to being perceived globally to be legitimate.[22] This is because we can expect that, in most cases, an intervener that reflects worldwide public opinion will be perceived globally to be legitimate and, on the other hand, an intervener that ignores worldwide public opinion will be viewed as acting illegitimately. And, as argued in Chapter 3, an intervener's global perceived legitimacy has instrumental significance. It follows, then, that there may be some contingent instrumental significance to an intervener's global external representativeness.[23]

5.4 CONCLUSION

The principal purpose of this chapter has been to highlight, and to make the case for, the moral significance of two largely overlooked factors for the legitimacy of humanitarian intervention: whether the intervener is representative of the opinions, firstly, of its citizens and, secondly, of those in the political community in which it intervenes.

There are three, largely complementary, reasons why the first factor, the intervener's internal representativeness, is important. The first is consequentialist: an internally representative intervener is more likely to be effective because it is more likely to commit the resources necessary for successful humanitarian intervention. The second is the Resources Argument: the intervener should take into account its citizens' opinions on the intervention because its citizens provide the financial and human resources for intervention. The third is the value of individual self-government on humanitarian intervention.

Three parallel reasons explain the importance of the second factor, the intervener's local external representativeness. The first is consequentialist: a locally externally representative intervener is more likely to be effective. The second is the Burdens Argument: the intervener should take into account the opinions of those in the political community in which it intervenes—and, in particular, the opinions of the victims and burdened bystanders—because humanitarian intervention may have a negative impact on these individuals' basic human interests. The third is the value of individual self-government.

Hence, internal and local external representativeness play a significant role in an intervener's legitimacy. For that reason, we need to pay them greater attention and, ultimately, to improve the extent to which current interveners are internally and locally externally representative. And although it can be difficult for an intervener to obtain accurate information on the opinions of both its constituents and those suffering the humanitarian crisis, these difficulties are not insurmountable. For the reasons given in this chapter, an intervener should make a concerted effort to obtain and to take into account such information and consequently be both internally representative and locally externally representative.

It is worth noting, lastly, that the arguments for the value of internal and local external representativeness cohere with the Moderate Instrumentalist Approach, which leaves room in its primarily consequentialist conception of legitimacy for secondary factors. Indeed, they reinforce the objection made in the previous chapter against the Extreme Instrumentalist Approach: effectiveness is not the sole moral concern when deciding who should intervene. In Chapter 6, I consider whether the Moderate Instrumentalist Approach should include three further potential factors in its account of the legitimacy of humanitarian interveners. These relate to the humanitarian credentials of the intervener: the importance of (*a*) possessing a humanitarian motive, (*b*) having a humanitarian intention, and (*c*) achieving a humanitarian outcome.

NOTES

1. That said, these issues, especially local external representativeness, have received some treatment. Of those who consider these issues, Buchanan (1999; 2006: 27), deLisle (2001: 552), ICISS (2001*a*: 36), and Tesón (2003: 105–7; 2005*c*: 132–5, 164–6) are the most constructive.

2. This caveat is important since, in Chapter 1, I argued that in *particularly serious cases*, the duty to assist non-citizens by intervening outweighs the duty to citizens. In other words, in such cases fiduciary obligations are outweighed by the duty to intervene and therefore the first reason—fiduciary obligations—cannot ground the rejection of the trusteeship model of representation. Nevertheless, humanitarian intervention should still be internally representative in such cases, given the second reason (which I consider below) for rejecting the trusteeship model of representation—the high moral stakes involved.

3. As I argue in Chapter 6, once we adopt a broader notion of the national interest, humanitarian intervention will often be in the interests of the state.

4. Although these three arguments could be applied to make the case for a delegate conception of representativeness for other governmental decisions, they are particularly pertinent for humanitarian intervention, given the two distinctive features outlined. For instance, one option would be to apply these three arguments to make the case for the representativeness of decisions that have lower moral stakes. The fact that these other decisions have lower moral stakes, however, means that these arguments would not be as persuasive as they are for humanitarian intervention. It is less important, for instance, that there is individual self-government on the issue of public transport than on the issue of humanitarian intervention.

5. One issue here is that the development of future standby arrangements for humanitarian intervention may require a binding, pre-arranged commitment to provide troops, potentially in contravention of public opinion (see Chapter 8 for a discussion of these arrangements). Such an intervener could lack internal representativeness, but play an important part in an effective humanitarian intervention.

6. In using this example, I am not claiming that the war on Iraq was a humanitarian intervention. See Chapter 6 for a rejection of the humanitarian credentials of this war.

7. Suppose a minority of two-fifths of the overall voting population oppose intervention, but the majority, three-fifths of the overall voting population, support it. The requirement of a supermajority of two-thirds of the voting population would mean that intervention would not occur.

8. It should be noted here that an intervener's local external representativeness may differ from its perceived legitimacy (the instrumental importance of which I defended in Chapter 3). An intervener's perceived legitimacy depends on the degree to which it is *perceived to be legitimate* by those in the political community in which it intervenes. By contrast, its local external representativeness depends on the degree to which the intervener *reflects, in its decision-making, the opinions* of those in the political community in which it intervenes. In theory, an intervener can be perceived to be legitimate, but lack local external representativeness—individuals may support an intervention even though their opinions are not reflected. For instance, an intervener may enjoy support because it halted a murderous rebel group but ignore all local opinion on the intervention. An agent, in theory, could also be locally externally representative, but lack perceived legitimacy. For instance, it may reflect in its decision-making local opinion, but still not be perceived to be legitimate, perhaps because it is ineffective or lacks Security Council authorization.

9. The ICRC also conducted its survey in a number of the states (such as the UK, the US, and France) who typically play a large role in any force undertaking humanitarian intervention. These provided information on citizens' views on whether and how intervention should be undertaken by their state. Similar surveys could be used therefore to help ensure an intervener's internal representativeness. Another example is the *Public Opinion Survey of UNMIL's Work in Liberia*, carried out by Jean Krasno (2006), which conducted questionnaires on the United Nations Mission in Liberia (UNMIL)'s perceived effectiveness, its conduct, and the form of any future humanitarian operations.

10. It is worth noting that the case for local external representativeness fits in with the ICISS's 2001*a*: 45 defence of the importance of 'local ownership' (although their focus is on the responsibility to rebuild and the post-conflict stage).

11. See, further, Mersaides (2005).

12. Similarly, McMahan (2010: 51) argues that humanitarian intervention can seldom promise rescue without endangering its intended beneficiaries and it is wrong to expose people to the risk of such harm in the absence of compelling evidence that they are willing to accept that risk—that is, their consent. He goes on to assert that the requirement of consent plays a 'second-order role' in the justification of humanitarian intervention, valuable because of the uncertainties and risks surrounding intervention.

13. There may be, however, an instrumental reason for taking into account the opinions of the accomplices and collaborators: such individuals are less likely to resist an intervener if they feel that their opinions are being represented.

14. Andrew Altman and Christopher Heath Wellman (2008: 244–5) reject the independent importance of an intervener's local external representativeness because it allows the majority of *victims* to reject intervention. This seems deeply unpersuasive, given the Burdens Argument and argument from self-government (discussed in Sections 5.2.2 and 5.2.3).

15. To be more specific than this would be a mistake. For instance, to specify the exact percentage of the support of the victims and the bystanders required for an intervener to be said to be locally externally representative would require too much detail. It would not fit in with the inexactness of establishing the opinions of those in the political community that is subject to the intervention. That is not to claim that an intervener cannot obtain a fairly accurate picture of the opinions of the victims and the bystanders. On the contrary, it can do so if it uses the measures outlined above. Rather, my point is that this information will not be easily quantifiable.

16. These categories could be further divided. For instance, the category of accomplices could be divided into those who are willing, those who are naive, and those who have little choice but to be accomplices. But the typology as presented captures the most morally relevant distinctions.

17. Strictly speaking, use of the term 'individual self-government' may not always be appropriate for local external representativeness because the intervener does not establish a government in the target state (unless it forms a transitional

administration). Nevertheless, the underlying principle is essentially the same: individuals should have some degree of control over their ruling institutions. To show the mirroring of the argument for internal representativeness, I will continue to use the term 'individual self-government'.

18. Weale phrases this in terms of 'interests', but the argument can be applied to well-being.

19. It may be replied that, on an objective list view of well-being, we can define the constituents of a good life and hence what is necessary for well-being. Within the broad categories of the values that contribute to the good life (such as friendship), however, the details of the good life for each individual cannot be known *a priori*. The particular individual is the best judge of these details.

20. Note that this is an argument for the worth of individual self-government, not communal self-government (which is sometimes used to defend non-intervention). Some accounts of the value of communal self-government would include communities with little or no individual self-government (e.g. Walzer 1980).

21. One example of this was the response by a number of Somalis to the proposal to send Kenyan, Ethiopian, and Djiboutian peacekeepers to Somalia in 2005. Their opposition to intervention by their neighbours (especially by Ethiopia) was so great that a brawl erupted in the Somali parliament and Somali warlords claimed they would target Ethiopian peacekeepers (BBC 2005*a*).

22. I say 'in practice' because, strictly speaking, there is a difference between global external representativeness and being perceived globally to be legitimate. An intervener may have worldwide support for its intervention (e.g. because it effectively contains a humanitarian crisis and has UN Security Council authorization), and therefore be perceived globally to be legitimate. Yet it may fail to reflect worldwide public opinion on how it intervenes (e.g. worldwide public opinion wants a greater show of force and a quick end to the crisis) and therefore lack global external representativeness.

23. Global public opinion can also play a 'jurying' role in deciding whether an intervener is or is not legitimate. See my discussion in Chapter 7.

6

An Intervener's Humanitarian Credentials: Motives, Intentions, and Outcomes

One of the most common criticisms of humanitarian intervention is that it is not really 'humanitarian' because the intervener is not acting for humanitarian reasons, but instead is pursuing self-interested economic or political goals. This renders its action illegitimate, the objection runs, since interveners should be driven by the humanitarian impulse of saving lives and helping to ensure the enjoyment of human rights. Accordingly, many theorists require humanitarian interveners to meet the equivalent of the *jus ad bellum* criterion of right intention. For instance, Lucas asserts that '[t]he intention in using force must be restricted without exception to purely humanitarian concerns' (2003*a*: 87). Intervening nations, he continues, must not possess financial, political, or material interests in the outcome of the intervention, apart from the general welfare sustained by having justice served. Similarly, the ICISS list 'right intention' as the first of their precautionary principles for those discharging the responsibility to protect: '[t]he primary purpose of the intervention, whatever other motives intervening states may have, must be to halt or avert human suffering' (2001*a*: XII).

There is, however, ambiguity and confusion in the meaning and requirements of right intention in the context of undertaking humanitarian intervention. It is often used when what is actually meant is 'right motive'. As a result, some prefer to ignore the significance of right intention and focus instead on the results achieved by the intervener. On this view, it does not matter whether an intervener acts for humanitarian reasons; what matters is that it successfully achieves a humanitarian outcome.

What are at stake, then, are the humanitarian credentials of the intervener. Must an intervener be driven by humanitarian reasons in order to be regarded as 'humanitarian'? Or is achieving a humanitarian outcome sufficient (and necessary) to render it a 'humanitarian' intervener? This is, to a certain extent, a definitional issue. We need to know what is required for an agent's intervention to be correctly deemed 'humanitarian'. But it is also normative. The humanitarian credentials of the intervener are often claimed (or implicitly assumed) to *justify* its intervention. An intervener that has a humanitarian intention, for instance, is not only said to be a 'humanitarian intervener' but also claimed to be a *legitimate* humanitarian intervener.

In what follows, I consider both the definitional and normative questions. That is, I assess whether the humanitarian credentials of an intervener should also be included as morally relevant qualities under the Moderate Instrumentalist Approach when deciding who should intervene. More specifically, I start by making the distinction between an intervener's (*a*) motives, its (*b*) intentions, and (*c*) the outcomes it achieves. I then consider both the definitional and normative importance of an intervener's motives (Section 6.2), its intentions (Section 6.3), and the outcomes it achieves (Section 6.4). I will largely reject the normative importance of all three factors for an intervener's legitimacy—as morally important qualities when deciding who should intervene—but affirm the definitional importance of an intervener's having a humanitarian intention. The final two sections use this analysis to consider two more practical issues. Section 6.5 asserts that an intervener's selectivity in where it intervenes, driven by ostensibly self-interested motives, does not render it an illegitimate intervener. Section 6.6 uses the accounts of motives and intentions to reject the humanitarian credentials of the 2003 war in Iraq.

6.1 THE DIFFERENCE BETWEEN HUMANITARIAN INTENTIONS, MOTIVES, AND OUTCOMES

It will help if I begin by clarifying the meaning of each of the three concepts that are the focus of this chapter. The first is a humanitarian 'intention', which means that the intervener has *the purpose of preventing, reducing, or halting the humanitarian crisis.* Such an intervener acts with the aim of bringing about humanitarian consequences. The *underlying reason* for the intervener's having this humanitarian intention, however, does not also have to be humanitarian. It could be, for instance, a self-interested reason. In this context, Terry Nardin argues that '[o]ne should distinguish a person's *goals*—what he or she aims at—from that person's dispositions and desires—*why* he or she is aiming at it. There are good reasons for keeping these two aspects of choice separate' (2006: 10; emphasis added). For example, South Africa might intervene to stop a humanitarian crisis in Mozambique, but its reason for doing so is because it desires to reduce the number of refugees entering its borders. By contrast, a war that lacks a humanitarian purpose, but which has expected humanitarian side-effects, would not be considered to have a humanitarian intention. If Russia intervenes in Uzbekistan with the purpose of establishing a puppet government, it would not have a humanitarian intention, even if the establishing of a puppet government increases the stability of Uzbekistan and improves the human rights situation, and therefore has humanitarian side-effects.

Second, if the intervener is to have a humanitarian 'motive', its reason for having a humanitarian intention must also be humanitarian. Hence, its motive is the *underlying reason* for undertaking humanitarian intervention. In the example above, if South Africa is to have a humanitarian motive, the reason for its wanting to intervene in Mozambique must be humanitarian. In other words, its humanitarian intention must not be due to some underlying self-interest, such as glory, power, or enrichment. On the contrary, it must be caused by an underlying humanitarian reason, that is, it must be motivated by the desire to save lives and to end human suffering.

As Tesón (2005a: 6) notes, this distinction is commonly made in criminal law. Consider, for instance, a criminal who steals—which is her intention—but receives a lighter sentence because she has the motive of feeding her starving family. He summarizes the difference:

> [i]ntention covers the contemplated act, what the agent wills to do. I see a person in distress, decide to rescue her, and do it. The action was an act of rescue. I intended to rescue the person, I committed to doing it, and did it. . . . By contrast, a motive is a *further* goal that one wishes to accomplish with the intended act. I rescued the person in danger, I intended to do it, so mine was an act of rescue. But suppose I did it because I wanted to appear as a hero in the local newspaper. I had an ulterior motive (Tesón 2005a: 5).[1]

Many of the objections to humanitarian intervention overlook this distinction between intention and motive. In particular, the frequent conflation of these two concepts leads to the conclusion that there can be no such thing as 'humanitarian intervention' since interveners rarely, if ever, possess humanitarian motives. What this overlooks (as we will see) is that humanitarian *motives*, unlike humanitarian *intentions*, are not a defining condition of 'humanitarian' intervention. Therefore, an intervener can be engaged in 'humanitarian intervention' without possessing a humanitarian motive.

Third, and more straightforward, if a humanitarian intervention succeeds in ending human suffering then it has a humanitarian 'outcome'. The intervener need not have a humanitarian motive or intention—for instance, it may intervene only to remove a hostile regime, and do so successfully, but its act may have significant humanitarian consequences.

6.2 HUMANITARIAN MOTIVES

Having distinguished between these three concepts, let us now consider the importance of an intervener's motives, both for the definition of a humanitarian intervener and for its legitimacy. The chief argument for *including* humanitarian motives is that an intervention cannot be humanitarian unless those intervening are motivated by humanitarian concerns. As Bhikhu Parekh puts it, humanitarian intervention is 'an act of showing concern for and helping our fellow human beings . . . born out of compassion and solidarity, not contempt and pity, and is motivated by a desire to help' (1997a: 64–5). It follows that an intervention which lacks a humanitarian motive would not be regarded as 'humanitarian' intervention.

There are two conceptual difficulties, however, with the reliance on humanitarian motives. The first problem is ontological: whose motives should count? It can be misleading to anthropomorphize the intervener, claiming that it has a particular motivation, for interveners are simply a collection of individuals.[2] The motivations of the individuals who collectively constitute the intervener cannot be easily collated so as to say that the intervener has a certain motive. As Shashi Tharoor and Sam Daws (2001: 24) suggest, every intervention arises from a complex and changing context of political aims, views, and positions in which motives are hard to isolate and interrogate.

Therefore, we need to specify exactly whose motives matter: should we take the motives of the intervener to be determined by (*a*) the motives of the intervener's ruling elite (i.e. the governing authority and leading decision-makers) or (*b*) the motives of all those individuals who collectively constitute the intervener? It is questionable, if we are to take motivation as a guide, whether we should limit this to (*a*) the ruling elite's motivation. The risk is that intervention that is otherwise humanitarian would be rejected as an instance of humanitarian intervention if the ruling elite were (as is perhaps inevitable) motivated by non-humanitarian motives, such as personal glory or electoral pressures. A better indicator then would seem to be (*b*) the motivation of all those who collectively constitute the intervener, such as American citizens and the US military if the intervener is the US. Although this broader approach is preferable, on this position, an intervener's motive would be impossibly complex, given the number of individuals with different motives involved. Thus, making motives a defining condition of humanitarian intervention risks either (*a*) disregarding obvious cases of humanitarian intervention or (*b*) having an unmanageably complex notion of an intervener's motive.

The second problem is epistemological: there are serious difficulties in ascertaining an intervener's motives. Assume, for example, that we take an intervener's motives to be determined by its ruler's motives. Establishing what motivated a ruler to decide to intervene is notoriously difficult. Even if we overlook the banal point that we can never know what someone else is thinking, attempting to discover a ruler's motives for intervening is decidedly tricky. For instance, did Bill Clinton want to intervene in Kosovo because he really cared about saving the lives of the Kosovan Albanians? Or was he more concerned with reducing the domestic political heat after the Monica Lewinsky affair? It is difficult to know and, as a result, making the definition of an intervention hang on such matters is problematic. The same applies, but on a much larger scale, if we were to take an intervener's motives as the motives of all those who collectively form the intervener; we would face the challenge of determining *all* these individuals' motives.[3]

Even if we were to overlook these conceptual problems and assume that we can easily establish an intervener's motives, it is doubtful whether an intervener's having a humanitarian motive is of much *moral* significance. As such, it should not be regarded as an important legitimating factor on the Moderate Instrumentalist Approach.

First, it is doubtful whether an intervener's having a humanitarian motive has substantial intrinsic value. The argument for humanitarian motives having intrinsic value revolves around the Kantian notion that people should do the right things for the right reasons. If, for instance, Jack rescues Jill from drowning, it should be because he wants to save her life, not because he knows that she will give him a big financial reward. To be sure, there does seem to be something intuitively attractive about this Kantian notion. As Nardin argues: '[m]otives are a necessary element in judgments of responsibility, of praise and blame, culpability and excuse' and are 'relevant in making moral judgments because we have moral duties to act from the proper motives' (2006: 10).

The moral significance of motivation, however, largely (but not completely) dissipates in the context of the humanitarian intervention and the use of military force more generally. In short, the intrinsic importance of a humanitarian motive seems small. It is certainly not a *necessary* condition of legitimate humanitarian intervention. As Tesón argues:

> [i]t puts too much stock in the agent's subjective state and, in doing so, disallows many actions that are objectively justified under any plausible moral theory. Take this obvious case: a political leader decides to stop genocide in a neighboring country (or, even less controversially, to defend that country against aggression) because he thinks that is the best way to

win reelection. If we require right *motive* and not merely right intent, that war would be unjust (2005*a*: 9).

Could an intervener's having a humanitarian motive nevertheless be a *significant*, if not *necessary*, condition of an intervener's legitimacy? Humanitarian intervention is a response to grievous suffering or loss of life, typically on a massive scale. In this context, the intrinsic importance of an intervener's having a humanitarian motive pales into insignificance, especially when contrasted with other values that *are* important to an intervener's legitimacy. In short, the mindset of those intervening is far less important than these other qualities. Consider the following hypothetical example, which demonstrates the difference in importance between an intervener's effectiveness and its motivation. There is a humanitarian crisis in Burundi. Zambia, for humanitarian reasons, wants to intervene, and has a reasonable expectation of saving 10,000 lives. Tanzania wants to intervene in Burundi as well, but this time for self-interested reasons (to stop border incursions) and has a reasonable expectation of saving 10,001 lives. Who should intervene, Zambia or Tanzania? Assuming, for the sake of example, that there are *no further differences* between the potential interveners, and that the different motivations for intervening have no impact on how the intervention is carried out, it is clear that we ought to prefer Tanzania's intervention because, despite its lacking a humanitarian motivation, one further life would be saved.

Similar arguments can be made to demonstrate the importance of other factors affecting the legitimacy of an intervener, such as its representativeness and the means it uses. If we have a choice between a representative yet self-interested intervener, and a less representative but well-motivated intervener, we should prefer the former. Likewise, if we face a choice between an intervener that uses humanitarian means yet undertakes intervention for self-interested reasons, and an intervener that drops bombs indiscriminately but that has a humanitarian motive, we should, again, prefer the former. My point, then, is that the value of an intervener's having a humanitarian motive is likely to be overshadowed by other, more morally important factors affecting the legitimacy of an intervener. By comparison, then, having a humanitarian motive is of little *intrinsic* moral value.

In response, one could claim that, in practice, an intervener's motivation is *instrumentally* important since it affects these other normative qualities: an intervener with a humanitarian motivation is much more likely to be effective, representative, and to adopt humanitarian means. Although these claims have some *prima facie* plausibility, they are difficult to substantiate, especially given the epistemological and ontological problems noted above. In fact, it is sometimes suggested that it is morally desirable that an intervener is *not* motivated by humanitarian concerns, since interveners that possess humanitarian motives are unlikely to be sufficiently committed to achieve effective humanitarian intervention. This is not the position that I defend here. My point, rather, is that we should not necessarily rebuke humanitarian interveners that seem to *lack* a humanitarian motivation. It does not follow that we must censure interveners that, on balance, seem to *possess* a humanitarian motivation. This leads us to an important point.

6.2.1 Mixed motives

The claim that an intervener's motives are morally important typically has a positive and a negative aspect. On the one hand, it asserts (positively) that interveners *should* possess a humanitarian motive. On the other hand, it asserts (negatively) that they *should not* possess a self-interested, ulterior motive.

It is often implied that interveners possess either purely humanitarian motives or purely self-interested motives. This is unduly narrow. As Walzer asserts, there are 'only mixed cases where the humanitarian motive is one among several' (2006: 101). The (perhaps caricatured) Realist position that states will always act purely on the basis of self-interest and the view that states can possess purely humanitarian motives are too crude, given the different individuals that collectively comprise the intervener, each with their own reasons for wanting to act (Jeangène Vilmer 2007: 208).

One alternative is to assert that interveners should be *predominantly* motivated by humanitarian motives and self-interested motives should play only a *marginal* role. The epistemological and ontological problems with determining motives, as well as the relative lack of importance of motivation in the context of humanitarian intervention, suggest that this alternative is unconvincing. These problems aside, there is a further difficulty with this view: it incorrectly repudiates interveners that are motivated out of self-interest. That is to say, there are a number of reasons why the negative element of the claim that an intervener's motives are morally important—that an intervener should not possess a self-interested motivation—is mistaken.

First, many theorists argue that it is morally desirable that an intervener is motivated by self-interest because a self-interested motive will ensure that the intervener will be sufficiently committed, and commitment is central to effective intervention.[4] Note that this argument differs from the claim rejected above that interveners should *not* possess a humanitarian motive because those that do so are unlikely to be sufficiently committed. The argument here does not assert that an intervener *should not* possess a humanitarian motive. It simply asserts that an intervener *should* possess a self-interested motive (it could still possess both a self-interested and a humanitarian motive).

There are strong and weak versions of this argument. The stronger version says that a sizeable element of self-interest is a *prerequisite* for effective intervention because this is the only way to ensure the necessary commitment, whereas the weaker version says that a sizeable element of self-interest will *improve the chances* of effective intervention because this makes the necessary commitment more likely. The weaker claim has some plausibility. Most theories of international relations admit that concerns about self-interest figure largely in states' foreign policy decisions. An intervener often needs a political motivation to undertake humanitarian intervention, which means that it can justify its commitment in terms of the interests of its citizens. As the ICISS assert, 'the budgetary cost and risk to personnel involved in any military action may in fact make it politically imperative for the intervening state to be able to claim some degree of self-interest in the intervention' (2001*a*: 36). Therefore, a strong element of self-interest makes it more likely that an intervener will provide the commitment necessary for effective humanitarian intervention, such as to provide substantial military resources over a sustained period of time. An intervener with a humanitarian motive alone is unlikely to commit the resources required to prevent egregious human suffering beyond its borders. It also follows that an intervener is more likely to be willing to undertake intervention in the first place if it has a self-interested motive for acting.

Second, the promotion of self-interest by interveners should not be considered to be 'selfish' in the usual sense of the term. Even on a narrow conception of self-interest, a state leader who promotes their state's interests is not necessarily acting selfishly, but is promoting the interests of other individuals—that is, their citizens' interests—as well. Accordingly, other things being equal, intervention by, for example, South Africa based on humanitarian and self-interested reasons for intervening (say, for instance, it will benefit from increased stability in South Africa) might be preferable to intervention by the UK that is based solely on a humanitarian reason for acting. To put it simply, more individuals might benefit from the intervention by the former than the latter (i.e. those enduring the humanitarian crisis *and* South Africans, compared to solely those enduring the humanitarian crisis if the UK acts). Moreover, if one holds that an intervener has a fiduciary obligation (although perhaps not an absolute) to promote its citizens' interests, it follows that it is morally important than an intervention is self-interested.[5]

Third, we need not adopt unquestionably the narrow, materialist view of self-interest as being comprised of power and/or security. Instead, as English

School and constructivist international relations theorists such as Wheeler (2000: 24) and Chris Brown (2003: 46) claim, a state's self-interest is also determined by its identity and shared values and principles, such as the promotion of democracy, freedom, and human rights.[6] It follows that, first, intervention that is self-interested in this broader sense may also not be morally problematic, assuming that these values are morally worthy. Second, the promotion of self-interest and humanitarianism are not mutually exclusive.

These arguments are perhaps not sufficient to show that interveners' *having* a self-interested motivation is an important factor in its legitimacy, given the problems outlined above of dealing with motivations in the context of humanitarian intervention. That aside, self-interested motives (narrowly conceived) may sometimes conflict with humanitarian ones. For instance, a head of state's motive of wanting to intervene to stop refugee flows may clash with their foreign minister's motive of wanting to save lives. The foreign minister's humanitarian motive could lead them to endorse the use of ground troops, whereas the head of state's self-interested motive could lead them to limit the intervention to the use of air power alone. Notwithstanding, these three points do help to show that, in addition to not objecting to humanitarian intervention because (*a*) it *lacks* a *humanitarian* motive, we should not necessarily reject humanitarian intervention because (*b*) it *has a self-interested* motive. This applies both to the definition and the legitimacy of humanitarian intervention.

6.3 HUMANITARIAN INTENTIONS

Having rejected the positive and negative elements of the claim that humanitarian motives are an important factor in defining humanitarian intervention and its legitimacy, let us turn to consider the importance of an intervener's intentions when deciding who should intervene. I will start with the definitional importance of intentions.

If an intervener is to be engaged in 'humanitarian' intervention, it must have a humanitarian intention. That is to say, to be 'humanitarian', an intervener must have the predominant *purpose* of preventing, reducing, or halting actual or impending loss of life and human suffering, whatever the *underlying reasons*—its motives—for wishing to do so. This assertion is well supported by the literature. Ellery Stowell says that humanitarian intervention is the 'reliance upon force for the justifiable *purpose* of protecting the inhabitants of another state'; Brownlie states that humanitarian intervention has 'the *object* of protecting human rights'; Adam Roberts says that humanitarian intervention has 'the *purpose* of preventing widespread suffering or death among the inhabitants' (in Chesterman 2001: 1–3; emphases added); and Parekh defines humanitarian intervention as having '*a view* to ending or at least reducing the suffering' (1997*b*: 5; emphasis added). Thus, one of the central reasons why the French, British, and American creation of safe havens and implementation no-fly zones in northern Iraq in 1991 is regarded as a case of humanitarian intervention is because its intention was humanitarian—to protect thousands of endangered Kurds.

It seems clear, then, that a humanitarian intervention must by definition have a humanitarian intention. Indeed, this is how we tend to classify actions. As Tesón asserts, the concept of intention 'allows us to *characterize* the act, to say that the act belongs to a certain class of acts, such as acts of rescue' (2005*a*: 5). In other words, a chief way to determine what a particular agent is doing—its action—is to look at its intentions. Thus, the intention of an intervener is key to determining its action. If an intervener has a humanitarian intention, then, *providing that it meets the other defining conditions* (delineated in Chapter 1), it is engaged in humanitarian intervention.

Those who deny the need for humanitarian intervention to have a humanitarian intention could make the following argument: a humanitarian intention is not required if there is a humanitarian outcome. This argument is unsatisfactory, as demonstrated by the following example. Suppose, in the middle of the night, the electrics in house No. 1 short-circuit, causing a small fire. The battery in their fire alarm has run out and so it does not sound. Soon after, a burglar breaks into the neighbouring house, No. 2, setting off their intruder alarm. It is so loud that it awakens the residents of house No. 1 before the fire in their house has time to spread and put their lives at risk. Indirectly, then, the burglar has saved the lives of inhabitants of No. 1. But we would not call the burglar's action humanitarian because, despite it yielding a humanitarian outcome, the *intention* was not to save the lives of the inhabitants of No. 1.

Now, if we apply this same reasoning to international intervention, an intervention that does not aim to have a humanitarian outcome cannot be called a humanitarian intervention even if it actually results in a humanitarian outcome. In this context, Tesón (2005*a*: 8) gives the example of the Falklands War. This resulted in a humanitarian outcome—the establishment of democracy in Argentina—but lacked a humanitarian purpose (Thatcher's intention was not to free the Argentines) and, for this reason, is not widely regarded as an instance of humanitarian intervention.

Note here that determining an intervener's intention is not subject to the same level of epistemological and ontological problems as determining its motive. First, its intention can be taken to be the intentions of the major actors that collectively comprise the intervener (e.g. the leaders who have authorized the use of force, the relevant governmental departments, and the armed forces). Second, ascertaining the intention of an intervener is easier than ascertaining its motives. As Bellamy argues, 'a number of tests can be applied to ascertain a state's intentions with reasonable accuracy' (2004: 227).[7] In particular, there are three ways we can do this, which, when combined, can help us to build a general picture of what the intervener's intention is.

The first way is to examine the *rhetoric* of the major actors that collectively comprise the intervener (Bellamy 2004: 227). We should look to the justifications offered and the rationales given for the intervention. But, in this context, Tesón claims that 'governments, like individuals, may lie about why they are doing what they are doing, or they may be mistaken about why they are doing what they are doing. . . . Words lack magical power, so whether the intervention is humanitarian cannot depend on the government saying so' (2005a: 4). Nevertheless, the rhetoric of the major actors can provide *some* indication of the intention of the intervener. First, in many cases, a government may not be lying or be mistaken about what it is doing. Second, once a government has offered a humanitarian justification for an intervention, it often becomes tied into that justification and has to follow a subsequent course of action that conforms to this justification. Hence, Wheeler argues, *pace* Tesón, '[t]he legitimating reasons employed by governments are crucial because they enable and constrain actions' (2000: 287). For instance, the (first) Bush and Clinton Administrations' invocation of humanitarian justifications for their interventions in northern Iraq, Somalia, and the Balkans constrained their subsequent actions by the need to defend these actions as being in conformity with their humanitarian claims (Wheeler 2000: 288).[8]

The second way to determine an intervener's intention is to consider the decisions taken by the major actors, such as the intervener's ruling elite, military officers, and soldiers. Do they result, or are they likely to result, in humanitarian action? In other words, we need to consider the intervener's *behaviour*. Thus, Tesón suggests that 'what the intervener *does* is the best evidence of its intention' (2005a: 8). Similarly, Bellamy asserts that 'intentions can be inferred from acts themselves' and '[w]hen a state embarks on a humanitarian intervention, the strategies it adopts allow us to infer its intentions' (2004: 227). As argued in Chapter 4, the means used by the intervener are crucial in this context. The intervener must follow closely the principles of internal and external *jus in bello*. For example, an intervener that relies heavily on indiscriminate weapons cannot be plausibly said to possess a humanitarian intention (Bellamy 2004: 229).

Third, we should look to the intervener's previous behaviour. How does its current intervention fit in with the intervener's general pattern of behaviour?

So to judge NATO's intention in Kosovo, for instance, we can (*a*) look to the statements of the NATO heads of states and governments; (*b*) consider NATO leaders, officers, and soldiers' subsequent behaviour (e.g. were they more concerned with protecting civilians or securing their economic and political interests?); and (*c*) see how these fit with the previous decisions taken by NATO. Given that NATO (*a*) repeatedly reaffirmed their desire to halt the humanitarian crisis in Kosovo, (*b*) took actions that evidenced a strong desire to end the humanitarian crisis (although NATO's use of cluster bombs and the refusal to use ground troops does cast some doubt on the humanitarian credentials of the intervention (see Chapter 4)), and (*c*) undertook similar action in Bosnia, it seems that NATO's intention in Kosovo was humanitarian.

6.3.1 Mixed intentions

As with motives, the claim that an intervener's intentions are important typically has a positive and a negative aspect. On the one hand, it asserts (positively) that an intervener *should* possess a humanitarian intention. On the other hand, it asserts (negatively) that it *should not* possess an ulterior, self-interested intention.

As I have argued, the positive claim that an intervener *should possess* a humanitarian intention is important in the definition of humanitarian intervention. Conversely, the negative claim that interveners must lack completely any other intentions can be rejected. That is to say, an intervener can be engaged in 'humanitarian' intervention and possess both a humanitarian and a self-interested intention. What matters is that the humanitarian intention is *predominant*: an intervener cannot be rightly classified as 'humanitarian' unless its purpose is predominantly humanitarian.

To exclude fully non-humanitarian intentions would disregard the mix of intentions that comes from an intervener not being a single, unitary actor. It is perhaps inevitable that there will be differences in intention between those authorizing the use of force and those carrying it out, between military leaders and governmental officials, between governmental institutions (such as defence and foreign ministries), and between soldiers and their commanding officers. Although such differences mean that an intervener is unlikely to possess a pure humanitarian intention, we should not discount interventions that *overall* are predominantly intended to be humanitarian by the various actors involved that collectively comprise the intervener. For instance, countries contributing troops to a multinational force may have different objectives. One state may attempt to use the intervention to protect its own nationals from harm. Another may have the intention of regime change. Nevertheless, if the intention of the other factions is humanitarian, with the result that the intervener overall is predominantly guided by the humanitarian purpose of tackling the humanitarian crisis, the intervention can still be classified as 'humanitarian'.[9]

6.3.2 The moral significance of intentions

We have seen an intervener needs to possess a humanitarian intention to be engaged in the action of humanitarian intervention. But is having a humanitarian intention *morally* significant and, specifically, an important factor in an intervener's legitimacy? Tesón asserts that 'intention, unlike motive, is ... relevant ... in *evaluating* the action morally' (2005a: 7). Similarly, Bellamy notes that 'the legitimacy of a humanitarian intervention ought to be evaluated according to whether the intervener *intended* to prevent or halt an injustice and promote peace' (2004: 227). On this view, then, a humanitarian intention contributes to the legitimacy of an intervener.

I do not endorse this position. A humanitarian intention is, for most part, only a *defining* condition of humanitarian intervention: an intervener needs to have a humanitarian intention in order to be engaged in 'humanitarian' intervention. It does little moral work in establishing an intervener's legitimacy and therefore is not an important concern under the Moderate Instrumentalist Approach. To be sure, intention, like motive, is commonly viewed as morally significant in moral philosophy and criminal law in the evaluation of an individual's behaviour. Why then is it not an important factor in the legitimacy of a humanitarian intervener?

Often when intentions are given moral significance it is because the actions that the intentions aim at are, in themselves, *prima facie* good or *prima facie* bad. For example, intending to kill someone is regarded as problematic because murder is *prima facie* bad. By contrast, intending to keep a promise is morally desirable because promise-keeping is *prima facie* good. When we learn more about the particulars of the case, our judgement of the overall justifiability of the action may alter (e.g. there may be mitigating circumstances). This is why the action is regarded only as '*prima facie* good' or '*prima facie* bad'. To judge fully someone's stealing of a loaf of bread, for instance, we need to know their motives for doing so, the ramifications of their actions, and how they went about doing so, not simply their intention to do so. But we still tend to think that their intentions play a role in judging their behaviour, since the action that they aim at—stealing—can be viewed as bad in the abstract. That is, the abstract justifiability of the action gives intention some significance, *independent of the particulars.*[10]

By contrast, humanitarian intervention cannot be classified in the abstract as good or bad; it is far too complex an issue morally. It involves the use of military force (which can cause significant harm to individuals' human rights), can undermine communal integrity, cause international instability, but, on the other hand, save thousands of individuals' lives. Accordingly, the action of humanitarian intervention *in the abstract* cannot be said to be *prima facie* good or bad. Instead, it is the *particulars* of the case that determine the justifiability of an intervention. It follows that an intervener's humanitarian intention is neither necessarily desirable, nor necessarily objectionable—any moral importance of an intervener's intention is *dependent on the particulars.*[11] That is, it is dependent on the other factors in an intervener's legitimacy, such as its likely success, the means it uses, its internal and external representativeness, and so on. Thus, intention is not an independent factor in an intervener's legitimacy.

To give an example, suppose that State A intends to intervene in State B, where there is an ongoing humanitarian crisis. Without any further information, we cannot properly assess the moral credentials of this action. We do not know *how* State A intends to intervene, *why* it intends to do so, or whether it would be *successful.* Now, suppose that State A's action would be unsuccessful—it is ill-equipped to mount such an operation—and, moreover, its action would result in a worsening of the humanitarian situation. State A is well aware of these facts, but attempts the intervention anyway. In this case, we can say that, *given the extra information*, its action was morally wrong. Or, suppose instead that State A's action would almost certainly be successful—it has the necessary military and non-military resources, support from the local population, and so on. In this case, we can say that, given the extra information, its action was morally right. But, if we learn further that State A uses landmines and cluster bombs, then we might question its legitimacy. There would therefore be a more complex moral picture of the justifiability of the intervention. My point, then, is that the agent's intention, on its own, does little to determine the moral justifiability of an intervener's action. Knowing that State A has a humanitarian intention of intervening in State B to stop the crisis there does little to tell us whether this action is *justifiable.* For this, we need to look to other factors. In Chapter 3, I claimed that the main factor contributing to an intervener's legitimacy is its expectation of success. It follows that an intervener that has a humanitarian intention may or may not be legitimate; but an intervener that is likely to be *successful* in fulfilling its humanitarian intention will go a long way towards being legitimate.

Certain *non*-humanitarian actions, such as self-defence, may also be neither *prime facie* objectionable nor *prime facie* problematic in the abstract. That said, there do exist less morally complex international actions that are *prima facie* good and *prima facie* bad in the abstract, such as colonial conquest. As such, *some* intentions of states may have *prima facie* moral weight. An intervener that possesses in part a *prima facie* bad intention such as conquest would lose significant legitimacy, even if humanitarian intentions are predominant overall.

Weiss (2007: 102–3) puts the point another way: using the term 'humanitarian' intervention stakes out the moral high ground prematurely, without adequate debate on the merits of a particular case. Rather than 'visceral accolades because of a qualifying adjective', what is needed is a serious discussion about the likely costs and benefits, particularly 'because analyses of intervention in the 1990s suggest that outside assistance can do more harm than good or can become entangled in a local political economy that favors war rather than peace' (Weiss 2007: 103).

Those who are much more in favour of humanitarian intervention in the abstract may be more willing to claim that it is, *prima facie*, a good action, and so possessing a humanitarian intention is *prima facie* desirable. Even if this point is granted, and the moral complexity and problems of humanitarian intervention overlooked, this would still fail to show that intentions play a *significant* role in an intervener's legitimacy. Intention would only predispose us towards the intervener. Other factors, such as the likelihood of success and means used, would, as in the example given, play the most important roles.[12] As such, intentions do not do much *positive* work in establishing a particular humanitarian intervener's legitimacy.

There are, however, two important caveats. First, possessing a humanitarian intention may have some instrumental significance. An intervener that is obviously intending to tackle the humanitarian crisis may be more likely to be perceived locally and globally as legitimate than an intervener whose intentions are less clear.

Second, although *possessing* a humanitarian intention does little to establish an intervener's legitimacy, *lacking* a humanitarian intention is morally problematic. My reasoning is as follows. There is a strong case to maintain a general prohibition on the use of force (e.g. for reasons of global stability), with only a few exceptions. The use of force in order to tackle a serious humanitarian crisis—humanitarian intervention—is generally regarded as one of these exceptions, even if not *prima facie* good. And to be such an exception, humanitarian intervention requires a humanitarian intention. Otherwise, it would be a different sort of intervention (say, for example, conquest) that is *prima facie* morally impermissible because it violates the general prohibition on the use of force (unless it falls under another exception to prohibition on the use of force, such as self-defence in response to aggression). Accordingly, an intervention that lacks a humanitarian intention (or another appropriate reason for the use of force) is *prima facie* morally impermissible because it is not using force for an acceptable reason. In this sense, possessing a humanitarian intention has some moral value in the negative sense. Those that lack a humanitarian intention are not engaged in 'humanitarian' intervention and their violation of the principle of non-intervention is (potentially) morally problematic. This does not mean that an intervener that possesses a humanitarian intention is necessarily a legitimate intervener. As I have argued, we need to know further information about the intervener in order to make this judgement and this further information does the moral work.

6.4 HUMANITARIAN OUTCOMES

Let us now focus on the question of humanitarian outcomes. One approach holds that intervention must result in an improvement in the humanitarian crisis in order to be defined as 'humanitarian intervention'. It follows that an intervention that does not reduce, halt, or prevent grievous loss of life and human suffering would not be deemed 'humanitarian', regardless of its motives or intentions.

There is good reason, however, not to insist that humanitarian intervention must have a humanitarian outcome. If we were to make humanitarian outcomes a defining condition of humanitarian intervention, we would have to wait until after intervention to see whether it was in fact humanitarian. As Tesón argues, if we were to include humanitarian outcomes in the definition of humanitarian intervention, 'actions could not be judged when they are contemplated, since we would have to wait for all the consequences of the action to unfold' (2005a: 8). This problem also means that we should reject outcomes as an important moral factor in an intervener's legitimacy. Including outcomes would contravene the forward-looking account of legitimacy defended in Chapter 1. What we are concerned with is the *ex ante* issue of who should intervene in the future when a serious humanitarian crisis occurs again, rather than an *ex post* assessment of the outcomes of an intervener's previous action.

To be sure, looking to see whether a previous humanitarian intervention by an intervener achieved a successful outcome in the past will help us to determine whether the intervener is likely to achieve a successful outcome in the future. In addition, it is vital that an intervener *attempts* to achieve a humanitarian outcome. Indeed, in Chapter 3, I placed significant emphasis on an intervener's effectiveness and claimed, in particular, that the likelihood of achieving a successful humanitarian outcome is central to an intervener's legitimacy. How does this cohere with the rejection of humanitarian outcomes?

The position I have defended places weight on an intervener's *likely* effectiveness at the time of intervention, rather than judging its effectiveness with the benefit of hindsight. That is, an agent's legitimacy depends on whether if, at the time when the decision is made to intervene, it can be reasonably expected to be effective, not whether it achieves a humanitarian outcome, perhaps fortuitously, after the event. More precisely, the position I have defended is a form of 'expected consequentialism', which judges things by whether they are *expected* to result in an increase in good consequences. By contrast, the inclusion of humanitarian outcomes in an intervener's legitimacy relies on 'actual consequentialism', which judges things by whether they *actually* result in an increase in good consequences. The problem with actual consequentialism is that it fails to provide moral guidance.[13]

6.5 SELECTIVITY

To recap: we can distinguish between (*a*) an intervener's motives, (*b*) its intentions, and (*c*) the outcomes that it achieves. It is important that an intervener possesses a humanitarian intention in order to be engaged in the activity of humanitarian intervention, although this, in itself, has little normative significance. Possessing a humanitarian motive and achieving a humanitarian outcome have little definitional or normative significance. Let us now use this analysis of intentions, motives, and outcomes to repudiate two major misunderstandings of the ethics of humanitarian intervention, both of which can confuse the assessment of who should intervene. The first is that an intervener's selectivity in where it intervenes renders it an illegitimate intervener. The second is that the 2003 war in Iraq was a case of justifiable humanitarian intervention.

One of the most frequent criticisms made of humanitarian intervention is that it is carried out inconsistently. The criticism might be, for instance, that NATO undertook intervention in Kosovo but not in DR Congo (Damrosch 2000). The problem with this selectivity is that it conveys the impression that 'some are more worth protecting than others' (ICISS 2001*b*: 150). If humanitarian intervention really is to be humanitarian, the objection continues, it has to be consistently applied whenever there is a serious humanitarian crisis. Mohammed Ayoob, for instance, claims that since humanitarian interventions 'are undertaken on a selective basis and the same criteria are not applied uniformly and universally in every case, such interventions lose legitimacy and credibility in the eyes of many, if not most, members of the international system' (2002: 86). Likewise, Edward Luttwak asks: 'what does it mean for the morality of a supposedly moral rule, when it is applied arbitrarily, against some but not others?' (2000: 4).

Although frequently made, this objection about selectivity is problematic. Some selectivity in the application of humanitarian intervention is, in fact, desirable. On the Moderate Instrumentalist Approach, an intervener should be reasonably expected to be effective and an intervener may be expected to be effective in one situation but not in another. For instance, suppose that Chad and Algeria both suffer serious humanitarian crises. France has a reasonable expectation of improving the situation in Chad—it would be locally external-ly effective—without destabilizing international order and without its intervention being extremely costly in French resources and lives. But suppose further that France does not have a reasonable expectation of improving the situation in Algeria. Given the history between these two countries, French intervention would face much resistance and so be unlikely to be locally externally effective. The intervention would also destabilize the surrounding region, and so lack global external effectiveness. What is more, the intervention would be likely to be bloody, with much fighting, and with a large number of French casualties, so the intervention would lack internal effectiveness. In these two cases, it is certainly desirable that France should be selective in where it intervenes. On the Moderate Instrumentalist Approach, France would be a legitimate intervener in Chad, but not in Algeria. Hence, as Tharoor and Daws note, 'selectivity is thus an inevitable consequence of the requirement of efficacy in intervention' (2001: 27). But, as Tharoor and Daws also note, this does not mean that we should overlook humanitarian crises in situations where intervention will not be effective. Other measures of the responsibility to protect should be employed instead, short of military intervention, such as international criminal prosecutions and military, diplomatic, and economic sanctions.

Moreover, having intervened in one country, the intervener may not have the resources (especially military resources) to intervene in another. For this reason, most interveners should be selective where they intervene. Furthermore, there are some countries in which a humanitarian intervener could *never* be legitimate (at least in the foreseeable future). For instance, intervention in Russia over the crisis in Chechnya or in China over the occupation of Tibet is likely to be globally externally ineffective—at worst, it might lead to nuclear war. Failing that, it is likely to be internally ineffective—if the US, for instance, were to intervene in either of these countries, the number of US casualties and the cost in resources would be excessive. In addition, intervention in either China or Russia would be unlikely to improve the situation of the Chechens or Tibetans.

There is, then, a strong case for a degree of selectivity in humanitarian intervention on the Moderate Instrumentalist Approach. But it is not only for consequentialist reasons that selectivity can be desirable. The other factors in the legitimacy of an intervener may also mean that interveners should be selective in where they intervene. For instance, an intervener may not be able to act in response to one humanitarian crisis without violating *jus in bello*, but can do so in response to another.

That said, it might be argued that selectivity is more of a problem for the legitimacy of interveners when they remain selective after these concerns have been taken into account. In other words, selectivity renders an intervener illegitimate when the intervener would be effective, internally and locally externally representative, and be able to follow the principles of *jus in bello* in a number of cases, but does not respond to them consistently.[14] For instance, suppose that there are two similar humanitarian crises, one in Niger, the other in Mali. The US has a reasonable expectation of successfully intervening in both states. The US decides to intervene in Niger. The apparent, underlying reason for the US's decision is that oil has been found in Niger (the instability caused by the humanitarian crisis makes it extremely difficult to access this oil). The US does not intervene in Mali, where there is no such potential oil supply. Is the US nevertheless a legitimate intervener in Niger? Many sceptics of humanitarian intervention would say that it is not. The selectivity of American intervention undermines its legitimacy because it intervenes in Niger where it has some interest at stake, but not in Mali, where it has none.

The underlying objection here is one about motives and runs as follows. The selectivity of interveners demonstrates that humanitarian intervention is undertaken only ever for the intervener's own interests—humanitarian justifications are a facade. Ayoob, for instance, argues that it is 'impossible to prevent considerations of national interest from intruding upon decisions regarding international intervention for ostensibly humanitarian purposes' (2002: 85) and therefore 'selectivity in humanitarian interventions seems to be inevitable' (2002: 86). The argument continues: humanitarian intervention undertaken for an intervener's own interest is illegitimate. Selectivity therefore demonstrates the illegitimacy of humanitarian intervention.[15]

There are good reasons, however, to doubt the validity of this claim. First, as noted above, we can question the importance of motives for an intervener's legitimacy. In the above example, the US is likely to be effective in Niger and it would be legitimate for this reason. When millions of lives are at stake, the motives of an intervener seem unimportant in comparison, at least intrinsically. Furthermore, we should not necessarily oppose a humanitarian intervener that seems to have a self-interested motivation, given my arguments in Section 6.2: a self-interested motive may make successful intervention more likely; the promotion of self-interest is not necessarily selfish; and, on broader conceptions, self-interest does not conflict with humanitarianism.

Second, this selectivity objection misses its target. When considering whether the US is a legitimate intervener in Niger, we have to consider the factors relevant *to that particular case*. So, when considering US intervention in Niger, we should ask: what is the right way to tackle the humanitarian crisis in Niger? According to the Moderate Instrumentalist Approach, the most important thing is that the humanitarian crisis in Niger is effectively tackled. For that reason, the US would be a legitimate intervener. My point, then, is that when considering whether an intervener is legitimate *in a particular case*, we should concentrate on the details *of that case* and, crucially, on whether it will be effective.[16] The other cases of humanitarian intervention are important for the legitimacy of the intervener only to the extent that they affect (or are affected by) *this* case. As Thomas Franck argues: '[t]he ultimate test of a humanitarian intervention's legitimacy is whether it results in significantly more good than harm, not whether there has been a consistent pattern of such interventions whenever and wherever humanitarian crises have arisen' (2002: 189). So, the seemingly obvious point that the selectivity objection overlooks is this: what an intervener does or does not do in one state should not change the judgement of the legitimacy of its intervention in another, unless it will actually affect this intervention.

Third, this is not to say that we should refrain from criticizing the US for not intervening in Mali. When considering the particular details of the Mali example, or when considering US foreign policy more generally, the US (and perhaps others) should be criticized for failing to fulfil the duty to end human suffering in the Mali example. In this sense, selective humanitarian intervention *is* morally problematic. Given that humanitarian intervention is a duty, it is wrong that agents fail to act on the duty to intervene when they could do so legitimately.[17] But this does not necessarily undermine the justification of humanitarian intervention *when it actually occurs*. We should not criticize states when they do intervene legitimately; we should criticize them when they do not. As the Supplementary Volume to the ICISS report asserts, 'even occasionally

doing the right thing well is certainly preferable to doing nothing rout-
inely' (2001*b*: 150).[18]

6.6 THE WAR IN IRAQ

Let us now consider whether, given the argument above, the 2003 war in Iraq
was a case of 'humanitarian intervention'. Tesón (2005*a*; 2005*c*) makes perhaps the strongest case that can be made in favour of the war being a
humanitarian intervention. Drawing on the distinction between an intervener's intention and motive, he argues that, although the British and Americans may have had dubious motives for intervening (personal enrichment, a
place in history, etc.), their intention was humanitarian. This intention
was regime change, to bring to an end Saddam Hussein's tyrannical rule
(Tesón 2005*a*).

Tesón is right to focus on the coalition's intention in Iraq. It is key to
understanding whether this war is a case of humanitarian intervention. This is
because it meets the other defining conditions listed in Chapter 1 (it was
military and forcible, it occurred in circumstances of grievous suffering, and it
was by an external party). But, *pace* Tesón, it is very doubtful whether the
coalition's intention was humanitarian. Rather, as Weiss rightly asserts,
'the primary purpose of the war in Iraq was not to halt human suffering'
(2005*b*: 179).[19]

Tesón's argument relies on the humanitarian credentials of regime change,
of ending Saddam Hussein's tyrannical rule. But, although it may have
humanitarian side-effects, removing a tyrannical dictator is not, in itself,
humanitarian. It can be consistent with having a non-humanitarian intention, such as protecting national security. There needs to be something extra
to establish the humanitarian credentials of a particular regime change. To be
sure, this is not an argument about motives. I agree with Tesón that we should
leave the underlying motives of leaders aside when assessing the humanitarian
credentials of intervention. An agent may undertake intervention to remove
two tyrannical dictators: one with the intention of securing national security
and the other with the intention of halting genocide. The leader's decisions in
both cases may be *motivated* by electoral pressures.

Tesón (2005*a*: 13) concurs that regime change, by itself, may not be enough
to ensure an intervention's humanitarian intention. But he argues that the
coalition had a humanitarian intention because not only did it remove a
vicious dictator, it also attempted to establish democracy, set up a liberal
constitution, and did not leave Iraq to anarchy. There is little evidence,

however, that the *predominant* intention of the regime change was humanitarian. We can see this by using the three tests of an intervener's intention outlined earlier.

First, the *rhetoric* of the British and American governments claimed that the predominant purpose of the war—of regime change—was in the national self-interest, primarily national and regional security (i.e. to remove weapons of mass destruction). In this context, Kenneth Roth, Executive Director of Human Rights Watch, asserts that the 'principal justifications offered in the prelude to the invasion were the Iraqi government's alleged possession of weapons of mass destruction, its alleged failure to account for them as prescribed by numerous UN Security Council resolutions, and its alleged connection with terrorist networks' (2006: 88). Although the UK and US employed the quasi-humanitarian rhetoric of promoting freedom and democracy, such justifications have largely been post-hoc rationalizations and played a significant role only after the failure to find the weapons of mass destruction. For example, Bush made no mention of liberating the Iraqi people in his letter to Congress in March 2003, which presented his official grounds for the use of force (R. Miller 2008: 57).

Second, the *behaviour* of the British and American governments cohered with the rhetoric—the decisions taken have not been directed at benefiting Iraqi civilians. Roth argues that

> if invading forces had been determined to maximize the humanitarian impact of an intervention, they would have been better prepared to fill the security vacuum that predictably was created by the toppling of the Iraqi government. It was entirely foreseeable that Saddam Hussein's downfall would lead to civil disorder (2006: 88).

In addition, the coalition employed measures, such as cluster bombs, that it was clear would result—and did result—in a large number of civilian casualties (Roth 2006: 89–90). Therefore, the behaviour of the coalition also showed that it did not possess a humanitarian purpose (also see Cottey 2008: 430).

Third, the *previous behaviour* of the British and American governments in imposing sanctions against Iraq fits in with this pattern of behaviour. These sanctions exacted a terrible humanitarian toll on Iraq. As many as 500,000 Iraqi children died of thirst, malnutrition, and preventable diseases as a result (Winston 2005: 49). Yet the US and the UK continued to support sanctions against Iraq, despite opposition to sanctions from many other governments.[20]

Thus, the coalition lacked a humanitarian intention. For this reason, the 2003 war on Iraq was not a case of 'humanitarian intervention'. Moreover, even if we overlook this point, on the Moderate Instrumentalist Approach that I have defended, the war was not a case of *justifiable* humanitarian intervention.[21]

To start with, it lacked a reasonable expectation of success. It has since been widely acknowledged that there was not a well-thought-out strategy for managing the situation after Saddam's forces had been defeated. Furthermore, it lacked just cause. As Roth (2006: 86) argues, there was not the same degree of the violation of human rights in March 2003 as in previous years (such as during the Anfal genocide). Although the tyranny and oppression of Saddam's rule were objectionable, it is questionable whether these were sufficiently egregious to render humanitarian intervention by the coalition justifiable.

Tesón (2005c: 398) disputes this. He claims that Saddam's ongoing tyrannical rule justified intervention. It is important, however, to separate two issues here. On the one hand, Saddam's regime was clearly illegitimate and, as such, the communal integrity and state sovereignty of Iraq were not persuasive reasons to reject intervention. On the other hand, the humanitarian crisis was not serious enough to justify humanitarian intervention. This is because the likely costs of any intervention outweighed the potential benefits. Recall the discussion of just cause in Chapter 1. I argued that, if an intervener is to have just cause, the intervener needs to be responding to a situation (typically, the mass violation of basic human rights) in which it has the opportunity to do enough good to outweigh the harm that it will cause. It is severely doubtful that the improvements in the enjoyment of human rights by the removal of Saddam's tyranny was sufficient to outweigh the foreseeable harms in terms of civilian and soldier casualties, as well as other more diffuse negative effects on the international system.

In reply, Tesón (2005a) claims that humanitarian intervention can be justifiable in response to *consummated* atrocities (such as the slaughter of the Kurds, Marsh Arabs, and southern Shiites). In defence of this position, he asserts that if ongoing crimes are the only proper target of intervention, then all mass murderers have to do to avoid being subject to humanitarian intervention is to speed up the executions (Tesón 2005c: 397). This reply is deeply problematic. In short, intervention in response to consummated atrocities benefits no one. The costs and dangers of humanitarian intervention heap further misery on a population that has already suffered major atrocities. Such costs can be justified only when the potential benefits outweigh them—when there are people to save and rights violations to halt. Military intervention launched to punish leaders, even if it succeeds, is more than likely to punish the population as well. To be sure, mass murderers should still, after the event, be subject to other forms of international coercion short of military intervention, such as international criminal prosecutions and targeted sanctions.[22]

Moreover, the coalition has violated the principles of internal and external *jus in bello* outlined in Chapter 4. There have been an extraordinarily high number of civilian casualties, with force protection often guiding military actions rather than non-combatant immunity and discrimination. Tesón (2005c: 407) asserts that civilian losses have been well within the boundaries permitted by the doctrine of double effect, since they are in proportion to the 'remarkable improvement' in the quality of life and prospects of the Iraqi population and their descendants. It is patent that this is mistaken. Any beneficial effects from the war (such as the potential establishment of democratic institutions) are massively disproportionate to deaths amongst the Iraqi population (widely cited estimates vary from 91,000 to 654,000) and the destabilizing effects of the war for the international system.[23]

For these reasons, the war in Iraq was not a case of (*a*) justifiable (*b*) humanitarian intervention.

6.7 CONCLUSION

Let me recap the argument of this chapter. I have been considering the importance of three factors often said to be central to the humanitarian credentials of an intervener and when deciding who should intervene: its motives, its intentions, and the outcomes of humanitarian intervention. First, possessing a pure or predominant humanitarian motive, to the extent that this can be determined, is not necessary for an intervener to be engaged in 'humanitarian intervention', nor is it an important factor in its legitimacy. In fact, it may be preferable that an intervener is motivated by self-interest. Second, an intervener's intentions are central to determining whether it is engaged in 'humanitarian intervention'. Like humanitarian motives, possessing a humanitarian intention does little non-instrumental work in establishing the legitimacy of an intervener (although it may be instrumentally important and *lacking* a humanitarian intention may be morally problematic). Third, whether an intervener's action results in a humanitarian outcome is irrelevant to the definition of humanitarian intervention and to its legitimacy. Thus, these three qualities should not be included in the Moderate Instrumentalist Approach, since they lack much independent significance when deciding who should undertake humanitarian intervention.

Using this analysis, we have seen that an intervener's selectivity in where it intervenes does not render it an illegitimate intervener when it *does* intervene;

the problem instead is *non*-intervention in other cases. In addition, the war in Iraq was not a case of justifiable humanitarian intervention since it lacked a humanitarian intention and failed to meet the requirements of the Moderate Instrumentalist Approach.

NOTES

1. The exact difference between intention and motive can be difficult to pinpoint. It is sometimes framed in terms of means and ends, short- and long-term goals, and motives as causal powers (and therefore different to intentions). See Kaufman (2003: 322–3) for a survey of these positions (and some of their inadequacies). That said, it is widely held in the philosophy of action, moral philosophy, legal theory and practice, and popular understandings that there *is* a difference between intention and motive. See, further, Anscombe (1976: 18–20). She suggests that it is held that '[a] man's intention is what he aims at or chooses; his motive is what determines the aim or choice' (Anscombe 1976: 18). For more on this difference in the context of humanitarian intervention, see Bellamy (2004: 225), Nardin (2006: 9–11), and Tesón (2005a: 4–9; 2005c: 113–21).
2. This is not to deny that states and other collective institutions can be said to possess motives or intentions. As Nardin (2006: 9) argues, it is perfectly intelligible to say that a group can choose amongst alternative actions, and the end or purpose of the action that it chooses is its intention (and its motive is its underlying reason for deciding on this course of action).
3. Indeed, the complexity of determining an agent's motive for action is one of the reasons why motives are not given a greater role in criminal law (see Kaufman 2003: 319–20).
4. See, for instance, Coates (2006: 76–9), Seybolt (2007: 20), Stein (2004: 31), and Walzer (2002: 27).
5. A similar point is made by Hegel (1991 [1821]) in part two of *The Philosophy of Right* (Möralitat) in response to the Kantian claim (as Hegel understands it) that, for any action to have moral worth, it must be done for duty's sake, and not with any element of self-interest. Hegel instead argues that it is our duty not only to respect others' interests ('right'), but also to promote our own interests ('welfare'), which together comprise the 'good'.
6. In the second Presidential Debate, Barack Obama asserted a broader view of national interest in response to a question about the crisis in Darfur: '[s]o when genocide is happening, when ethnic cleansing is happening somewhere around the world and we stand idly by, that diminishes us. And so I do believe that we have to consider it as part of our interests, our national interests, in intervening where possible' (CNN 2008).

7. Likewise, in criminal law, intention is required in virtually every case since it is easier to infer from the surrounding circumstances than motives, despite some difficulties with subjectivity (Kaufman 2003: 319–20).

8. Wheeler relies on the philosophy of Quentin Skinner here. Skinner asserts that whether an actor is sincere or not is beside the point. What matters is that, once an agent has accepted the need to justify behaviour, he is committed to showing that his actions 'were in fact motivated by some accepted set of social and political principles. And this in turn implies that, *even if the agent is not in fact motivated by any of the principles* he professes, *he will nevertheless be obliged to behave in such a way* that his actions remain compatible with the claim that these principles genuinely motivated him' (in Wheeler 2000: 9).

9. According to certain formulations of the principle of right intention in Just War Theory, the focus should be on the intentions of the decision-makers. This would mean that we should overlook the intentions of those carrying out the intervention. Yet such a conception of right intention is outmoded and gives a false picture of an intervener's intentions. Those authorizing the use of force may have very different intentions to those carrying it out. This was the allegation made against the actions of the private military company Executive Outcomes in Sierra Leone in 1995. Although the government of Sierra Leone hired Executive Outcomes for essentially what was a humanitarian purpose (to defeat the murderous RUF), it was alleged that Executive Outcomes became more interested in securing access to the diamond mines than protecting civilians. Given this potential for disjuncture between the intentions of those authorizing the use of force and the intentions of those undertaking or assisting the use of force, we may need to roll out the principle of right intention to cover both those authorizing force and those using it (or assisting in its use). That is, if we hold that the Just War Theory principle of right intention is important, it is also vital that those *undertaking* the use of force possess right intention. See Pattison (2008*b*: 144–9).

10. For more on how intention is not always central to moral responsibility, see Shaw's (2006) detailed discussion of the role of intention in ethics.

11. Humanitarianism in other, non-military contexts may be *prima facie* desirable, but in the context of humanitarian *military* intervention, the matter is more complex.

12. Tesón (2005*c*) gets close to this position when he highlights intentions as important yet gives weight to other factors.

13. See Hooker (2000), Lenman (2000), Dale Miller (2003), and M. Singer (1977; 1983). Those who defend actual consequentialism include Smart (1973) and Temkin (1978).

14. Wheeler takes a similar position: he asserts that it is important to distinguish 'between actions that are selective because of considerations of selfish interests, and those that would have to be ruled out because the human costs of intervention would outweigh the humanitarian benefits' (2000: 134). Also see Chris Brown on what he calls 'triage' (2003: 35–6).

15. One target that those who make this sort of argument may have in their sights is the suggestion that humanitarian intervention is justified *because* it is undertaken *with* a humanitarian motive (or intention). As Pretap Bhanu Mehta (2006: 280) asserts, this can occlude the moral issues at stake. I agree with the critics here: just as the motives of the intervener do not undermine its legitimacy, nor do they establish it.

16. It is important to remember here that one aspect of effectiveness is global external effectiveness. This means that, when concentrating on the details of a particular case, we should also consider the likely effects of intervention on international order, stability, and future humanitarian interventions.

17. Note that, if humanitarian intervention is held to be only a *right*, selectivity seems far less problematic, since on this position states are not *obliged* to intervene. Intervention is merely permissible. They do nothing wrong by failing to act.

18. One sense in which selectivity may be said to be problematic is if interveners act in response to a less serious humanitarian crisis and then are no longer able to intervene in response to a more serious one. This may be because of overstretch and political factors, such as adversity towards political casualties after previous interventions. One of the criticisms of the war in Iraq was that the extent of British and American involvement meant that it was politically and militarily impossible to conduct a similar intervention in Darfur (although Iraq was not a case of humanitarian intervention—see Section 6.6). Again, however, the focus should be on where the agent has failed to act, rather than where it has acted. The agent should be criticized for failing to act in the more serious case. But it still, presumably, would have a duty to intervene in the less serious case and therefore cannot be robustly criticized for doing its duty.

19. The underlying *motive* of the war might be claimed to have been, more broadly, to promote democracy and freedom in the Middle East. Mozaraffi (2005) defends the war on these grounds. But even if this was the case, the *intention* was still regime change and not humanitarian.

20. For a detailed critique of the British government's case for sanctions against Iraq, see Herring (2002).

21. Those who discuss the justifiability of the war in Iraq as a case of humanitarian intervention include Cushman (ed.) (2005), McMahan (2004*b*), R. Miller (2008), Nardin (2005), Roth (2004; 2006), and Tesón (2005*a*; 2005*b*; 2005*c*). Also see Heinze (2006), who argues that the justifiability of the invasion of Iraq is more nuanced than often claimed.

22. A more interesting argument is from Heinze (2006), who argues that the war could potentially have been justifiable, like NATO intervention in Kosovo, on the basis of the likely *future* mass violation of basic human rights. Given Saddam's track record, it was only a matter of time before he carried out another large-scale mass killing against the Kurdish and Shiite populations. The problem, however, with this argument is that it seems to justify preventa-

tive war in response to distant aggression, as opposed to pre-emptive wars in response to more immediate aggression (such as Kosovo). See N. Crawford (2005), Lee (2005), Luban (2004), and R. Miller (2008) on the problems of preventative wars.

23. At the time of writing (May 2009), the Iraqibodycount.org claims that there have been in between 91,924 and 100,348 documented civilian deaths. This is a much lower figure than the total likely deaths, since it is not an estimate but a record of documented deaths from media reports and review of hospital, morgue, NGO, and official figures. The Iraq Family Health Survey Study Group (2008) estimates the number of violent deaths at 151,000 from March 2003 through June 2006. A Lancet study (Burnham et al. 2006) estimates that, as of July 2006, there have been 654,965 excess Iraqi deaths as a consequence of the war. Many of these deaths are not a direct result of the violation of *jus in bello* by the US and UK, but caused by the wider civil disruption.

7

Assessing Current Interveners

The previous chapters have delineated the qualities that interveners need to be legitimate. This chapter will answer who should actually intervene. To do this, I will first bring together the findings of the previous chapters to provide a complete conception of legitimacy for humanitarian intervention. This conception of legitimacy (the Moderate Instrumentalist Approach), with its emphasis on effectiveness, provides the framework for determining which agent of intervention would be morally preferable. Second, the chapter will use the conception of legitimacy outlined to answer the two central questions identified in Chapter 1: (*a*) 'who has the right to intervene?' and (*b*) 'who has the duty to intervene?' In answer to the first question, I suggest that any agent that has an *adequate degree of* legitimacy has the right to intervene. In answer to the second question, I argue that (amongst those that meet the threshold level) the duty to intervene should fall on the *most legitimate* intervener which, in most cases, will be the *most effective* intervener. Assigning the duty to intervene raises additional issues of distributing responsibilities, such as that of fairness, which cannot be captured simply by setting a threshold level for when an agent's intervention is morally permissible. Therefore, Section 7.2 will defend the view that the most legitimate agent has the duty to intervene against both three leading alternatives and the claim that this is unfair on the most legitimate agent. Third, in Section 7.3, I will consider who, out of the currently existing agents of intervention (NATO, states, the UN, regional organizations, and private military companies), (*a*) has an adequate degree of legitimacy, and therefore the *right* to intervene, and (*b*) is the most legitimate agent, and therefore has the *duty* to intervene. I conclude that, although some agents of intervention have a *degree* of legitimacy, no currently existing agent is *fully* legitimate according to the conception of legitimacy that I have outlined.

7.1 OUTLINE OF THE COMPLETE CONCEPTION OF LEGITIMACY

This first section will bring together the features of legitimacy identified in previous discussions into a complete conception of legitimacy for humanitarian intervention—the Moderate Instrumentalist Approach. Recall that, in Chapter 1, I outlined my use of legitimacy as the morally justifiable use of political power. A legitimate agent will have certain qualities that mean it can justifiably wield political power. I take legitimacy to be scalar, that is, a matter of degree. We can distinguish between an intervener that possesses full legitimacy and an intervener that possesses an adequate degree of legitimacy. Intervention by an intervener possessing an adequate degree of legitimacy is morally acceptable. It is desirable, however, to have an intervener that possesses a more than adequate degree of legitimacy and, in particular, an intervener that is fully legitimate, for the simple reason that such an intervener's use of power would be more morally justified.

The most important factor for the legitimacy of an intervener is its effectiveness. This reflects the intuitive plausibility of consequentialist thinking on humanitarian intervention. According to the Moderate Instrumentalist Approach, what matters most is that we can expect the intervener to achieve good consequences—that it will successfully prevent, halt, or decrease the egregious violations of human rights.

There are three forms of effectiveness. The first type of effectiveness is 'local external effectiveness', which depends on whether an intervener is likely to promote or harm the enjoyment of human rights (and primarily the basic rights) of those in the political community that is subject to its intervention. In other words, to be locally externally effective, an intervener needs to be successful at tackling the humanitarian crisis (and preventing its reoccurrence). The second type of effectiveness is 'global external effectiveness'. This depends on whether an intervener promotes or harms the enjoyment of the human rights in the world as a whole, apart from the intervener's citizens and those subject to its intervention. The third type of effectiveness is an intervener's 'internal effectiveness', which depends on the consequences for the intervener's own citizens. Given the importance of an intervener's being effective in these three senses, it follows that an intervener's overall effectiveness is a necessary condition of its legitimacy. If, when combining its local external effectiveness, global external effectiveness, and internal effectiveness, an intervener is ineffective overall, it cannot be legitimate.

If they are to be effective, interveners need to have a number of characteristics. These include adequate military and non-military resources and a suitable strategy to use these resources successfully. Interveners also need to have the commitment to intervene successfully. Regional interveners are likely to do well in this regard: their geographical proximity gives them extra reason to ensure that the humanitarian crisis is resolved and, in addition, means that fewer resources are required. It is also important for an intervener to intervene in a timely manner, that is, quickly and when the situation is ripe for humanitarian intervention, and to possess international support for the intervention.

The overall effectiveness of an intervener depends, firstly, on the degree to which it has these characteristics and, secondly, on the circumstances in which it is acting. Both the probability and the magnitude of an intervener's effectiveness will vary according to the circumstances. When an intervener has a high probability of achieving a success with a large magnitude, effectiveness can be not only a necessary but also a sufficient condition for it to have an adequate degree of legitimacy. Consequently, effectiveness can be sufficient for an adequate degree of legitimacy in unusual circumstances where hugely beneficial consequences are more than likely. In most cases, however, effectiveness will not be sufficient because an intervener will not have a very high probability of achieving a very sizeable success. Typically, then, an intervener's legitimacy depends also on the degree to which it possesses other qualities.

Moreover, even where hugely beneficial consequences are more than likely, and effectiveness is sufficient for an intervener to have an adequate degree of legitimacy, the intervener will not be fully legitimate unless it possesses all of the relevant qualities. Hence, at most, effectiveness can be sufficient only for an adequate degree of legitimacy and, in the majority of circumstances, it will not be sufficient even for this. This is because the legitimacy of an intervener also depends on three other, non-consequentialist qualities.

The first of these non-consequentialist qualities is fidelity to the principles of *jus in bello*. These principles limit the means that an intervener can use to undertake humanitarian intervention. The first set of principles—principles of 'external *jus in bello*'—is concerned with how the intervener should treat the population subject to its intervention. These include a strict rule of non-combatant immunity, which maintains that civilian casualties are impermissible, and a principle of proportionality, which limits the harm that the intervener can cause to combatants. The second set of principles—principles of 'internal *jus in bello*'—is concerned with how the intervener should treat its own citizens. These include a restriction on the sort of soldiers that the intervener can use (e.g. not conscripts or child soldiers) and a prohibition on the use of methods that cause the intervener's own soldiers excessive and avoidable harm.

In Chapter 5, I highlighted two other factors that are non-instrumentally valuable (as well as instrumentally valuable) for an intervener's legitimacy. Both concern whether the intervener represents the opinions of two sets of people in its decision-making. First, it should represent the opinions of those individuals from whom it is collectively formed—it needs to be 'internally representative'. Second, it should represent the opinions of those individuals in the political community that is subject to its intervention (and particularly the victims of the humanitarian crisis)—it needs to be 'locally externally representative'. To establish that it is internally representative, an intervener can conduct referenda on humanitarian intervention, carry out opinion polls on some of the population, and, less scientifically, consider other indicators of the public mood. To ensure that it is locally externally representative, it can ascertain directly the opinions of those in the political community that is subject to its intervention, or, given that this is often difficult, it can use indirect indicators, such as information provided by reliable intermediaries.

However, other factors commonly cited as having non-consequentialist importance have, at best, small significance for the legitimacy of an intervener. It is sometimes suggested that having proper legal authorization—UN Security Council authorization—is valuable. Yet this proper legal authorization is, at best, a minor non-consequentialist factor for the legitimacy of an intervener. The gap between the current international law and the demands of morality is too large: *lex lata* bears little relation to *lex ferenda*. As such, a legal intervener is by no means certain to be a legitimate intervener. That legality may have some small, independent value means that it is, to some extent, desirable. But it is far from being a necessary or even important non-consequentialist factor for the legitimacy of humanitarian intervention.

The argument that an intervener's motives are an important independent factor in its legitimacy can also be challenged. It is crucial to note the difference between a humanitarian intention and a humanitarian motive. An intervener with a humanitarian intention has the goal of preventing, reducing, or halting the humanitarian crisis. The reason for the intervener's having this humanitarian goal, however, does not have to be humanitarian as well. By contrast, if an intervener is to have a humanitarian motive, not only must its goal be humanitarian but also its reason for having that goal. Both an intervener's motives and intentions do little non-instrumental work in establishing an intervener's legitimacy. An intervener may have purely humanitarian motives, mixed motives, or purely self-interested motives, and yet still be legitimate. And, although having a humanitarian intention is a necessary condition of any intervener being deemed 'humanitarian', it does not follow that having a humanitarian intention does much *positive*, independent work in establishing an intervener's legitimacy: we need to have further information in order to judge the legitimacy of an intervener.

Two other commonly cited factors do not contribute much non-instrumentally to the legitimacy of an intervener. First, as argued in Chapter 5, it does not matter whether an intervener's decision-making reflects the opinions of those individuals in the world at large (global external representativeness). Second, as argued in the previous chapter, an intervener may be selective in its intervention and still be legitimate. This goes against the argument that an intervener is illegitimate in State A because it has not intervened in a similar situation in State B.

Although having proper legal authorization, possessing a humanitarian intention, and being globally externally representative do not have much independent moral significance, this does not mean that they play *no* role in an intervener's legitimacy. On the contrary, these three qualities have instrumental significance. An intervener is more likely to be effective if it has proper authority and a humanitarian intention, and is globally externally representative. The three non-consequentialist values—fidelity to the principles of *jus in bello*, internal representativeness, and global external representativeness—are also instrumentally significant. An intervener that is internally and locally externally representative and has a high degree of expected fidelity to the principles of internal and external *jus in bello* is also more likely to be effective. Accordingly, the conception of legitimacy presented (the Moderate Instrumentalist Approach) is more complex than having effectiveness on the one hand and the non-consequentialist factors on the other. Effectiveness is also determined in part by the extent to which an intervener possesses these three non-consequentialist qualities.

So, to be *fully* legitimate, an intervener needs to be internally effective, globally externally effective, locally externally effective, to follow principles of internal *jus in bello*, to follow principles of external *jus in bello*, to be internally representative, and to be locally externally representative. To have *an adequate degree of* legitimacy, an intervener does not need to have all of these qualities. Whether it has an adequate degree of legitimacy depends on whether it possesses enough of these qualities cumulatively. An intervener could have an adequate degree of legitimacy, yet lack one of these qualities. It may, for instance, lack internal representativeness, but have an adequate degree of legitimacy overall because it is locally externally representative, follows closely all the principles of *jus in bello*, and will be highly effective. Similarly, an intervener could have an adequate degree of legitimacy yet meet some of these qualities only *partially*. For instance, there are different levels of local external representativeness, ranging from none to full representativeness (depending on the degree to which an intervener represents the opinions of those suffering the humanitarian crisis). An intervener can have an adequate degree of legitimacy even though it is only *partially* representative of those in the political community subject to intervention, perhaps because it will be extremely effective overall.

The only *necessary* condition of legitimacy is effectiveness. This is because of the overwhelming significance this quality has for the legitimacy of an intervener. Indeed, in exceptional circumstances, where extremely beneficial consequences are highly likely, effectiveness can be a *sufficient* condition for the legitimacy of an intervener. That effectiveness can be, on occasion, sufficient for an adequate degree of legitimacy shows, first, the impact of circumstances on my conception of legitimacy for humanitarian intervention. Circumstances determine whether qualities other than effectiveness are required if an intervener is to possess an adequate degree of legitimacy and, if so, the degree to which these are required. Whether an intervener is likely to possess these qualities also depends on the circumstances (for instance, if it is likely to be locally externally representative). Second, it reflects the dominant position of effectiveness amongst the qualities which contribute to an intervener's legitimacy. Thus, my conception of legitimacy is, in large part, consequentialist, as encapsulated by the Moderate Instrumentalist Approach. This is with good reason: consequentialist thinking on humanitarian intervention is intuitively compelling. What seems to matter, above all else, is that an intervener prevents, halts, or decreases egregious violations of human rights. But my account is not wholly consequentialist. In most cases, the degree to which an intervener possesses certain non-consequentialist qualities—internal representativeness, local external representativeness, and fidelity to principles of *jus in bello*—plays a large role in its legitimacy. And even when local external effectiveness is sufficient for an adequate degree of legitimacy, an intervener needs these non-consequentialist qualities to be fully legitimate.

7.1.1 Vagueness and institutions

It might be claimed that the conception of legitimacy I have developed is too vague. First, it leaves open the possibility that an intervener can possess varying amounts of the morally relevant qualities outlined, including very little of some, yet still have an adequate degree of legitimacy. Second, the qualities identified are somewhat indeterminate: there can be differing interpretations and judgements about whether an intervener possesses them. These two problems, it might be objected, mean that it will be difficult in practice to determine whether an intervener is legitimate. Moreover, given this indeterminacy, agents may be able to claim, with some plausibility, that they possess the morally relevant qualities, and are therefore legitimate, even when they are not.[1] This could, the argument runs, increase the risk of abusive non-humanitarian intervention or illegitimate humanitarian intervention.

There are a number of points to make in response. To start with, the conception of legitimacy outlined above is not that vague. I have been careful to specify what exactly is required to possess the morally relevant qualities. For instance, for an intervener to be effective, I argued that it must be reasonably expected to make an improvement in the enjoyment of human rights (and primarily of basic rights) in the long term, compared to the counterfactual, of those suffering humanitarian crisis, of the intervener's citizens, or in the world at large. In practice, this means that the intervener must be responding to a serious humanitarian crisis, where the degree of violations of human rights is both qualitatively and quantitatively significant, and have a number of qualities, such as the necessary military and non-military resources, a suitable strategy, sufficient commitment, the ability to intervene in a quick and timely manner, and be likely to be perceived to be legitimate. Similarly, when discussing the importance of fidelity to the principles of *jus in bello*, I detailed what exactly is required for each of the principles. In Chapter 1, I delineated when an agent can be said to be engaged in 'humanitarian intervention' and, in Chapter 6, what constitutes a humanitarian intention. Consequently, it would be difficult for a non-humanitarian, abusive, or illegitimate agent to claim plausibly that they are a legitimate humanitarian intervener.

Given the varying characteristics of humanitarian crises, and the different considerations involved, it would be a mistake to be more determinate. We need to retain a degree of flexibility in the relevant normative factors so that we can apply them to the differing situations that will arise. The risk in being more determinate is that we may deny the legitimacy of an intervener in a particular case because it does not meet all the details of a certain factor, yet the specifics of the case—and commonsense—tell us that the intervener is legitimate overall (Chopra and Weiss 1992). For instance, although the assessment of an intervener's effectiveness might be easier if we took this to be measured by whether the intervener fulfils its mandate, this would rule out cases where an intervener has does not fulfil its mandate (or goes beyond its mandate), yet we still generally regard it as having been effective. Hence, Weiss asserts that, in the messy world of humanitarian intervention, '[a]nalyses and not formulas are required. The task is thus to be flexible rather than to take preset criteria and apply them rigidly' (2005*a*: 213).[2]

One solution to the problem of indeterminacy, favoured by many (e.g. Buchanan and Keohane 2004; Pogge 2006), is to have institutions that formally decide whether an intervener possesses the morally relevant qualities. The goal here is to establish something akin to a (model) domestic legal system, which has set processes to determine an agent's intention, as well as to make judgements on other morally relevant concerns (such as its likely effectiveness). It would silence much of the contestation by listening to competing claims and deciding in a fair and accurate manner which is correct. If put in place at the international level, such a system would be able to adjudicate on which intervener is most likely to be effective. It would also be able to take into account the particularities of the case and rule accordingly, that is, either authorize or reject the intervention.

The development of an international adjudicating institution would, of course, be highly desirable. Indeed, one of the benefits of the cosmopolitan democratic institutions that I propose in the next chapter is that they would be able to decide in a fair manner whether to authorize intervention. But we must tread carefully here: not all institutions are appropriate for this function. As it stands, the Security Council is not a suitable candidate to act as an adjudicating institution. Central to the credibility of an adjudicating institution is, firstly, that its processes are fair, transparent, and procedurally just, and secondly, that it makes the right judgement in most cases. The Security Council fails on both counts. As argued in Chapter 2, the functioning of the Security Council is highly problematic. In addition, it has failed to authorize humanitarian interventions that were legitimate overall (e.g. NATO intervention in Kosovo) and its permanent members have opposed a number of potential humanitarian interventions that might have been legitimate, had they been undertaken (e.g. UN action in Darfur before UNAMID). The Security Council therefore lacks just procedures and regularly does not make the right decisions. For these reasons, it would be mistaken to let it decide whether an intervener is legitimate; it could not be relied upon to make this decision in a morally responsible way. As Chesterman argues, 'it is misleading to suggest that the Council ever worked effectively as an objective arbiter in the area of peace and security—or that it was ever realistically expected to do so. The Council was and remains an inherently political body' (2005: 159).[3]

What is *currently* the best way then of deciding whether an agent possesses the morally relevant qualities and would therefore be a legitimate intervener? A seemingly more promising solution, defended by Franck (2003; 2006), is to have various actors play a 'jurying' function. They could evaluate the justifiability of an intervener's action, including its motives, proportionality, and likely effectiveness. Indeed, Franck argues that such jurying already takes place. Examples include the defeat in the Security Council of Russia and China's attempt to admonish NATO's action in Kosovo, the silent acquiescence in response to Tanzania's intervention in Uganda, and the mildness of the disapprobation of India's intervention in Bangladesh (Franck 2006: 151).[4] According to Franck (2003: 228–9), jurying is conducted in three forums: the International Court of Justice; international political forums, that is, the Security Council and General Assembly; and the 'court of public opinion' informed and guided by the global media and NGOs. In these forums, Franck argues, states should make the ultimate decision, although the UN secretariat and agencies, the media, and NGOs have an important role in the assessment process.

The notion of jurying is a plausible way of determining legitimacy. Franck's own account, however, is too state-centric and unduly optimistic about the impartiality of states. As Pogge (2006: 170) argues, a jury of states is susceptible to undue influence, such as the pressure put on members of the Security Council in the build-up to both Iraq wars to reach the 'right decision'. Moreover, certain states may be overly cautious in their judgement because, on the one hand, they generally oppose humanitarian intervention, asserting instead the sanctity of state boundaries, or, on the other, are concerned that they would be required to intervene or provide resources. For this reason, it is important that non-state perspectives should be included in any jurying role.[5] In particular, the decisions on an intervener's legitimacy should incorporate leading NGOs and global public opinion, as well as states. Even though such actors may have questionable partiality as well, they will help to balance states' views on humanitarian intervention.[6]

It may be objected, first, that these actors (states, NGOs, and global public opinion) will frequently fail to make a coherent, unified decision on humanitarian intervention and, second, even if they do make a decision, it will be difficult to determine what this is. Both these criticisms are, to a certain extent, correct and provide further reason for why we should look to develop a more formalized adjudicating institution. But we should not discount completely the ability of these actors to make a clear decision, such as the widespread condemnation of Israeli action in Lebanon in 2006. Nor is it impossible to determine what this decision is. The opinions of states can be inferred from resolutions in the General Assembly and Security Council, pronouncements by regional organizations, and from statements by heads of states and governmental officials. NGOs also frequently publicize their opinions, such as the strong refutation of the humanitarian credentials of the Iraq War by Roth (2004; 2006). Similarly, a sense (if not a perfect measurement) of worldwide public opinion can be obtained from sources such as the Eurobarometer and WorldPublicOpinion.org.

A further criticism is that any decisions by these actors would fail to constrain powerful states. Again, this is often true. Indeed, any scheme to decide the applicability of international rules and norms is likely to face this problem. But many states are influenced by the opinions of their peers, the criticism of NGOs, and global public opinion, if for no other reasons than wanting to be seen as good international citizens and domestic electoral pressures. Indeed, it can be plausibly claimed that the jurying function of states, NGOs, and global public opinion has *already* played a significant role in constraining states. Consider, for instance, the widespread view, despite the claims of the US and the UK, that the 2003 war on Iraq was illegal and largely unjustifiable. This view, although not sufficient to constrain these states at the time, seems to have had a large impact on their behaviour, and international relations more generally, since.

7.2 ANSWERING THE TWO CENTRAL QUESTIONS

In Chapter 1, I said that this book is concerned with two central questions:

1. 'Who has the right to intervene?' or 'who may intervene?' and
2. 'Who has the duty to intervene?' or 'who should intervene?'.

I will now briefly sketch my answer to these two questions by drawing on the conception of legitimacy defended, that is, the Moderate Instrumentalist Approach. In the answer to the first question ('who has the *right* to intervene?'), any intervener that possesses *an adequate degree of* legitimacy according to this account will have the *right* to intervene. In effect, this sets a threshold level for *when* humanitarian intervention will be permissible. As we saw above, to possess an adequate degree of legitimacy, it is necessary that the agent is likely to be effective overall—and effectiveness can be sufficient for an adequate degree of legitimacy in exceptional circumstances where extremely beneficial consequences are likely. In most cases, however, an agent will also need to possess a number of other qualities (such as being representative and following principles of *jus in bello*) in order to have an adequate degree of legitimacy and therefore the right to intervene. In addition, an agent would need to be reacting to circumstances that meet the just cause threshold outlined in Chapter 1 (typically, the mass violation of basic human rights). It would also need to be engaged in 'humanitarian intervention' to have a right to undertake humanitarian intervention. In other words, it would need to meet the four defining conditions of humanitarian intervention (also listed in Chapter 1): it would need (*a*) to be engaged in military and forcible action; (*b*) to be responding to a situation where there is impending or ongoing grievous suffering or loss of life; (*c*) to be an external agent; and (*d*) to have a humanitarian intention, that is, a predominant purpose of preventing, reducing, or halting the ongoing or impending grievous suffering or loss of life.

In answer to the second question ('who has the *duty* to intervene?'), an agent would need to meet the threshold level so that it first has the *right* to intervene. It would need to possess, at the very least, an adequate degree of legitimacy (and meet the just cause threshold and be engaged in 'humanitarian intervention'). To put this another way, for an agent's intervention to be *obligatory*, it is necessary that it is first *permissible*. Amongst those agents that have the right to act (amongst those that have at least an adequate degree of legitimacy), it is the *most* legitimate agent that has the *duty* to intervene. If this agent fails to intervene, the duty falls on the next most legitimate intervener, and so on. Given the importance that the Moderate Instrumentalist Approach places on an intervener's effectiveness, the most *effective* intervener will often be the most *legitimate* intervener.

It might be asked, however, why the duty to intervene should be assigned to the most legitimate intervener. Assigning the duty to intervene is not as straightforward as setting a threshold level above which an intervener has the right to intervene. There are additional issues that concern how the duty should be assigned. These issues include whether the distribution should reflect historical responsibility and special relationships, and the fairness of the distribution of the duty. Therefore, I will now, first, consider three leading alternative ways of assigning the duty to intervene. These are that we should look to the intervener that (*a*) is responsible for creating the humanitarian crisis, (*b*) has a special relationship with those suffering the humanitarian crisis, or (*c*) has the institutionalized responsibility to intervene.[7] Second, I will consider the objection that looking to the most legitimate intervener is *unfair* on this intervener.

7.2.1 Alternative ways of assigning the duty to intervene

The first alternative is that the intervener that is responsible for creating the humanitarian crisis should intervene. It may, for instance, be a former colonial master whose misrule and reckless departure has led to chronic instability. Or it could be an international hegemon that has previously destabilized the region. The intuition at work here is, to put it crudely, that those that create the mess should clear it up.

The second alternative is a special relationship between those suffering the humanitarian crisis and the intervener.[8] In this context, Tan (2006*a*: 98) gives an example of a man drowning off a beach that has no lifeguard on duty. Out of everyone on the beach, the drowning man's spouse would be identified as the appropriate agent because of her special relationship to him. In the case of humanitarian intervention, the special relationship might be historical, religious, or cultural. A humanitarian crisis, for instance, in a commonwealth state might mean that the UK and other commonwealth states possess an obligation to act.

Whether these two alternatives are persuasive ways of assigning the duty to intervene depends, to a certain extent, on the position taken on the duties of humanitarian intervention. To see this, it helps to return to the two approaches to the duty to intervene outlined in Chapter 1. On what I called the 'General Right Approach', for *most* agents humanitarian intervention is only supererogatory: it is morally permissible, but not morally obligatory. This is because, on this approach, there exist *negative* duties to non-compatriots, for instance, not to cause them harm. But there exist few, if any, *positive* duties to non-compatriots, particularly one as demanding as humanitarian intervention. In other words, although there is a general *right* to intervene, there is not a general, unassigned *duty* to do so. Nevertheless, a certain agent might still have the duty to intervene. For it to do so, there needs to be a strong reason why it should act. It is not simply a case of *assigning* the duty to intervene. Rather, the duty to intervene needs to be *generated*.

One reason why, on the General Right Approach, an intervener could possess the duty to intervene is that it caused the humanitarian crisis. It violated its negative duty to avoid harming non-compatriots, and therefore has a duty to resolve this crisis. Another way that the duty to intervene could be generated on this approach is from special ties. Although we have negative duties towards non-compatriots, the argument runs, we possess positive duties towards fellow citizens, for instance, to provide welfare. It may also follow that we also have positive duties towards certain non-citizens that we have close affinities to, particularly when they are in extreme peril.

By contrast, being the intervener most likely to be legitimate does not seem to be able to *generate* the duty to intervene. It may be argued that assigning the duty to intervene to the most legitimate intervener is unfair on that intervener since it places an unduly heavy burden on this intervener. This, of course, is an important issue (I consider it in detail in the next section), but the objection here is more fundamental. It is not simply a question of the unfairness of *assigning* the duty to intervene, which assumes that there is a duty to be assigned. Rather, it is a question of the *existence* of this duty. Unlike in the cases of the existence of special ties or the causing of the humanitarian crisis, there does not seem to be a strong enough reason why the most legitimate intervener is obliged to go beyond its negative duty to refrain from harming those beyond its borders. Simply being the most legitimate actor does not generate a positive duty to act. So, if one adopts the General Right Approach, looking to the most legitimate intervener seems deeply unpersuasive. The two alternatives, which depend on special relationships and can generate the duty to intervene, seem more plausible.

Yet recall that, in Chapter 1, I argued that there are significant problems with the General Right Approach and instead defended the 'General Duty Approach', which is similar to that endorsed by the ICISS. On this view, there is a general, unassigned duty to undertake humanitarian intervention, which needs to be assigned to a particular agent. To assign this duty, we need to look to an additional reason (or an 'agency condition'), such as being the most legitimate or responsible for the crisis. I will not repeat in full my argument in defence of this approach here. To summarize, I claimed that the existence of a general, unassigned duty to undertake humanitarian intervention is the following: intuitively compelling; can be defended on the basis solely of negative duties; is a logical corollary of the right to intervene; is a logical corollary of basic human rights; and stems from the moral obligation to respect humanity and, more specifically, the duty to prevent human suffering.

When one holds the General Duty Approach—the view that humanitarian intervention is generally a duty—it is not necessary to generate the duty to intervene since this duty *already* exists. In other words, we are not concerned with finding ways of justifying why a particular agent has the duty to intervene. Rather, we are looking for the *most appropriate way of assigning this duty*. It follows that looking to historic responsibility for the crisis or special ties might still be desirable ways of assigning the duty to intervene, yet this is less obviously the case.

In fact, these two alternative solutions are not plausible ways of allocating the general, unassigned duty to intervene on the General Duty Approach. (Some of the objections that I raise will also show that these two solutions are unconvincing even if one adopts a General Right Approach.) Let me start with the first alternative, which holds that the intervener that is somehow responsible for the crisis has the duty to intervene. An obvious difficulty is that identifying the actors that are responsible for the humanitarian crisis can be tricky. Sometimes this is all too obvious, but, at other times, it can be difficult to disentangle the role that a potential intervener played in causing the humanitarian crisis from the roles that other, especially domestic, actors played.[9] It might be argued in response that intervention by the agent responsible for the crisis is required for some sort of reparative justice—and that this should trump other concerns. But this would be an odd, and largely unconvincing, notion of justice in this context: those who suffered the injustice in the first place—those suffering the humanitarian crisis—could end up being worse off. This is because those that are responsible for the crisis, if they were to intervene, could face high levels of resistance amongst the local population.

Likewise, the second alternative (that we should look to the intervener that has a special bond with the intervener) also has its problems. It is doubtful whether many special bonds exist amongst international actors that are sufficiently strong.[10] It is not clear, for instance, that the communal affinity of the *umma* (the Muslim community) is sufficient to identify a Muslim state as the appropriate intervener when another Muslim state is suffering a humanitarian crisis (see Hashmi 2003). Furthermore, even if there were a few special bonds strong enough to make a difference, in many other cases there would not be. This would leave us with the original problem of specifying which agent should intervene in these cases.[11]

Furthermore, it is not clear why an agent that is responsible for the crisis or one that has special ties with those suffering the crisis should be preferred to the most legitimate intervener, which, according to the Moderate Instrumentalist Approach, will often be the most effective intervener. If one takes humanitarian intervention generally to be a duty, as the General Duty Approach does, what seems to matter most is that this duty is effectively discharged. The ICISS argue that the language of responsibility and duties 'focuses the international searchlight back where it should always be: on the duty to protect communities from mass killing, women from systematic rape and children from starvation' (2001*a*: 17). And when the focus is on those suffering the humanitarian crisis, what is most important is that their suffering is ended. This seems more morally urgent than an intervener making up for its past injustices or assisting those with which it has ties.

7.2.2 Institutionalizing the duty to intervene

Having largely rejected two alternative ways of assigning the duty to intervene, let us now consider a third solution. This involves the clear designation of the duty to intervene to a specific institution, such as the UN, AU, EU, or a new agent specifically designed to discharge this duty, such as a permanent UN rapid-reaction force.

The same problem arises for this solution as for the other two alternatives: it would fail to identify any current intervener since, at present, no agent has the institutionalized duty to undertake humanitarian intervention. Nevertheless, this solution might seem to be the best way of assigning the duty to intervene *in the future*. Indeed, this alternative could be preferable for a number of reasons. First, formally assigning this duty to a particular agent could ensure that this agent discharges it when the situation demands. In doing so, it could (further) respond to the objection considered in the previous chapter: that humanitarian intervention is selectively carried out in response to certain humanitarian crises, but not others (Tan 2006*b*: 296). Institutionalizing the duty to intervene could also help to ensure that, when it does occur, humanitarian intervention is effective. It may be, for instance, that other agents pool resources so that they are more efficiently used by the agent with the institutionalized duty to intervene.

This institution may also gain significant experience in undertaking humanitarian intervention. Institutionalizing the duty to intervene could also remove much of the current contestation surrounding humanitarian intervention by judging whether intervention would be justifiable. Formally designating the duty to intervene to a specific institution could also help to discourage abusive intervention that claims to be humanitarian. This is because, by formally designating who should intervene, the only agent that could legitimately claim to be engaged in humanitarian intervention would be the designated intervener.

Furthermore, we could combine this solution with the approach that I have defended: the most legitimate intervener could have the institutionalized the duty to intervene. We could do this either by first identifying the most legitimate intervener, and then assigning it the legal duty to intervene, or by ensuring that the organization that has the legal duty to intervene is the most legitimate (for instance, by providing it with the resources necessary for effective intervention). On this combined approach, the agent that would be the most legitimate humanitarian intervener would have the institutionalized duty to intervene and having this institutionalized duty to intervene should mean that in general it undertakes intervention when necessary. One way of implementing this combined approach, which I consider in the next chapter, is to increase regional organizations' capacity to undertake humanitarian intervention within their own regions, so that they are the most legitimate interveners, and to institutionalize this by reforming regional organizations' constitutions so they have the legal duty to intervene. But we should go further than this. It should not be merely the *most* legitimate intervener that has the institutionalized duty to intervene, but the intervener that is *fully* legitimate according to the conception outlined above. We could potentially achieve this goal if we act on the proposals, also considered in the next chapter, for a large-sized cosmopolitan UN force in the hands of cosmopolitan democratic institutions.

The problem, of course, is that we are a long way from achieving this solution; current international institutions are far from this ideal. It would require significant reform of current international institutions. This is not to detract from the desirability of this solution. It is simply to admit that such an institution would require significant reform of the international system and, for this reason, we may need to pursue other ways of assigning the duty to intervene in the short to mid term.

One apparent alternative is to assign the duty to intervene to a currently existing institution. We could formally assign the duty to intervene, for instance, to the UN as it currently exists. Yet this option seems less persuasive than looking to the most legitimate intervener. The risk with such a solution is that we could assign the duty to intervene to an institution that has significant difficulty in discharging this duty. Indeed, it may lack many of the advantages of the institutional solution outlined. For example, if we were to institutionalize the duty to intervene at the UN in its current form, it would have real trouble intervening in response to all—or even most—of the severe humanitarian crises worldwide. In addition, it may be too conservative in its assessments of when the permissibility criteria for justifiable humanitarian intervention have been met. For instance, Russia and China, being generally opposed to humanitarian intervention, would be likely to be overly cautious in their assessments. So, although the ideal institutional arrangement is the most desirable way of assigning the duty to intervene, problems of feasibility may mean that we should instead look to the most legitimate intervener, at least in the short term.[12]

One immediate objection is that looking to the most legitimate intervener gives priority to unilateralism over multilateralism. In response, it is worth noting that, as I will argue in Section 7.3, the most legitimate institution may still be the UN, especially given its degree of perceived legitimacy amongst conflicting parties. Likewise, regional organizations may sometimes be more likely to be effective than states because of their geographical proximity. The problem is that institutionalizing the duty to intervene in these organizations in their current form would task them with humanitarian intervention in *all* situations, including those that they are not best placed to deal with. Alternative, unilateral options, such as India's intervention in East Pakistan in 1971, Tanzania's intervention in Uganda in 1979, and NATO's intervention in Kosovo in 1999—all of which lacked multilateral support but helped to prevent and halt mass violations of basic human rights—would be foreclosed. My point, then, is that until we develop a legitimate institutional arrangement to undertake humanitarian intervention, both unilateral *and* multilateral solutions should be on the table in response to serious humanitarian crises.

7.2.3 Fairness and legitimacy

It may be objected that the Moderate Instrumentalist Approach's assertion that the duty to intervene should be assigned to the most legitimate intervener imposes an unreasonably heavy burden on this agent. For instance, it would be unfair on NATO if it always has the duty to intervene. States, the UN, and regional organizations should do their bit too. This objection is a version of a standard objection to consequentialism: it is excessively demanding. In this case, the objection is that this solution is excessively demanding on the most legitimate intervener.[13]

It is important to note here that this objection has force only against legitimacy being used to decide the *duty* to intervene. If humanitarian intervention is held to be only a *right*, then there is a straightforward response to the objection: looking to the most legitimate intervener is not unfair because this intervener can choose whether to exercise its right to act. There are, however, (at least) three ways that the issue of unfairness could arise when using legitimacy to assign the *duty* to intervene.

First, having the most legitimate agent intervene could be unfair because that agent has to do all the intervening. The duty to intervene may fall on the same agent in a number of different cases. Other agents would not have the duty to intervene because their intervention would not be the most legitimate. The second and third potential types of unfairness differ from this in that they involve the most legitimate agent covering for other agents' non-compliance with their duties. In the second, other interveners fail to intervene and so the duty to intervene falls on an intervener that has already done its fair share. Suppose, for instance, that States A and B would be the two most legitimate interveners, but are unwilling to act. The duty then falls on State C to intervene since it is the third most legitimate intervener. This seems unfair on State C because it has already done its fair share. It has already undertaken humanitarian intervention a number of times recently. The third type of case in which the issue of unfairness could arise would be when the most legitimate intervener has to act because of the behaviour of those that caused the humanitarian crisis (e.g. governmental persecution of a certain ethnicity). It is because of these individuals' non-compliance with their duty to protect their citizens that the most legitimate intervener has the burden of intervention. In these three ways, then, adopting the most legitimate intervener as the preferred agent can be unfair to that intervener.

In response, there are a number of points that, to a certain extent, mitigate this potential unfairness. First, as suggested above, there currently exists an unassigned duty to intervene. As such, an intervener's legitimacy does not have to *generate* the duty to intervene. Rather, legitimacy merely *specifies* who has the duty to intervene. That this is unfair on the most legitimate intervener is still an issue, but it is less of an issue because this intervener *already* has a duty (albeit an unassigned one) to intervene.

Second, which intervener possesses the duty to intervene may vary according to the circumstances since different interveners may be effective in different circumstances. Indeed, if an intervener is already intervening somewhere else, or if it has already intervened somewhere else recently, then, for reasons of overstretch, it is unlikely to be the most effective agent for a further intervention and therefore unlikely to be the most legitimate intervener. The duty to intervene would therefore fall on another agent.

Third, although other agents may not have the duty to undertake humanitarian intervention, they may nevertheless have other, associated duties, related to the responsibility to protect and the prevention of human suffering, which are equally demanding. These might include funding the intervention and providing equipment, and these will further offset any apparent unfairness. This reply also helps to repudiate a further criticism: the most legitimate interveners have an incentive to run down their capabilities and other agents have an incentive to fail to develop their capabilities so that they do not possess the duty to intervene (see deLisle 2001: 546). Actors that fail to maintain their capacity to intervene would violate these other duties.

Nonetheless, this objection about fairness might still be claimed to have some purchase. But we can modify this solution so that it is not so demanding. One option would be a principle of beneficence that asserts that the demands on a complying agent should not exceed what they would be if everyone complied with the principle that should govern their conduct (see L. Murphy 2000). For our purposes, those complying with the duty to prevent human suffering would not be required to do more than they would have to if everyone complied with this duty. This principle of beneficence, however, is not best suited to humanitarian intervention, since intervention always involves cases where someone has failed to comply with their duty, that is, where a government is unable or unwilling to fulfil its duty to uphold its citizens' human rights. So, humanitarian intervention requires at least one agent to do more (i.e. to intervene) than would be required if there were full compliance with the duty to prevent human suffering.

My alternative suggestion to tackle the problem of the unfairness on the most legitimate intervener is that we amend the duty to prevent human suffering so that agents have a duty to make a *reasonable and substantial effort* to protect populations suffering. This means that the duty to intervene still falls on the most legitimate intervener, but if this agent has already made significant effort to prevent human suffering in a number of ways which go beyond what would be reasonably required of it (such as by undertaking a number of recent humanitarian interventions), then, for reasons of fairness, the duty to intervene should fall on the next most legitimate intervener. In practice, however, most agents have not done their bit to prevent human suffering given the number of humanitarian crises and amount of human suffering that currently go unchecked. The duty to intervene, according to this condition, is therefore likely to continue to fall on the most legitimate intervener.

Thus, we have seen that any agent that has at least an *adequate degree of* legitimacy has the right to intervene (providing that they also have just cause and are engaged in humanitarian intervention). The *most* legitimate agent has the *duty* to intervene, although this should be moderated to take into account fairness. In the future, we should work towards institutionalizing the duty to intervene in an agent that is *fully* legitimate according to the Moderate Instrumentalist Approach, although we should be wary of institutionalizing the duty to intervene in the immediate future.

7.3 WHICH CURRENT AGENT SHOULD INTERVENE?

Let us now use the conception of legitimacy outlined above to assess the current agents of intervention and see who exactly has the right and/or duty to intervene. To do this, I will assess the track record of humanitarian interveners to see how they measure up to the conception of legitimacy that I have developed. An intervener's track record is only partially useful, however. An intervener may have been effective in the past because it has acted only in more straightforward cases, so it might not be similarly effective in the future. Therefore, it is also important to consider the institutional characteristics of the intervener to assess whether its track record is likely to be repeated.

Some, such as Daniele Archibugi (2005), doubt the legitimacy of *all* current agents of humanitarian intervention, and argue that only reformed or new agents could be legitimate. If this view is correct, no one should intervene until we develop intervening agents that are more satisfactory. As will become apparent, my reading of the current situation is less pessimistic. As argued above, it is not necessary for an intervener to be *fully* legitimate for its intervention to be justified, although, of course, full legitimacy is preferable. It is necessary, however, for an intervener to have *an adequate degree of* legitimacy. Given that a large number of the humanitarian interventions previously undertaken have had some degree of success as defined in Chapter 3 (and are likely to continue to do so), a number of the current agents of humanitarian intervention are likely to possess some degree of legitimacy.[14] Whether this is sufficient for an adequate degree of legitimacy largely depends on the other morally relevant factors, but, overall, we should expect a number of current interveners to meet the threshold required for an adequate degree of legitimacy. Hence, a number of interveners are likely to possess the *right* to intervene. A further concern is who, amongst these, is the *most* legitimate agent of humanitarian intervention—who has the *duty* to intervene.

In what follows, I consider the five main potential interveners in descending order of legitimacy: (*a*) NATO, (*b*) states and coalitions of the willing, (*c*) the UN, (*d*) regional and subregional organizations, and (*e*) private military companies. This ranking can be only approximate at best. Given the degree to which circumstances can affect an intervener's effectiveness (as well as other factors, such as its local external representativeness), interveners that are generally less legitimate may, in specific cases, be more legitimate and therefore sometimes be the preferred choice.

7.3.1 NATO

Amongst currently existing interveners, NATO would probably rank as the most likely to be legitimate. This is because of its effectiveness, which can be seen both in its success in previous missions (such as in Bosnia and in Kosovo) and in its level of military infrastructure. In Bosnia, the 1995 NATO air campaign forced the Bosnian Serbs to agree to peace after three unsuccessful years of UNPROFOR intervention. In Kosovo, although NATO's bombing campaign at first escalated the extent of the Serbian oppression, it avoided ethnic cleansing on the scale of that seen in Bosnia. The effectiveness of these two operations was no coincidence. NATO has tremendous military and logistical resources (including a well-equipped rapid-reaction force, the NATO Response Force). In addition, when NATO does intervene, it tends to do so with the commitment to ensure, firstly, a rapid resolution to the humanitarian crisis and, secondly, long-term peace and stability. As Terry Terriff (2004*a*: 128) asserts, NATO's post-conflict reconstruction efforts in the Balkans demonstrate its desire to stabilize these regions in order to provide democracy, rule of law, and human rights.[15] Even if NATO's interventions tend to be ultimately due to political, rather than humanitarian, motivations (e.g. to reassert its relevance), this is not necessarily problematic, given the rejection of the importance of an intervener's motives in Chapter 6.

In addition, NATO intervention is likely to be internally representative. Its decision-making depends on consensus; each member state must consent to the use of force. Every NATO member state is a democracy and, as argued in Chapter 5, democratic states are most likely to be responsive to their citizens' opinions on the use of force. It follows that NATO decision-making is likely to be responsive to the opinions of citizens within the alliance.[16]

It is questionable, however, whether NATO always uses humanitarian means. As we saw in Chapter 4, the Kosovo intervention was heavily criticized for its sole use of airpower and its reluctance to deploy ground troops. The bombing campaign damaged vital infrastructure and killed a number of civilians, far more than probably would have occurred if the alliance had been willing to undertake slightly more risky operations or to employ ground troops.[17] On the other hand, Stromseth (2003: 249) claims that NATO made great efforts to conform to the law of armed conflict in the Kosovo campaign. Moreover, even if NATO's fidelity to the principles of *jus in bello* was doubtful in Kosovo, Terriff (2004*a*: 128) expects NATO to undertake any future humanitarian intervention as humanely as possible, with a minimum number of civilian casualties.

That said, NATO has faced two major challenges that have raised doubts over its purposes and capabilities. The first is disagreement over potential members of NATO, most notably the former-Soviet states Ukraine and Georgia. This has called into question the unity and direction of NATO, and its role in the post-Cold War world vis-à-vis Russia and the EU.[18] The second is the difficulty that the International Security Assistance Force (ISAF) in Afghanistan has had in securing the requisite troop numbers. Certain NATO members, such as Germany and Italy, have been reluctant to contribute their troops both in general and in the Taliban strongholds of the south (Whitlock 2009). This has raised doubts over whether any future humanitarian intervention conducted by NATO would have sufficient commitment. This should be put in the context, however, of what is already a sizeable and sustained commitment—as of June 2009, 61,130 troops (NATO 2009: 1)—of NATO members in the notoriously harsh conditions of Afghanistan.

Despite these challenges, if it is willing to intervene, NATO is still likely to be the most legitimate agent, primarily because of its effectiveness. What matters most for legitimacy is the intervener's likely success at halting the humanitarian crisis and NATO is, at the moment, the agent most likely to be successful, given its substantial military, political, and financial capabilities. But when is NATO willing to act? Although NATO now has a much broader notion of security and has widened the geographical scope of its mandate, it remains essentially a collective defence organization, and this determines its decision-making (Terriff 2004*a*). Hence, in most cases it lacks the willingness to undertake humanitarian intervention. This does not undermine its legitimacy when it *does* act (as argued in the previous chapter, selectivity does not harm an intervener's legitimacy), but it does mean that we need to consider other options.

7.3.2 States and coalitions of the willing

The track record of humanitarian intervention by states and coalitions of the willing is somewhat uneven, but, on the whole, shows that they tend to be effective (Seybolt 2007: 271–2). On the one hand, the following interventions by states and coalitions of the willing were probably not effective: the US-led mission in Somalia to protect humanitarian corridors in 1992[19]; French intervention in Rwanda in 1994, which was too late to stop the genocide and instead halted the advance of the Rwandan Patriotic Front—a Tutsi force, thereby allowing the unchecked exodus of the *interahamwe* murder squads to

DR Congo; and the 2002 French intervention in Côte d'Ivoire to halt growing violence, which has arguably exacerbated the situation.

On the other hand, the following interventions by states and coalitions of the willing were probably successful: India's 1971 intervention in East Pakistan that brought an end to the Pakistani oppression of Bengalis (Wheeler 2000: 55); Tanzania's 1979 intervention in Uganda that removed Idi Amin from power (Wheeler 2000: 111); France's 1979 intervention in the Central African Republican that engineered a bloodless coup against Emperor Bokassa (ICISS 2001*b*: 63); the creation by the US, the UK, and France of safe havens and no-fly zones in northern Iraq to protect the Kurds in 1991; the Australian-led 1999 intervention to protect the East Timorese from the Indonesian army after the Timorese had voted for independence; and the British intervention in Sierra Leone in 2000 to prevent the United Nations Mission in Sierra Leone (UNAMSIL) from collapse.[20]

Overall, then, the number of successful interventions by states are greater than the number of unsuccessful interventions. Can we expect this trend to continue? Much depends on which particular state intervenes. In particular, many mid- and large-sized Western, liberal democratic states have the required military and non-military resources, and are therefore likely to be effective. But this effectiveness is likely to be limited: a number of these states would face a high level of local resistance. For instance, Archibugi (2005: 224) argues that, after the war on Iraq, the US does not have credibility in the eyes of the world to carry out humanitarian intervention. Where it does intervene, it is likely to face extreme local opposition (which can harm the chances of a successful outcome) and lack local perceived legitimacy. Similarly, ex-colonial masters intervening in their former colonies may also be highly unpopular amongst the local inhabitants. Such states may also lack global perceived legitimacy, which will also harm an intervener's likely effectiveness. Conversely, non-Western states, which might face less resistance, are limited to intervention in nearby or neighbouring states at best, given their lack of resources.

Nearly all states are highly selective interveners, choosing to stand by on many occasions. As with NATO, this does not necessarily undermine the legitimacy of a state's humanitarian intervention. What it does mean, however, is that, on many occasions, no state is willing to undertake humanitarian intervention. So, again, we have to look for the next best option.

7.3.3 The UN

The discussion that follows will consider intervention by the UN itself, rather than UN-authorized humanitarian intervention. The latter option—Security

Council-authorized intervention—encompasses a number of possible inter-veners, including NATO, states (or coalitions of the willing), and regional organizations. To provide a more detailed analysis, I consider these options individually.

UN interventions have been subject to a number of criticisms, which have led many to doubt its suitability to carry out humanitarian intervention. To start with, when the UN has intervened itself, the results have often been mixed at best. The following three interventions, for example, are often highlighted for their questionable effectiveness. First, in Bosnia as many as 230,000 people died during the UNPROFOR mission (ICISS 2001*b*: 94). Second, the UN mission in Rwanda, UNAMIR, was unable to prevent the genocide of Tutsis and moderate Hutus, and was even downgraded in the middle of the killing. Third, the 1999 UN intervention in Sierra Leone, UNAMSIL, was unable to stop the atrocities committed by the RUF and was at the point of collapse until the British intervention in 2000 (ICISS 2001*b*: 109).

The lack of success of these missions is frequently attributed to the way in which UN operations are undertaken (e.g. Seybolt 2007: 273). Rather than having a standing army of its own, readily available for quick deployment, the UN has to rely on ad hoc contributions of troops from member states. Member states are reluctant to commit their soldiers and, as a result, UN missions often do not have enough troops to fulfil their mandates. An example is the recent United Nations Mission in Darfur (UNAMID), which has had real difficulties in getting up to its full strength of 26,000 personnel. Western states, in particular, have shown a reluctance to contribute troops, which is unfortunate since their troops tend to be the best trained and to have the most equipment (Bellamy and Williams 2009).

Furthermore, the system of ad hoc troop deployment is laborious. First, it takes time for states to decide whether they will volunteer troops. If they do decide to commit troops, deployment can be painfully slow. For instance, after NATO intervention in Kosovo, it took the UN 'over a year to deploy an adequate number of civilian police (CIVPOL), which led to the absence of police in regions and was a key contribution to the initial failure to establish the rule of law' (Bhatia 2003: 79). In addition to delays in deployment, it can also take the Security Council much time to authorize a UN intervention in the first place.

When the troops do actually arrive, they frequently lack the necessary equipment. They also tend to lack standardized equipment and many have inadequate training (Kinloch-Pichat 2004: 176). Hence, according to Carl Conetta and Charles Knight: '[t]he UN peace operations system is . . . like a volunteer fire department in which all the firefighting assets are privately owned, and no assurance exists that volunteers will deploy to fires on time or with all of their necessary equipment in tow' (1995: 6). In the field, there is frequently a lack of clear lines of command and control, so that it is not clear whose orders troops should be following, the orders of the UN commander or the orders of their national commander. Troops also have trouble integrating; the multinational make-up of the force means that troops speak different languages and have different cultures (Kinloch-Pichat 2004: 176–7).

In addition to these problems of ineffectiveness, Stephen Kinloch-Pichat (2004: 178) argues that a lack of discipline, amoral personal behaviour, and the corruption of the contingents participating in UN missions have been recurrent themes in UN interventions. The difficulty of legally sanctioning those involved in violations of human rights exacerbates these problems (Kinloch-Pichat 2004: 186). Hence, UN troops do not always seem to show adequate fidelity to the principles of *jus in bello*.

All that said, it is important not to over-exaggerate these problems. There have been several improvements to the UN's procedures and capabilities. For instance, the Security Council is now more willing to give its troops a civilian protection mandate supported by Chapter VII authorization (unlike many of the UN operations in the early 1990s). Under the current UN Secretary General, Ban Ki-Moon, the Department of Peacekeeping Operations (DPKO) has been reorganized and the Department of Field Support has been created, which aims to provide financial, logistical, and technical support and expertise to UN peace operations. The UN has also improved its flexibility, being able to shift forces between missions (e.g. from Liberia to Côte d'Ivoire). In addition, it has worked to improve its forces' fidelity to the principles of *jus in bello*. The DPKO makes a point of highlighting that holding personnel accountable is a 'major priority' and it argues that it 'has adopted a comprehensive three-pronged strategy (prevention, enforcement, and remediation) to address the issue of sexual exploitation and abuse by UN personnel' (UN 2008*b*: 2). The DPKO also highlights its relative cost-effectiveness: '[w]hen costs to the UN per peacekeeper are compared to the costs of troops deployed by the US, other developed states, the North Atlantic Treaty Organization (NATO) or regional organizations, the United Nations is the least expensive option by far' (UN 2008*b*: 2).

Moreover, the difficulties that UNAMID has had in getting up to strength in Darfur and the reluctance of certain Western states to contribute to major UN peace operations should be put into the context of what is a boom time for UN peace operations. According to the DPKO (UN 2009), as of May 2009, there are 114,577 troops, police, observers, and other officials serving on 16 UN peace operations. Moreover, the frequently highlighted inefficiencies of the UN are, in practice, often overshadowed by the understated, but notable, successes that it has with its peace operations. Even in the three operations discussed above, which are often presented as examples of the UN's ineffectiveness, UN intervention was partially effective and clearly better than no intervention at all. First, in Bosnia, the UN intervention provided humanitarian aid to 4.3 million victims and frustrated the war aims of Bosnian Serbs and the Milosevic government for a greater Serbia (Gizelis and Kosek 2005: 370; ICISS 2001*b*: 94). Second, in Rwanda, Roméo Dallaire was widely credited for protecting a number of civilians, who would have been slaughtered if it were not for his leadership. Third, the UN mission in Sierra Leone, even though it needed support from the British, has since largely stabilized the country and has helped to establish a war crimes tribunal.

Overall, then, the UN has a significant resources gap because of its reliance on ad hoc troops and this gap undermines its effectiveness. Although the UN is not the most effective agent, even its interventions commonly regarded as ineffective have achieved some measure of success. And, given its recent improvements, we can probably expect humanitarian intervention by the UN to have some success in the future. Indeed, the UN may sometimes be the most legitimate intervener, particularly when intervention by NATO or militarily capable Western states would face international and local resistance.

7.3.4 Regional and subregional organizations

In general, intervention by regional organizations has had varied results. The central problem is that the majority of regional organizations do not possess the infrastructure, expertise, mandate, and finance to tackle effectively a humanitarian crisis (Diehl 2005). Of course, as with state intervention, much depends on which particular regional or subregional organization intervenes.

The EU is by far the most capable regional organization and is the only regional organization able to intervene beyond its borders. The Helsinki Headline Goal, adopted in 1999, requires the EU to develop a 60,000-strong military force, to be deployable within sixty days and sustainable for at least one year in the field (Terriff 2004*b*: 152).[21] The EU scaled back these proposals, however, to the less ambitious 'battlegroups' concept, which became operational in January 2007. There are thirteen rapidly deployable battlegroups, each consisting of 1,500 soldiers (and support), two of which are deployable in the field simultaneously for up to 120 days. Although the development of these battlegroups has provided the EU with notable rapid-reaction capability, their limited size and the EU's lack of significant heavy air-lift capacity means that it does not possess the ability to undertake a large-scale humanitarian intervention. In 2003, the EU intervened in Bunia (in DR Congo) in response to growing international concern, but deployed its force (Operation Artemis) only for a short space of time. Similarly, the EU mission in Chad and the Central African Republic (EUFOR Tchad/RCA) in 2008 provided some civilian protection, but it was too small (around 3,000 troops) and lacked the mandate to provide widespread protection to the threatened population (Germain and Herz 2008).

Article 4 (h) of the Charter of the African Union allows for the AU to intervene in grave circumstances (war crimes, genocide, and crimes against humanity) in countries that have signed up to the treaty. There are also proposals for an African Standby Force, in the control of the AU, to be in place by 2010. This would comprise five brigades of around 4,000 military personnel that would be able to respond to a variety of crises (P. Williams 2008: 314). If put in place, this could be seen as a notable step towards realizing the much-heralded 'African solutions for African problems'.

But, although a great improvement on its predecessor, the Organization of African Unity, the AU suffers from massive shortfalls in funding and equipment, and has relied heavily on external funding and equipment. For instance, the African Union Mission in Somalia (AMISOM) had difficulties in deploying its authorized strength of 8,000 troops, largely due to financial and logistical constraints (Center on International Cooperation 2008: 3). Similarly, its mission in Darfur, AMIS, faced serious shortfalls in military equipment, resources, and even basic supplies, and, as a result, was unable to do much to halt the *janjaweed* raids on the local population. Accordingly, the 'African solutions for African problems' view is misleading, since, as Paul Williams (2008: 316–18) asserts, the problems are not solely African—under the responsibility to protect they are global—and the solutions cannot be solely African either, given the limited capacity of the AU.[22]

ECOWAS is perhaps the most notable subregional organization for humanitarian intervention. It plans to develop a 6,500-strong standby force as part of the African Standby Force, which would give it the ability to deploy 1,500 troops within thirty days, to be followed by the remaining 5,000 troops within ninety days (Holt and Berkman 2006: 69). Previous interventions by ECOWAS, however, have had questionable effectiveness. Although its intervention in Liberia in 1990 (ECOMOG) successfully pushed back the rebel advances and restored law and order in Monrovia, it became more like a party in the conflict and was unable to establish authority in the interior (ICISS 2001*b*: 81–4). In addition, its peacekeepers allegedly committed abuses against a number of civilians and suspected rebels and provided arms support to factions opposed to Charles Taylor, thereby aiding the proliferation of rebel groups (Nowrojee 2004).[23] Similarly, although its 1997 intervention in Sierra

Leone was able to restore the ousted president, rebels remained in control in rural areas and continued to brutalize the civilian population and, in 1999, overran Freetown, murdering thousands before ECOMOG could regain control (ICISS 2001*b*: 107). ECOWAS has also intervened in Côte d'Ivoire, but its efforts stalled and it has had insufficient resources and ultimately necessitated French intervention (Nowrojee 2004). Thus, although ECOWAS has been willing to undertake a long-term engagement in the country concerned, like the AU, and as the recent action in Côte d'Ivoire has demonstrated, it ultimately lacks the funding and resources to intervene successfully.[24]

Other regional organizations have more limited capacity still. Some even have the principle of non-intervention enshrined in their constitutions. An example is the Association of Southeast Asian Nations (ASEAN), which explicitly rejects the notion of intervention to protect people against large-scale abuses of human rights and lacks the provision even for peacekeeping (Emmers 2004: 145).[25]

At the moment, therefore, regional organizations have limited legitimacy. They do not have the military capability to undertake a major intervention, which limits the prospective effectiveness, and ultimately the legitimacy, of any future intervention by a regional organization in response to a large-scale humanitarian crisis. Nonetheless, regional and subregional organizations are often more willing to intervene, given their geographical proximity to the humanitarian crisis, which means that they have a stake in local stability. If they had more resources to undertake humanitarian intervention, they might be willing to intervene more frequently than other agents. Hence, the Stanley Foundation report, *Issues Before the UN's High-Level Panel—The Use of Force*, asserts that '[r]egional organizations are useful for what they can become, not what they are' (2004: 4).

7.3.5 Private military companies

The final option is to hire private military companies (PMCs).[26] PMCs have increasingly become part of the military landscape as many of the traditional functions of the regular military have been outsourced (see Singer 2003*a*).[27] Their use has been well documented in Iraq, where the widely estimated 20,000-plus contractors have been involved in several roles, from providing logistics to protecting key officials. In fact, PMCs have already played significant roles in several previous humanitarian interventions. For instance, in 2007, Pacific Architect Engineers, Inc. were awarded a $250 million contract for the establishment and provision of camps for UNAMID in Darfur. In East Timor, Defence Systems Limited supplied logistical and intelligence for the UN-sanctioned force and DynCorp provided helicopters and satellite communications (Bures 2005: 538). Most notably, in 1995, the government of Sierra Leone employed Executive Outcomes, who, because of their military superiority, were able to successfully end the murderous RUF's siege of Freetown (see Howe 1998).

There are three sorts of role that PMCs could play in humanitarian intervention (see Gantz 2003; P.W. Singer 2003*a*: 184–8). The first is the most likely: PMCs could be used in a non-combat capacity to bolster another intervener's military capabilities. They could provide logistics, lift capacity, military training, communications, and other support services. In doing so, they could improve this agent's effectiveness or make an intervention possible that would otherwise struggle to get off the ground. For instance, a regional organization lacking in lift capacity could hire a PMC to provide transport for its troops. Some of the normative concerns surrounding the use of PMCs are perhaps less serious in this first sort of role, since the PMC would not be providing frontline combat services. Nevertheless, there are still concerns over the openness of the processes by which PMCs win their contracts and the potential for conflicts of interest (Singer 2003*a*: 151–68).

By contrast, the second and third roles involve PMCs in combat. In the second role, PMCs could provide troops or bolster another agent's intervention. For instance, a UN force that is struggling to receive sufficient contributions of troops from member states could hire a PMC to fill the gaps. In addition, PMCs could provide a rapid-reaction force to intervene in response to humanitarian crisis whilst a larger, more long-term UN or regional organization force is being put together. Or, they could be hired to protect key officials and infrastructure.[28] In this second role (like the first), then, PMCs would not be undertaking intervention themselves. Instead, they would be part of a larger, hybridized force, the benefits of which I will discuss in the next section.

In the third potential role, PMCs would undertake humanitarian intervention by themselves. A PMC (or several PMCs) would be hired by a state, a group of states, or an international organization to intervene, to resolve the crisis, and to rebuild afterwards. It is currently unlikely that a PMC would be employed in such a role. To start with, it is doubtful whether PMCs currently have the capacity to take on such a role. Most firms could not deploy and organize the size of force necessary for a major operation (i.e. over 20,000 personnel). There would also be notable political obstacles to PMCs undertaking humanitarian intervention by themselves, given the current levels of political opposition to their use (especially in the Global South).

Furthermore, the use of a PMC in a combat role poses several normative concerns. These include the potentially profit-driven intentions of a private force, which may distract from the humanitarian objectives (Pattison 2008*b*: 144–9), and the lack of regulation of the private military industry, meaning that private contractors can violate principles of external *jus in bello* largely with impunity (Pattison 2008*b*: 150–3).[29] The use of PMCs also raises concerns over internal *jus in bello* and, in particular, an intervener's responsibility of care for those fighting on its behalf. Deaths of private contractors are seldom covered by the media. Political leaders are often less concerned about the loss of private contractors than regular soldiers and private contractors do not receive the same level of support if injured in action (Krahmann 2008: 260). In addition, private contractors have frequently failed to receive the correct equipment promised to them when signing up (such as flak jackets) and, accordingly, have been at much greater risk than necessary. For instance, Blackwater have been sued for allegedly sending an undermanned and poorly equipped detail by the families of four ex-employees killed in Fallujah (*USA Today* 2007). More-over, PMCs are unlikely to be effective when undertaking a combat role. Although they might have the requisite military muscle, they are likely to lack many of the other qualities of effectiveness necessary for successful interven-tion, such as non-military resources, a suitable post-war strategy for building and maintaining a peaceful resolution to the crisis, and, more indirectly, perceived legitimacy at the local and global levels (which may be harmed by the perceptions of the force as mercenaries).

7.3.6 Hybrid solutions

Thus far, I have largely focused on intervention by agents acting singularly. A growing trend, however, has been for humanitarian intervention to be undertaken by agents acting together in hybrid operations. There are three forms of hybrid operation.[30] The first, 'sequential operations', involve differ-ent interveners succeeding each other. This includes what Alex Bellamy and Paul Williams (2009: 47) call 'spearhead' operations, where Western troops prepare the security environment on the ground in order to hand over to the UN or a regional organization. Examples are the Australian-led intervention in East Timor (INTERFET), before the establishment of the UN transitional administration, and French Operation Licorne in the Côte d'Ivoire before the arrival of the ECOWAS force. Second, 'parallel operations' involve interveners operating in response to the same crisis, but under different command. Such operations often involve a more militarily capable Western state providing additional enforcement capabilities or the threat of such force. Examples include NATO action in Bosnia in support of UNPROFOR, British action in Sierra Leone in support of UNAMSIL, and Operation Artemis in support of MONUC in DR Congo in 2003. The third, 'integrated operations', involve interveners operating in response to the same crisis under unified or joint command, such as the UN–AU operation in Darfur (UNAMID).

There has also been a growth in supportive arrangements, where one agent assists another's intervention. These involve, first, the supply of equipment and training by another intervener to bolster capacity, such as the US' Global Peace Operations Initiative, which aims to provide 75,000 extra peacekeepers worldwide. Second, they involve the provision of funding and equipment (including from PMCs) for a particular operation. For instance, the EU provided $120 million for the AU's force in Darfur and NATO provided lift capacity (Piiparinen 2007: 371).

Hybrid operations and supportive arrangements can combine the strengths of particular agents and, as a result, perhaps offer the best hope for effective—and legitimate—humanitarian intervention. On the one hand, they provide Western states, NATO, and the EU with a politically viable way to intervene without committing themselves to a drawn-out occupation. On the other hand, they offer the UN (and regional organizations) much-needed funding and military capability (including access to the rapid-reaction capabilities of the NATO Response Force and EU battlegroups), and can utilize the UN's expertise in longer, peace-building operations. In addition, hybrid operations enhance flexibility and can make possible an intervention that would otherwise struggle to get off the ground (such as the AU's operation in Darfur). Indeed, some of the most successful interventions have been part of a larger hybrid operation (e.g. British action in Sierra Leone and the Australian-led intervention in East Timor). In fact, *most* recent humanitarian interventions have been hybrid missions and future interventions can be expected to continue to rely on a combination of agents. Hybrid solutions have, for these reasons, been receiving much support.[31]

Some, however, see such solutions as a way for Western states to circumvent their duties. Touko Piiparinen cites the objection that 'the provision of logistical, technical, and training support by NATO and the EU may be used as a facade, a rhetorical tool, by which Western countries portray themselves as "doing their bit" in alleviating African suffering, when in reality the AU urgently needs not only Western hardware, but also professional soldiers from the world's most sophisticated armies' (2007: 376). Even when the West does provide military personnel (such as in a spearhead role), these troops, Bellamy and Williams (2009: 52) argue, might save more lives if they were integrated into a larger UN operation. As such, although the increased flexibility and the potential combination of strengths of hybrid options can be beneficial, they should not be seen as a panacea. It is important that they are not regarded by the West as a way of avoiding contributing troops. Moreover, hybrid solutions can be only the sum of their parts and, as we have seen, the parts—the individual agents—suffer from a number of problems.

7.3.7 Who should intervene and the responsibility to protect

We have seen then that, overall, no current agent of humanitarian intervention is fully legitimate according to the conception of legitimacy outlined. Nevertheless, a number of agents of intervention—NATO, certain states, the UN, certain regional organizations, and hybrid combinations—would probably possess an adequate degree of legitimacy in many cases. Of these agents, NATO or a hybrid operation that pairs a major Western power (i.e. the EU or NATO) with the UN would be most desirable, given that it would probably be the most effective. Let us now use this survey of the various agents to respond to the two central sets of questions identified in Chapter 1. The first two questions are: (*a*) 'Who has the right to intervene?' and (*b*) 'Who has the duty to intervene?'

As discussed above, in response to question (*a*), any intervener that possesses *an adequate degree of* legitimacy has the right to act (providing that they have just cause and are engaged in humanitarian intervention). It will often be the case that several of the current interveners will possess an adequate degree of legitimacy, since they will make an improvement in the enjoyment of the human rights of those suffering the crisis (and largely possess the other qualities). As such, a number of interveners may possess the *right* to intervene in a particular situation. Of course, there will be cases, such as Tibet and Chechnya, where no agent could effectively, and thus legitimately, intervene.

In response to question (*b*), it is the *most* legitimate agent of humanitarian intervention that has the *duty* to act. The *most* legitimate agent will often be NATO or a hybrid operation that pairs a major Western power with the UN. If this agent(s) fails to intervene, the duty falls on the next most legitimate intervener, and so on.[32]

Let me now consider who should undertake humanitarian intervention according to the responsibility to protect doctrine. The central question varies according to the interpretation of the responsibility to protect favoured. If we endorse the ICISS version of the doctrine, the question is:

> Amongst the interveners that meet the precautionary principles, who has the duty to intervene when a state is unable or unwilling to halt actual or apprehended large-scale loss of life or ethnic cleansing within its borders?

If we defend the version of the doctrine agreed at the World Summit, the question is:

who has the right to intervene when a state is manifestly failing to prevent genocide, war crimes, ethnic cleansing, and crimes against humanity within its borders and when the Security Council authorizes intervention?

The basic answer that I have defended provides the answer to both questions. That is, when military intervention is required to fulfil the responsibility to protect on both the ICISS and World Summit versions of the doctrine, intervention should be undertaken by a hybrid solution or NATO. If these agents fail to act, the responsibility to protect then falls on states, coalitions of the willing, the UN, and regional organizations (and PMCs) in descending order.

Both versions of the responsibility to protect largely require interveners to possess Security Council authorization. This does not mean that intervention without Security Council authorization would necessarily be illegitimate. Rather, such intervention could not be included under the doctrine (although there is more scope for it to be included under the ICISS doctrine if, for instance, it received authorization under the Uniting for Peace procedure). Nor does this mean that only the UN can discharge the responsibility to protect. Other interveners, providing that they have Security Council authorization (or host state consent), can intervene militarily to fulfil the responsibility.

There is, however, one potentially significant point of difference between the answer to who should intervene according to the ICISS report and the World Summit agreement. In short, when concerned with the latter, the Summit agreement, an intervener's effectiveness is likely to take on greater significance still. This is because this version of the responsibility to protect sets the bar for humanitarian intervention higher: that is when a state is 'manifestly failing' to tackle the 'genocide, ethnic cleansing, crimes against humanity, and war crimes' within its borders. As such, it is likely to be even more important that the humanitarian crisis is tackled successfully. According to the Moderate Instrumentalist Approach, an intervener that is highly likely to tackle effectively such a serious crisis will go a long way to possessing an adequate degree of legitimacy, even without possessing the other characteristics, since it would have a high probability of achieving a success with a particularly large magnitude.[33]

7.4 INADEQUACIES OF THE CURRENT AGENTS AND MECHANISMS

In this chapter, then, I have outlined the complete conception of legitimacy—the Moderate Instrumentalist Approach—and considered which current agents have the right to intervene, the duty to intervene, and should discharge the responsibility to protect. My conclusions have been largely positive: a number of interveners will possess the right to intervene in certain cases and there have been some notable improvements in the agents of intervention, particularly with the rise of hybrid solutions. That said, there is significant room for improvement and we cannot be satisfied with the current abilities of interveners. Indeed, the inadequacies of the current situation have been highlighted by three major humanitarian crises.

The first is Somalia, often cited as the archetypal 'failed state' because it has not had an effective government since 1991. When the Union of Islamic Courts gained control of Mogadishu in 2006, Ethiopia intervened (with non-humanitarian intentions) in support of the weak Transitional Federal Government. The subsequent conflict and power vacuum have significantly worsened the already-poor situation of the Somali citizens. According to Human Rights Watch's *World Report 2009*, both sides in the conflict have committed war crimes 'with complete impunity and with devastating impact on Somalia's civilian population' (2009: 110). The report also documents that more than three million Somalis are in need of humanitarian assistance, but attacks on humanitarian workers and piracy have impeded delivery (Human Rights Watch 2009: 110). The AU launched a peacekeeping mission, AMISOM, in 2007, but this has been significantly understrength and the few troops that have been deployed have been restricted to protecting basic installations in Mogadishu.

The second is the DR Congo. Since the removal from power of President Mobutu Sese Seko in 1997, the DR Congo has been subject to major fighting between rival factions, which have been supported by Burundi, Rwanda, and Uganda on the one side and Chad, Angola, Namibia, and Zimbabwe on the other. According to the International Rescue Committee (2008), this conflict has resulted in around 5.4 million deaths since 1998, making it the most deadly conflict since World War II. The UN peacekeeping mission, MONUC, deployed in 2001, has been unable to tackle fully the humanitarian crisis. In 2003, the French led an EU mission (Operation Artemis) to contain clashes in Ituri, but this intervention was only short lived. Subsequent deaths and displacements in 2005 resulted in the UN describing eastern DR Congo as the 'world's worst humanitarian crisis' (in International Crisis Group 2008*a*). In 2008, a further 400,000 people fled their homes, pushing the total number of displaced persons in the North and South Kivus to over 1.2 million (Human Rights Watch 2009: 61). To be sure, MONUC has improved civilian protection in certain areas. Yet, violent clashes have continued elsewhere as it has struggled with limited capacity and troop numbers (Human Rights Watch 2009: 64–5). For instance, Médecins Sans Frontières (2009) have criticized

MONUC for failing to protect civilians in the Haut-Uélé region from the Lord's Resistance Army, which has massacred more than 900 civilians since September 2008.[34]

The third is the conflict in Darfur. This has led to 300,000 deaths and the displacement of 2.5 million people (UN 2008*a*). In 2004, the AU authorized a peacekeeping force, but this struggled for enough money to keep running, with its troops going unpaid for months at a time, and perpetually ran short of basic supplies, such as fuel and food (Polgreen 2006: 14). In the few places where it was deployed, it has had some success. But in the vast swathes of Darfur without an AU presence, the *janjaweed* (with the support of the Sudanese government) continued to terrorize and to murder the local population. The Security Council passed a number of resolutions on the crisis, but these were watered down at the insistence of the Chinese, who have significant oil interests in Sudan (Farer 2005*a*: 246). In July 2007, the Security Council authorized the hybrid UN/AU force (UNAMID). The deployment of UNAMID, however, was severely delayed by the lack of cooperation from the Sudanese government and the slowness of the contributors (UN 2008*a*). It has also faced massive shortfalls in troop numbers, as well as transport and aviation assets (such as helicopters) (UN 2008*a*).[35] In the meantime, the Sudanese government, *janjaweed*, and other militia have continued to torment the civilians of Darfur.

These three crises, together with the preceding analysis, demonstrate that the current agents and mechanisms of humanitarian intervention face two serious problems. First, there are too many times when humanitarian intervention should be undertaken, but is not. Too often NATO and capable states fail to act or act too late, and Security Council authorization for UN operations is too often stymied. The result is that many humanitarian crises continue unabated. Second, even when there is intervention, no existing intervener is fully legitimate. This means that, when humanitarian intervention *does* occur, it will probably have some significant flaws. In particular, the intervener(s) is likely to have at least one of the following failings: (*a*) it will have deficiencies in its local external effectiveness and therefore fail to tackle the humanitarian crisis fully; (*b*) it will lack global external effectiveness and so harm the enjoyment of human rights globally; (*c*) it will be internally ineffective and so harm its own citizens' enjoyment of human rights; (*d*) it will show inadequate fidelity to the principles of internal *jus in bello*; (*e*) it will show inadequate fidelity to the principles of external *jus in bello*; (*f*) it will not be properly internally representative and, consequently, fail to represent fully the opinions of those providing the resources needed to undertake the intervention; and (*g*) it will be lacking in local external representativeness and therefore fail to take into account properly the opinions of those suffering the humanitarian crisis. Thus, it seems clear that there needs to be significant improvements to the agents and mechanisms of humanitarian intervention. It is to these I now turn.

NOTES

1. See Bellamy (2006*b*) for some further problems with such indeterminacy.
2. Section 8.1 on reforming international law in the next chapter has further discussion of these issues.
3. See, further, Chesterman and von Einsiedel (2005: 755–6). It might be claimed that the Security Council does have one major draw: it has a significant ability to constrain agents. That is, intervention opposed by the Security Council is much less likely to go ahead than intervention opposed by the international community in general. This means that the Security Council's decision on whether an intervener would be legitimate has more power to ensure compliance. As argued in Chapter 2, however, it is far from certain that the Security Council does have the ability to constrain agents, especially powerful ones.
4. Franck's primary focus is on cases where humanitarian intervention is morally justifiable but of questionable legality according to a strict reading of the UN Charter.
5. See, further, Catherine Lu (2006*a*: 205), who argues that non-state perspectives should be included since it is the protection of the members of the wider community of humanity that ultimately grounds the justification of humanitarian intervention. Farer (2005*a*: 220) argues for a jury of leading state officials, the UN Secretary General, heads of prominent NGOs, religious leaders, public intellectuals, and newspaper editors.
6. As such, 'jurying' is best seen as a metaphor. It is less formalized than a domestic jury is and global 'jurors' may not meet the standards that we would expect in a domestic setting. The decisions would also be political rather than legal (although they may gain legal force over time).
7. These three categories are based on Tan's discussion (2006*a*) of the duty to protect. I also discuss these three alternatives in Pattison (2008*c*). For a reply to my article, see Roff (2009).
8. deLisle (2001: 550) seems to endorse this position.
9. These difficulties in determining causality may also apply to the institutional cosmopolitan case for the general, unassigned duty to intervene, considered in Chapter 1.
10. That these relationships are not sufficiently strong poses even greater problems for this solution when adopting the General Right Approach, since these relationships are required to *generate*, rather than *specify*, the duty to intervene.

11. Tan cites the opposite problem where 'there may be more than one potential agent with historical ties to those in need of protection, in which case the agency problem reappears' (2006*a*: 102).

12. It may be responded that a non-ideal institutional arrangement is a necessary stepping stone to achieve an ideal institutional solution. But this is speculative and the transaction costs in terms of the ineffective prevention of human suffering may be significant (and more certain).

13. Indeed, this is the reason why Tan (2006*a*: 102) shies away from placing the duty to intervene on the most capable agent.

14. Recall that I argued in Chapter 3 that an intervener's success should not be measured simply by whether it has succeeded in its mandate, secured the peace, or protected civilians, but more broadly by its effects on the enjoyment of human rights (especially basic rights) over the long term, compared to the counterfactual.

15. This likely effectiveness may, however, be diminished by the lack of the perceived legitimacy of participating members.

16. In this context, NATO is also likely to be consistent with the Resources Argument because the US, which contributes the most towards NATO interventions, usually has the most control in NATO's decision-making.

17. Its campaign in Afghanistan has also been criticized for indiscriminate bombing. See, for instance, Human Rights Watch's report (2008) *'Troops in Contact' Air-strikes and Civilian Deaths in Afghanistan*, which highlights the violation of non-combatant immunity when air strikes are not pre-planned (although, according to this report, civilian casualties have been minimized when the strikes are pre-planned).

18. See Evans (2008*b*: 192–3) on the potential future roles for NATO.

19. This intervention is generally regarded as unsuccessful, largely because of the infamous 'Blackhawk Down' incident in which a number of US Rangers' bodies were dragged through the streets of Mogadishu, and also because Somalia remains a failed state (e.g. Gizelis and Kosek 2005: 369). The Supplementary Volume to the ICISS report (2001*b*: 97) suggests, however, that the mission was not without its success; the impact of the famine was alleviated and perhaps only 50,000–100,000 of the 1.5 million threatened by starvation actually died. Robert Oakley (1993) also claims that it was successful.

20. For a defence of the success of British action in Sierra Leone, see P. Williams (2002).

21. See Olsen (2002) and Rasmussen (2002) for further analysis of EU plans for a reaction force.

22. The 'African solutions for African problems' view is also problematic because it can be used by Western states to justify their inaction and by certain African leaders to block potentially justifiable non-African humanitarian intervention (P. Williams 2008: 320–2).

23. ECOWAS redeployed in Liberia in 2003 after the country had descended into civil war again in 2000. Its intervention calmed the situation in the capital and paved

the way for the deployment of 15,000 UN troops, although it was not able to subdue the violence elsewhere (Nowrojee 2004).

24. Similar criticisms are made of the ECOWAS mission in Liberia (ECOMIL) by the *Report of the African Union–United Nations Panel on Modalities for Support to African Union Peacekeeping Operations* (UN 2008c: 12), which highlights the inability of ECOWAS to fulfil its mandate because of an acute lack of resources.

25. Although the idea of an ASEAN peacekeeping force has been proposed by Indonesia, the Thai and Singaporean foreign ministers rejected the idea, the latter arguing that '[w]e think that ASEAN is not really a security organization or a defense organization' (Washington Post 2004).

26. I consider this option in more detail—and its potential problems—in Pattison (forthcoming *b*). Also see Bellamy, Williams, and Griffin (2004: 203–9), D. Brooks (2000), D. Brooks and Chorev (2008), Bures (2005), the Foreign Affairs Committee (2002), the Foreign and Commonwealth Office's Green Paper (2002), Gantz (2003), Ghebali (2006), O'Hanlon and Singer (2004), P.W. Singer (2003*a*: 182–7; 2003*b*), and Spearin (2005).

27. These firms are sometimes referred to as 'private security companies', 'private military firms', or 'private military and security companies'. I adopt Simon Chesterman and Chia Lehnardt's definition of PMCs as 'firms providing services outside their home states with the potential for use of lethal force, as well as of training and advice to militaries that substantially affects their war-fighting capacities' (2007: 3). As Chesterman and Lehnardt note, this definition does not rely on the dubious distinction between 'offensive' and 'defensive' operations, which is sometimes used to distinguish between 'private military companies' and 'private security companies'.

28. A number of humanitarian organizations, such as CARE, Save the Children, and World Vision, have hired PMCs to improve the security of their personnel and infrastructure in the field. See Olsson (2007), Spearin (2008), and Stoddard, Harmer, and DiDomenico (2008).

29. I discuss these problems further in Pattison (forthcoming *b*). There are a number of other normative problems raised by PMCs, which may also count against their use for humanitarian intervention (even in minor roles). These include the undermining of democratic accountability and deeper concerns about the justifiability of private force. I consider these in Pattison (2008*b*; forthcoming *a*).

30. I draw here on the Center on International Cooperation (2008: 10). For further discussion of hybrid operations, see Bellamy and Williams (2009: 47–9).

31. For instance, Romeo Dallaire has argued that 'a mixture of mobile African Union troops supported by NATO soldiers equipped with helicopters, remotely piloted vehicles, night-vision devices and long-range special forces could protect Darfur's displaced people in their camps and remaining villages, and eliminate or incarcerate the Janjaweed' (in Piiparinen 2007: 368).

32. By asserting that hybrid agents possess the duty to intervene, it might be claimed that the answer that I have presented is vague since it does not identify one

specific agent as having the duty to intervene. We will therefore run into the problems surrounding the unassigned duty to intervene considered in Chapter 1. In response, although hybrid solutions have various combinations, when faced with a particular crisis it may be very clear what sort of hybrid solution should be adopted. It might, for instance, be clear that UN intervention supported by a strong firefighting force from NATO would be the most likely to be effective. In such cases, it falls on the potential participants both to offer their services and to coordinate an effective response to the humanitarian crisis.

33. Moreover, it might be argued that, since the interveners will possess UN Security Council authorization (or have host state consent), concerns over abuse will largely diminish and an intervener's effectiveness becomes even more important still. I argued in Chapter 2, however, that UN Security Council authorization will do little to forestall abusive intervention.

34. Also see Wild (2009) and the reply by Alan Doss (2009), Special Representative of the Secretary General for the DR Congo.

35. For further criticisms of the international intervention in Darfur, see de Waal (2007) and Tinsley (2009).

8

Reforms to the Agents and Mechanisms of Humanitarian Intervention

From the discussion in Chapter 7, it is clear that we need to improve the agents and mechanisms of humanitarian intervention so that we can legitimately tackle egregious violations of human rights on a much more frequent basis. In the words of David Gompert (2006), former president of RAND Europe and Special Assistant to George Bush Sr., we need to develop the *capability to protect* if we are to discharge effectively the *responsibility to protect*. But what can we do to ensure this? Using the conception of legitimacy outlined in the previous chapters, this chapter considers proposals for reform.

I evaluate five sets of proposals. The first three are the codification of criteria for humanitarian intervention in international law, the extension of UN standby arrangements, and the creation of a small cosmopolitan UN force. Although most of these proposals would have some merit if put in place, none would completely tackle the difficulties we currently face. I therefore present two further suggestions for reform. The first is a more long-term aim: the creation of a large-sized cosmopolitan UN force under the control of cosmopolitan democratic institutions. Such an intervener could be fully legitimate according to the complete conception of legitimacy I have outlined. The second is a more short-term goal: the improvement of the capacity of regional organizations to undertake humanitarian intervention. Although this second option might not lead to fully legitimate intervention, it would, firstly, ensure a greater degree of legitimacy than interveners have at the moment (primarily because of increased effectiveness) and, secondly, enable humanitarian intervention to be undertaken on a more frequent basis.

8.1 REFORM OF INTERNATIONAL LAW

As I argued in Chapter 2, there is a gap between international law and legitimacy for humanitarian intervention: an intervener that is legal—one that has UN Security Council authorization—is not necessarily legitimate. One option to improve the legitimacy and frequency of humanitarian intervention is to reform the international law on humanitarian intervention, so that *lex lata* bears more relation to *lex ferenda*, thereby narrowing the gap between legal and legitimate interveners. Most of the proposals for reform of international law suggest doing this by codifying certain criteria for humanitarian intervention in international law. These criteria usually constitute some form of the traditional Just War principles of *jus ad bellum* (i.e. just cause, right intention, legitimate authority, last resort, proportionality, formal declaration of war, and reasonable prospects of success).

The codifying of criteria for humanitarian intervention in international law has received renewed attention with the rise of the responsibility to protect. The suggestion is that those discharging the responsibility to protect by military intervention should meet the 'just cause threshold', possess the 'right authority', and meet the four additional precautionary principles identified by the ICISS (right intention, last resort, proportional means, and reasonable prospects). The ICISS (2001*a*: 74) argues that the Security Council should embrace the set of guidelines outlined in their report to govern the Council's responses to claims for humanitarian intervention. In his report, *In Larger Freedom*, Kofi Annan (2005: 33) proposes that the Security Council should adopt a resolution setting out criteria and expressing its intention to be guided by them when deciding whether to authorize the use of force. Similarly, *A More Secure World* (UN 2004: 57–8) proposes a set of guidelines—'five criteria of legitimacy'—which the Security Council should consider when deciding whether to authorize military force.[1] These guidelines, it argues, should be embodied in declaratory resolutions of the Security Council and General Assembly.[2]

For our purposes, the criteria to be codified in international law would be the same as the factors of legitimacy outlined in the previous chapters: local external effectiveness, global external effectiveness, internal effectiveness, fidelity to the principles of internal and external *jus in bello*, internal representativeness, and local external representativeness. In order to ensure that such a law would apply only to interveners that are engaged in humanitarian intervention, it would also be necessary to include the defining qualities (outlined in Chapter 1) that are implicit in the meaning of humanitarian intervention. An intervener needs: (*a*) to be engaged in military and forcible action; (*b*) to be responding to a situation where there is impending or ongoing grievous suffering or loss of life; (*c*) to be an external agent; and (*d*) to have a humanitarian intention, that is, a predominant purpose of preventing, reducing, or halting the ongoing or impending grievous suffering or loss of life.

In addition (as also suggested in Chapter 1), there would need to be a just cause criterion that sets the bar for justifiable humanitarian intervention fairly high.

These criteria could be codified in international law in three ways.[3] The first strategy is to change international law so that the interveners that are already legal according to the current international law—those that have Security Council authorization—have to meet these criteria as well. If an intervener were not to meet one of these criteria, or if it were not to receive Security Council authorization, then its intervention would be illegal. Given that this proposal adds extra legal restrictions to the status quo, I shall call this the 'Restrictive Approach'. The proposals for criteria for the responsibility to protect usually assume that Security Council authorization will be necessary, so, in effect, adopt this approach.[4] The second approach is to create a new legal right of humanitarian intervention which permits certain agents (such as states and regional organizations) to intervene legally without Security Council authorization as long as they meet these criteria. This is what I will call the 'Additional Right Approach', for it supplements the current international law with an additional legal provision on humanitarian intervention. Interveners authorized by the Security Council would still be legal and would not need to meet these criteria. The third approach is both to create a new legal right of humanitarian intervention and to reform current international law, so that *all* legal interveners, including those that receive the Security Council's authorization, meet these criteria. This is what I will call the 'Comprehensive Right Approach'. Unlike the second approach, which asserts that Security Council-authorized interventions need to meet only the requirements of *current* international law, on this approach Security Council-authorized interventions must also conform to the criteria.

All three approaches aim to improve the legitimacy of interveners. The Restrictive Approach would increase the legitimacy of interveners authorized by the Security Council, but would do little to alter the legitimacy of unauthorized interveners. By contrast, the Additional Right Approach would improve the legitimacy of unauthorized interveners, but would do little to alter the legitimacy of interveners authorized by the Security Council. The third approach, the Comprehensive Right Approach, would improve the legitimacy of both interveners authorized by the Security Council and unauthorized interveners. For this reason, this would seem to be, on the face of it, the best approach.

8.1.1 Objections to the reform of the international law on intervention

There are various objections to reforming international law in each of these three ways. The first set of objections claim that a legal right of humanitarian intervention would allow for *too much* intervention. These objections apply to the Additional Right Approach and the Comprehensive Right Approach since they envisage a new legal right to intervene for unauthorized interveners. (The Restrictive Approach, by contrast, does not propose a new legal right to intervene, but a modification of the current legal provisions on humanitarian intervention.) Some of these objections are similar to those encountered in Chapter 2 and so do not need to be considered in detail.

Thomas Franck and Nigel Rodley argue that a legal right to undertake humanitarian intervention would be 'an unlimited fiat for larger states to oppress their smaller neighbors' (1973: 304). To be sure, the concern is not that such a legal right would lead to more cases of *humanitarian* intervention (as defined in Chapter 1). Rather, it is that, if such a rule existed, states would have more opportunity to undertake abusive (i.e. *non*-humanitarian) intervention. They would cite humanitarian justifications to justify abusive, imperialistic wars. Franck and Rodley (1973: 284) give the example of Hitler's letter to Chamberlain in 1938, which claimed justification for the invasion of Czechoslovakia because of that country's poor treatment of ethnic Germans.[5]

It is questionable, however, whether a new legal right of humanitarian intervention would provide many additional opportunities for states to undertake abusive interventions (Farer 2003: 79). Against this argument, codification of criteria for humanitarian intervention in international law would restrict the opportunity for abuse. Generally, Franck and Rodley's objection underestimates the constraining power of international law and international norms. A large number of states would probably behave as if they were constrained by these criteria. Furthermore, even if a few states attempted to present a mendacious humanitarian justification for an abusive war, it would be difficult for them to maintain, with any plausibility, to their domestic publics and to the international community that they meet these criteria. Such states would have to claim and to appear to meet *all* these criteria. This would be quite demanding. It would not be enough that they simply claim and appear to be acting with a humanitarian intention (which would be all that is required if one were to create instead a new legal right to undertake unauthorized humanitarian intervention without codifying the accompanying normative criteria). As Jarat Chopra and Thomas Weiss assert, a 'high degree of proof could be demanded from states claiming this right of intervention' (1992: 3).

It might be argued that a few states would disregard the opinions of their domestic publics and world public opinion, and undertake abusive intervention anyway. But for these states, establishing a new legal right of humanitarian intervention would not provide many *additional* opportunities to undertake abusive intervention. States that are determined to undertake abusive wars, regardless of the plausibility of justification, would be able to invoke self-defence as the justification for their force. As the Supplementary Volume to the ICISS report suggests, the argument that 'the promotion of an international regime of humanitarian intervention would give interveners a legal pretext ignores one fact. Strong states which are—for reasons good or bad—determined to intervene in a weak state have no shortage of legal rationalizations for their actions' (2001*b*: 67).

A more plausible objection to codifying criteria for humanitarian intervention in international law is that it would not tackle one of the main problems that the current international system faces: the lack of willingness to undertake humanitarian intervention. As Chesterman argues, 'the problem is not the legitimacy of humanitarian intervention but the overwhelming prevalence of inhumanitarian nonintervention' (2003: 54).[6] Reforming the legal architecture of humanitarian intervention is unlikely to mean that states would be more willing to undertake humanitarian intervention. Hence, Chris Brown argues, 'setting up a system of rules designed to prevent them [states] from acting seems a somewhat pointless activity. Instead, we ought to be thinking of ways of encouraging states to intervene more often' (2005: 227).

Although strictly correct, this objection misses the point of the codification of criteria for humanitarian intervention in international law. It should not be seen as an attempt to tackle the problem of reluctance to undertake humanitarian intervention. Instead, its aim is to tackle the other problem that besets current humanitarian intervention: the lack of legitimacy of those that undertake it. By insisting that interveners meet certain normative criteria, an intervener would (we can presume for now) be legitimate if its intervention were legal. The objection claims that reforming international law in this way would lead to *better* humanitarian intervention, when what is really needed are *more* cases of humanitarian intervention. In fact, both are needed: more and better humanitarian intervention. Codification of criteria for humanitarian intervention in international law could help to achieve the latter.

That said, there is a risk that establishing criteria for humanitarian intervention in international law could lead to *too little* humanitarian intervention. Certain states may use the excuse of not meeting the criteria to avoid fulfilling their moral obligation to undertake humanitarian intervention (ICISS 2001*b*: 172). Further, an agent might claim that its intervention would not meet these criteria when in fact it would.

The Restrictive Approach could certainly be criticized for leading to too little humanitarian intervention since, by limiting occasions on which the Security Council could legally authorize humanitarian intervention, it would decrease opportunities for legal humanitarian intervention. The Comprehensive Right Approach may also be subject to this criticism since it too would

restrict the ability of the Security Council to authorize humanitarian intervention. But, for the Additional Right Approach, and perhaps for the Comprehensive Right Approach, this objection might be too harsh. At the
moment, states can use the excuse of illegality for not undertaking humanitarian intervention. They can hide behind the fact that they require Security
Council authorization for their intervention to be legal and never seek that
authorization. Legal criteria that allow states and regional organizations to
intervene, without Security Council authorization, would remove the ability
of states to use the Security Council as an excuse for their inaction.

At this point, the following question might be asked: why is it problematic
if the Restrictive Approach and the Comprehensive Right Approach restrict
humanitarian interveners that do not meet the relevant criteria? Surely, if an
intervener does not satisfy these criteria, it would be illegitimate. But this line
of reasoning is mistaken. In fact, it leads us to a significant problem with the
codifying of legal criteria for humanitarian interveners in international law: it
requires a categorical approach to legitimacy.

On the categorical approach, an intervener that does not meet even one
factor would be illegal. To be legal, an intervener needs to possess *all* of the
relevant qualities. But on the conception of legitimacy I outlined in Chapter 7
(and in Chapter 1), which adopts a scalar approach, an intervener can be
legitimate even though it lacks one of these qualities (depending on the other
factors, the circumstances, and providing that it is effective). So, there is a
problem with creating a new international law using strict criteria: it would
still leave a gap between legal and legitimate interveners. Some legitimate
interveners would be legal, but other legitimate interveners would be illegal.
For instance, State A might intervene effectively to stop genocide in State B
and be careful to conduct intervention in the manner desired by those
suffering the humanitarian crisis, but fail to follow closely principles of
internal *jus in bello* (e.g. it uses conscripts). In this case, although State A
would be legitimate overall, it would be illegal because of its contravention of
the principles of internal *jus in bello*. What is more, if all potential agents were
to obey this reformed international law, a number of legitimate, but illegal,
interveners would not intervene. This could lead to further instances of non-
intervention.[7]

A further problem with codifying criteria for humanitarian intervention in
international law is that achieving the necessary agreement amongst states for
the amendment of existing treaties (such as the UN Charter) or the creation
of a new treaty would be difficult (Bellamy 2008: 622–30). For instance, to
amend the UN Charter, there needs to be two-thirds majority support in the
General Assembly and unanimous support amongst the permanent members
of the Security Council, both of which are unlikely to be achieved (Buchanan

2003: 138; Stromseth 2003: 259; Wheeler 2005*a*: 237). The other potential way of reforming international law—by the gradual evolution of customary international law—is notoriously unpredictable and would be unlikely to deliver these particular criteria.

Moreover, there is significant political opposition to the development of legal criteria for intervention. The agreement reached on the responsibility to protect at the World Summit, for instance, does not refer to the ICISS precautionary principles. Although during the negotiations in the build-up to the Summit several African states endorsed criteria as essential to making the Security Council's decisions transparent, India, Russia, China, and other states, were concerned that such criteria could be used to circumvent the Council (Bellamy 2008: 626) and more generally lead to greater interventionism. By contrast, the US has opposed efforts to establish guidelines on intervention in the fear that it will restrict their freedom of manoeuvre or require them to intervene when they do not wish to (Wheeler 2005*b*: 7).

Even if it were possible to achieve agreement on a new, treaty-based international law permitting humanitarian intervention when certain criteria are met, it is unlikely that states would agree to the criteria outlined above. A different list of criteria would further increase the discrepancy between legal and legitimate interveners. A different list of criteria may also be far more restrictive, including morally dubious clauses (such as a literal account of last resort and a highly restrictive criterion of just cause), which would further decrease the number of humanitarian interventions.[8] As Stromseth asserts, '[a]t worst, a document severely restrictive of any future humanitarian interventions would emerge' (2003: 260).

One solution would be to reject the categorical, criteria-based approach to reform of international law and to adopt a scalar approach instead. Interveners would be legal even though they failed to meet certain criteria. To be specific, they would be required to meet six criteria, four of which are defining conditions necessary for their intervention to be 'humanitarian intervention' (the fifth would be a just cause criterion). The only necessary condition affecting an intervener's legitimacy would be that it is effective. The other factors affecting the legitimacy of humanitarian interveners would not be legal criteria. There would be no legal requirements for an intervener to be internally representative, locally externally representative, have fidelity to the principles of internal *jus in bello*, or have fidelity to the principles of external *jus in bello*.

This scalar approach is not without its difficulties, however. The danger is that there could still be a significant gap between legal and legitimate interveners. This gap, however, would be the inverse of the gap discussed before. All legitimate interveners would be legal, but so too would some *illegitimate* interveners. For instance, State A might be expected to make a small improvement in State B, but be internally and externally unrepresentative and cause a number of civilian casualties. Although its intervention would be illegitimate, it would still be legal.

We therefore face a dilemma: a criteria-based approach to codifying factors in international law may be too restrictive, but a scalar-based approach may be too permissive. This dilemma cannot be easily overcome. Perhaps the most desirable solution would be to adopt a criteria-based approach, but to admit that, on certain occasions, there may be mitigating circumstances that permit the overriding of a particular criterion. This solution gains in persuasiveness if we use the Additional Right Approach, which is the least restrictive of the three.[9] Overall, then, if we use the Additional Right Approach in this way, the creation of a new legal right to undertake humanitarian intervention would be desirable. It would certainly be an improvement on the current situation, which is much more restrictive, given that only interveners authorized by the Security Council can intervene legally.

But, perhaps a more desirable, long-term aim would be to insist not only that there is a legal right to undertake intervention when certain criteria are met, but also that there is a legal duty to do so. This might take the form of giving the responsibility to protect greater legal significance. The international community or a particular agent would be legally obliged to act when a state is failing to protect its civilians. A model might be Article 1 of the Convention on the Prevention and Punishment of the Crime of Genocide which, on some views, legally obliges states to intervene in cases of genocide.[10] Having a legal duty to intervene would also help to tackle the problem of the lack of willingness to undertake intervention. All agents that can intervene legitimately would be not only morally, but also legally, compelled to do so.

In reality, the establishment of a legal duty—or even a new legal right—to undertake humanitarian intervention is unlikely in the near future. As already discussed, it is not foreseeable (in the short term at least) that states would agree on a morally appropriate set of principles. Nonetheless, we need not abandon legal reform. The law on humanitarian intervention can be reformed in another way that does not involve the adoption of criteria. That is, we can reform regional organizations' legal structures so that they can legally undertake humanitarian intervention within their own regions without *ex ante* Security Council authorization (and are legally obliged to intervene). This reform would create an additional legal basis for humanitarian intervention (in the form of a treaty). The starting point here could perhaps be the African Union's (AU's) constitution, which, recall, allows the AU to intervene in grave circumstances in countries that have signed up to the treaty.[11] Additional reform may be needed to permit regional organizations to intervene without Security Council authorization (given that the UN Charter takes precedence over other international treaties). Such reform does not require a criteria-based approach and is therefore not so restrictive. A regional organization could intervene when it deems that its intervention would be legitimate. Consequently, this approach to reforming the international legal system places trust in regional organizations. This trust would be more justified if regional organizations were to adopt the reforms suggested in Section 8.5.

Yet, legal solutions can be only ever part of the solution. Even if we could establish a legal duty to undertake legitimate humanitarian intervention, this duty would have little merit unless it were accompanied by the capacity to undertake humanitarian intervention. Reform of the legal architecture cannot be sufficient. This also applies to the reform of regional legal structures—we need to strengthen regional organizations' capabilities to intervene if the legal right or duty is to have moral significance. In short, legal solutions are not enough: we need practical and political ones. Let us now consider these.[12]

8.2 ENHANCEMENT OF UN STANDBY ARRANGEMENTS

The second potential reform to current mechanisms and agents of humanitarian intervention is for the enhancement of UN standby arrangements. Under the United Nations Stand-by Arrangements System (UNSAS), member states make conditional commitments of troops and resources (such as military formations, specialized personnel, and equipment) to the UN. The resources which member states commit are on standby in their home countries until they are needed. By April 2005, eighty-three member states had signed up to UNSAS.

There are several levels of commitment.[13] These range from providing a list of capabilities that describes the kind of resources that might be made available, to a memorandum of understanding with the UN that specifies exact resources, response times, and conditions for employment. At the rapid deployment level, states pledge resources that can be deployed to a UN mission within thirty days of a traditional mission and within ninety days of a complex mission from receiving the Security Council mandate.

This system provides the UN with a detailed knowledge of the forces and other capabilities that states have available in a state of readiness. H. Peter Langille (2000*a*) notes that the system also helps with planning, training, and preparation, and provides the UN with a variety of potential options if certain member states choose not to participate in an operation. Furthermore, although these arrangements are conditional, it may be that states that have committed to providing resources will be more forthcoming than would have otherwise been the case, since they can plan and budget for participation in a UN peace operation.

A potential solution to the current problems with the agents of humanitarian intervention—and specifically to the problems that the UN faces—is to extend and enhance the UN's standby arrangements (see Roberts 2008: 130). This would involve (*a*) the continued development, expansion, and improvement of UNSAS; (*b*) the creation of rapid-response units, perhaps based on the now-disbanded Stand-by High Readiness Brigade for United Nations Operations (SHIRBRIG), to provide significant capacity at the rapid deployment level;[14] and (*c*) the extension of the mandates of these standby arrangements to clearly include Chapter VII peace enforcement operations such as humanitarian intervention (these arrangements are largely limited to Chapter VI operations).[15]

Such developments would improve the capacity of the UN to undertake humanitarian intervention itself. An enhanced UNSAS would mean that the UN would have a wide knowledge of available troops, have improved planning of humanitarian operations, and be able to deploy troops more quickly. The extension of this conditional agreement may also mean that member states would be more willing to commit troops and resources. Rapid-reaction units would provide the UN with quickly deployable units, readily available to fulfil the mandates of the Security Council.

8.2.1 Does standby mean standing by in the face of a humanitarian crisis?

Little can be said against any moves to enhance these standby arrangements. They would clearly improve the UN's ability to undertake legitimate humanitarian intervention. But these proposals are limited: although an improvement, they fail to resolve some of the fundamental problems that are inherent in the system of voluntary, ad hoc contributions by member states to UN missions.

Like the current UN arrangements, these standby arrangements would face a shortage in a number of areas, including headquarters, communications, and sea and airlift capacity (Langille 2000*a*). The problems with the integration of troops, command and control, and logistical issues are likely to persist. Furthermore, the deployment of UNSAS depends on Security Council approval, which may not be forthcoming, and even if forthcoming, can be time consuming, thereby reducing rapid reaction.

The greatest problem with these arrangements, though, is that, like any UN mission dependent on the ad hoc contribution of troops, deployment under the UNSAS depends on national approval. States retain the prerogative on whether to deploy troops. To be sure, this is not necessarily a bad thing, given the value of internal representativeness. Yet, the requirement of national authorization is often time consuming and can slow deployment (Kinloch-Pichat 2004: 173). This will further decrease rapid-reaction capability. Most significantly, the need for national approval means that, on many occasions, states choose not to provide troops. Consequently, the need for national approval means that a UN mission may lack the necessary number of troops or may not be undertaken at all.

One potential solution would be to remove the need for national approval. Once states had signed up to the UNSAS or a similar model, they would be legally bound to provide troops. In addition to tackling the problem of member states' lack of willingness to contribute troops, this would also mean that states would have to retain their troops in a higher state of readiness and would therefore provide the UN with a stronger rapid-reaction capability. Yet it is unlikely that, firstly, states would sign up to such an agreement and, secondly, even if they did sign up to it, would act as if bound by it. Moreover, even if states did agree to be bound to commit troops under such an automated standby system, the UN missions would lack legitimacy because they would not be internally representative. Those providing the resources for the intervention—the citizens of the various member states who signed up to UNSAS or a similar alternative—would have no say in whether, where, and how these resources are used.[16]

Overall, then, enhancing UN standby arrangements cannot be the solution to the problems with the current mechanisms and agents of humanitarian intervention because such standby arrangements suffer from the same inherent weaknesses as the UN ad hoc national contingents (Kinloch-Pichat 2004: 175). That is, with a *standby* system, states will simply *stand by* in the face of a humanitarian crisis on too many occasions. This inherent problem of UN standby forces cannot be overcome easily. Perhaps a better option would be to concentrate instead on developing a UN *standing* force. Conetta and Knight argue that '[i]f the goal is a truly rapid, multilateral capability to deploy for peace operations, there is no good substitute for a UN standing force' (1995: xiii). The next section will consider whether they are right.

8.3 CREATION OF A (SMALL) COSMOPOLITAN UN FORCE

There have been many proposals for a UN standing army, from Trygve Lie (the first UN Secretary General) in the 1950s, Brian Urquhart (a former UN

Under-Secretary-General) in the early 1990s, to a number of proposals more recently.[17] A related suggestion is a United Nations Emergency Peace Service (UNEPS) to provide a robust military presence as well as police and civilian units.[18] Although these proposals differ in detail, most of them share the same core ideas. Essentially, what is envisaged is a standing military force of around 5,000–15,000 troops to undertake humanitarian intervention. This force would be authorized by the Security Council and deployable within a few days. The troops would be truly cosmopolitan in character: they would be volunteers (rather than conscripts, although still paid); they would not have any national allegiance; and many may be motivated by considerations of humanity (Kinloch-Pichat 2004). They would also be an elite force, similar to the French Foreign Legion, and have a strong *esprit de corps*.

The attractiveness of such a cosmopolitan force is clear: rather than the current situation where the UN has to beg, often unsuccessfully, for ad hoc contributions of troops from unwilling member states in order to fulfil its mandates, there would be a readily available standing army to deploy quickly and effectively whenever needed. This force would also overcome three of the central problems outlined with any standby arrangement such as UNSAS (Kinloch-Pichat 2004). First, these troops would not be subject to national authorization, since they would have no national allegiance. Second, the troops would be able to train together, and so would be much more integrated. Third, this force would provide a real rapid-reaction capability.

Would such a UN force be able to ensure that serious humanitarian crises can legitimately be tackled on a more frequent basis? Let me begin with two common, but unpersuasive, objections. The first objection is that the creation of such a force is unfeasible. It is claimed that states would not agree to a cosmopolitan UN force for a number of reasons. For instance, the anti-UN stance of many in the US means that it would block any moves to establish a standing army for the UN. Similarly, Evans (1993: 58) argues that states in the Global South would also strongly oppose such a force, for fear it may be used against them. Thus, Marrack Goulding, a former Under-Secretary-General for Peacekeeping Operations, claims that a cosmopolitan military force 'will continue to be a bigger pill than sovereign states will feel able to swallow' (2004: 114). Yet, although there may be political difficulties in establishing such a force, these problems are not innate to the international system. The proposed force would be fairly small and, as such, its creation would not be excessively demanding. It would not take *that* much effort to achieve. Although the estimated cost of $2 billion to set up and $900 million per year certainly raises funding issues, this expense is not so large as to be insurmountable.[19] Further, such a force might be seen as a cheaper option since an effective rapid response to a humanitarian crisis before it escalates is cost effective (Axworthy and Rock 2009: 61)—it avoids the need for a much more extensive (and expensive) mission later on.[20]

A second common objection concerns not the feasibility of a cosmopolitan force, but its desirability. The suggestion is that a UN standing army would lead to an increase in supranational governance, which, it is feared, would ultimately result in a tyrannical world state.[21] As Langille (2000*a*) points out, if the small cosmopolitan UN force proposed gains a reputation for being successful, there probably *would* be moves to extend its size and power. Yet, even if this were true, we would still be a very long way from a world state. Furthermore, although one may rightly reject a world state, supranational governance short of this might well be desirable. As Archibugi (2004*a*) and David Held (1995*b*) assert, there is a need to increase the amount of (demo-cratic) supranational governance given the current lack of democratic and effective control over a number of significant global issues. In sum, even if we admit that a cosmopolitan UN force sits on a slippery slope that could end in supranational governance, this is not necessarily a bad thing, and it would be a long slide to a world state.

A more telling objection to the proposed force is that it would be severely limited in what it could do. Given the size of the force envisaged (5,000–15,000 troops) it would be too small to intervene successfully in many situations (Hillen 1994: 62; Kinloch-Pichat 2004: 142; Wheeler 2000: 306). Most human-itarian crises require a much greater number of troops. For instance 20,000 British, American, and French troops were required to implement the no-fly zones in northern Iraq in 1991 (ICISS 2001*b*: 88); 21,000 troops were needed for the multinational force in Haiti in 1994 (ICISS 2001*b*: 104); and over 50,000 NATO troops were needed to keep Kosovo peaceful (Goulding 2004: 106). So, the problem is this: a cosmopolitan UN force of only 5,000–15,000 troops would not be able to respond to many humanitarian crises.

To be fair, most of its proponents would accept this criticism. They tend to see such a force as having three roles: first, to deploy rapidly in the early stages of a crisis, thereby achieving a successful resolution without needing to be replaced; second, to deploy rapidly with ad hoc troops replacing it after a few months; and third, to fill gaps in ad hoc coalitions where member states have not contributed enough troops. Hence, the role of the cosmopolitan UN force, as envisaged by its proponents, would not be to replace the role of ad hoc UN coalitions or other agents, who would still be needed, especially for large-scale missions (Kinloch-Pichat 2004: 219). Rather, it would be to fill gaps in current UN capacity, especially its lack of a rapid-reaction capability.

But there would be two problems with having such a force fulfil these three roles. First, as discussed earlier, the existing options on humanitarian intervention are inadequate and offer little guarantee that effective action will be taken to halt a serious and large-scale humanitarian crisis, such as Darfur. The three roles outlined for the cosmopolitan UN force are quite limited and would seem to do little to change this situation. Second, this force would have difficulty performing even these three quite limited roles. To start with, if the force fulfilled one of its roles in one region in the world, it would not be able to intervene elsewhere. Yet it is common for there to be more than one humanitarian crisis at a time that needs tackling. Hence, Wheeler states, '[t]he UN Fire Brigade could not have been sent to save Rwandans, because it would already have been committed to firefighting in Somalia or Bosnia' (2000: 304). In addition, too few of the proposals take into account the need for troop rotation. The need for rotation of troops means that, after undertaking one mission, the force would not be available for a number of months afterwards whilst its troops regenerate. Furthermore, if the force were used as an initial rapid-reaction force, no backup troops may be forthcoming from member states to replace it (Hillen 1994: 61). This would confront the cosmopolitan force with the unenviable dilemma of either leaving, thereby letting the humanitarian crisis go unresolved, or staying, thereby depriving others of access to its protection (although there may be some pressure on states to provide back-up). Lastly, having funded the force, states would most likely expect it to remove some of their peacekeeping and humanitarian intervention burden, and therefore may be less willing to provide troops themselves. As a result, the gaps in UN ad hoc missions may be much larger. The upshot is that a cosmopolitan UN force, as proposed, would be likely to have little utility. Proposals that lead to one legitimate, but limited, agent of intervention, and to much non-intervention, are far from the solution to the problem of who should intervene.

It would not be only the size of the force proposed that would limit its utility. First, it would have to rely on powerful states—especially the US—for lift capacity, communications, and logistics, which would reduce its ability to operate independently of the wishes of powerful states (Kinloch-Pichat 2004: 210–11). Second, the force would likely be dependent on the financial contributions of member states (again, especially the US), who could use this dependency to control the force (Kinloch-Pichat 2004: 206–11). Third, and perhaps most serious, it would be dependent on Security Council authorization. The UN force would not be used against any of the permanent members of the Security Council (although this might be justified on grounds of prudence) or against any other states they wished to shield (Kinloch-Pichat 2004: 237). Indeed, the permanent members would most likely authorize its use only where they did not deem their interests to be at stake.[22] So, even if the force were large enough and had the military, logistical, and financial resources to intervene, it would not have been deployed in Darfur, given China's opposition, or in Kosovo, given Russia's opposition, and perhaps not even in Rwanda, given the behaviour of the permanent members at that time.[23] Hence, Kinloch-Pichat (2004: 211) argues that the idea of a UN force, which was designed by its proponents to relieve the dependence of the UN on powerful states for humanitarian intervention, brings us back to square one. Its deployment would be dependent on the wishes of powerful states, which are likely to block humanitarian intervention on a number of occasions, meaning that threatened populations would be left to their fate.

8.4 A LARGER COSMOPOLITAN UN FORCE AND COSMOPOLITAN DEMOCRATIC INSTITUTIONS

We should not abandon the idea of a cosmopolitan UN force, however. There are serious problems with the current agents of humanitarian intervention and the situation clearly needs improving. Moreover, a cosmopolitan UN force would, as suggested earlier, certainly have some merit, such as being an elite force and providing a rapid-reaction capability. Yet to have substantial moral worth—to be a significant goal worth working towards—it is necessary to make two amendments to the existing proposals. Indeed, such a force, if revised, could be fully legitimate according to the conception of legitimacy outlined.

As the first objection shows, a cosmopolitan UN force would need to be much larger. Michael O'Hanlon (2003: 85) argues that 200,000 troops would be needed to tackle all the humanitarian crises in the world at any one time, which translates into 600,000 troops after taking into account the need for rotation. Given the elite nature of the cosmopolitan UN force, it would perhaps require 75,000 troops to be available at any time, with support staff and rotation taking this to 175,000 troops (although this might still be too optimistic). Such a force would be able to intervene in larger humanitarian crises, such as Darfur, and be able to intervene in more than one place at a time. It would also be able to continue its deployment without reliance on ad hoc troops for replacement.[24]

As the second objection shows, the force would also need to have the necessary autonomy. For this, it would need to be provided with financial, military, and logistical resources, and freed from the self-interested decision-making of major states. However, we should not simply place the decision on where and when to authorize the force in the hands of the Secretary General and the Secretariat. Although this would reduce the influence of major states, and therefore help the force to be more autonomous, it would give much power to unelected officials, who could easily abuse it. It is important then that this force should be accountable, and, specifically, democratically accountable.[25] A satisfactory level of democratic accountability could not come from having the Security Council in its current form in charge of the force. In addition to restricting the potential usefulness of such a force by making its deployment dependent on the self-interested decision-making of major states, both the functioning of the Council, which heavily favours the permanent five members and lacks transparency, and its composition, which includes three European permanent members but none from the South, are undemocratic.

Given the problems with the democratic credentials of the current international system, to achieve a satisfactory level of democratic control over the large-scale cosmopolitan UN force we would need to develop cosmopolitan democratic institutions by reforming current institutions and developing new ones. The sort of institutions that would fit the bill include the following: a reformed Security Council, with regional organizations replacing the current permanent members and a watering down (and ultimate removal) of the veto[26]; an intelligence-gathering and monitoring institution to help to decide when and where intervention would be appropriate; a larger Secretariat with the ability to manage the deployment of the force; international legal institutions with greater jurisdiction and resources, including the capacity to prosecute those who commit egregious violations of basic human rights (thereby creating the need for humanitarian intervention in the first place) and the ability to ensure that the cosmopolitan UN force follows principles of internal and external *jus in bello*; and a global parliament formed of representatives from constituencies of the same size.

These institutions would be in charge of authorizing, running, and monitoring the use of force by the cosmopolitan UN standing army. Here is how they might work. The intelligence-gathering institution would report to the global parliament a serious humanitarian crisis which it believes could be tackled by the cosmopolitan UN force. The global parliament would meet quickly to debate the deployment of the force in this case and perhaps resolve that the force should undertake humanitarian intervention to remedy this crisis.[27] The reformed Security Council would retain the power to block the intervention, but only if there were a level of consensus in the Council (since none of the permanent members, who would be regional organizations, would have the power of veto). The international legal institutions would make recommendations on the legality of the proposed intervention to both the global parliament and the reformed Security Council. In addition, they would review the intervention afterwards, making detailed assessments of the action and recommendations for the future.

It would be necessary to ensure that the cosmopolitan democratic institutions would authorize humanitarian intervention in the right cases and not in the wrong ones. In other words, we should take steps to avoid a tyranny of the global majority in which the global demos authorizes abusive, non-humanitarian intervention against a minority (such as the Roma) (see, further, Pattison 2008a: 135–7). I have already indicated that the global parliament's decision to deploy the cosmopolitan UN force could be blocked by the reformed Security Council. A further check on the power of the global *demos* would be the codification of certain criteria in international law to restrict when humanitarian intervention can be legally authorized. Legal criteria such as this, if subject to independent judicial review (by strengthened international legal institutions), would limit the opportunities that the global parliament would have to authorize abusive intervention.

Hence, there are two parts to this proposal. First, there should be a new agent to *undertake* humanitarian intervention—a large-sized cosmopolitan UN force. Second, existing institutions should be reformed and new international institutions should be created to *authorize* humanitarian intervention—to decide when the relevant normative criteria have been met and if an intervener would be legitimate. Indeed, an additional benefit of such institutions is that they would be able to act as legitimate authorizing institutions. That is to say, they would also be able to authorize other agents' humanitarian interventions and the stamp of approval from these institutions would legitimize the authorized agents.

In the hands of such cosmopolitan democratic institutions, a large cosmopolitan UN force could intervene effectively to prevent humanitarian crises in challenging situations on a much more frequent basis and with much greater democratic control. It could also be assigned formally the duty to intervene and the task of discharging the responsibility to protect when the state in question is failing to tackle a serious humanitarian crisis within its borders. Accordingly, this two-part proposal would be a highly desirable solution to the problems faced by the current agents and mechanisms of humanitarian intervention. In short, it could potentially be *fully* legitimate according to the conception of legitimacy outlined.

An obvious objection to this proposal is that both aspects, the intervening force and the authorizing institutions, are unattainable. The existence of the EU and the UN, however, proves that transnational institutions can be created (Held 1998: 28).[28] Indeed, there has already been considerable evolution of state sovereignty as the forces of cosmopolitanism (e.g. individual human rights and human security) and the forces of globalization (e.g. transnational trade) have challenged the moral and political significance of state borders. As Archibugi notes, '[t]here is a perceptible tendency towards widening the international community, which implies an irreversible shift towards a progressive *de facto* reduction of the sovereignty of individual states' (1995: 157). Moreover, it is important to note that this proposal is a long-term normative goal to work towards—to help guide our future reforms—rather than a policy prescription that can be implemented instantaneously. As such, concerns over immediate feasibility are largely irrelevant. As Held argues, '[t]he question of political feasibility can't simply be set up in opposition to the question of political ambition' (1995*a*: 285).

The proposal, then, is best seen instead as a mid- to long-term solution to the problems with the current agents and mechanisms of humanitarian intervention. As the desirability of a cosmopolitan UN force is increased by making the two changes suggested earlier (by increasing its size and by putting it under the control of cosmopolitan democratic institutions), the likelihood of achieving this goal in the short-term diminishes. Creating a small-scale cosmopolitan UN force, such as that proposed by Urquhart and others, is more likely to be attainable, yet its lack of autonomy and utility limit the desirability of this reform.

For this reason, it may be more fruitful to concentrate our immediate efforts elsewhere. To that extent, a better short-term option would be to strengthen certain regional and subregional organizations so that they have a greater ability to undertake effective humanitarian intervention within their regions. This has more immediate political viability than a small-scale standing UN force (given the likely opposition to this force). It is also more desirable. As argued earlier, a small-scale standing UN force would have limited utility (for instance, it would be able to tackle only one humanitarian crisis at a time) and would be reliant on major states. By contrast, regional organizations, if improved, could intervene without being subject to the whims of major states and could provide the capacity to tackle a number of different humanitarian crises in different regions across the world at the same time.

8.5 IMPROVED REGIONAL ORGANIZATIONS

As suggested in Chapter 7, regional organizations often have the willingness to intervene. The proximity of regional interveners means that they typically have a vested interest in resolving the crisis (ICISS 2001*b*: 210). A nearby humanitarian crisis may cause border incursions, an influx of refugees, financial hardship, and political instability for the whole region. Indeed, it would be odd if the member states of regional organizations did *not* benefit from humanitarian intervention within their regions. This element of self-interest makes the necessary commitment—as well as the willingness to undertake intervention—more likely to be forthcoming. It is often in regional organizations' interests to stay the course, thereby ensuring a successful resolution to the humanitarian crisis in the long term. The problem, though, with regional organizations at the moment is that they lack the resources to undertake humanitarian intervention successfully. I discussed the problems of ECOWAS, the EU, and the AU in this respect in Chapter 7. The suggestion, then, is to utilize the potential willingness of regional organizations to undertake humanitarian intervention by strengthening their capabilities to do so.[29]

Particular attention should be paid to the strengthening of African regional organizations, such as the AU and ECOWAS, given the large number of humanitarian crises on this continent and the general reluctance of other agents to intervene in what are regarded as African quagmires. There are a number of potential improvements that might be made. The first concerns the funding of regional organizations and, in particular, the AU. As it stands, the AU relies heavily on external funding for peace operations, but this is ad hoc and unreliable. Jakkie Cilliers (2008: 158–9) proposes that there be a single point of entry for international funders wanting to assist the AU which would replace the current donor scramble and duplication of efforts.[30]

The second improvement is the further training of African troops in peacekeeping with programs such as the Global Peace Operations Initiative. This would help to overcome some of the previous problems with African peacekeepers' abuse of civilians (Nowrojee 2004), as well as broadly developing African capacity for peace operations.[31]

This relates to the third, most obvious improvement: increase the military resources of regional organizations. The AU, African subregional organizations, and the EU have begun to address their lack of capacity with development of the African Standby Force and the EU battlegroups respectively, both of which, when fully operational, will offer notable rapid-reaction capability. Although already ambitious, the 25,000 troops projected for African Standby Force will probably need to be increased further, given the number of conflicts in Africa and the need for a sustained troop presence (and the expected increased reliance on this force). Likewise, although a positive development, the capacity and size of EU battlegroups need to be increased (perhaps to include greater lift capacity and logistics) so that the EU can successfully intervene to tackle large-scale humanitarian crises beyond its borders.

A fourth improvement would be to increase cooperation between agents, that is, further 'hybridization'. As Ban Ki-Moon (2009: 28) argues in his report on the responsibility to protect, *Implementing the Responsibility to Protect*, increased global–regional collaboration is key to operationalizing the responsibility to protect. Kofi Annan's report (2005: 52), *In Larger Freedom*, proposes more specifically that there be a memorandum of understanding between regional organizations and the UN which would place the capacities of each organization within the UNSAS. For its part, the UN would amend the rules of its peacekeeping budget to give it the option of using its assessed contributions to finance operations by regional organizations (Annan 2005: 52). Similarly, Piiparinen (2007: 386) proposes a memorandum of understanding between NATO and the AU for a standby system of NATO equipment and logistics for use by the AU in response to 'another Darfur'. Gompert (2006: 14) also proposes a more active role for NATO, having its members reinforce AU troops if escalation is necessary. This partnership, he argues, is both consistent with NATO's new aim of extending security beyond Europe and would be sustainable politically in the West and in Africa (Gompert 2006).[32]

A fifth improvement would be to reform certain regional organizations' treaties or constitutions so that humanitarian intervention by the relevant regional organization within its own borders is legally permissible. I discussed this option briefly in Section 8.1. Such reform could mean that regional organizations would be able to intervene legally within their own regions without requiring Security Council authorization. This would place much power in the hands of regional organizations. A potential objection here is that this power would be abused by regional hegemons that would use the cover of legality to engage in abusive intervention. The trust in regional organizations would be more justified if regional organizations were reformed so that they were more democratic, both in composition (by the democratization of member states) and in functioning (by increasing transparency and by ensuring a large role for regional parliaments). These revisions would mean that humanitarian intervention undertaken by regional organizations is much more likely to be internally representative and, ultimately, legitimate. Such democratic reforms, however, would not be necessary for regional organizations to have a satisfactory degree of legitimacy in the short term. Although these proposals for improving the *authorizing* mechanism of regional organizations are desirable, the immediate aim is to improve the capacity of regional organizations to *undertake* intervention within their regions.

It is important that these proposals for strengthened regional organizations—and in particular African regional organizations—would not lead to the rest of the international community completely washing their hands of other regions' crises (Bellamy and Williams 2005: 195; Weiss 2001: 423).

Other agents, such as states and the UN, still have a moral duty to undertake humanitarian intervention even if there are regional mechanisms in place. In anticipation of this problem, it would be judicious, firstly, to strengthen regional organizations' capability to intervene even further so that other agents' lack of willingness to intervene would not be too detrimental and, secondly, for regional organizations to highlight that they may not always be able to act and that other agents still may have the responsibility to protect.

Thus, given that it would be a highly motivated, elite force with rapid-reaction capability, a large-scale cosmopolitan UN force would be the most desirable, long-term solution to the problem of a lack of legitimate inter-veners to undertake humanitarian intervention.[33] Yet, in the short term, it would be more fruitful to improve regional organizations in these five ways so that they have a greater ability to undertake effective humanitarian interven-tion within their regions.

8.6 CONCLUSION

To recap, in this chapter I have considered various proposals for reform. All of the proposals surveyed are likely to be an improvement on the current agents and mechanisms of humanitarian intervention. But the most desirable reforms would, first, be to develop the capacities of regional organizations, which would be a short- to mid-term solution to the problem of who should intervene. Second, in the long term, to achieve fully legitimate humanitarian intervention, we would need the sort of democratic and effective intervention that can come only from a large UN force under control of cosmopolitan democratic institu-tions. Although this is not on the cards today, nor will it be tomorrow, or any time in the near future, it is in the realm of the possible. And, as Urquhart argues (when outlining his more limited proposal), '[t]here are plenty of arguments against such a force. There is one overwhelming argument for it. It is desperately needed' (2003). In Chapter 9, I will consider how these reforms, necessary for legitimate humanitarian intervention, can be realized.

NOTES

1. These five criteria of legitimacy are seriousness of threat, proper purpose, last resort, proportional means, and balance of consequences.

2. Although these proposals for guidelines to govern the Security Council's use of force may be only recommendations initially, and so not legally binding, if followed closely they could become part of customary international law.

3. The ensuing discussion builds upon categories detailed by the Danish Institute of International Affairs (DUPI) (1999) and Stromseth (2003).

4. Archibugi (2005: 224) also endorses this position. Likewise, the British and Dutch governments have attempted to formalize criteria to govern the circumstances in which the Security Council should be prepared to authorize intervention (Blair 1999; Advisory Council on International Affairs and Advisory Committee on Issues of Public International Law 2000). That said, the UK has since changed its stance on criteria for intervention (Bellamy 2005: 36).

5. Many of those who are opposed to criteria for the responsibility to protect fear that they will be adopted on the basis of these approaches, that is, they are concerned that interveners will not always need UN Security Council authorization for the intervention if they meet the requisite criteria. See Bellamy (2008: 626).

6. Pogge (2006), Weiss (2005a: 235), and Wheeler (2005b: 241) make similar points.

7. It might be argued that, if humanitarian intervention were more clearly demarcated in international law, dictators would be less willing to violate their citizens' rights, so there would be less need for humanitarian intervention. See Caney (2005: 256). Yet, there is already provision for humanitarian intervention in current international law (i.e. when it is authorized by the Security Council). The deterrent effect that would be gained by allowing other interveners to intervene if they met certain criteria would probably add little to the deterrent effect of current international law.

8. A literal account of last resort is problematic because it would require all other options short of military intervention to be pursued first, regardless of their likely success. See Chapter 3.

9. This approach may be the most difficult on which to reach agreement, however, given the current political opposition to a general rule permitting humanitarian intervention without the need for Security Council authorization.

10. It states: '[t]he Contracting Parties confirm that genocide, whether committed in time of peace or in time of war, is a crime under international law which they undertake to prevent and to punish'.

11. There are problems with the AU's arrangements for humanitarian intervention, however. First, as Bellamy (2006b) points out, it is not entirely clear how the AU would authorize intervention against a host state's consent. The AU Assembly must defer its responsibility to the AU's Peace and Security Council, but the Assembly meets only annually and requires a two-thirds majority, which might be hard to achieve (Bellamy 2006b: 158). Second, it could lead to the UN Security Council deferring to the AU even though the AU lacks the capacity to act effectively (Bellamy 2006b: 159–60). Third, again as Bellamy (2006b: 160) notes, it may lend credence to the notion that the Security Council ought to refrain from imposing its will on Africans and thereby risk further increasing Western pretexts for standing by.

12. Buchanan and Keohane (2004) propose the creation of a democratic coalition to authorize preventative war, including humanitarian intervention. This coalition would be based on agreement amongst its members, with its practice becoming part of customary international law (Buchanan and Keohane 2004: 19). The coalition would be a second body to refer to if the Security Council opposes intervention. There are a number of problems with this proposal (in relation to humanitarian intervention), however. First, it would be likely that powerful non-democratic states, such as Russia and China, would vehemently oppose such a coalition. This is because it would, in effect, water down their veto—any proposed intervener that had its intervention blocked by a Russian or Chinese veto could still be legal if authorized by the coalition. Second, it is not clear what such a coalition would add to the status quo and, in particular, how it would better NATO or the EU undertaking or authorizing intervention without UN Security Council approval (perhaps with the open support of other democratic states). Third, adding another level of bureaucratic decision-making is likely to lead to delays and innocent lives would be lost in the meantime. Last, it does not tackle the problem of a lack of willingness to intervene. Creating such a coalition would do little to make actors keener to intervene to stop egregious violations of human rights. See Bellamy (2006a: 10) for further criticisms of this proposal.

13. I draw here on UN (2003).

14. SHIRBRIG was a Danish-led initiative, formed in response to the calls for such a force in Boutros Boutros-Ghali's *Supplement to an Agenda for Peace*. It comprised sixteen states which together aimed to provide a standby rapid-reaction force of 4,000–5,000 troops deployable within fifteen to thirty days for a maximum of six months (SHIRBRIG 2003). It was supposed to offer the UN relatively prompt access to a pre-established, well-trained, cohesive, and versatile force (Langille 2000b). Although SHIRBRIG was employed largely successfully in the border between Eritrea and Ethiopia, it was disbanded in 2008. This was largely because its member states did not provide it with the troops needed (see von Freiesleben 2008).

15. For more detailed proposals, see Langille (2000a).

16. Such arrangements might still lead to legitimate humanitarian intervention overall. For example, an automated UNSAS might mean that a sufficient number of troops are contributed for a UN mission to tackle genocide. Given the arguments in Chapter 3, the effectiveness at tackling this genocide is more important to legitimacy than concerns over internal representativeness.

17. See, for instance, Abramowitz and Pickering (2008), Caney (2005), Conetta and Knight (1995), Held (1995a; 1998), Langille (2004), Smith (1998), Urquhart (2003), and Woodhouse and Ramsbotham (2005). Kinloch-Pichat (2004) provides a detailed history of the proposals for a UN standing army. Also see Roberts (2008). A different yet interesting proposal (although largely heuristic) is made by Bernard Williams (1995). He suggests the creation of an international rescue army of private relief agencies such as Oxfam, which would be funded by

billionaire philanthropists, consist of idealistic soldiers, and be guided by a committee of reputable international figures.

18. The UNEPS is proposed by Johansen (2006). Axworthy and Rock (2009), Citizens for Global Solutions (2008), Global Action to Prevent War and Armed Conflict, Langille (2009), and the World Federalist Movement have endorsed the proposed force. Also see Herro, Lambourne, and Penklis (2009), who consider the roles that such a force could have played in Rwanda and Darfur.

19. This is the estimated cost of the UNEPS proposed by Johansen (2006).

20. Interestingly, the proposal for a UN standing force has much public support worldwide (see Chicago Council on Global Affairs/WorldPublicOpinion.org 2007: 2).

21. As Kant argues in *Perpetual Peace*, if there were 'an amalgamation of the separate nations under a single power', laws would 'progressively lose their impact as the government increases its range, and a soulless despotism, after crushing the germs of goodness, will finally lapse into anarchy' (1991 [1795]: 113). See, also, Scully (2000) and Zolo (1997: 121). On a world state more generally, see Cabrera (forthcoming), Craig (2008), Lu (2006*b*), and Wendt (2003).

22. A related objection here is that the authorization of the UN force would still be reliant on the morally objectionable Security Council, which lacks insufficient representation and equality (Abbot 2005: 6; Kinloch-Pichat 2004: 235). Although this is a telling procedural criticism of the functioning and representation of the Council, my point is more instrumental: it would restrict the ability of the force to act.

23. See Pogge (2006: 161–7) on the abhorrent behaviour of the permanent members during the genocide in Rwanda.

24. This was the sort of size of force originally envisaged under Article 43 of the UN Charter, which, although never implemented, was meant to provide a large number of troops readily available to the UN Security Council. The US estimated that it would provide 300,000 troops under this Article (Urquhart 1993: 3).

25. My reason for holding democratic accountability as valuable mirrors the arguments given in Chapter 5 for an intervener's internal representativeness. Intrinsically, democratic decision-making (or, more specifically, majoritarian control) maximizes individual self-government and, instrumentally, democratic decision-making tends to be more likely to deliver the right results. I discuss the importance of democratic accountability of such a force in more detail in Pattison (2008*a*: 132–3).

26. James Paul and Cecile Nahory (2005) suggest this can be done if Japan, Brazil, India, and Germany press for reform rather than campaigning to become permanent members (which is unlikely to be successful anyway).

27. Archibugi (2004*b*: 10) also believes that a world parliament is the ideal institution to deliberate on humanitarian intervention. He also goes on to propose the creation of a UN army. His proposal, unlike mine, is for a *standby* rather than a *standing* army. The (main) problem with such standby arrangements, as argued in Section 8.2, is that states retain the prerogative of whether or not to deploy troops,

and this means that, on many occasions, states do not provide troops. For further criticisms of Archibugi's proposal, see Farer (2005*b*: 246–7).

28. As Richard Falk and Andrew Strauss (2001) assert, even the most ambitious part of this proposal—a global parliament—is achievable. They argue that, like the early European Parliament, a relatively weak assembly, created by global civil society and business leaders (perhaps with the endorsement of a relatively small number of countries to start with), and initially equipped with largely advisory powers, could begin to address concerns about democratic deficit, whilst posing only a long-term threat to the realities of state power. Formal powers could follow as the assembly becomes the practical place for clashing interests to be resolved.

29. Kinloch-Pichat (2004: 235) also proposes improving regional organizations' capability to intervene. My proposal differs from his in that he suggests creating a UN standing army *before* pursuing regional options. This gets things the wrong way round: it would be far simpler and more beneficial to improve regional organizations' capabilities first.

30. This idea is also supported by the *Report of the African Union–United Nations Panel on Modalities for Support to African Union Peacekeeping Operations* (UN 2008*c*: 23), which proposes two new financial mechanisms to support the AU: UN-assessed funding on a case-by-case basis to support Security Council-authorized AU missions and a voluntary, multidonor trust fund that focuses on capacity and institution-building.

31. Some argue (e.g. Bhatia 2003: 143) that such training programmes ought to be treated carefully because of the danger of increasing the conflict capabilities of unstable states. For a reply, see O'Hanlon (2003: 104–5).

32. Another proposal is from Deane-Peter Baker (2007: 123), who suggests using retired Western navy vessels to bolster AU capacity.

33. There are two other reasons for favouring a large-scale UN force in the hands of cosmopolitan democratic institutions in the long term. First, the proposals for regional organizations are still for standby solutions and may therefore face problems similar to the UNSAS. (These problems may not be on the same scale, given that Security Council authorization would not be necessary. The location of member states to the crisis may also mean that they are willing to stand up and provide troops that they have offered on a standby basis.) Second, beyond the issue of humanitarian intervention, cosmopolitan democratic institutions are required if we are to tackle poverty, nuclear proliferation, and environmental concerns effectively and democratically (Pogge 1992*b*: 62–4).

9

Conclusion: Realizing Legitimate Humanitarian Intervention

My aim in this book has been to consider a central issue in the ethics and politics of humanitarian intervention and the responsibility to protect: when the world is faced with a serious humanitarian crisis, which international actor, if any, should undertake humanitarian intervention to help those suffering? Drawing on the Moderate Instrumentalist Approach, I have argued that an intervener that possesses an adequate degree of legitimacy possesses the right to intervene—which may, in practice, mean that many interveners can permissibly intervene—and that the most legitimate agent has the duty to intervene—which may, in practice, mean that NATO or a hybrid force is morally obliged to do so. I have also argued that the current agents and mechanisms of humanitarian intervention are inadequate. In particular, interveners are often unwilling to step forward and, when they do intervene, humanitarian intervention is typically far from being fully legitimate. For this reason, Chapter 8 considered various proposals for improving the agents and mechanisms of humanitarian intervention and defended two reforms in particular: in the long term, the development of a cosmopolitan UN force in the hands of cosmopolitan democratic institutions and, more immediately, the strengthening and reform of regional organizations.

Since Chapter 7 provided a detailed summary of the normative arguments from the previous chapters, I will not recap the main points here. Instead, I want to finish by considering how we can achieve legitimate humanitarian intervention in the future. The challenges are threefold. First, as we have seen, there are too many occasions when humanitarian intervention should be undertaken, but is not. The result is that many serious humanitarian crises continue unabated. How, then, can the general willingness of potential interveners to undertake humanitarian intervention be increased? Second, too often the most legitimate agent, such as NATO, fails to act. How can we, then, improve the likelihood of the most legitimate agent intervening? Third, there need to be significant reforms to the agents and mechanisms of humanitarian intervention. How can these reforms be realized?

In response to these challenges, I first re-emphasize our duties to meet these challenges. Second, I offer some proposals for amending states' perceptions of their national interest. Third, I emphasize that humanitarian intervention is an important, but limited, part of the responsibility to protect.

9.1 THE DUTY TO REFORM

Before considering more practical proposals for achieving legitimate human-itarian intervention, it is worth reiterating the duties that fall on us to strive towards this goal. In Chapter 1, I defended the General Duty Approach, which asserts that there is a general, unassigned duty to undertake humanitarian intervention in certain circumstances. This duty needs to be assigned to be effectively claimable. I have argued that it should be assigned to the most legitimate agent which, according to the Moderate Instrumentalist Approach, will often be the intervener that is most likely to be effective. In practice, this may be NATO or a hybrid force—much depends on the particular circum-stances. But once we know the details of the case, it should be made clear to the intervener most likely to be legitimate that it has the duty to undertake humanitarian intervention. If it fails in this duty, then it is morally culpable. However, this lack of action would not justify the non-intervention of other interveners. The duty to intervene will fall then on the next most legitimate intervener and so on.

In Chapter 1, I suggested that the general, unassigned duty to intervene largely stems from the more fundamental duty to prevent human suffering, which asserts that there is a duty to do what we can to prevent, to halt, and to decrease substantial human suffering, such as that found in genocide and large-scale violations of basic human rights. If we take this duty seriously, it falls on most international actors to work towards improving the capacity to undertake legitimate humanitarian intervention. As Tan argues, 'all members are obliged to *do what is necessary* to establish and support the cooperative arrangement required to carry out the duty to protect' (2006*a*: 104). To prevent human suffering legitimately and frequently, we need to create a cosmopolitan UN force and place it in the hands of cosmopolitan democratic institutions. Again as Tan argues, the duty to intervene 'can generate the duty to create a global humanitarian defence force if the creation of this force is required to ensure that the response to humanitarian emergencies is accept-ably efficient' (2006*a*: 105). Thus, there is a duty to create a large-scale cosmopolitan UN force with accompanying democratic institutions and to enhance regional organizations' capabilities to intervene because these are central to ensuring that substantial human suffering is tackled. So, although only the most legitimate intervener has the duty to intervene, it falls on all of us to act on the duty to reform the current agents and mechanisms of humanitarian intervention.

9.2 WILL AND INTEREST

It is important not to be too pessimistic about the likelihood of these duties being fulfilled, that is, of the chances of achieving legitimate humanitarian intervention by increasing the willingness to intervene and realizing the two main reforms suggested in Chapter 8. There has already been a significant increase in the number of humanitarian interventions since the end of the Cold War. In addition, the agreement to the doctrine of the responsibility to protect at the World Summit was something of a watershed moment for humanitarian intervention. It marked the universal acceptance of the permissibility of humanitarian intervention in certain circumstances. In particular, it asserts the permissibility of Security Council-authorized intervention (in certain circumstances) and, in doing so, rejects absolute non-interventionism. It also acknowledges that a state's sovereignty is conditional on the treatment of its population. These are important milestones in the history of humanitarian intervention, the responsibility to protect, and state sovereignty more generally.

Moreover, support for humanitarian intervention has generally been maintained over the past decade, despite the fear that the War on Terror and the 2003 war on Iraq would undermine the support for military action in the name of humanitarianism. The US- and UK-led operation in Iraq, in particular, threatened to damage the credibility of humanitarian intervention irrevocably, since one of the justifications offered by George Bush and Tony Blair was essentially humanitarian: to end the violation of human rights by the Ba'athist regime and to bring freedom and democracy to Iraq. That this war used force indiscriminately, involved the abuse of civilians, and has led, in effect, to civil war, could have created an unrelenting cynicism and rejection of any international action for apparently humanitarian purposes. The risk of world public opinion and elites being against any future international action with a purported humanitarian justification was increased further by the degree of worldwide attention on—and condemnation of—the war. Indeed, the War on Terror and the 2003 war on Iraq led Weiss to conclude that 'the sun of humanitarian intervention has set for now' (2004: 149).

However, there have still been a number of humanitarian interventions since the launch of the War on Terror. More specifically, although there has been a decline in the number of the classical forms of humanitarian interventions of the 1990s (such as NATO's intervention in Kosovo), there has been an expansion in robust UN and regional peace operations—the grey area between traditional peacekeeping and classical humanitarian intervention discussed in Chapter 1. Examples include intervention in Côte d'Ivoire by France, the UN, and ECOWAS, MONUC and the EU's Operation Artemis in DR Congo. In fact, as discussed in Chapter 7, it is a boom time for UN peace operations. In addition, there continue to be calls for humanitarian intervention to be undertaken in a number of other places where the mass violation of basic human rights currently goes unchecked (such as for the deployment of a UN force to Somalia).

Moreover, the fact that there have been a number of *proposals* for reform, such as for the creation of the African Standby Force, demonstrates that there is a certain degree of will in the international community to reform the current mechanisms of humanitarian intervention. Furthermore, the fact that there have been a number of *actual* reforms, such as improvements made to the UN and the development of EU battlegroups, demonstrates that this will is sometimes sufficiently strong to achieve reform. To be sure, as detailed in Chapter 7, there are still too many humanitarian crises that currently go unchecked and, when humanitarian intervention does occur, it often has significant flaws. Much still needs to be done to improve the current levels of willingness and the capabilities of potential interveners. Nevertheless, my point is that the improvements that there have been and the continued, if occasional, willingness to intervene—despite the War on Terror and the war in Iraq—show that attempting to improve further current humanitarian interveners is not unduly idealistic. Of course, we need to increase significantly the will to reform and the will to undertake humanitarian intervention if we are to achieve legitimate humanitarian intervention on a much more frequent basis.

Central to improving the will to reform the mechanisms and agents of humanitarian intervention is improving the will to undertake humanitarian intervention. If international actors are keener to intervene to tackle egregious violations of human rights, then they will be more likely to push for reforms to the current mechanisms and agents of humanitarian intervention that will enable them to do so more effectively and, ultimately, legitimately. On the other hand, one way to improve the international community's will to intervene is to improve the agents and mechanisms of humanitarian intervention. Most of the reforms discussed in Chapter 8, if put in place, would help, to some extent, to overcome the reluctance to undertake intervention. In particular, one of the benefits of increasing the ability of regional organizations to undertake humanitarian intervention is that this would take advantage of their greater willingness to intervene, which is currently limited by their lack of capacity (Hirsh 2000: 6).[1]

One way of improving the will to undertake humanitarian intervention and to reform the current mechanisms and agents of intervention is to encourage a subtle adjustment in states' perceptions of their national interest. In this context, Kofi Annan has called for a new, broader definition of the national interest in which states recognize that the collective interest is identical with their national interest (Abbott 2005: 7). To that extent, humanitarian intervention carried out effectively by states (or other agents) can have massive potential benefits for that intervener, such as increased international status, greater standing in regional organizations, and the opening up of new foreign markets. More generally, most of us have an interest in a just global order. A more narrow understanding of the national interest misses such benefits.

Furthermore, Chris Brown (2005: 227) argues that we need to get away from treating humanitarianism as a separate category of state behaviour. This is the product of a Realist mindset, he argues, since it takes states to be rational egoists who act in the pursuit of their material interest, with anything that varies from this requiring explanation. The danger with this mindset is that it will be reinforcing. That is to say, it will lead to a lack of humanitarian intervention, with states regarding standing by in the face of a humanitarian crisis as the behaviour expected of them, unless there is a material interest clearly involved. Brown (2005: 228) proposes instead that we adopt a more ideational notion of interests, which would remove the need for a separate category of humanitarian action. On this more ideational view, tackling humanitarian crises may be, in fact, in the national interest because, as Evans asserts, '[e]very country has an interest in being, and being seen to be, a good international citizen' (2008*b*: 229).

But even on narrow understandings of self-interest, humanitarian intervention can be justified. There has been a growing realization that the disruption caused by a humanitarian crisis far away can have significant domestic effects. For instance, failed (and failing) states often lead to large refugee flows and are increasingly being regarded as breeding grounds for international terrorism (Terriff 2004*a*; Welsh 2004: 189). Evans argues that 'states that cannot or will not stop internal atrocity crimes are the kind of states that cannot or will not stop terrorism, weapons proliferation, drug and people trafficking, the spread of health pandemics, and other global risks' (2008*b*: 229). It is important, therefore, that these links between humanitarian intervention and national interest be emphasized, thereby tapping into a potential source of political will to undertake humanitarian intervention and to implement reform.

9.3 UTILIZING THE RESPONSIBILITY TO PROTECT

Perhaps the greatest hope for improving the will to intervene and to implement reform, and thereby respond to the three challenges, lies with the responsibility to protect. This doctrine has received significant international attention since the original ICISS report in 2001. Changes to the agents and mechanisms of humanitarian intervention are now often cast in terms of 'realizing' the responsibility to protect.[2] By contrast, the lack of an effective response to serious humanitarian crises is said to constitute a 'failure' in the implementation of the responsibility to protect.[3] In other words, this doctrine has significant rhetorical and political force and, as such, is central to improving the willingness and legitimacy of humanitarian intervention. For instance, Ban Ki-Moon has identified operationalizing the responsibility to protect as one of his key priorities and appointed Edward Luck as his special adviser on the doctrine (Wheeler and Egerton 2009: 115). Several research and advocacy centres have also been set up, including in Accra, Brisbane, Madrid, New York, and Oslo (Wheeler and Egerton 2009: 115). State officials, NGOs, aid workers, and diplomats are increasingly using the language of the responsibility to protect in relation to conflict situations, and global worldwide public opinion (including in non-Western states) appears to support the doctrine (Cottey 2008: 436). Casting the reforms in terms of the responsibility to protect may make their realization more likely as international actors treat acting on this responsibility as morally and politically urgent.

Yet, to make use of the will surrounding the responsibility to protect to achieve these reforms, it is important to reiterate that (*a*) humanitarian intervention is *only one part* of the doctrine of the responsibility to protect, but that (*b*) it *is* a part of the responsibility to protect. As discussed in Chapter 1, humanitarian intervention is both broader and narrower than the responsibility to protect. It is broader since certain forms of humanitarian intervention are clearly ruled out by the ICISS and World Summit versions of the responsibility to protect. For instance, on the version of the responsibility to protect endorsed at the World Summit, humanitarian intervention may fall under the responsibility to protect only when it has Security Council authorization and is in response to a state's manifest failure to tackle ethnic cleansing, crimes against humanity, war crimes, and genocide. Humanitarian intervention in other cases—without UN Security Council authorization and in response to less serious situations—could not be included under the responsibility to protect. Conversely, humanitarian intervention is narrower since the responsibility to protect involves much more than humanitarian intervention. Military intervention is only one part of the responsibility to react, which in turn is only one part of the responsibility to protect—the responsibility to prevent and the responsibility to rebuild are other central elements of the doctrine.

In fact, a limited version of the responsibility to protect, such as that agreed to at the World Summit, where military intervention is less pronounced, may receive greater support and political will, and thus (perhaps paradoxically) may best help to achieve the reforms required. Let me explain. Despite the increased acceptance of humanitarian intervention, intervention is still controversial. Many state leaders, especially those in the Global South, fear that they will be subject to humanitarian intervention. In some cases, this might be because they are involved in the abuses of their population's human rights. Others fear (perhaps erroneously) that humanitarian intervention will be used as a Trojan Horse to engage in abusive intervention.[4] Other states are less concerned that they will be subject to intervention themselves, but are concerned about the potentially destabilizing effects of humanitarian intervention for their surrounding region and that a general doctrine of humanitarian intervention will weaken their state sovereignty.[5] To guard against abuse and to limit the occasions of intervention, many assert that unauthorized intervention is impermissible. Likewise, China and Russia insist that there must be Council approval for any authorization (Bellamy 2006*b*: 151), partly because this ensures that they can veto any intervention not to their liking.

This opposition to humanitarian intervention—and, in particular, *certain forms* of humanitarian intervention (i.e. unauthorized, unilateral interventions)—means that to maintain agreement around the responsibility to protect, it is necessary to limit it to a narrow doctrine, such as that endorsed at the World Summit. Indeed, within expert and policy-making circles many use the more conservative World Summit form of the responsibility to protect for fear of undermining the international support.[6] This is not simply a fop to dictators and violators of human rights. The responsibility to protect has enormous potential if it can be taken forward. As I have argued, it could prompt the reforms necessary to undertake legitimate humanitarian intervention and, ultimately, lead to less suffering worldwide. There are other reasons for trying to maintain support for the responsibility to protect. It could become a clear and established legal norm that reinforces the conditionality of state sovereignty on the protection of human rights, could motivate states to improve their human rights records, and could lead to the development of early warning and other preventative capacities. A central aim, therefore, of the responsibility to protect is to avoid the need for military intervention. By acting on the responsibility to prevent by, for instance, developing early-warning capacity, violent disturbances may be checked before they become serious humanitarian crises that require military intervention.

My suggestion, then, is that the responsibility to protect be treated fairly narrowly, as in the World Summit agreement, but that humanitarian intervention is still clearly demarcated as one aspect of the responsibility to protect doctrine. Indeed, to achieve the reforms and improvement in willingness necessary for legitimate humanitarian intervention, it is important to emphasize that humanitarian intervention (albeit only certain, less controversial forms of humanitarian intervention) *is* still part of the responsibility to protect. In fact, Nicholas Wheeler and Frazer Egerton argue that humanitarian intervention is the area where the responsibility to protect has 'the greatest potential to save strangers, and yet faces its greatest challenges at the same time' (2009: 116). If we ignore, overlook, or exclude forcible military intervention from the responsibility to protect, we will be adopting a head-in-the-sand approach about the hard choices that will sometimes need to be made about military intervention.[7] Humanitarian crises may still sometimes become serious enough to warrant intervention and this should be viewed as a potential option. And if it is seen as one, perhaps extreme option, then it is necessary that there is the capacity to undertake legitimately this option when needed. In other words, reform of the agents and mechanisms of humanitarian intervention is part of operationalizing the responsibility to protect. Clearly marking out a circumscribed role for humanitarian intervention under the responsibility to protect may make the most of the impetus for reform surrounding this doctrine. For instance, former Canadian foreign affairs minister, Lloyd Axworthy, and former ambassador of Canada to the UN, Allan Rock, (2009: 60–1), argue for the development of the United Nations Emergency Peace Service (UNEPS) as part of the 'unfinished business' of realizing the responsibility to protect.

It is also important to reiterate that other forms of humanitarian intervention can occur *outside* the remit of the responsibility to protect, most notably interventions without the authorization of the Security Council, such as the NATO action in Kosovo. The fact that they are not included within the responsibility to protect doctrine should not rule them out completely. The danger is that the responsibility to protect could end up being used as a major impediment to legitimate humanitarian intervention. It could place all the decisions to intervene in the hands of the Security Council, whose permanent five may block intervention and set the bar for intervention very high. The result could be that certain tyrannical and authoritarian leaders do what they want to their citizens as the previously more willing agents refuse to intervene for fear of violating the responsibility to protect doctrine. Defenders of the responsibility to protect assert that one of its key draws is that it offers a wide variety of different responses to serious humanitarian crises, rather than solely military intervention. If we are concerned with a broad array of measures, then humanitarian intervention that is outside the remit of the responsibility to protect should also be on the table as part of the potential responses to serious humanitarian crises.[8]

Conceptualizing humanitarian intervention and the responsibility to protect in these ways will help to draw on the appeal of the responsibility to protect doctrine. This, in turn, could improve the willingness to intervene and to reform the current agents and mechanisms of intervention. Such improvements are vital if we are to legitimately tackle and prevent serious humanitarian crises in the future.

NOTES

1. See, further, Evans (2008*b*: 223–41), who argues that from his (notable) experience, there are four key elements to mobilizing political will: knowledge of the problem; concern to do something about it; suitable institutions to deliver; and effective leadership.
2. See, for instance, Bellamy (2009*a*) and a recent report by One World Trust (Herman 2009).
3. For instance, the East Timor and Indonesia Action Network, Life is Life, and the West Papua Advocacy Team cite the responsibility to protect in their attempt to persuade the US government to investigate human rights abuses in West Papua (ETAN 2009). Likewise, a joint letter by Amnesty International, Human Rights Watch, the Global Centre for the Responsibility to Protect, and the International Crisis Group (International Crisis Group 2009) to the Japanese prime minister invokes the responsibility to protect. This was as part of the effort to convince Japan to support the reporting of the humanitarian situation in Sri Lanka in 2009 to the Security Council.
4. See, for example, the statement by Hugo Chavez that the responsibility to protect doctrine is 'very suspicious . . . tomorrow or sometime in the future, someone in Washington will say that the Venezuelan people need to be protected from the tyrant Chavez, who is a threat' (in Santos 2005). Also see Bellamy (2009*a*) and Focarelli (2008) for surveys of states' lingering fears of abusive humanitarian intervention and the responsibility to protect.

5. It is worth noting that this is not simply a North versus South issue: several states in the Global South supported the responsibility to protect in the negotiations around the 2005 World Summit. Useful collections of government statements by region on the responsibility to protect can be found at <http://www.responsibilitytoprotect.org/index.php/government_statements/c129>.
6. Examples include Ban Ki-Moon (2008), Bellamy (2008), Evans (2008a), and Luck (2008).
7. See, further, Welsh's (2009) warnings of the dangers of focusing solely on conflict prevention at the expense of the 'hard power' measures of coercive action, which will still sometimes be required.
8. This may seem to go against the spirit of the ICISS's (2001a) attempts to integrate humanitarian intervention as part of the responsibility to protect. As I have discussed, however, the responsibility to protect doctrine has since taken on a broader significance beyond the issue of humanitarian intervention and the agreement at the World Summit (which is favoured by many) adopts a narrower account of humanitarian intervention. This makes it necessary to leave scope for humanitarian intervention outside the remit of the doctrine.

Bibliography

Abbott, Chris (2005). 'Rights and Responsibilities: The Dilemma of Humanitarian Intervention', *Global Dialogue*, 7/1–2: 1–15.

Abiew, Francis Kofi (1999). *The Evolution of the Doctrine and Practice of Humanitarian Intervention* (London: Kluwer Law International).

Abramowitz, Morton and Thomas Pickering (2008). 'Making Intervention Work', *Foreign Affairs*, 87/5: 100–8.

Advisory Council on International Affairs and Advisory Committee on Issues of Public International Law (2000). *Advisory Report 13: Humanitarian Intervention.* Available at <http://cms.web-beat.nl/ContentSuite/upload/aiv/doc/AIV_13_Eng.pdf> (accessed 04/06/09).

Altman, Andrew and Christopher Heath Wellman (2008). 'From Humanitarian Intervention to Assassination: Human Rights and Political Violence', *Ethics*, 118/2: 228–57.

Annan, Kofi (1999). *Secretary-General's Bulletin: Observance by United Nations Forces of International Humanitarian Law*, ST/SGB/1999/13, 6 August 1999. Available at <http://www.unhcr.org/refworld/docid/451bb5724.html> (accessed 04/06/09).

—— (2005). *In Larger Freedom: Towards Development, Security and Human Rights for All*, A/59/2005. Available at <http://www.un.org/largerfreedom/contents.htm> (accessed 04/06/09).

Anscombe, G.E.M. (1976). *Intention*, Second Edition (Oxford: Basil Blackwell).

Arbour, Louise (2008). 'The Responsibility to Protect as a Duty of Care in International Law and Practice', *Review of International Studies*, 34/3: 445–58.

Archibugi, Daniele (1995). 'From the United Nations to Cosmopolitan Democracy', in Daniele Archibugi and David Held (eds), *Cosmopolitan Democracy: An Agenda for a New World Order* (Cambridge: Polity Press), pp. 121–62.

—— (2004*a*). 'Cosmopolitan Democracy and its Critics: A Review', *European Journal of International Relations*, 10/3: 437–73.

—— (2004*b*). 'Cosmopolitan Guidelines for Humanitarian Intervention', *Alternatives*, 29/1, 1–21.

—— (2005). 'Cosmopolitan Humanitarian Intervention Is Never Unilateral', *International Relations*, 19/2: 220–4.

Arneson, Richard (2005). 'Sophisticated Rule Consequentialism: Some Simple Objections', *Philosophical Issues*, 15/1: 235–51.

Atack, Iain (2002). 'Ethical Objections to Humanitarian Intervention', *Security Dialogue*, 33/3: 279–92.

Axworthy, Lloyd and Allan Rock (2009). 'R2P: A New and Unfinished Agenda', *Global Responsibility to Protect*, 1/1: 54–69.

Ayoob, Mohammed (2002). 'Humanitarian Intervention and State Sovereignty', *International Journal of Human Rights*, 6/1: 81–102.

Badescu, Christina G. (2007). 'Authorizing Humanitarian Intervention: Hard Choices in Saving Strangers', *Canadian Journal of Political Science*, 40/1: 51–78.

Bagnoli, Carla (2006). 'Humanitarian Intervention as a Perfect Duty: A Kantian Argument', in Terry Nardin and Melissa S. Williams (eds), *NOMOS XLVII: Humanitarian Intervention* (New York: New York University Press), pp. 117–40.

Baker, Deane-Peter (2007). 'The AU Standby Force and the Challenge of Somalia', *African Security Review*, 16/2: 120–3.

Ban Ki-Moon (2008). 'On "Responsible Sovereignty: International Cooperation for a Changed World"', 15 July 2008, Berlin, SG/SM/11701. Available at <http://www.un.org/News/Press/docs/2008/sgsm11701.doc.htm> (accessed 15/06/09).

BBC (2005*a*). 'Peacekeepers for Somalia Approved', *BBC*, 18 March 2005. Available at <http://news.bbc.co.uk/1/hi/world/africa/4363021.stm> (accessed 09/06/09).

—— (2005*b*). 'UN Attacks DR Congo Militia Camps', *BBC*, 2 April 2005. Available at <http://news.bbc.co.uk/2/hi/africa/4403841.stm> (accessed 09/06/09).

Beitz, Charles R. (1979). *Political Theory and International Relations*, First Edition (Princeton, NJ: Princeton University Press).

—— (1980). 'Nonintervention and Communal Integrity', *Philosophy & Public Affairs*, 9/4: 385–91.

Bellamy, Alex J. (2004). 'Motives, Outcomes, Intent and the Legitimacy of Humanitarian Intervention', *Journal of Military Ethics*, 3/3: 216–32.

—— (2005). 'Responsibility to Protect or Trojan Horse? The Crisis in Darfur and Humanitarian Intervention after Iraq', *Ethics & International Affairs*, 19/2: 31–53.

—— (2006*a*). 'Preventing Future Kosovos and Future Rwandas: The Responsibility to Protect After the 2005 World Summit', Policy Brief No. 1 of the Initiative: Ethics in a Violent World: What Can Institutions Do? (New York: Carnegie Council).

—— (2006*b*). 'Whither the Responsibility to Protect? Humanitarian Intervention and the 2005 World Summit', *Ethics & International Affairs*, 20/2: 143–69.

—— (2008). 'The Responsibility to Protect and the Problem of Military Intervention', *International Affairs*, 84/4: 615–39.

—— (2009*a*). 'Realizing the Responsibility to Protect', *International Studies Perspectives*, 10/2: 111–28.

—— (2009*b*). *Responsibility to Protect: The Global Effort to End Mass Atrocities* (Cambridge: Polity Press).

—— and Paul D. Williams (2005). 'Who's Keeping the Peace? Regionalization and Contemporary Peace Operations', *International Security*, 29/4: 157–95.

—— —— (2009). 'The West and Contemporary Peace Operations', *Journal of Peace Research*, 46/1: 39–57.

—— —— and Stuart Griffin (2004). *Understanding Peacekeeping* (Cambridge: Polity Press).

Bhatia, Michael V. (2003). *War and Intervention: Issues for Contemporary Peace Operations* (Bloomfield, NJ: Kumarian Press).

Blair, Tony (1999). 'Doctrine of the International Community', Speech to the Economic Club, Chicago, 24 April 1999. Available at <http://www.pm.gov.uk/output/Page1297.asp> (accessed 09/06/09).

Blocq, Daniel S. (2006). 'The Fog of UN Peacekeeping: Ethical Issues Regarding the Use of Force to Protect Civilians in UN Operations', *Journal of Military Ethics*, 5/3: 201–13.

Bodansky, Daniel (1999). 'The Legitimacy of International Governance: A Coming Challenge for International Environmental Law?', *American Journal of International Law*, 93/3: 596–624.

Brandt, R.B. (1972). 'Utilitarianism and the Rules of War', *Philosophy & Public Affairs*, 1/2: 145–65.

Breau, Susan C. (2006). 'The Impact of the Responsibility to Protect on Peacekeeping', *Journal of Conflict & Security Law*, 11/3: 429–64.

Brooks, Doug (2000). 'Messiahs or Mercenaries? The Future of International Private Military Services', *International Peacekeeping*, 7/4: 129–44.

—— and Matan Chorev (2008). 'Ruthless Humanitarianism: Why Marginalizing Private Peacekeeping Kills People', in Andrew Alexandra, Deane-Peter Baker, and Marina Caparini (eds), *Private Military and Security Companies: Ethics, Policies and Civil-Military Relations* (New York: Routledge), pp. 116–30.

Brooks, Thom (2002). 'Cosmopolitanism and Distributing Responsibilities', *Critical Review of International Social and Political Philosophy*, 5/3: 92–7.

Brown, Adèle (2008). 'Reinventing Humanitarian Intervention: Two Cheers for the Responsibility to Protect', House of Commons Research Paper 08/55, 17 June 2008. Available at <http://www.parliament.uk/commons/lib/research/rp2008/rp08–055.pdf> (accessed 09/06/09).

Brown, Chris (2003). 'Selective Humanitarianism: In Defence of Inconsistency', in Deen K. Chatterjee and Don E. Schied (eds), *Ethics and Foreign Intervention* (Cambridge: Cambridge University Press), pp. 31–50.

—— (2005). 'What, Exactly, Is the Problem to Which the "Five-Part Test" Is the Solution?', *International Relations*, 19/2: 225–9.

Brownlie, Ian (1963). *International Law and the Use of Force by States* (Oxford: Clarendon Press).

—— (1973). 'Thoughts on Kind-Hearted Gunmen', in Richard B. Lillich (ed.), *Humanitarian Intervention and the United Nations* (Charlottesville, VA: University Press of Virginia), pp. 139–48.

Buchanan, Allen (1999). 'The Internal Legitimacy of Humanitarian Intervention', *Journal of Political Philosophy*, 7/1: 71–87.

—— (2000). 'Justice, Legitimacy, and Human Rights', in Victoria Davion and Clark Wolf (eds), *The Idea of a Political Liberalism: Essays on Rawls* (Oxford: Rowman and Littlefield), pp. 73–89.

—— (2002). 'Political Legitimacy and Democracy', *Ethics*, 112/4: 689–719.

—— (2003). 'Reforming the International Law of Humanitarian Intervention', in J.L. Holzgrefe and Robert O. Keohane (eds), *Humanitarian Intervention: Ethical, Legal and Political Dilemmas* (Cambridge: Cambridge University Press), pp. 130–73.

—— (2004). *Justice, Legitimacy, and Self-Determination: Moral Foundations for International Law* (Oxford: Oxford University Press).

—— (2006). 'Institutionalizing the Just War', *Philosophy and Public Affairs*, 34/1: 2–38.

Buchanan, Allen and Robert O. Keohane (2004). 'The Preventative Use of Force: A Cosmopolitan Institutional Proposal', *Ethics & International Affairs*, 18/1: 1–22.

Bures, Oldrich (2005). 'Private Military Companies: A Second Best Peacekeeping Option?', *International Peacekeeping*, 12/4: 533–46.

Burnham, Gilbert, Riyadh Lafta, Shannon Doocy, and Les Roberts (2006). 'Mortality After the 2003 Invasion of Iraq: A Cross-sectional Cluster Sample Survey', *The Lancet*, 368/9545: 1421–8.

Byers, Michael and Simon Chesterman (2003). 'Changing the Rules About Rules? Unilateral Humanitarian Intervention and the Future of International Law', in J. L Holzgrefe and Robert O. Keohane (eds), *Humanitarian Intervention: Ethical, Legal and Political Dilemmas* (Cambridge: Cambridge University Press), pp. 177–203.

Cabrera, Luis (forthcoming). 'World Government: Renewed Debate, Persistent Challenges', *European Journal of International Relations*.

Caney, Simon (2005). *Justice Beyond Borders: A Global Political Theory* (Oxford: Oxford University Press).

Card, Robert F. (2007). 'Inconsistency and the Theoretical Commitments of Hooker's Rule-Consequentialism', *Utilitas*, 19/2: 243–58.

Caron, David D. (1993). 'The Legitimacy of the Collective Authority of the Security Council', *American Journal of International Law*, 87/4: 552–88.

Carr, E.H. (2001 [1939]). *The Twenty Years' Crisis 1919–1939: An Introduction to the Study of International Relations*, Michael Cox (ed.) (Basingstoke: Palgrave Macmillan).

Center on International Cooperation (2008). *Briefing Paper: Annual Review of Global Peace Operations 2008*. Available at <http://www.cic.nyu.edu/internationalsecurity/docs/Final2008briefingreport.pdf> (accessed 09/06/09).

Chandler, David (2002). *From Kosovo to Kabul: Human Rights and International Intervention* (London: Pluto Press).

Chesterman, Simon (2001). *Just War or Just Peace? Humanitarian Intervention and International Law* (Oxford: Oxford University Press).

—— (2003). 'Hard Cases Make Bad Law: Law, Ethics, and Politics in Humanitarian Intervention', in Anthony F. Lang Jr. (ed.), *Just Intervention* (Washington, DC: Georgetown University Press), pp. 46–61.

—— (2005). 'Legitimacy and the Use of Force in Response to Terrorism—a Comment', in Paul Eden and Thérèse O'Donnell (eds), *September 11, 2001: A Turning Point in International and Domestic Law?* (New York: Transnational Publishers), pp. 149–61.

—— and Chia Lehnardt (2007). 'Introduction', in Simon Chesterman and Chia Lehnardt (eds), *From Mercenaries to Market: The Rise and Regulation of Private Military Companies* (Oxford: Oxford University Press), pp. 1–10.

—— and Sebastian von Einsiedel (2005). 'Dual Containment: The US, Iraq and the U.N. Security Council', in Paul Eden and Thérèse O'Donnell (eds), *September 11, 2001: A Turning Point in International and Domestic Law?* (New York: Transnational Publishers), pp. 725–56.

Chicago Council on Global Affairs/WorldPublicOpinion.org (2007). *World Publics Favor New Powers for the UN*. Available at <http://www.worldpublicopinion.org/pipa/pdf/may07/CCGA+_UN_article.pdf> (accessed 09/06/09).

Chopra, Jarat and Tanja Hohe (2004). 'Participatory Intervention', *Global Governance*, 10/3: 289–305.

—— and Thomas G. Weiss (1992). 'Sovereignty Is No Longer Sacrosanct: Codifying Humanitarian Intervention', *Ethics & International Affairs*, 6/1: 95–117.

Christiano, Thomas (1996). *The Rule of the Many: Fundamental Issues in Democratic Theory* (Oxford: Westview Press).

Cilliers, Jakkie (2008). 'The African Standby Force: An Update on Progress', *Institute for Security Studies Paper*, 160. Available at <http://www.iss.co.za> (accessed 09/06/09).

Citizens for Global Solutions (2008). *United Nations Emergency Peace Service: One Step Towards Effective Genocide Prevention*. Available at <http://www.globalsolutions.org/files/general/UNEPS_1step.pdf> (accessed 09/06/09).

Clarke, John (2001). 'A Pragmatic Approach to Humanitarian Intervention', *Journal of Humanitarian Assistance*. Available at <http://www.jha.ac/articles/a072.pdf> (accessed 16/06/09).

CNN (2008). 'Transcript of Second McCain, Obama Debate', *CNN.com*, 7 October 2008. Available at <http://www.cnn.com/2008/POLITICS/10/07/presidential.debate.transcript> (accessed 09/06/09).

Coady, C.A.J. (2002). 'The Ethics of Armed Humanitarian Intervention', *US Institute of Peace, PeaceWorks Report No. 45*. Available at <http://www.usip.org/pubs/peaceworks/pwks45.pdf> (accessed 09/06/09).

Coates, Anthony (2006). 'Humanitarian Intervention: A Conflict of Traditions', in Terry Nardin and Melissa S. Williams (eds), *NOMOS XLVII: Humanitarian Intervention* (New York: New York University Press), pp. 58–83.

Conetta, Carl and Charles Knight (1995). *Vital Force: A Proposal for the Overhaul of the UN Peace Operations System and for the Creation of a UN Legion*, Project on Defense Alternatives Research Monograph 4 (Cambridge, MA: Commonwealth Institute).

Cook, Martin L. (2003). '"Immaculate War": Constraints on Humanitarian Intervention', in Anthony F. Lang Jr. (ed.), *Just Intervention* (Washington, D.C.: Georgetown University Press), pp 145–54.

Cottey, Andrew (2008). 'Beyond Humanitarian Intervention: The New Politics of Peacekeeping and Intervention', *Contemporary Politics*, 14/4: 429–46.

Craig, Campbell (2008). 'The Resurgent Idea of World Government', *Ethics & International Affairs*, 22/2: 133–42.

Crawford, Neta C. (2005). 'The Justice of Preemptive and Preventative War Doctrines', in Mark Evans (ed.), *Just War Theory: A Reappraisal* (Edinburgh: Edinburgh University Press), pp. 25–49.

Crawford, Timothy W. and Alan J. Kuperman (eds) (2006). *Gambling on Humanitarian Intervention: Moral Hazard, Rebellion and Civil War* (New York: Routledge).

Cushman, Thomas (ed.) (2005). *A Matter of Principle: Humanitarian Arguments for War in Iraq* (Berkeley, CA: University of California Press).

Dahl, Robert A. (1989). *Democracy and its Critics* (London: Yale University Press).

Damrosch, Lori Fisler (2000). 'The Inevitability of Selective Response? Principles to Guide Urgent International Action', in Albrecht Schnabel and Ramesh Thakur (eds), *Kosovo and the Challenge of Humanitarian Intervention* (New York: United Nations University), pp. 405–19.

Danish Institute of International Affairs (DUPI) (1999). *Humanitarian Intervention. Legal and Political Aspects* (Copenhagen: Danish Institute of International Affairs).

de Waal, Alex (ed.) (2000). *Who Fights? Who Cares? War and Humanitarian Action in Africa* (Trenton, NJ: Africa World Press).

—— (2007). 'Darfur and the Failure of the Responsibility to Protect', *International Affairs*, 83/6: 1039–54.

deLisle, Jacques (2001). 'Humanitarian Intervention: Legality, Morality, and the Good Samaritan', *Orbis*, 45/4: 535–56.

Diehl, Paul F. (2005). 'Nations Agree Genocide Must Be Stopped. Can They Find the Mechanism to Do It?', *Washington Post*, 15 May 2005. Available at <http://www.globalpolicy.org/security/peacekpg/reform/2005/0515again.htm>(accessed 10/06/09).

—— (2008). *Peace Operations* (Cambridge: Polity Press).

Doppelt, Gerald (1980). 'Statism Without Foundations', *Philosophy & Public Affairs*, 9/4: 398–403.

Doss, Alan (2009). 'Letter to Ms. Laurence Gaubert, Head of Mission for MSF in Congo', *MONUC.org*. Available at <http://monuc.unmissions.org/Portals/MONUC/Letters/Final 6.02.2009 Letter SRSG Response to MSF Press release 4 Feb.pdf> (accessed 13/06/09).

Doyle, Michael W. (2001). 'The New Interventionism', *Metaphilosophy*, 32/1–2: 212–35.

Emmers, Ralph (2004). 'Regional Organisations and Peacekeeping: A Study of the ARF', in Lorraine Elliott and Graham Cheeseman (eds), *Forces for Good: Cosmopolitan Militaries in the Twenty-first Century* (Manchester: Manchester University Press), pp. 134–49.

Estlund, David (2007). 'On Following Orders in an Unjust War', *Journal of Political Philosophy*, 15/2: 213–34.

ETAN (2009). 'Groups Urge U.S. Action on West Papua Rights as Security Situation Deteriorates', *ETAN.org*, 9 April 2009. Available at <http://www.etan.org/news/2009/04papua.htm> (accessed 14/06/09).

Evans, Gareth (1993). 'A UN Volunteer Military Force—Four Views', *New York Review of Books*, 24 June 1993, 40/12: 58.

—— (2008a). 'Facing Up to Our Responsibilities', *The Guardian*, 12 May 2008. Available at <http://www.guardian.co.uk/commentisfree/2008/may/12/facinguptoourresponsibilities> (accessed 14/06/09).

—— (2008b). *The Responsibility to Protect: Ending Mass Atrocity Crimes Once and For All* (Washington, DC: Brookings Institution Press).

Falk, Richard and Andrew Strauss (2001). 'Toward Global Parliament', *Foreign Affairs*, 80/1: 212–20.

Farer, Tom J. (1991). 'Human Rights in Law's Empire: The Jurisprudence War', *American Journal of International Law*, 85/1: 117–27.

—— (2003). 'Humanitarian Intervention Before and After 9/11: Legality and Legitimacy', in J.L. Holzgrefe and Robert O. Keohane (eds), *Humanitarian Intervention:*

Ethical, Legal and Political Dilemmas (Cambridge: Cambridge University Press), pp. 53–90.

—— (2005*a*). 'Cosmopolitan Humanitarian Intervention: A Five-Part Test', *International Relations*, 19/2: 211–20.

—— (2005*b*). 'Response to the Commentators', *International Relations*, 19/2: 242–7.

Fixdal, Mona and Dan Smith (1998). 'Humanitarian Intervention and Just War', *Mershon International Studies Review*, 42/2: 283–312.

Focarelli, Carlo (2008). 'The Responsibility to Protect Doctrine and Humanitarian Intervention: Too Many Ambiguities for a Working Doctrine', *Journal of Conflict & Security Law*, 13/2: 191–213.

Foot, Philippa (1988). 'Utilitarianism and the Virtues', in Samuel Scheffler (ed.), *Consequentialism and its Critics* (Oxford: Oxford University Press), pp. 224–41.

Foreign Affairs Committee (2002). *Private Military Companies: Response of the Secretary of State for Foreign and Commonwealth Affairs* (London: The Stationery Office). Available at <http://www.fco.gov.uk/resources/en/pdf/7179755/2002_oct_ninth_report> (accessed 14/06/09).

Foreign and Commonwealth Office (2002). *Private Military Companies: Options for Regulation* (London: The Stationery Office). Available at <http://www.fco.gov.uk/resources/en/pdf/pdf4/fco_pdf_privatemilitarycompanies> (accessed 14/06/09).

Franck, Thomas M. (2002). *Recourse to Force: State Action Against Threats and Armed Attacks* (Cambridge: Cambridge University Press).

—— (2003). 'Interpretation and Change in the Law of Humanitarian Intervention', in J.L. Holzgrefe and Robert O. Keohane (eds), *Humanitarian Intervention: Ethical, Legal and Political Dilemmas* (Cambridge: Cambridge University Press), pp. 204–31.

—— (2006). 'Legality and Legitimacy in Humanitarian Intervention', in Terry Nardin and Melissa S. Williams (eds), *NOMOS XLVII: Humanitarian Intervention* (New York: New York University Press), pp. 143–57.

—— and Nigel S. Rodley (1973). 'After Bangladesh: The Law of Humanitarian Intervention by Military Force', *American Journal of International Law*, 67/2: 275–305.

Gantz, Peter (2003). 'The Private Sector's Role in Peacekeeping and Peace Enforcement', *Refugees International*, 18 November 2003. Available at <http://www.globalpolicy.org> (accessed 14/06/09).

Germain, Nicolas and Virginie Herz (2008). 'The Limits to Eufor's Mandate', *France 24*. Available at <http://www.france24.com/en/20080928-limit-eufor-mandate-chad-darfur-peacekeeping-eu-report-oxfam> (accessed 14/06/09).

Ghebali, Victor-Yves (2006). 'The United Nations and the Dilemma of Outsourcing Peacekeeping Operations', in Alan Bryden and Marina Caparini (eds), *Private Actors and Security Governance* (Berlin: LIT Verlag), pp. 213–30.

Gheciu, Alexandra and Jennifer M. Welsh (2009). 'The Imperative to Rebuild: Assessing the Normative Case for Postconflict Reconstruction', *Ethics & International Affairs*, 22/2, 121–46.

Gizelis, Theodora-Ismene and Kristin E. Kosek (2005). 'Why Humanitarian Interventions Succeed or Fail: The Role of Local Participation', *Cooperation and Conflict*, 40/4: 363–83.

Gompert, David C. (2006). 'For a Capability to Protect: Mass Killing, the African Union and NATO', *Survival*, 40/1: 7–18.

Goodman, Ryan (2006). 'Humanitarian Intervention and Pretexts for War', *American Journal of International Law*, 100/1: 107–41.

Goulding, Marrack (2004). 'Cosmopolitan Purposes and the United Nations', in Lorraine Elliott and Graham Cheeseman (eds), *Forces for Good: Cosmopolitan Militaries in the Twenty-first Century* (Manchester: Manchester University Press), pp. 101–16.

Graham, Gordon (1987). 'The Justice of Intervention', *Review of International Studies*, 13/2, 133–46.

Gray, Christine (2000). *International Law and the Use of Force*, First Edition (Oxford: Oxford University Press).

Green, Leslie (1988). *The Authority of the State* (Oxford: Clarendon Press).

Gueli, Richard (2004). 'Humanitarian Intervention in Africa: Towards a New Posture', *Scientia Militaria: South African Journal of Military Studies*, 32/1: 120–42.

Hall, Stephen (2001). 'The Persistent Spectre: Natural Law, International Order and the Limits of Legal Positivism', *European Journal of International Law*, 12/2: 269–307.

Hare, R.M. (1972). 'Rules of War and Moral Reasoning', *Philosophy & Public Affairs*, 1/2: 166–81.

Hart, H.L.A. (1994). *The Concept of Law*, Second Edition (Oxford: Clarendon Press).

Hashmi, Sohail H. (2003). 'Is There an Islamic Ethic of Humanitarian Intervention?', in Anthony F. Lang Jr. (ed.), *Just Intervention* (Washington, DC: Georgetown University Press), pp. 62–83.

Hegel, Georg Wilhelm Friedrich (1991 [1821]). *Hegel: Elements of the Philosophy of Right*, Allen W. Wood (ed.) and trans. H.B. Nisbet (Cambridge: Cambridge University Press).

Hehir, Aidan (2008). *Humanitarian Intervention After Kosovo: Iraq, Darfur and the Record of Global Civil Society* (Basingstoke: Palgrave Macmillan).

Heinze, Eric A. (2004). 'The Moral Limits of Humanitarian Intervention: Reconciling Human Respect and Utility', *Polity*, 36/4: 543–58.

—— (2005). 'Commonsense Morality and the Consequentialist Ethics of Humanitarian Intervention', *Journal of Military Ethics*, 4/3: 168–82.

—— (2006). 'Humanitarian Intervention and the War in Iraq: Norms, Discourse, and State Practice', *Parameters: US Army War College Quarterly*, 36/1: 20–34.

—— (2009). *Waging Humanitarian War: The Ethics, Law, and Politics of Humanitarian Intervention* (Albany, NJ: SUNY Press).

Held, David (1995a). *Democracy and the Global Order: From the Modern State to Cosmopolitan Governance* (Cambridge: Polity Press).

—— (1995*b*). 'Democracy and the New International Order', in Daniele Archibugi and David Held (eds), *Cosmopolitan Democracy: An Agenda for a New World Order* (Cambridge: Polity Press), pp. 96–120.

—— (1998). 'Democracy and Globalization', in Daniele Archibugi, David Held, and Martin Köhler (eds), *Re-imagining Political Community: Studies in Cosmopolitan Democracy* (Oxford: Polity Press), pp. 11–27.

Henckaerts, Jean-Marie and Louise Doswald-Beck (2005). *Customary International Humanitarian Law: Volume I: Rules* (Cambridge: Cambridge University Press).

Herman, Lyndall (2009). 'Too Quiet on the Western Front: Why Failing to Find Political Solutions to Overstretch in UN Peacekeeping Could Scupper the Realisation of the Responsibility to Protect', One World Trust Briefing Paper 105, May 2007. Available at <http://www.oneworldtrust.org/> (accessed 15/06/09).

Herring, Eric (2002). 'Between Iraq and a Hard Place: A Critique of the British Government's Narrative for UN Economic Sanctions', *Review of International Studies*, 28/1: 39–56.

Herro, Annie, Wendy Lambourne, and David Penklis (2009). 'Peacekeeping and Peace Enforcement in Africa: The Potential Contribution of a UN Emergency Peace Service', *African Security Review*, 18/1: 49–62.

Hillen, John F. III (1994). 'Policing the New World Order: The Operational Utility of a Permanent U.N. Army', *Strategic Review*, 22/2: 54–62.

Hirsh, Michael (2000). 'Calling All Regio-Cops: Peacekeeping's Hybrid Future', *Foreign Affairs*, 79/6: 2–8.

Hodge, Carl Cavanagh (2003). 'The Port of Mars: The US and the International Community', *Journal of Military Ethics*, 2/2: 107–21.

Holt, Victoria K. and Tobias C. Berkman (2006). *The Impossible Mandate? Military Preparedness, the Responsibility to Protect and Modern Peace Operations* (Washington, DC: Henry L. Stimson Center).

Holzgrefe, J.L. (2003). 'The Humanitarian Intervention Debate', in J.L. Holzgrefe and Robert O. Keohane (eds), *Humanitarian Intervention: Ethical, Legal and Political Dilemmas* (Cambridge: Cambridge University Press), pp. 15–52.

Hooker, Brad (2000). *Ideal Code, Real World: A Rule-Consequentialist Theory of Morality* (Oxford: Clarendon Press).

—— (2004). 'Rule Consequentialism', in Edward N. Zalta (ed.), *The Stanford Encyclopedia of Philosophy*, Spring 2004 Edition. Available at <http://plato.stanford.edu/archives/spr2004/entries/consequentialism-rule/> (accessed 14/06/09).

—— (2005). 'Reply to Arneson and McIntyre', *Philosophical Issues*, 15/1: 264–81.

—— (2007). 'Rule-Consequentialism and Internal Consistency: A Reply to Card', *Utilitas*, 19/4: 514–19.

Howe, Herbert M. (1998). 'Private Security Forces and African Stability: The Case of Executive Outcomes', *Journal of Modern African Studies*, 36/2: 307–31.

Human Rights Watch (2008). *'Troops in Contact', Airstrikes and Civilian Deaths in Afghanistan*. Available at <http://www.hrw.org/sites/default/files/reports/afghanistan0908webwcover_0.pdf> (accessed 15/06/09).

Human Rights Watch (2009). *Human Rights Watch World Report 2009*. Available at <http://www.hrw.org/sites/default/files/reports/wr2009_web.pdf> (accessed 15/06/09).

Hurka, Thomas (2005). 'Proportionality in the Morality of War', *Philosophy & Public Affairs*, 33/1: 34–66.

—— (2007). 'Liability and Just Cause', *Ethics & International Affairs*, 21/2: 199–218.

ICISS (2001*a*). *The Responsibility to Protect: Report of the International Commission on Intervention and State Sovereignty* (Ottawa: International Development Research Centre).

—— (2001*b*). *The Responsibility to Protect: Research, Bibliography, Background: Supplementary Volume to the Report of the International Commission on Intervention and State Sovereignty* (Ottawa: International Development Research Centre).

Independent International Commission on Kosovo (2000). *The Kosovo Report* (Oxford: Oxford University Press).

International Committee of the Red Cross (2000). *The People on War Report: ICRC Worldwide Consultation on the Rules of War*. Available at <http://www.icrc.org/Web/Eng/siteeng0.nsf/htmlall/p0758/$File/ICRC_002_0758.PDF!Open> (accessed 15/06/09).

International Crisis Group (2008*a*). 'Conflict History: DR Congo'. *Crisisgroup.org*. Available at <http://www.crisisgroup.org/home/index.cfm?action=conflict_search&l = 1&t = 1&c_country = 37> (accessed 15/06/09).

—— (2008*b*). 'Conflict History: Somalia'. *Crisisgroup.org*. Available at <http://www.crisisgroup.org/home/index.cfm?action = conflict_search&l = 1&t = 1&c_country = 98> (accessed 15/06/09).

—— (2009). 'Joint Letter to Japanese Prime Minister on Sri Lanka', *Crisisgroup.org*, 11 May 2009. Available at <http://www.crisisgroup.org/home/index.cfm?id = 6096> (accessed 15/06/09).

International Rescue Committee (2008). 'IRC Study Shows Congo's Neglected Crisis Leaves 5.4 Million Dead; Peace Deal in N. Kivu, Increased Aid Critical to Reducing Death Toll', *Theirc.org*. Available at <http://www.theirc.org/news/irc-study-shows-congos0122.html> (accessed 15/06/09).

Iraq Family Health Survey Study Group (2008). 'Violence-Related Mortality in Iraq from 2002 to 2006', *New England Journal of Medicine*, 358/5: 484–93.

IRIN (2008). 'DRC: Anti-MONUC Protest in Rutshuru Turns Violent', *IRIN*, 3 September 2008. Available at <http://www.irinnews.org/Report.aspx?ReportId = 80149> (accessed 15/06/09).

Jeangène Vilmer, Jean-Baptiste (2007). 'Humanitarian Intervention and Disinterestedness', *Peace Review*, 19/2: 207–16.

Joffe, George (1994). 'Sovereignty and Intervention: The Perspective from the Developing World', in Marianne Heiberg (ed.), *Subduing Sovereignty: Sovereignty and the Right to Intervene* (London: Pinter), pp. 68–95.

Johansen, Robert C. (ed.) (2006). *A United Nations Emergency Peace Service: To Prevent Genocide and Crimes Against Humanity* (New York: World Federalist Movement).

Kaldor, Mary (1999). *New and Old Wars: Organized Violence in a Global Era* (Cambridge: Polity Press).

—— (2008). 'Responsible Intervention', *Survival*, 50/4: 191–200.

Kant, Immanuel (1991 [1795]). 'Perpetual Peace: A Philosophical Sketch', in *Kant: Political Writings*, Hans S. Reiss (ed.) and trans. H.B. Nisbet, Second Edition (Cambridge: Cambridge University Press), pp. 93–130.

Kaufman, Whitley (2003). 'Motive, Intention, and Morality in the Criminal Law', *Criminal Justice Review*, 28/2: 317–35.

Kinloch-Pichat, Stephen (2004). *A UN 'Legion': Between Utopia and Reality* (London: Frank Cass).

Kovach, Karen (2003). 'The International Community as Moral Agent', *Journal of Military Ethics*, 2/2: 99–106.

Krahmann, Elke (2008). 'The New Model Soldier and Civil-Military Relations', in Andrew Alexandra, Deane-Peter Baker, and Marina Caparini (eds), *Private Military and Security Companies: Ethics, Policies and Civil-Military Relations* (New York: Routledge), pp. 247–65.

Krasno, Jean (2006). *Public Opinion Survey of UNMIL's Work in Liberia*, External Study for the Peacekeeping Best Practices Section, United Nations Department of Peacekeeping Operations. Available at <http://www.peacekeepingbestpractices. unlb.org/PBPS/Library/Liberia_POS_final_report_Mar_29.pdf> (accessed 15/06/09).

Krisch, Nico (2002). 'Review Essay: Legality, Morality and the Dilemma of Humanitarian Intervention After Kosovo', *European Journal of International Law*, 13/1: 323–35.

Kuperman, Alan J. (2001). *The Limits of Humanitarian Intervention: Genocide in Rwanda* (Washington, DC: Brookings Institution Press).

Kurth, James (2006). 'Humanitarian Intervention After Iraq: Legal Ideas vs. Military Realities', *Orbis*, 50/1: 87–101.

Ladley, Andrew (2005). 'Peacekeeper Abuse, Immunity and Impunity: The Need for Effective Criminal and Civil Accountability on International Peace Operations', *Politics and Ethics Review*, 1/1: 81–90.

Langille, H. Peter (2000a). 'Conflict Prevention: Options for Rapid Deployment and UN Standing Forces', *Global Polity Forum*. Available at <http://www.globalpolicy. org/security/peacekpg/reform/canada2.htm> (accessed 15/06/09).

—— (2000b). 'SHIRBRIG: A Promising Step Towards the United Nations that Can Prevent Deadly Conflict', *Global Policy Forum*. Available at <http://www.globalpolicy. org/security/peacekpg/reform/canada.htm> (accessed 15/06/09).

—— (2004). 'Preventing Genocide: Time for a UN 911', *Globe and Mail*, 19 October 2004. Available at <http://www.globalpolicy.org/security/peacekpg/reform/2004/ 1019timefor.htm> (accessed 15/06/09).

—— (2009). 'UN Emergency Peace Service Question Goes Unasked', *Embassy.Mag*, 7 January 2009. Available at <http://www.embassymag.ca/page/view/langille-1-7– 2009> (accessed 04/03/09).

Lango, John (2001). 'Is Armed Humanitarian Intervention to Stop Mass Killing Morally Obligatory?', *Public Affairs Quarterly*, 15/3: 173–91.

—— (2007). 'The Just War Principle of Last Resort: The Question of Reasonableness Standards' *Asteriskos: Journal of International and Peace Studies*, 1/1–2: 7–23. Available at <http://www.igesip.org/asteriskos/1_2/galego/art1.pdf> (accessed 16/06/09).

—— (2009a). 'Before Military Force, Nonviolent Action: An Application of a Generalized Just War Principle of Last Resort', *Public Affairs Quarterly*, 23/2: 115–33.

—— (2009b). 'Military Operations by Armed UN Peace-keeping Missions: An Application of Generalised Just War Principles', in Th. A. van Baarda and D.E.M. Verweij (eds), *The Moral Dimension of Asymmetrical Warfare: Counter-terrorism, Western Values and Military Ethics* (Leiden: Martinus Nijhoff), pp. 115–33.

Lee, Steven (2005). 'A Moral Critique of the Cosmopolitan Institutional Proposal', *Ethics & International Affairs*, 19/2: 99–107.

Lenman, James (2000). 'Consequentialism and Cluelessness', *Philosophy & Public Affairs*, 29/4: 342–70.

Lepard, Brian D. (2002). *Rethinking Humanitarian Intervention: A Fresh Legal Approach Based on Fundamental Ethical Principles in International Law and World Religions* (Pennsylvania: Pennsylvania State University Press).

Lu, Catherine (2006a). 'Whose Principles? Whose Institutions? Legitimacy Challenges for "Humanitarian Intervention"', in Terry Nardin and Melissa S. Williams (eds), *NOMOS XLVII: Humanitarian Intervention* (New York: New York University Press), pp. 188–216.

—— (2006b). 'World Government', in Edward N. Zalta (ed.), *Stanford Encyclopedia of Philosophy*, Winter 2006 Edition. Available at <http://plato.stanford.edu/archives/win2006/entries/world-government> (accessed 15/06/09).

Luban, David (1980a). 'Just War and Human Rights', *Philosophy & Public Affairs*, 9/2: 160–81.

—— (1980b). 'The Romance of the Nation-State', *Philosophy & Public Affairs*, 9/4: 392–7.

—— (2004). 'Preventive War', *Philosophy & Public Affairs*, 32/3: 207–48.

Lucas, George R. Jr. (2003a). 'From *jus ad bellum* to *jus ad pacem*: Re-thinking Just-War Criteria for the Use of Military Force for Humanitarian Ends', in Deen K. Chatterjee and Don E. Scheid (eds), *Ethics and Foreign Intervention* (Cambridge: Cambridge University Press), pp. 72–96.

—— (2003b). 'The Role of the "International Community" in Just War Tradition—Confronting the Challenges of Humanitarian Intervention and Preemptive War', *Journal of Military Ethics*, 2/2: 122–44.

Luck, Edward C. (2008). 'International Disaster Assistance: Policy Options', Subcommittee on International Development, Foreign Assistance, Economic Affairs and International Environmental Protection, Committee on Foreign Relations of the US Senate, 17 June 2008. Available at <http://www.ipinst.org/asset/file/370/disaster.pdf> (accessed 15/06/09).

Luttwak, Edward N. (2000). 'No-score War', *Times Literary Supplement*, 14 July 2000. Available at <http://tls.timesonline.co.uk/article/0,,25368–1942387_1,00.html> (accessed 17/06/09).

Lyons, David (1965). *Forms and Limits of Utilitarianism* (Oxford: Oxford University Press).

Macklem, Patrick (2008). 'Humanitarian Intervention and the Distribution of Sovereignty in International Law', *Ethics & International Affairs*, 22/4: 369–93.

Mason, Andrew (2000). *Community, Solidarity and Belonging: Levels of Community and their Normative Significance* (Cambridge: Cambridge University Press).

—— and Nicolas J. Wheeler (1996). 'Realist Objections to Humanitarian Intervention', in Barry Holden (ed.), *The Ethical Dimensions of Global Change* (London: Macmillan), pp. 94–110.

Matthews, Max W. (2008). 'Tracking the Emergence of a New International Norm: The Responsibility to Protect and the Crisis In Darfur', *Boston College International & Comparative Law Review*, 31/1: 137–52.

May, Larry (2008). *Aggression and Crimes Against Peace* (Cambridge: Cambridge University Press).

Mayall, James (2000). 'The Concept of Humanitarian Intervention Revisited', in Albrecht Schnabel and Ramesh Thakur (eds), *Kosovo and the Challenge of Humanitarian Intervention* (New York: United Nations University), pp. 319–33.

McClean, Emma (2008). 'The Responsibility to Protect: The Role of International Human Rights Law', *Journal of Conflict & Security Law*, 13/1: 123–52.

McDougall, Derek (2004). 'Intervention in Solomon Islands', *The Round Table*, 93, 213–23.

McIntyre, Alison (2001). 'Doing Away with Double Effect', *Ethics*, 111/2: 219–55.

—— (2005). 'The Perils of Holism: Brad Hooker's *Ideal Code, Real World*', *Philosophical Issues*, 15/1: 252–63.

McMahan, Jeff (1996). 'Intervention and Collective Self-Determination', *Ethics & International Affairs*, 10/1: 1–24.

—— (2004a). 'The Ethics of Killing in War', *Ethics*, 114/4: 693–733.

—— (2004b). 'Unjust War in Iraq', *The Pelican Record*, XLI/5: 21–33. Available at <http://leiterreports.typepad.com/blog/2004/09/the_moral_case_.html> (accessed 15/06/09).

—— (2005). 'Just Cause for War', *Ethics & International Affairs*, 19/3: 1–21.

—— (2006). 'On the Moral Equality of Combatants', *Journal of Political Philosophy*, 14/4: 377–93.

—— (2008). 'The Morality of War and the Law of War', in David Rodin and Henry Shue (eds), *Just and Unjust Warriors: The Legal and Moral Status of Soldiers* (Oxford: Clarendon Press), pp. 19–43.

—— (2009). *Killing in War* (Oxford: Clarendon Press).

—— (2010). 'Humanitarian Intervention, Consent, and Proportionality', in N. Ann Davis, Richard Keshen, and Jeff McMahan (eds), *Ethics and Humanity: Themes from the Philosophy of Jonathan Glover* (New York: Oxford University Press), *forthcoming*.

McMahan, Jeff (forthcoming). 'Child Soldiers: The Ethical Perspective', in Scott Gates and Simon Reich (eds), *Child Soldiers in the Age of Fractured States* (Pittsburgh: University of Pittsburgh Press).

Médecins Sans Frontières (2009). 'Lack of Protection for Victims of Violence in North-Eastern Congo (DRC)', *MSF.org.uk*. Available at <http://www.msf.org.uk/lack_of_protection_in_drc_20090204.news> (accessed 15/06/09).

Mehta, Pratap Bhanu (2006). 'From State Sovereignty to Human Security (via Institutions?)', in Terry Nardin and Melissa S. Williams (eds), *NOMOS XLVII: Humanitarian Intervention* (New York: New York University Press), pp. 259–85.

Mersaides, Michael (2005). 'Peacekeeping and Legitimacy: Lessons from Cambodia and Somalia', *International Peacekeeping*, 12/2: 205–11.

Miller, Dale E. (2003). 'Actual-Consequence Act Utilitarianism and the Best Possible Humans', *Ratio*, 16/1: 49–63.

Miller, David (2001). 'Distributing Responsibilities', *Journal of Political Philosophy*, 9/4: 453–71.

—— (2007). 'The Responsibility to Protect Human Rights', Working Paper Series, SJ006, Centre for the Study of Social Justice, University of Oxford, May 2007.

Miller, Richard B. (2008). 'Justifications of the Iraq War Examined', *Ethics & International Affairs*, 22/1: 43–67.

Mozaffari, Medhi (2005). 'Just War Against an "Outlaw" Region', in Thomas Cushman (ed.), *A Matter of Principle: Humanitarian Arguments for War in Iraq* (Berkeley, CA: University of California Press), pp. 106–24.

Munck, Gerardo L. and Chetan Kumar (1995). 'Civil Conflicts and the Conditions for Successful International Intervention: A Comparative Study of Cambodia and El Salvador', *Review of International Studies*, 21/2: 159–81.

Murphy, Liam B. (2000). *Moral Demands in Nonideal Theory* (New York: Oxford University Press).

Murphy, Ray (2000). 'International Humanitarian Law Training for Multinational Peace Support Operations—Lessons from Experience', *International Review of the Red Cross*, 840: 953–68.

Nardin, Terry (2003). 'The Moral Basis for Humanitarian Intervention', in Anthony F. Lang Jr. (ed.), *Just Intervention* (Washington, DC: Georgetown University Press), pp. 11–28.

—— (2005). 'Response to "Ending Tyranny in Iraq": Humanitarian Imperialism', *Ethics & International Affairs*, 19/2: 21–6.

—— (2006). 'Introduction', in Terry Nardin and Melissa S. Williams (eds), *NOMOS XLVII: Humanitarian Intervention* (New York: New York University Press), pp. 1–28.

NATO (2009). 'International Security Assistance Force and Afghan National Army Strength & Laydown', NATO.int <http://www.nato.int/isaf/docu/epub/pdf/placemat.pdf> (accessed 21/06/09).

Nickel, James W. (2007). *Making Sense of Human Rights*, Second Edition (Oxford: Blackwell).

Nowrojee, Binaifer (2004). 'Africa on Its Own: Regional Intervention and Human Rights', *Human Rights Watch World Report*. Available at <http://199.173.149.120/ wr2k4/download/4.pdf> (accessed 15/06/09).

Nozick, Robert (1974). *Anarchy, State, and Utopia* (Oxford: Blackwell).

O'Hanlon, Michael E. (2003). *Expanding Global Military Capacity for Humanitarian Intervention* (Washington, DC: Brookings Institution Press).

—— and P.W. Singer (2004). 'The Humanitarian Transformation: Expanding Global Intervention Capacity', *Survival*, 46/1: 77–100.

Oakley, Robert (1993). 'A UN Volunteer Force—the Prospects', *New York Review of Books*, 15 July 1993, 40/13: 52–3.

Olsen, Gorm Rye (2002). 'The EU and Conflict Management in African Emergencies', *International Peacekeeping*, 9/3: 87–102.

Olsson, Christian (2007). 'The Politics of the Apolitical: Private Military Companies, Humanitarians and the Quest for (Anti-)Politics in Post-intervention Environments', *Journal of International Relations and Development*, 10/4: 332–61.

Orend, Brian (2006). *The Morality of War* (Ontario: Broadview Press).

Parekh, Bhikhu (1997*a*). 'Rethinking Humanitarian Intervention', *International Political Science Review*, 18/1: 49–69.

—— (1997*b*). 'The Dilemmas of Humanitarian Intervention: Introduction', *International Political Science Review*, 18/1: 5–7.

Pattison, James (2008*a*). 'Humanitarian Intervention and a Cosmopolitan UN Force', *Journal of International Political Theory*, 4/1: 126–45.

—— (2008*b*). 'Just War Theory and the Privatization of Military Force', *Ethics & International Affairs*, 22/2: 143–62.

—— (2008*c*). 'Whose Responsibility to Protect? The Duties of Humanitarian Intervention', *Journal of Military Ethics*, 7/4: 262–83.

—— (2009). 'Humanitarian Intervention, the Responsibility to Protect, and *jus in bello*', *Global Responsibility to Protect*, 1/3: 364–91.

—— (Forthcoming *a*). 'Deeper Objections to the Privatisation of Military Force', *Journal of Political Philosophy*.

—— (Forthcoming *b*). 'Outsourcing the Responsibility to Protect: Humanitarian Intervention and Private Military Companies'.

Paul, James and Celine Nahory (2005). 'Theses Towards a Democratic Reform of the UN Security Council', *Global Policy Forum*, 13 July 2005. Available at <http://www. globalpolicy.org/security/reform/2005/0713theses.htm> (accessed 15/06/09).

Pfaff, Tony (2000). *Peacekeeping and the Just War Tradition*, Strategic Studies Institute, US Army War College. Available at <http://www.strategicstudiesinstitute.army.mil/ pdffiles/PUB302sd.pdf?> (accessed 15/06/09).

Piiparinen, Touko (2007). 'The Lessons of Darfur for the Future of Humanitarian Intervention', *Global Governance*, 13/3: 365–90.

Pitkin, Hanna F. (1967). *The Concept of Representation* (London: University of California Press).

Pogge, Thomas (1992*a*). 'An Institutional Approach to Humanitarian Intervention', *Public Affairs Quarterly*, 6/1: 89–103.

Pogge, Thomas (1992*b*). 'Cosmopolitanism and Sovereignty', *Ethics*, 103/1: 48–75.

Pogge, Thomas (2006). 'Moralizing Humanitarian Intervention: Why Jurying Fails and How Law Can Work', in Terry Nardin and Melissa S. Williams (eds), *NOMOS XLVII: Humanitarian Intervention* (London: New York University Press), pp. 158–87.

—— (2008). *World Poverty and Human Rights*, Second Edition (Cambridge: Polity Press).

Polgreen, Lydia (2006). 'Shaky Peace in Darfur at Risk, as a New Confrontation Looms', *New York Times*, 31 August 2006. Available at <http://www.nytimes.com/> (accessed 13/06/09).

Quinn, Warren S. (1989). 'Actions, Intentions, and Consequences: The Doctrine of Doing and Allowing', *Philosophical Review*, 98/3: 287–312.

Ramsbotham, Oliver and Tom Woodhouse (1996). *Humanitarian Intervention in Contemporary Conflict: A Reconceptualization* (Cambridge: Polity Press).

Rasmussen, Mikkel Vedby (2002). 'Turbulent Neighbourhoods: How to Deploy the EU's Rapid Reaction Force', *Contemporary Security Policy*, 23/2: 39–60.

Rawls, John (1999*a*). *A Theory of Justice*, Revised Edition (Oxford: Oxford University Press).

—— (1999*b*). *The Law of Peoples* (London: Harvard University Press).

Raz, Joseph (1986). *The Morality of Freedom* (Oxford: Clarendon Press).

—— (1989). 'Facing Up: A Reply', *Southern California Law Review*, 62: 1153–235.

Roberts, Adam (1993). 'Humanitarian War: Military Intervention and Human Rights', *International Affairs*, 69/3: 429–49.

—— (2008). 'Proposals for UN Standing Forces: A Critical History', in Vaughan Lowe, Adam Roberts, Jennifer Welsh, and Dominik Zaum (eds), *The United Nations Security Council and War: The Evolution of Thought and Practice since 1945* (Oxford: Oxford University Press), pp. 99–130.

Roff, H. M. (2009). 'Response to Pattison: Whose Responsibility to Protect?', *Journal of Military Ethics*, 8/1: 79–85.

Roth, Kenneth (2004). 'War in Iraq: Not a Humanitarian Intervention', *Human Rights Watch World Report 2004*. Available at <http://hrw.org/wr2k4/3.htm> (accessed 15/06/09).

—— (2006). 'Was the Iraq War a Humanitarian Intervention?', *Journal of Military Ethics*, 5/2: 84–92.

Santos, Diego (2005). 'Chavez Criticizes UN Reforms in Speech', *Associated Press*, 17 September 2005. Available at <http://www.globalpolicy.org/empire/humanint/2005/0917chavezun.htm> (accessed 15/06/09).

Scheffler, Samuel (1988). 'Introduction', in Samuel Scheffler (ed.), *Consequentialism and Its Critics* (Oxford: Oxford University Press), pp. 1–13.

—— (2004). 'Doing and Allowing', *Ethics*, 114/2: 215–39.

Scully, Sean (2000). 'Armed Troops Sought for UN', *Washington Times*, 1 June 2000. Available at <http://www.globalpolicy.org/security/peacekpg/reform/mcgovern.htm> (accessed 15/06/09).

Seybolt, Taylor B. (2007). *Humanitarian Military Intervention: The Conditions for Success and Failure* (Oxford: SIPRI and Oxford University Press).

Shaw, Joseph (2006). 'Intention in Ethics', *Canadian Journal of Philosophy*, 36/2: 187–224.

SHIRBRIG (2003). 'Facts', *SHIRBRIG Online*. Available at <http://www.shirbrig.dk/html/facts.htm> (accessed 15/06/09).

Shraga, Daphna (2000). 'UN Peacekeeping Operations: Applicability of International Humanitarian Law and Responsibility for Operations-Related Damage', *American Journal of International Law*, 94/2: 406–12.

Shue, Henry (1996). *Basic Rights: Subsistence, Affluence, and U.S. Foreign Policy*, Second Edition (Princeton, NJ: Princeton University Press).

—— (2003). 'Bombing to Rescue?: NATO's 1999 Bombing of Serbia', in Deen K. Chatterjee and Don E. Scheid (eds), *Ethics and Foreign Intervention* (Cambridge: Cambridge University Press), pp. 97–117.

—— (2004). 'Limiting Sovereignty', in Jennifer M. Welsh (ed.) *Humanitarian Intervention and International Relations* (Oxford: Oxford University Press), pp. 11–28.

Simmons, A. John (1999). 'Justification and Legitimacy', *Ethics*, 109/4: 739–71.

Singer, Marcus G. (1977). 'Actual Consequence Utilitarianism', *Mind*, 86/341: 67–77.

—— (1983). 'Further on Actual Consequence Utilitarianism', *Mind*, 92/366: 270–4.

Singer, P.W. (2003a). *Corporate Warriors: The Rise of the Privatized Military Industry* (New York: Cornell University Press).

—— (2003b) 'Peacekeepers, Inc.', *Policy Review*, 119. Available at <http://www.hoover.org/publications/policyreview/3448831.html> (accessed 11/06/09).

Singer, Peter (2002). *One World: The Ethics of Globalization* (London: Yale University Press).

Smart, J.J.C. (1973). 'An Outline of a System of Utilitarian Ethics', in J.J.C. Smart and Bernard Williams (eds), *Utilitarianism: For and Against* (Cambridge: Cambridge University Press).

Smith, Michael J. (1998). 'Humanitarian Intervention: An Overview of the Ethical Issues', *Ethics & International Affairs*, 12/1: 63–79.

Spearin, Christopher (2005). 'Between Public Peacekeepers and Private Forces: Can There Be a Third Way?', *International Peacekeeping*, 12/2: 240–52.

—— (2008). 'Private, Armed and Humanitarian? States, NGOs, International Private Security Companies and Shifting Humanitarianism', *Security Dialogue*, 39/4: 363–82.

Stahn, Carsten (2007). 'Responsibility to Protect: Political Rhetoric or Emerging Legal Norm?', *American Journal of International Law*, 101/1: 99–120.

Stanley Foundation (2000). *Problems and Prospects for Humanitarian Intervention*, the Stanley Foundation's Thirty-Fifth United Nations of the Next Decade Conference. Available at <http://www.stanleyfoundation.org/publications/archive/UNND00.pdf> (accessed 16/06/09).

—— (2004). *The Use of Force*, Issues Before the UN's High-Level Panel. Available at <http://reports.stanleyfoundation.org/UNHLP04a.pdf> (accessed 15/06/09).

Stein, Mark S. (2004). 'Unauthorized Humanitarian Intervention', *Social Philosophy & Policy*, 21/1: 14–38.

Steinhoff, Uwe (2008). 'Debate: Jeff McMahan on the Moral Inequality of Combatants', *Journal of Political Philosophy*, 16/2: 220–6.

Stoddard, Abby, Adele Harmer, and Victoria DiDomenico (2008). 'The Use of Private Security Providers and Services in Humanitarian Operations', *Humanitarian Policy Group Policy Report 27*, October 2008 (London: Overseas Development Institute). Available at <http://www.odi.org.uk/resources/download/2816.pdf> (accessed 23/06/09).

Stromseth, Jane (2003). 'Rethinking Humanitarian Intervention: The Case for Incremental Change', in J.L. Holzgrefe and Robert O. Keohane (eds), *Humanitarian Intervention: Ethical, Legal and Political Dilemmas* (Cambridge: Cambridge University Press), pp. 232–72.

Tan, Kok-Chor (2006a). 'The Duty to Protect', in Terry Nardin and Melissa S. Williams (eds), *NOMOS XLVII: Humanitarian Intervention* (New York: New York University Press), pp. 84–116.

—— (2006b). 'The Unavoidability of Morality: A Commentary on Mehta', in Terry Nardin and Melissa S. Williams (eds), *NOMOS XLVII: Humanitarian Intervention* (New York: New York University Press), pp. 286–98.

Temkin, Jack (1978). 'Actual Consequence Utilitarianism: A Reply to Professor Singer', *Mind*, 87/347: 412–14.

Terriff, Terry (2004a). 'NATO: Warfighters or Cosmopolitan Warriors?', in Lorraine Elliott and Graham Cheeseman (eds), *Forces for Good: Cosmopolitan Militaries in the Twenty-first Century* (Manchester: Manchester University Press), pp. 117–33.

—— (2004b). 'The European Union Rapid Reaction Force: An Embryonic Cosmopolitan Military?', in Lorraine Elliott and Graham Cheeseman (eds), *Forces for Good: Cosmopolitan Militaries in the Twenty-first Century* (Manchester: Manchester University Press), pp. 150–67.

Tesón, Fernando R. (1998). *A Philosophy of International Law* (Oxford: Westview Press).

—— (2003). 'The Liberal Case for Humanitarian Intervention', in J.L. Holzgrefe and Robert O. Keohane (eds), *Humanitarian Intervention: Ethical, Legal and Political Dilemmas* (Cambridge: Cambridge University Press), pp. 93–129.

—— (2005a). 'Ending Tyranny in Iraq', *Ethics & International Affairs*, 19/2: 1–20.

—— (2005b). 'Reply to Terry Nardin: Of Tyrants and Empires', *Ethics & International Affairs*, 19/2: 27–30.

—— (2005c). *Humanitarian Intervention: An Inquiry into Law and Morality*, Third Edition (New York: Transnational Publishers).

—— and William Twining, Ward Farnsworth, and Stefan Vogenauer (2003). 'The Role of Academics in the Legal System', in Peter Cane and Mark Tushnet (eds), *The Oxford Handbook of Legal Studies* (Oxford: Oxford University Press), pp. 920–49.

Thakur, Ramesh and Thomas G. Weiss (2009). 'R2P: From Idea to Norm—and Action?', *Global Responsibility to Protect*, 1/1: 22–53.

Tharoor, Shashi and Sam Daws (2001). 'Humanitarian Intervention: Getting Past the Reefs', *World Policy Journal*, 18/2: 21–30.

Tinsley, Rebecca (2009). 'The Failure of Unamid', *The Guardian*, 1 January 2009. Available at <http://www.guardian.co.uk/commentisfree/2009/jan/01/darfur> (accessed 23/02/09).

UN (2003). *UN Standby Arrangements System Military Handbook.* Available at <http://www.un.org/Depts/dpko/rapid/Handbook.html> (accessed 06/06/09).

—— (2004). *A More Secure World: Our Shared Responsibility*, Report of the High-Level Panel on Threats, Challenges and Change, A/59/565. Available at <http://www.un.org/secureworld/report.pdf> (accessed 15/06/09).

—— (2005). *2005 World Summit Outcome*, A/RES/60/1. Available at <http://www.un.org/summit2005/documents.html> (accessed 15/06/09).

—— (2008a). 'Darfur—UNAMID—Background', *UN.org*. Available at <http://www.un.org/Depts/dpko/missions/unamid/background.html> (accessed 23/02/09).

—— (2008b). *Fact Sheet: United Nations Peacekeeping.* Available at <http://www.un.org/Depts/dpko/factsheet.pdf> (accessed 15/06/09).

—— (2008c). *Report of the African Union-United Nations Panel on Modalities for Support to African Union Peacekeeping Operations*, A/63/666–S/2008/813. Available at <http://www.un.org/ga/search/view_doc.asp?symbol = S/2008/813> (accessed 13/06/09).

—— (2008d). *United Nations Peacekeeping Operations: Principles and Guidelines* (New York: Department of Peacekeeping Operations).

—— (2009). *Background Note: United Nations Peacekeeping Operations.* Available at <http://www.un.org/Depts/dpko/dpko/bnote.htm> (accessed 21/06/09).

Urquhart, Brian (1993). 'For a UN Volunteer Military Force', *New York Review of Books*, 10 June 1993, 40/11: 3–4.

—— (2003). 'A Force Behind the UN', *New York Times*, 7 August 2003. Available at <http://www.nytimes.com> (accessed 31/05/09).

US Catholic Bishops (1992). 'The Challenge of Peace: God's Promise and Our Response: The Pastoral Letter on War and Peace' in Jean Bethke Elshtain (ed.), *Just War Theory* (New York: New York University Press), pp. 77–168.

USA Today (2007). 'Blackwater: Fallujah Deaths Unavoidable', *USA Today*, 24 October 2007. Available at <http://www.usatoday.com/news/washington/2007-10-24-blackwater-deaths_N.htm> (accessed 14/06/09).

Vernon, Richard (2008). 'Humanitarian Intervention and the Internal Legitimacy Problem', *Journal of Global Ethics*, 4/1: 37–49.

Vincent, R.J. (1986). *Human Rights and International Relations* (Cambridge: Cambridge University Press).

von Freiesleben, Jonas (2008). 'Denmark Remains Committed to UN Peacekeeping—but Is Contemplating SHIRBRIG Pull-Out', *Center for UN Reform*. Available at <http://www.centerforunreform.org/node/359> (accessed 15/06/09).

Walzer, Michael (1980). 'The Moral Standing of States: A Response to Four Critics', *Philosophy & Public Affairs*, 9/3: 209–29.

—— (2002). 'Arguing for Humanitarian Intervention', in Nicolaus Mills and Kira Brunner (eds), *The New Killing Fields: Massacre and the Politics of Intervention* (New York: Basic Books), pp. 19–35.

Walzer, Michael (2004). *Arguing About War* (London: Yale University Press).

—— (2006). *Just and Unjust Wars*, Fourth Edition (New York: Basic Books).

Washington Post (2004). 'Singapore Sidesteps ASEAN Peacekeeping Force', *Washington Post*, 4 March 2004. Available at <http://www.washingtonpost.com/wp-dyn/articles/A29542–2004Mar4.html> (accessed 15/06/09).

Weale, Albert (1999). *Democracy* (New York: St Martin's Press).

Weiss, Thomas G. (2001). 'Researching Humanitarian Intervention: Some Lessons', *Journal of Peace Research*, 38/4: 419–28.

—— (2004). 'The Sunset of Humanitarian Intervention? The Responsibility to Protect in a Unipolar Era', *Security Dialogue*, 35/2: 135–53.

—— (2005*a*). 'Cosmopolitan Force and the Responsibility to Protect', *International Relations*, 19/2: 233–7.

—— (2005*b*). *Military-Civilian Interactions: Humanitarian Crises and the Responsibility to Protect*, Second Edition (New York: Rowman and Littlefield Publishers, Inc).

—— (2007). *Humanitarian Intervention: Ideas in Action* (Cambridge: Polity Press).

—— (2010). 'Reinserting "Never" into "Never Again": Political Innovations and the Responsibility to Protect', in David Hollenbach (ed.), *Driven from Home: Human Rights and the New Realities of Forced Migration* (Washington, DC: Georgetown University Press), *forthcoming*.

Welsh, Jennifer M. (2004). 'Authorizing Humanitarian Intervention', in Richard M. Price and Mark W. Zacher (eds), *The United Nations and Global Security* (Basingstoke: Palgrave Macmillan), pp. 177–92.

—— (2009). 'Policy Briefing: Implementing the "Responsibility to Protect"', Oxford Institute for Ethics, Law, and Armed Conflict. Available at <http://www.elac.ox.ac.uk/downloads/R2P_policybrief_180209.pdf> (accessed 20/05/09).

Wendt, Alexander (2003). 'Why a World State is Inevitable', *European Journal of International Relations*, 9/4: 491–542.

Wheeler, Nicholas J. (2000). *Saving Strangers: Humanitarian Intervention in International Society* (Oxford: Oxford University Press).

—— (2005*a*). 'A Victory for Common Humanity? The Responsibility to Protect after the 2005 World Summit', paper presented at The UN at Sixty: Celebration or Wake?, Faculty of Law, University of Toronto, Canada, 6–7 October 2005.

—— (2005*b*). 'Legitimating Humanitarian Intervention: A Reply to Farer's Five-Part Test', *International Relations*, 19/2: 237–41.

—— (2008). 'Operationalising the Responsibility to Protect: The Continuing Debate Over Where Authority Should Be Located for the Use of Force', Norwegian Institute of International Affairs (NUPI) Report, No. 3. Available at <http://www.nupi.no> (accessed 20/05/09).

—— and Frazer Egerton (2009). 'The Responsibility to Protect: "Precious Commitment" or a Promise Unfulfilled?', *Global Responsibility to Protect*, 1/1: 114–32.

—— and Tim Dunne (2001). 'East Timor and the New Humanitarian Interventionism', *International Affairs*, 77/4: 805–27.

Whitlock, Craig (2009). 'Afghanistan Appeal May Temper European Allies' Ardor for Obama', *Washington Post*, 6 February 2009. Available at <http://www.washingtonpost.com/wp-dyn/content/article/2009/02/05/AR2009020503786_pf.html> (accessed 22/02/09).

Wight, Martin (1991). *International Theory: The Three Traditions*, Gabriele Wight and Brian Porter (eds), with an introductory essay by Hedley Bull (Leicester: Leicester University Press).

Wild, Franz (2009). 'Congo Will Start New Rebel Hunt, UN Mission Head Says', *Bloomberg.com*, 23 February 2009. Available at <http://www.bloomberg.com/apps/news?pid = 20601116&sid = ajDKbcBOIqIs&refer = africa> (accessed 15/06/09).

Williams, Bernard (1995). 'Is International Rescue a Moral Issue?', *Social Research*, 62/1: 67–75.

Williams, Paul D. (2002). 'Fighting For Freetown: British Military Intervention in Sierra Leone', in Colin McInnes and Nicholas J. Wheeler (eds), *Dimensions of Western Military Intervention* (London: Frank Cass), pp. 140–68.

—— (2008). 'Keeping the Peace in Africa: Why "African" Solutions Are Not Enough', *Ethics & International Affairs*, 22/3: 309–29.

Windsor, Philip (1984). 'Superpower Intervention', in Hedley Bull (ed.), *Intervention in World Politics* (Oxford: Clarendon Press), pp. 45–65.

Winston, Morton (2005). 'The Humanitarian Argument for the Iraq War', *Journal of Human Rights*, 4/1: 45–51.

Woodhouse, Tom and Oliver Ramsbotham (2005). 'Cosmopolitan Peacekeeping and the Globalisation of Security', *International Peacekeeping*, 12/2: 139–56.

Zolo, Danilo (1997). *Cosmopolis: Prospects for World Government* (Cambridge: Polity Press).

Index